Everyone Loves Live Music

Big Issues in Music *A project of the Chicago Studies in Ethnomusicology Series*

Edited by Philip V. Bohlman

Also in this series:

Music and the New Global Culture: From the Great Exhibitions to the Jazz Age
by Harry Liebersohn

Everyday Creativity: Singing Goddesses in the Himalayan Foothills
by Kirin Narayan

Music and Capitalism: A History of the Present
by Timothy D. Taylor

Everyone Loves Live Music
A Theory of Performance Institutions

FABIAN HOLT

The University of Chicago Press CHICAGO AND LONDON

The University of Chicago Press, Chicago 60637
The University of Chicago Press, Ltd., London

Published 2020
Printed in the United States of America

29 28 27 26 25 24 23 22 21 20   1 2 3 4 5

ISBN-13: 978-0-226-73840-6 (cloth)
ISBN-13: 978-0-226-73854-3 (paper)
ISBN-13: 978-0-226-73868-0 (e-book)
DOI: https://doi.org/10.7208/chicago/9780226738680.001.0001

Library of Congress Cataloging-in-Publication Data

Names: Holt, Fabian, author.
Title: Everyone loves live music : a theory of performance institutions / Fabian Holt.
Other titles: Big issues in music
Description: Chicago : The University of Chicago Press, 2020. | Series: Big issues in music | Includes bibliographical references and index.
Identifiers: LCCN 2020024372 | ISBN 9780226738406 (cloth) | ISBN 9780226738543 (paperback) | ISBN 9780226738680 (ebook)
Subjects: LCSH: Rock music—Social aspects—United States. | Rock music—Social aspects—Europe. | Music festivals—Social aspects—United States. | Music festivals—Social aspects—Europe.
Classification: LCC ML3918.R63 H65 2020 | DDC 780.78—dc23
LC record available at https://lccn.loc.gov/2020024372

♾ This paper meets the requirements of ANSI/NISO Z39.48–1992 (Permanence of Paper).

In Heaven's court, from which I have returned,
one finds so many fair and precious gems
that are not to be taken from that kingdom:
one of those gems, the song those splendors sang.
He who does not take wings to reach that realm,
may wait for tidings of it from the mute.

After those ardent suns, while singing so,
had wheeled three times around us, even as
stars that are close to the fixed poles, they seemed
to me like women who, though not released
from dancing, pause in silence, listening
until new notes invite to new dancing.

And from within one light I heard begin:
"Because the ray of grace, from which true love
is kindled first and then, in loving, grows,
shines with such splendor, multiplied in you,
that it has led you up the stair that none
descends who will not climb that stair again . . ."

DANTE ALIGHIERI, *The Divine Comedy*
([1320] 1984, CANTO 10, LINES 70–87)

Contents

1 Introduction: The Social Study of Musical Performance Institutions 1
2 Conceptualizing Musical Performance Culture 41

Clubs in Everyday Urban Life

3 The Social Study of Music in Cities 65
4 The Commercial Institutionalization of the Rock Club in New York 74
5 How Did the Rock Club Evolve in Europe? 123

Music Festivals in the Summer Season

6 A Worldview History of Music Festivals 157
7 The Evolution of Anglophone Global Culture 183
8 Three Industry Evolutions That Changed Festival Culture 220
9 Festival Video and Social Media 239

10 Conclusion 262

Acknowledgments 285
Notes 289
Works Cited 299
Index of Names 333
Index of Subjects 339

: 1 :

Introduction: The Social Study of Musical Performance Institutions

Scholarly interest in musical performance has grown in music studies in the early twenty-first century. A new understanding is emerging of how performance culture has been shaped by dominant technologies and ideologies in modernity. Scholars are questioning media-centric understandings of performance and musical culture, drawing on evolving literatures in anthropology, ethnomusicology, and music psychology dating back to the 1970s (e.g., Cook 2013; Frith 2007; Wald 2009). In popular music, this book's main area of inquiry, electronic media have been particularly powerful, culturally and economically. The recording sector of the music industry had hegemonic status in the late twentieth century. Digitalization weakened its hegemony, and this stimulated the exploitation of commodity forms other than the sound recording, especially the music festival. The recession in the recording sector stimulated a general shift of emphasis to the performance sector and accelerated its international corporatization and branding as a live music industry. Euphoric narratives about live music caught the attention of popular media, policy makers, and scholars. Notable popular music scholar Simon Frith (2007) began exploring the transformation, but a sociology of musical performance has not yet matured. Instead, industry discourse of live music has been adopted rather uncritically into popular music studies at a substantial intellectual disadvantage.

This book evolves from this current moment of thinking about musical performance in music studies and aims to contribute a long-overdue critical and historically grounded analysis of the commercial institutionalization of Anglophone popular music performance culture in the United States and Western Europe. This project involves the development of new foundational analytical narratives of the field and its history. Discarding "live music" as a master concept, this book instead develops a discourse of musical performance culture in modernity. The argument put forth here pays particular attention to market-based institutions of musical performance since these institutions provide a focal point from which the commercial institutionalization of the culture can be analyzed. The intellectual project is to develop an analytical narrative of commercial performance institutions and demonstrate its potentials for the social study of musical performance and of music more broadly.

The first task is to understand popular music's live music moment not only as a symptom of change in the economy of music and as a marketing invention, but also as a reproduction of the media logics that have governed musical performance culture for about a century. The dualism between live and recorded music is an important dynamic in musical culture, but it has also become a discursive framing of musical performance culture, and as such it is simplified and reproduces media hegemony. By contrast, this book conceives live music as a particular formation within musical performance culture that has its own institutions and cultural histories in musical culture and not just in a contemporary industry or in consumer culture. Musical performance cannot be adequately understood only in terms of its difference from media production and consumption of music. Global musical performance cultures have existed long before the advent of electronic media and can be identified as performance cultures through their distinct institutions, ontologies, and histories.

In modernity, commercial performance institutions such as the concert hall, music festival, dance hall, cabaret, and popular music club have been central to the production and experience of musical performance and shaped musical performance cultures. These institutions have also been important institutions of musical and cultural life, supporting musical traditions, genres, and urban cultures. Festivals have created powerful moments of cultural festivity in musical and social life. As commercial institutions, however, they have not only been governed by an interest in protecting and celebrating music and culture. Rather, they have functioned as institutions of leisure and operated under market conditions. The institutionalization of musical performance as a commodity is an outcome of capitalism. Organizations need to sell performance events with a certain frequency to exist in the market. Moreover, the institutionalization of standardized commodities with a high level of consistency is a capitalist impulse to create stability in constantly changing markets. A potential conflict therefore exists in modernity between cultural and commercial perspectives on what constitutes a better place for music. This book shows that international corporations have gained unprecedented dominance in fields of Anglophone professional popular music performance and contributed to the institutionalization of popular music as consumer culture. As a humanist inquiry, however, this book does not limit its discussion to this development, but situates it historically and introduces comparative cultural perspectives.

This leads us to the main research question: How can the commercial institutionalization of Anglophone popular music performance that accelerated in the 1990s be situated in the broader history of musical performance institutions in modernity? This book uses two institutions, the club and the festival, as focal points for examining the process in the two major domains of popular music performance: everyday urban life and the summer season. It will conceptualize these two domains and analyze how the outlook and function of musical performance institutions have changed within them. The book thus responds to the accelerated commercial institutionalization, specifically international corporatization, on two levels. Conceptually, it constructs a historically and systematically grounded alternative to the predominant live music discourse. Empirically, it maps and analyzes the commercial institutionalization of clubs in urban economies and of festivals in media flows of Anglophone popular music and culture. The empirical investigations reconstruct the history of the club and the festival institution within musical and cultural histories and highlight how their evolution into the same system of international corporate ownership in the early twenty-first century has transformed them into institutions of broader consumer culture demographics.

This agenda requires more than a cultural critique. Above all, it requires a systematic analysis of the history of the field and its institutions. Such an analysis does not yet exist. There is little precedent for studying national and international fields of professional musical performance and how they transform. Fields of musical performance have been examined indirectly through literatures on individual musical traditions and genres. But there is no tradition, for instance, for more general and comparative analysis of the relationship between musical performance institutions such as the concert hall, the club, and the festival across different musical traditions and how their outlook and functions have changed as part of broader changes in society. Existing scholarly literatures focus on individual concert halls, clubs, and festivals, and on their particularity within individual musical traditions. Moreover, the performative turn in music studies has led to arguments about the fundamentally performative nature of music (e.g., Cook 2013), but these arguments are yet to explore social theory of performance and event cultures in modern societies. The field of performance studies has similarly ignored the commercial history of performance and all but continues to neglect music (Auslander 2004, 1–4). This book engages area literatures in its conception of the social study of music and musical performance institutions. The empirical argument for this is that musical performance is part of musical culture and requires a form of expertise that is not acknowledged in the universalizing, postdisciplinary narrative of performance studies (Kirshenblatt-Gimblett 2002/2004, 43). Performance studies and the more recent field of event studies will be valuable resources, but not the main disciplinary and theoretical ground.

The commercial institutionalization of the field calls for greater attention to social theory and particularly to sociological theory for conceptualizing musical performance institutions in modernity. This book constructs a new and more general discourse on these institutions by adopting and developing sociological discourse on leisure institutions and cultural production into music studies and then analyzing the transformation of these institutions in music history. Sociology will provide key concepts and a narrative of performance institutions in evolving culture markets. However, these institutions are not simply general commercial institutions. Rather, they belong to broader cultural histories of music and therefore require expertise in music studies. A more detailed discussion of methodology is reserved for the concluding chapter.

Following the above objectives, the inquiry progresses through a number of steps, from the construction of discourse and theory of the study object in the opening chapters (1–2) to more specific theory and analysis of individual types of institutions (chapters 3–9). The investigations are organized into two major sections, each focusing on one of the two domains (everyday urban life in chapters 3–5 and the summer season in chapters 6–9) and on two core institutions in these domains, the club and the festival. The overall structure does not unfold as a linear history or a single ethnography, but is rather structured by the systematic distinction between domains on the premise that the domains shape fundamentally different types and dynamics of performance institutions and that they can therefore be meaningfully theorized and analyzed as separate but interconnected entities. This organization creates a focus on the distinctness of the two domains, but the analyses also reveal connections. In particular, the urban domain has historically constituted a ground from which seasonal festivity has evolved, and the festival boom reflects and impacts on the challenged situation of the everyday urban domain. The overall structuring of the inquiry has the further advantage that the simpler institution of the club is examined before moving to the larger and more complex institution of the festival, which involves several performances, more intense media dynamics, and has a longer history.

The inquiry, moreover, expands historically and geographically. The theory is developed by expanding the analysis of institutions from recent popular music history into the longer history of music in modernity, with the wider aim of situating the contemporary world against the history from which it has evolved. Geographically, the inquiry examines developments in the professional field of Anglophone popular music performance, expanding from postwar centers of this culture, such as London, New York, and San Francisco—all of which had a defining impact on the club and the festival institution—into Continental Europe and the North Atlantic, illustrating the dynamics of media flows into Scandinavia, Hungary, Iceland, Spain, and Russia, for instance.

The music's media circulation is a constitutive factor in the field's international expansion. It explains evolutions in international touring, systems of ownership, music programming, and spatial design across Continental Europe. But how are the cultural boundaries of circulation regulated? And why do some forms of music have dedicated buildings of high professional standards in central parts of many cities, while others don't? The forms of music that have a more peripheral or sporadic presence and exist under less prestigious conditions tend to be music of minoritized and lower-class populations. Hegemonic ideologies in the cultural industries and in society shape the conditions and norms of performance institutions, which to some extent are articulations of societal structures. Even genres such as blues, salsa, Latin pop, hip hop, and grime that are popular in the Global North do not enjoy the same level of institutionalization as Anglophone rock and pop, the privileged domain of white patriarchy. Festivals of Anglophone pop have featured a small number of world music stars, beginning with Ravi Shankar and Bob Marley and continuing with the waves of exotic interest in African, Balkan, and Icelandic music stars and more recently Rosalía and the K-Pop band Blackpink. But these festivals present such artists while they are novelties and do not provide regular platforms for the musical cultures they represent. The representation of black popular music, and especially hip hop, grew in the 2010s, but how does the pop festival represent black popular music, and how does it serve black audiences? Social groups excluded from powerful cultural institutions have historically tended to mobilize in less institutionalized networks or in institutions that are not dedicated to individual art forms. In a Senate hearing in 1966, at the height of the Civil Rights movement, Ralph Ellison noted that the strongest institution for black people is the black church, well aware that its function had been defined by a history of racial segregation. In music, this history had involved segregated unions, performance venues, and traveling conditions (Monson 2007). Ellison pointed out that the government, by contrast, is an institution for all population groups and thus has an obligation to end segregation laws ("Statement of Ralph Ellison"). His statements are a reminder that dedicated arts institutions still tend to be a privilege reserved for some populations and that their values are defined within broader structures in society.

Overview of Chapters

The remainder of this introductory chapter (1) details the critique of live music discourse; (2) contemplates the disciplinary challenge in bringing sociology of performance institutions into music studies, specifically into the social study of music that includes ethnomusicology; and (3) introduces a narrative of commercial institutionalization and a conceptual framework of performance institutions.

Chapter 2 conceptualizes musical performance culture as part of the reconstruction of the study object that looks beyond live music. The chapter builds a systematic understanding of ontologies of musical performance culture that are often discussed separately, and their relationship is crucial. The ontologies have far-reaching implications for theory and disciplinarity. An understanding of the complex ontologies of the study object is not only important to musicology and sociology. It is also important for thinking critically about how musicologists and sociologists engage with understandings of performance culture in event studies, festival studies, urban studies, and media studies.

The first part (chapters 3–5) begins by taking stock of the intellectual history of music in cities to develop the conceptual foundations for studying performance institutions in the urban domain and to situate them in the cultural history of music in cities across the Global North. Chapter 3 argues that a long history of specialization into individual urban musical cultures has produced valuable insights but that a greater field-sensitivity can be developed by thinking more about shared knowledge interests and comparing the role of performance institutions in different urban musical cultures. In the process, the review illustrates potentials of the interdisciplinary social study of music. It concludes with the literature on popular music culture in contemporary cities, which is the focus area of the subsequent two chapters.

Chapters 3–4 examine the commercial institutionalization of the rock club in different kinds of cities and societies, focusing on one American metropolis and a few capital cities in small European countries. The objective is to understand how various models of the rock club have evolved as part of broader changes in cities and their fields of rock music. These models result from changes in the urban economies and value systems of this institution. The general argument of the two chapters investigating different cities in the Global North is that the transformation of the rock club can be interpreted as an ongoing adaptation to gentrification and the music industry's exploitation of more popular and conformist forms of indie rock. The rock club illustrates both general and particular implications of changing urban economies at the level of cultural production and human experience in performance. In the process, the chapters show how a sociology of performance institutions can complement thinking about collectivity, aesthetics, and ideology in urban musical and cultural studies.

Chapter 4 provides a comprehensive analysis of the club's emergence and transformation in the gentrification of a city, taking New York City as its example. The chapter analyzes how clubs of institutional significance to the rock field evolved in neighborhood transformations of this field. Based on ethnographic fieldwork in clubs and neighborhoods in the early 2010s and follow-up digital research in the late 2010s, the chapter registers the cultural and historical complexity of rock music in New York City, while using the institutional perspective to conceptualize different models of the rock club in broader structural change. The informal club of neo-bohemian neighborhood scenes declined in the 1990s and a new model has come to dominate—the indie rock concert theater—which is more focused on concert consumption and governed by other values and networks. This model is more bureaucratic and efficient for business and consumption on a larger scale, and it provides better aesthetic and technological conditions of concert consumption, but it also limits the existential social and psychological potentials of performance. The chapter concludes with a historically informed vision for performance institutions and human life in contemporary cities.

Chapter 5 provides a comparative perspective, showing that a similar commercial institutionalization of the rock club has occurred in small Continental European cities at the periphery of the genre's metropolitan centers, but that public policy in countries with the highest level of subsidizing of rock music in the world has sustained other values. A historical investigation into discourses on the rock club, based on interviews with club managements and on policy documents, reveals that the club was initially conceived within social policy of youth culture before finding a place in arts policy of music. Case studies of clubs in Amsterdam, Brussels, and Copenhagen show that city and state governments created a system of nonprofit ownership that built on local traditions of voluntary associations and continue to support unprofitable parts of the ecosystem of Anglophone rock and pop music. However, the chapter also argues that neither clubs nor policy makers have harnessed the potentials of a public culture conception of clubs and that city governments became more interested in arenas and mass culture events in the 2000s. The conclusion addresses this potential of performance institutions as institutions of public culture.

The second part (chapters 6–9) employs the theoretical framework to advance knowledge of music festival history in general and the recent history of Anglophone popular music festivals in particular. Institutional theory is central for analyzing the emergence and development of music and culture festivals in modernity and for interpreting the broader historical and cultural significance of popular music festivals. The festival chapters adopt a focus on how the music festival has evolved in different traditions as an institution governed by not just abstract social norms but also by specific cultural worldviews in those traditions. The worldview concept is developed with inspiration from symbolic anthropology and the sociology of festive events. This involves a theorization of the basic institutional functions that a festival has for a culture. The chapters further introduce an analytical narrative of festivals in a broader history of cultural festivity to theorize the distinctness and dynamism of the festival as a form of institutionalized festivity that evolves in cultural tradition. Festivals have frequently evolved from and been defined against less institutionalized forms of festivity.

Chapter 6 begins by introducing these core concepts and explores the potentials for integrating music festivals into the social study of music. The chapter then initiates an investigation into the history of the music festival institution that is continued in subsequent chapters. It outlines the trajectories of cultural worldviews that defined the music festival institution up to World War II through a comparative exploration of the institution's international history. This history reveals that the pioneering bourgeois music festival traditions in Europe evolved from the church into the secular sphere of civic associations and were influenced by Enlightenment ideas of authentic cultural citizenship. The powerful idea of civic and social becoming through cultural festivity has remained a core mythical dimension of the institution, exploited in such diverse contexts as totalitarian regimes and transnational cultural industries. In addition, the chapter identifies a major shift in European modernity from national festival cultures in the eighteenth century into Anglophone global cultures in the late twentieth century. Chapter 7 nuances this genealogy of the large pop festival through analysis of its evolution in the hippie movement and its influences from the culture of the happening in metropolitan arts scenes. The chapter shows how this model of the festival institution transformed in the process of commercial institutionalization, interpreting it as an institution of Anglophone global culture and a vehicle of a hegemonic form of globalization in the Global North that was accelerated by evolutions in media technologies and corporate ownership. The chapter introduces a distinction between two variations, the broad pop festival and the niche festival, and then illustrates how they have adapted differently to cultural worldviews promoted by transnational cultural industries and internet corporations.

How has the music festival transformed in the process of its corporate institutionalization? How has this process affected its symbolic order, its cultural worldview? Based on industry ethnography and theory of industry-driven popularization, chapter 8 argues that corporate exploitation has changed not only the business culture but also the functions of the festival and the norms that regulate its evolution and meanings. As the festival has been co-opted into corporate networks and become exploited in general commodity markets, it is governed more by norms of mainstream business and society and less by culture worlds of music and social movements. The chapter identifies and explores three functions that have developed since international corporatization began in the 1990s. These functions explain how the festival has evolved in institutionalized arrangements with city governments and advertising industries. The chapter includes the rock-based pop festival and the festival for popular forms of electronic dance music, the EDM pop festival, arguing that these two models are regulated in organizational fields with similar and overlapping corporate structures.

Chapter 9 develops the analysis by exploring a new media development. It analyzes how a new type of music marketing video, which I call music festival video, was developed by festival marketers in the early years of YouTube and Facebook and eventually transformed the design and experience of the popular music festival, particularly the EDM pop festival. Based on festival ethnography, interviews with marketers, and analysis of the videos and their circulation, the chapter argues that the commercial exploitation of social media videography involved a new ordering, expansion, and consumption of images within the annual festival cycle and that it coevolved with storytelling and design in the physical sphere of the festival. Music festival video transformed the EDM pop music festival into a more glamorous global consumer culture, and it transformed festival performance culture further into media culture. The conclusion suggests that a core dynamic in this process is the fetishization rather than the abandonment of seasonal performance culture. The main chapter case study is the Tomorrowland festival in Belgium in 2013, which was a culminating moment for music festival video and for the EDM pop festival.

The concluding chapter summarizes the main insights of the inquiry and reflects on the logic of this form of interpretative humanist scholarship, with a perspective on the broader theory and history of musical performance institutions in modernity. The chapter begins by summarizing the interpretative steps in the theoretical framework and how the investigations of individual institutions led to insights into the seasonal domains. After the discussion of the book's main objectives, I evaluate the structural conditions of popular music performance in contemporary societies. Have the central popular music performance institutions become better places for this musical culture and for human experience? I argue that alternatives to narratives of commercial growth and consumer satisfaction are needed and turn to ideas of human growth and conceptions of the good life in moral philosophy. The final section reflects on the changing conditions of humanistic scholarship, interpreting this book as a product and critique of hegemonic conditions in European universities.

A Few Things This Book Is Not

This book develops theory of relevance to many musical cultures and to other forms of culture, but the core framework is focused on two central institutions of Anglophone popular music and demonstrates only some of the potential applications of this framework.

The analytical objectives require engagement with a range of disciplines and area studies formations, but to reach meaningful depth and focus and to structure the conversation, I limit myself to intellectual traditions that are central to the social study of music, primarily music studies and sociology. As an interdisciplinary work, this book cannot privilege either of the two; it explores their distinct logics both in combination and separately. It adopts a sociological narrative of institutions and brings this narrative into continuous dialogue with specialized literatures in music studies: the narrative does not float above those literatures.

Moreover, this book concentrates on processes of institutionalization and uses institutions as focal points, not musicians and audiences. This is a matter of focus, since these processes are analyzed broadly, but with an emphasis on the changing outlook, functions, and values of performance institutions. A performance institution is not just a venue or a venue organization; it also involves the norms, practices, and networks through which musical performance events are constituted and regulated. Club and festival promoters and the events they produce are central units for institutional analysis of musical performance. This book highlights general implications of commercial institutionalization, such as changes in types of music, experiences, audiences, and architectures, but not so much from the perspectives of musicians. Part of the reason is the difficulty in getting access to the star performers who are central to the process, but a study of their perspectives based on more interviews and biographies, for instance, would refine rather than refute the framework and thesis of this book, showing how a small number of celebrities exploit the lucrative festival market as touring headliners and develop identities as top-tier industry professionals and stars of glamorous shows. Meanwhile, many lesser-known artists are playing smaller festival stages and clubs under precarious labor conditions, adopting identities as young talents or generic craftspeople. More experimental artists tend to perform in independent or DIY spaces, and many women and people of color are experiencing alienation and exclusion from clubs and festivals. The concluding chapter turns to Beyoncé's performance at Coachella in 2018, a performance of great cultural significance, to reflect on the agency of the pop celebrity in the rare instances where they challenge the norms of pop festivals.

Moreover, the lacuna of research on performance culture and modernity motivates this book's focus on the institutional and symbolic over the material and sensory dimensions of culture. The material and sensory dimensions are important, but analysis of common forms of performance in modern societies can do more to recognize how these dimensions are structured by cities, media, markets, and bureaucracy. In my ethnographic experience, I witnessed how these forces of modernity weaken the sovereignty of performing bodies and other core elements in performance culture, such as community, ritual, trance, and orality. The limited attention to institutions in the literatures on performance and on "live music experiences" has resulted in neglect of the political economy of the field.

Finally, this book is a humanist inquiry without utilitarian or commercial interests. My analysis of the scholarly live music literature will question the impact of such interests and show that scholarship on performance culture and modernity is still in its emerging stages. This book is written on the premise that more critical social analysis of Anglophone popular music performance culture and its organizational fields is essential to guiding future debate and public policy in this area. High levels of humanist expertise in the area are needed to educate the public about the history and future of this culture and its political regulation. Live music branding of cities, for instance, tends to narrow the cultural imagination of the city, and debates about the decline of small performance spaces tend to ignore fundamental aspects of gentrification. Saving neighborhood cultural scenes would require regulation of real estate capitalism. Similarly, arguments for experimental concert design in classical music (Tröndle 2009/2011) might usefully consider design as an element in the broader institutional regulation of performance culture and the social contract between audiences and organizations in a changing society. The evolution of participatory festival culture, moreover, has appealed to consumers (Robinson 2015) and sugarcoated growing levels of consumerism.

The Problems with Live Music

How could live music become a master concept in industry, policy, and research discourse on musical performance in the early twenty-first century? This systemic discursive development resulted from a rebranding of the concert industry and a psychological response in public consciousness to a major transformation in the economy of music. Music industry magazines and popular media played a key role in interpreting this transformation. They published several stories about "live music" becoming more profitable and growing numbers of festivals. These stories drew on a long history of declinist narratives of musical performance and of community and authenticity in modernity. This chain of associations in public consciousness was not made explicit, but it can be understood by situating the new enthusiasm for live music in the context of twentieth-century narratives about musical performance.

Throughout most of the twentieth century there were widespread concerns that musical performance had become an endangered species. Media evolutions made the consumption of music technologically independent from performing musicians. Recorded music replaced and challenged the status of some performance practices; it also contributed to shifts from public to domestic consumption (Frith 2007, 2; "live, adj. 1, n., and adv. 10a"). The terms "piped" and "canned" music indicated that performance was considered the more authentic form. In the middle of the century, musicians' unions in the United States and the United Kingdom reacted against specific consequences of mediatization by promoting ideas about live music's centrality to the survival of authentic musical culture. Sarah Thornton analyzed this evolution of what she calls a live ideology, structured by dichotomies such as life versus death, human versus mechanical, and creative versus imitative (Thornton 1995, 42). A similar ideology surfaced in the *New York Times* during the 1950s along with the consumer discourse of performance events as "live music" (Taubman 1953, 1955, and 1956; Antek 1957). In a discussion about choosing a hi-fi system, critic Howard Taubman wrote that most people still had opportunities to hear live music nearby and would find greater pleasure in experiencing music live, too (Taubman 1954). Positive meanings of the word "live" surfaced in multiple places, from "live electronics" in the 1960s avant-garde to signs outside the honky-tonk, pub, or bar advertising "we have live music." There was not yet a live music industry, however, and the declinist narratives continued to evolve. In the 1970s, for instance, disco was blamed for replacing musicians and for the presumed death of musical culture (Thornton 1995). Live ideology thus also ignored and repressed evolutions in electronic practices that created other types of experiences and freedoms from rockism (Lawrence 2004).

French minister of culture Jack Lang summed up decades of anxiety in 1981, at the peak of the recording industry's dominance, by stating that "music is everywhere but concerts are nowhere" ("Historique de la Fête de la Musique"). The statement served to motivate the establishment of an annual day of musical performance, Fête de la Musique, which is now celebrated in more than 800 cities around the world. Was musical performance really risking neglect to the extent that it needed a day of celebration like the library, the environment, and the labor union? Conventional notions of performance transformed further in subsequent decades as DJs began to appear at traditional rituals, such as weddings and the Olympics.[1]

Anglophone popular music studies has primarily been concerned with media culture of music since the formative years of the field in the 1970s, having been strongly influenced by cultural studies. Musicologists, such as Richard Middleton (1990), wrote insightfully about the performative dimension of popular music within the realm of electronic media. Middleton initiated a tradition for analyzing performativity in sound recordings and music videos, as opposed to in-person experience in performance events. The literature on music scenes brought attention to the spaces of such events, but it did not produce comprehensive theories and histories of musical performance culture. Will Straw's (1991) meditation on the impact of media circulation on local scenes introduced a perspective with great potential for the analysis of dynamics in many scenes, but it primarily conceptualized media logics. Music scholars such as Sara Cohen (1991), Barry Shank (1994), and Harris Berger (1999), on the other hand, produced ethnographies of local scenes. Their work offered valuable alternatives to the media-centric discourse of popular music studies, but did not develop models for analyzing broader national and transnational developments.

Arguments about a qualitative historical shift in the status and function of musical performance culture in cultural life emerged in the late twentieth century. These arguments were grounded in media theory. Andrew Goodwin suggested that electronic media were transforming musical aesthetics and erasing the boundary between human and automated performance (Goodwin 1988). He also argued that pop concerts were increasingly valued for the in-person experience of celebrity and less as a unique form of musical experience. It was Philip Auslander's book-length study a decade later that defined the most popular version of the declinist narrative, however. His polemic *Liveness: Performance in a Mediatized Culture* (1999), published in the last year of the century, punctured the romantic idea of performance as an alternative to media culture, arguing instead, as part of a broader argument about the hegemony of television in contemporary culture, that the music video had gained primary status. Pop concerts were reproducing sound recordings and music videos, and their main function was to allow audiences to experience the celebrity in person. Auslander's book explains important dynamics in pop culture, but also has considerable limitations. The most critical of these is that the book's methodology reproduces the media-centric culture it investigates. It does not distinguish between performance within and outside media spaces. It is therefore unclear why the book primarily discusses TV shows and arena concerts based on secondary sources and why it does not research performance from in-person perspectives in spaces such as the private home, the street, the bar, or the club. Auslander's key argument is about the hegemony of television as a medium, and the argument has major strengths for explaining particular media aesthetics and dynamics. But at no point does the book explore performance in spaces outside television, except indirectly and in fragments through discussions of general themes in the literature. The book portrays a world in which musical performance exists only as freestanding events in TV shows and arenas. It ignores how popular music performance culture evolves in institutions and urban markets. Music festivals are absent.

A New Collective Psychology of Growth and Vitality

Public sentiments about musical performance in mass media shifted from a set of anxieties about decline to enthusiasm for growth and vitality in the 2000s. I conceive the structure of this shift in collective consciousness and the mechanisms by which they operated as a new psychology of live music. The change in attitudes was stimulated by countless industry reports on business growth in concerts and festivals in trade magazines and news media (e.g., Slade 2004; Waddell 2000, 2001a, 2001b, 2006a, 2006b, 2007, 2008a, 2008b, 2009; McGowan 2007; Sisario 2009a; Jurgensen 2010). The master narrative in music business journalism during the first decade of this century linked the decline of the recording industry with the rise of the live music industry. The boom in music festivals was interpreted in celebratory terms until skepticism about massification began to appear, such as when the *New York Times* questioned the cultural relevance of large popular music festivals and announced it would no longer cover them with the same frequency (Pareles, Ratliff, and Caramanica 2016). But in general, the mass-media enthusiasm for "live music" was so strong that everyone seemed to have forgotten about past anxieties and the industry's co-option of the term. Live music passed as a cooler term for musical performance and an umbrella term for concerts and festivals. The folk narratives I encountered among industry professionals and fans in Denmark featured the idea that screen fatigue and the fragmentation of the media landscape created a need for in-person social experiences. Among the journalists and audiences who had discovered the trend, concerts and festivals were imagined as exotic novelties.[2]

To take stock of the new psychology of live music, let us consider a three-minute feature on live music that was broadcast during the BBC Music Awards in 2014 (BBC 2014). This was at the peak of industry growth. Motivated by stories about the festival boom, broadcasters and other media outlets began covering festivals more intensely and producing their own events. *Pitchfork* and iHeartRadio Music created their own festivals, NPR created Tiny Desk, and BBC created Live Lounge and an annual music awards show. The blaring enthusiasm for live music in the early 2010s is illustrated by this three-minute feature. The feature is a series of brief statements about the wonders of live music and its abundance, combined with footage from famous events. The message is validated by BBC hosts, including Jools Holland, and a string of mostly white, male stars such as Coldplay, Ed Sheeran, Calvin Harris, and Bryan Ferry. The first artist statement is by a member of Take That, who says, "I think it is amazing that the BBC can do so much live music!" with a pronunciation of "live music" that feels studied. The feature leaves little doubt as to its psychological investment in the term. The mere appearance of the term is believed to make a sentence meaningful.

A striking act performed by the term "live music" in this conversation is the removal of music's capacity to produce history and difference, not just immediacy and sameness. The BBC feature represents a mediatized consumer culture gaze on musical performance. This gaze, projected into the image of live music, validates experiences of musical events in simplistic terms without acknowledging how music is made and what it entails. It limits music's cultural dimensions in favor of the decontextualized commodity of the individual event. Implicitly, however, the feature reproduces a racial-and gender-biased narrative of mass-market Anglophone rock and pop music. The stars are white, male performers of rock, pop, and mainstream forms of country, soul, and dance music. Many forms of musical performance culture are absent, including amateur and street music. The absence of postcolonial Britain, moreover, raises questions about how the live music gaze relates to multiculturalism and migration. Art music appears in the form of brief footage from the Last Night of the Proms, but this event is not discussed.

Meanwhile, the term "live music" was spreading to consumer journalism. What used to be "concert" and "gig" listings, for instance, increasingly became "live music" listings in mainstream magazines such as *Time Out*. More specialist publications with scene expertise, such as *Brooklyn Vegan*, did not participate in this rebranding and continued to write about performance culture in more nuanced terms. *Brooklyn Vegan* provides listings of concerts in New York, Chicago, and Austin, and generally uses the term "show," a term that has been common in everyday popular music discourse for several decades. *Brooklyn Vegan* also provides reportage by specialist reporters and hosts conversations among frequent concertgoers.

The Institutionalization of Live Music Discourse

The mass-media enthusiasm discussed above was stimulated by a broad industry-driven institutionalization of live music discourse that spread from the concert industry into media, policy, and research. The idea of a live music industry evolved in the 1980s following a decade of growth and professionalization in the rock concert industry in the United Kingdom and the United States. In the 1970s, the dominant trade magazine *Billboard* organized annual conventions for the growing arena concert business. These conventions were called "*Billboard*'s International Talent Forum" since the business was focused on artists, not consumer experiences. The terms "live entertainment industry" and "live music industry" appeared in the magazine's own reports on the conventions, but it was not yet the standard industry designation ("2nd Talent Forum June 1–4"; "*Billboard*'s Third International Talent Forum"). At the time, the term "live entertainment" had a specific history in Las Vegas, where for decades entertainers had been promoted by the casino gambling industry to attract customers (Skolnick 1978, 51 and 84).

The evolution of the rock concert business into a live music industry was advanced by a convention in London. A few promoters started the International Live Music Forum (ILMF) in 1989 as an international networking event for professionals in the field. The Anglophone concert and festival industries were growing economically and geographically, so promoters from Continental Europe, for instance, had an interest in meeting representatives of the Anglophone industry in person. In addition to ILMF, the trade magazines *Audience* and *IQ Magazine* were created in 1999 and 2004, respectively. *Audience* now regularly publishes two magazines plus directories and guides to promoters and venues around the world. It also runs a subsidiary that has produced the convention Live UK Summit since 2007, among other things. Meanwhile, ILMF has grown into a large event. In 2018, it had more than one thousand participants from more than sixty countries ("Meeting of Minds"; "About the ILMC").

A similar formation occurred in the United States, where the industry reached a new level of corporatization with the development of SFX Entertainment, which was purchased by media giant Clear Channel in 2000 and renamed Live Nation in 2004. In the 2000s, *Billboard* developed more systematic and frequent coverage of the business. Veteran reporter Ray Waddell was the editor responsible for this area, writing reports on industry growth, while using the term "concert industry" well into the 2000s. These reports influenced investors at home and abroad and stimulated confidence in the industry, continuing a role that the magazine has fulfilled since the 1950s (Peterson 1997, 189). *Billboard* created awards based on ticket sales numbers and profits from tours, and it created a new convention. "*Billboard*'s Touring Conference and Awards" started in 2004 and moved from New York to Los Angeles, where the corporate live music industry became concentrated in the mid-2010s. In 2018, it was renamed "*Billboard* Live Music Summit." At the 2013 convention in New York, I witnessed how the live music gold rush attracted corporate professionals from afar, but few independent professionals. I met a top executive from Sony's headquarters in Japan, for instance, but not independent professionals from New York. *Billboard*'s close relationship with the corporate industry was evident throughout. The convention highlighted social media and electronic dance music as the new frontiers of the live music industry.

In Continental Europe, national associations of independent rock clubs adopted the English term and renamed themselves "live music" associations in the early 2010s. They understood how this appellation afforded them communicative power, as they aspired to grow as an industry and lobbied for public subsidies. At the same time, these independent rock clubs were suffering from growing corporatization and losing market share to festivals (chapter 5).

Public sector institutions generally began to take interest in "live music" in the mid-2010s and adopted the term into evolving economic policies of popular music.[3] In city marketing, Austin, Texas, has branded itself the "Live Music Capital of the World" since 1991 (O'Meara and Tretter 2013), and many cities started to support popular music events in the 1990s as part of the broader notion of the eventful city (Richards and Palmer 2010). Commercial interests also drove UNESCO's City of Music program, which gained traction in the early 2010s. In many of these initiatives, the folk ideology of live music was co-opted into worlds of business and consumption to project an aura of cultural values and civic authenticity. In the process, discourse on music in general was co-opted into these worlds. It seemed that everyone could love live music because it was a flexible signifier with many positive but also imprecise meanings. The mayor of London's 2015 taskforce "to save live music" (Ellis-Petersen 2015), for instance, set out to save clubs but did not spell out the criteria for supporting this particular culture or recognize the paradox that live music is a product of the capitalist system that destroyed the neighborhood ecologies of musical performance culture.

In Europe, the term "live music" has been taken up by the highest level of government. The European Union's interest in popular music had been insignificant and restricted to the independent sector into the mid-2010s. The rise of economic policies of culture and the psychology of austerity, however, made the corporate industry discourse on live music a welcome opportunity for retooling the EU's music policy. In 2016, the European Commission crafted a new agenda for music around this discourse under influence of industry lobbyists. I interviewed Karel Bartak, the person in charge of this process:

Author: The live music business experienced a boom in the 2000s. The number of festivals doubled in many countries. Have you thought about this?

Karel Bartak: Yes, of course. We are fully aware of this phenomenon. We are trying somehow to adapt to it and support it, especially the festivals that are a bit different and innovative and attract new and international audiences. This is of course an important phenomenon for us. We are busy trying to figure out how to help and thinking what we could be doing better in the next period [2020–2027]. . . . We have engaged in discussions with the sector for more than a year now to see how the support could evolve in the future because there is a change of mindset within the European Union. The notion of cultural and creative industries is much better recognized than it was in the past, so we do not have a representative sample but some data that can serve these arguments and prove that this sector is not only important for supporting art and

> music—and I don't know musicians and songwriting and composing and all this—but at the same time it is important from the economic point of view. Our big aim is to collect really representative data across Europe for making this statement about the economic value of live music and what is happening around the festivals, including the cross-border tourism and the revenue flows of companies. (Karel Bartak, Head of Culture Programme Unit, Directorate General for Education and Culture, European Commission, interview with the author, October 7, 2016)[4]

It is striking how Bartak's response shifts from cultural to economic policy. He explained to me that he and his team had met with many stakeholders from "the music world" and that they were open to meeting with "anyone." All of the examples he mentioned, however, were from the industry, mostly representatives of international industry associations but also Facebook and Google, for instance. The EU increasingly conceived its role in the cultural field as a supporter of industry. If a music policy centered on the live music industry were introduced, it would affect policies at the national and municipal levels across the EU. It would stimulate the field's further transformation into a for-profit value system and eliminate alternatives to this value system.

In just two decades, live music discourse has taken center stage in the industry, in mass media, in consumer culture, and in public policy. This institutionalization of live music discourse has escaped discussion in journalism and scholarship. The discourse's hegemony is illustrated by its adoption by independent rock clubs in Continental Europe, even though this made it more difficult for the clubs to distinguish themselves from the corporate industry (chapter 5). Moreover, the exploitation of folk discourse of live music can be interpreted as a general instance of how capitalism exploits human desires. Who, after all, does not value authentic and intimate experiences of musical performance? The situation parallels the marketing of commodities as sources of existential emotions such as happiness, love, and friendship. L'Oréal's slogan since 1973, for instance, states that all women are worthy of luxury, but it exploits human desires. It also exploits a feminist motif through commodified images of women.[5]

The Live Music Literature

A scholarly literature on live music emerged in Anglophone popular music studies in the late 2000s. The most influential proponent was Simon Frith. He pioneered this literature with his essay "Live Music Matters" in 2007 and co-led a research project based in Edinburgh in the early 2010s, which aimed to produce a three-volume "history of live music in the United Kingdom" (Frith 2007; Frith et al. 2013). The first strong wave of industry enthusiasm about live music came in 2007, and Frith's essay of that year explores sociological explanations for the industry boom. The essay makes a strong case for the general social and experiential values of live music consumption and is deservedly recognized as a landmark essay, but it also has some of the typical limitations of a pioneering effort. Above all, the essay is not investigating the term "live music" and its discursive operations. This has fundamental implications for the construction of the object of study and explains the lack of attention to its boundaries and to other social constructions of the object. The essay does not recognize the political economy and the cultural boundaries of live music discourse. Moreover, the discussion is framed in terms of the dualism of live and recorded music, which is relevant for identifying a specific dynamic in musical culture, but inadequate as a conceptual framing of performance culture. Live music replaces other ontologies in musical culture, including ontologies of music, performance, institutions, and architecture. These limitations are typical of the live music literature, including my own early contribution (Holt 2010), which similarly traced industry growth and suffered from methodological media-centrism.

Frith's essay makes gestures toward a sociology of musical performance that has not yet been fully developed. Typical of his writing style, Frith offers a number of very insightful statements with potential for further conceptualization, and he makes a compelling argument about synergy between live and recorded music. A systematic conceptualization does not materialize, however. The same is true for the first volume of his coauthored history of live music (Frith et al. 2013).[6] The volume begins with a brief statement about scholarly neglect of the live music sector and promises to explore the relationship between live and recorded music. However, the book does not promise or deliver much in terms of theory. It is an empirical history of musical performance cultures in the United Kingdom, with case studies of Bristol, Glasgow, and Sheffield in 1962. It is a valuable cultural history that provides great insight into the field and does not focus on live music discourse. The lack of critical thinking about the term is problematic, however, for the analytical and political reasons suggested above. The generally high quality of Frith's writings about live music notwithstanding, these writings contributed to the uncritical adoption of the term in the humanities.

A particular strand of live music literature is concerned with "the live music experience" and promotes a discourse structured by the live versus media dualism. This is illustrated by a pioneer research project funded by the Norwegian government. The project focused on the relationship between the consumption of live and recorded music. Two of the participants, Yngvar Kjus and Anne Danielsen (2014), conceptualized "the live music experience" in systematic terms, drawing on psychology and sociology. The literatures on performance in music studies are strikingly absent, however. Kjus and Danielsen thus indirectly illustrated the exclusionary work of live music discourse at the disciplinary level. Like their British colleagues, Kjus and Danielsen offered valuable insights. They shed light on the role of music festival consumption in music discovery and on how studio productions are adapted into a concert setting (see also Kjus 2018). By the late 2010s, the uncritical discourse continued in otherwise valuable work on "the live music experience" (e.g., Burland and Pitts 2014; Baxter-Moore and Kitts 2016) and in "live music" panels at the annual conferences of the International Association for the Study of Popular Music (IASPM).

This book does not merely introduce a critique of live music discourse in popular music studies; it also rejects it as an analytical discourse and develops an alternative. Live music is not a neutral term, it is not universal, and there are competing terms. It has a history as a folk and marketing term, but it has major limitations as an analytical term. The limitations pointed out above are considerable and cannot be overcome by perfecting the discourse. Key among these are (1) an uncritical reproduction of industry and consumer culture discourse and of methodological media-centrism; (2) an ignorance of the transformation of musical performance cultures in capitalism; (3) a lack of grounding in the cultural and intellectual histories of music and performance; and (4) a white, patriarchal ideology of Anglophone popular music. This book proposes an alternative discourse of musical performance culture in which live music is one among other ontologies and a powerful discourse that coevolved with the corporate institutionalization of Anglophone popular music performance in late modernity.

Finally, a critique of the live music literature can consider the corporate institutionalization of the humanities. Governments in Australia, Holland, Norway, and Scotland have funded research projects on live music with industry-related objectives and involved industry collaborations (Johnson and Homan 2002; Frith et al. 2013; Kjus and Danielsen 2014; "POPLIVE"). These research teams have not celebrated commercialism, and the Norwegian team made an important point in expanding the perspective from business to consumption, but they have not been critical of live music discourse or recognized how its ontologies and genealogies are constructed, particularly with respect to musical performance. The passive adoption of this discourse thus had considerable implications for the quality of research and for the capacity of the humanities to respond to a transformation in musical culture. I plead guilty to failing my own responsibility and hope to correct my mistake in this book. I experienced the neoliberal dilemma in the late 2000s: university professors had new opportunities for government research funding and for industry collaboration, but there was little space for critical humanist research. During my field experience in the festival industry (see p. 221), I began to feel alienated and eventually decided to not apply for funding for live music research out of my interest in maintaining political autonomy. I reflect further on the book's immanent critique of the challenged academic freedom in the humanities in the concluding chapter.

The Disciplinary Challenge

The limitations of live music scholarship identified above point to a lack of broader theorizations of musical performance culture in modernity. Sociologists have theorized fields of cultural production, but little sociological groundwork has been laid in the area of musical performance. This book looks beyond the nominal field of music sociology and instead adopts a discourse of the social study of music. The book draws on broader fields of sociology and on the anthropology of music, or ethnomusicology, in which important social theory of musical performance has evolved. In Anglophone scholarship, music sociology is a discourse rather than a field or discipline, and its knowledge interests center on microlevel analysis and on audience engagements with recorded music. The objectives of this book require another kind of analytical discourse. The main disciplinary challenge is to integrate a sociological narrative of institutions into music studies. At first, sociology has a complementary function by delivering institutional theory lacking in music studies, but the relationship between these two disciplines evolves throughout the book. Rather than seeking a synergy that erases disciplinary difference, the book allows the logic of each discipline to take center stage at different points in its analysis to potentially challenge each other with competing explanations. The logic of inquiry expands further in the integration of disciplines with area literatures.

Just Another Market Evolution?

To illustrate the centrality of a broad sociological interpretation, let us recognize how the transformation of the field has followed an evolutionary path typical in capitalism. The symptoms are strikingly familiar from the evolution of many other commodity markets in the past. Is it not true, for instance, that the music industry has developed performance events into standardized mass-market commodities and created narratives to make them authentic and induce consumer needs? The concert and festival industries have done this, for instance, by presenting more star performers in popular genres and transforming clubs and festivals into more glamorous spaces. These industries have also retooled themselves as a live music industry of consumer experiences. The growing spending on concerts and festivals in the 2000s, moreover, reflects growing levels of affluence for broader populations in capitalist societies in modernity, even when the historic growth in income inequality (and the decline in labor conditions and welfare services) in neoliberal capitalism are taken into account (Mueller 2012, 4; Milanovic 2013; Du Gay and Morgan 2013). Is the festival boom in the 2000s not a case of what German sociologist Werner Sombart imagined more than one hundred years ago (Sombart [1913] 1967), namely that with the progression of capitalist society nonessential goods would be produced for ever-larger groups of people as democratized luxuries that many can only afford during holidays? Bruno Frey's study of festival growth in classical music suggested that growing affluence and more leisure time over the course of the twentieth century were key factors in their growth (Frey 1994), and this argument applies to popular music festivals, too. Might desires for luxury explain the enthusiasm for the spectacle of mega stars, gourmet food, "glamping," and VIP packages? Moreover, could the frequent boredom and chatter among audiences in the past decade be a symptom of consumerist attitudes and unfulfilled desires?[7]

Knowledge of commodity markets is also relevant for understanding how institutions of Anglophone pop have evolved in Continental Europe. The live music industry has built on the accelerating media circulation of rock, pop, and electronic dance music in Europe since the 1980s with the deregulation of international media markets and the rise of corporate Anglophone streaming services and retailers such as Amazon, Apple, Netflix, Spotify, and YouTube (chapter 7). The scale of these newly deregulated markets created the basis for the international corporatization of popular music performance. The corporatization began in the rock industry in the 1990s, resulting in the duopoly of AEG and Live Nation, and evolved in the electronic dance music industry in the 2000s with SFX Entertainment and, again, Live Nation. SFX went bankrupt in 2016 but was revived as LiveStyle later that year.

The effects of the evolving media circulation and corporatization can be identified across Continental Europe: the number of concerts in urban clubs doubled in several cities in Continental Western Europe in the 1990s and 2000s, from Barcelona in the south to Stockholm in the north (chapter 5). The number of festivals and the size of their crowds also doubled. In the 1980s, for instance, Europe had a few dozen rock festivals with day crowds of about 25,000. By the 2010s, there were more than two hundred rock and EDM festivals with such day crowds and about forty of them had day crowds of more than 50,000 people, all of them owned or dominated by a few international corporations (chapter 8).[8] The market expanded eastward in the 2000s, as promoters such as Mikołaj Ziółkowski in Poland and Ivan Milivojev in Serbia created festivals that became part of Live Nation's touring circuit. Formerly more diverse national cultures of popular music performance are becoming more standardized with the internationalization of Anglophone popular culture. National broadcasters, moreover, are losing ground to Anglophone internet broadcasters such as YouTube, Boiler Room, and Red Bull TV. Corporate promoters have increased the circulation of international superstars, a small number of "cash cows," to a growing number of events with similar designs, giving local audiences in a wider territory the opportunity to experience international connectivity with Anglophone global culture (chapter 7).

The transformation of the field cannot only be explained in market terms, however. This book draws from sociology, but situates musical performance institutions in musical and cultural history. To this end, music studies is needed.

The Social Study of Music

This book builds on a development in music studies since the 1990s in which cultural and social theoretical approaches to music are integrated into a scholarly practice that combines interdisciplinarity with area studies specialization. A pioneer contribution to this tradition is the edited volume *The Cultural Study of Music* (Clayton, Herbert, and Middleton 2003/2012), which advanced cultural musicology and the more interdisciplinary term "the cultural study of music." Interdisciplinary sensibilities have continued to evolve, with music scholars becoming more eclectic in their inspirations from the social sciences (Shepherd and Devine 2015a, 2). An interdisciplinary conception of the social study of musical performance is especially relevant because major advances in social theory of performance have been made in ethnomusicology but escaped other areas of musicology as well as music sociology. This book draws on ethnomusicology to conceptualize performance culture (chapter 2) and to develop a cultural critique of music festival theory and historiography (chapters 6–7).

How might the book contribute to music sociology? While music sociology has achieved a limited level of institutionalization in the Anglophone world, it continues to evolve as a discourse on how music can be interpreted sociologically. There are no handbooks, journals, societies, or departments of music sociology, nor any established textbooks. During the 2000s, music sociology gravitated toward microlevel analysis. This trend is evident in the work of sociologists with long-term specialization in music, such as Antione Hennion, David Hesmondhalgh, and Tia DeNora. These scholars moved beyond Adorno's influential grand theory approach to instead create a more empirically and often ethnographically grounded sociology (DeNora 2015). One of the major advantages of this development is that sociology is brought into closer contact with a broader range of ordinary musical practices and experiences (Hesmondhalgh 2013, chapter 2; see also Kassabian 2013). Sociology is also brought into closer contact with music studies. The aforementioned scholars generally engage more with specialized music literatures and musicological arguments than scholars with a more general profile in cultural sociology. The work of the latter type can be found in journals such as *Cultural Sociology* and *Poetics*.

The evolution of a stronger microsociology of music has unfortunately involved the decline of interest in societal analysis and systemic formations of power and ideology. Georgina Born has critiqued the tendency to reduce music sociology to microsociology and argued for the inclusion of other levels of analysis (Born 2011, 378; Born 2012). This critique is relevant to scholarship on musical performance culture. How is it possible, for instance, that a major transformation in popular music's performance institutions in many countries has gone unnoticed in music sociology? How could music sociology ignore the impacts of global gentrification on local ecosystems of music cultures? Or the exploitation of live ideology in marketing and public policy? These are not minor developments with implications in a few locales, but rather broad, structural changes in the conditions of musical life and in the societal construction of music. These changes call for more meso- and macrolevel analysis as well as more critical social theory. DeNora's (2000) and Hesmondhalgh's (2013) books on music in everyday emotional life are deeply insightful, and they closed major gaps in the literature, but they do not situate music and emotional culture in broader social formations or discuss geographic and cultural boundaries in much detail. Hesmondhalgh has written insightfully about music and cultural difference in the past (e.g., Born and Hesmondhalgh 2000), and his monograph on music can be read as a contribution to a particular moment in sociological thinking about music. There is little societal analysis in current music sociology. Even *The Routledge*

Reader on the Sociology of Music devotes little attention to capitalism and consumer culture, for instance (Shepherd and Devine 2015b). The present book focuses its contribution on the social study of musical performance in urban social history and cultural globalization and in the commercialization of performance institutions.

The need for analysis of societal issues and systemic formations is demonstrated by the interest in capitalism that is strangely growing outside music sociology in popular music studies and in economic ethnomusicology (e.g., Goldschmitt 2011, 2019; Morcom 2015; Taylor 2016; Beaster-Jones 2016; James 2015). Taylor's *Music and Capitalism: A History of the Present* (2016) makes the case that musical scholarship has ignored neoliberal capitalism. The book asserts that neoliberalism has brought changes to all areas of social life and introduces a range of ideas and concepts, including capitalism's cultural turn and the brand commodity. The book explores the implications of neoliberalism in the music industry, focusing on its media sectors. The general argument about capitalism as an important context for understanding popular music and music production is important. However, the book's sensitivity to the universalizing effects of neoliberalism sediments in a monolithic narrative that ignores some of the diversity in capitalism, including the dynamics between rural and urban areas and, conceptually, between structure and agency. The book to some extent privileges superstructure. Moreover, like James (2015), Taylor treats capitalism thematically and does not situate music in a broader analysis of capitalist society and its institutions.

This book is not about the general relationship between music and capitalism, but it takes capitalism into account as a social system and ideology that shapes the conditions of culture. In basic terms, capitalism is "an imperative to unlimited capital accumulation by formally peaceful means" within a system of production and consumption based on private ownership of the means of production (Du Gay and Morgan 2013, 12). Capitalism is guaranteed by a set of institutions, including large corporations, banks, and financial markets (Mueller 2012, 3). This system governs contemporary societies and therefore deserves critical attention. Any analysis of it can recognize the system's strengths, such as efficiency and the historically broad distribution of wealth, but also its weaknesses, social injustices, and its more problematic forms, including neoliberalism, which has had detrimental impacts on society and accelerated climate change. Such analysis requires humanistic interpretation and debate. The corporate information technology, airline, and finance industries may be efficient and serve many customers, for instance, but how do they affect people's lives, society, and the environment? Are higher levels of productivity and consumption of music a path to richer and more meaningful lives and societies today? Or might more civic and public ownership over the means of production balance interests in commerce and consumption and create more space for broader conceptions of music and culture? Could such change be achieved through education and conversations in civil society, or does it also require regulation of capitalism's institutions?

Institutions in Everyday Urban Life and in the Summer Season

The commercial institutions of musical performance that have evolved since the eighteenth century in Europe and North America can be interpreted as a specific subset of leisure institutions. Concert halls, cabarets, dance halls, and festivals are places where people have spent money to enjoy music, socialize, drink, and dance outside regular working hours. Sociological literatures on institutions and on leisure more specifically provide valuable insights that can be developed further in the area of music.

The concept of institutions is central to sociology's interest in the structure of social life and the evolution of distinct domains in society. It builds on the insight that collective behavior is not simply an aggregate consequence of individual choice or individual-level properties (DiMaggio and Powell 1991, 2). Theories of institutions share an interest in overcoming atomistic accounts that describe individual situations with little attention to general social dynamics and societal context. A core analytical entity in institutional theory is organizations. Karl Marx pioneered the idea that social forces act on and through organizations, and Max Weber analyzed organizational bureaucracy as a defining aspect of modern society. Weber argued that bureaucracy emerged from market competition, state governments, and bourgeois demands and replaced earlier forms of domination that were less "rational" in that they were not governed by the same precise rules of coercion, forms of permanent administrative office regulation, and logics of means-ends calculus and matter-of-factness (Weber 1922/1978, 956 and 1002). Much institutional theory has been concerned with the large engines of society, with government and industry. This explains the emphasis on bureaucratic processes and formal regulation. These aspects have been less central to leisure institutions, which have historically been small and local and constituted by their difference from the functional spheres of society. Herbert Spencer's conception of this structural differentiation of modern society is echoed in contemporary notions of institutions as sectors or organizational fields (Scott 1995/2014, 10–11).

The social study of music can take inspiration from these sociological insights. Scholarship of performance in organized musical life in modern society is somewhat atomistic in that scholars routinely analyze examples or case studies with little attention to institutional dynamics. Performance is typically studied as an individual event. Concert halls, clubs, and festivals are studied as venues. Performance culture is studied within an individual genre.

I conceive of a performance institution as a form of organized performance culture that is spatially articulated. A performance institution is a model of production and consumption in a particular type of performance space that has become socially meaningful and symbolically important in cultural life through frequent repetition and experience of the culture's rituals and values. It is a relatively stable aesthetic and social arrangement that is articulated in a performance space and its ritual ordering, mythology, and programming. Performance institutions are structured by seasonal dynamics and the norms of a culture, including genre norms. They complement each other and compete within the leisure seasons and evolving music markets. Their meanings and functions are contingent to changing structures in their respective organizational fields and urban environments. Variations of each institution result from diversity and differentiation within genres and cities. Market competition drives the structuration of the organizational field of each institution and the evolution of variations that are adapted to mass-market demographics. This structuration can lead to a situation in which a few commercial models replace a more diverse range of older models (DiMaggio and Powell 1983). Such situation is characterized by a high level of cultural homogeneity and bureaucracy. The concept of institutions can be further delineated along four dimensions:

1. *Symbolic*. A performance institution produces its own symbolic order, such as the ritual and mythology of the festival. It also interprets the wider symbolic order of the genre and cultural sphere to which it belongs. It provides a space in which artists and audiences reproduce and potentially transform, if only momentarily, a symbolic order through their performative engagement with materials, symbols, and cognitive schemes. This conception builds on insights from Émile Durkheim's study of religion as a symbolic system that regulates behaviors and enables individuals to adopt collective subject positions, such as the sacred and the profane, and to experience a connection with society (Durkheim [1912] 2001). Talcott Parsons sought to synthesize Weber's and Durkheim's ideas in his conception of institutions as normative frameworks that govern practices (Scott 1995/2014, 16). I explore how norms and values govern practices, drawing

from symbolic approaches to festive events in anthropology and sociology and from New Institutionalism in organizational sociology. The symbolic dimension informs this book's interpretation of the functions and mythologies of clubs and festivals in musical culture, and it is central to its theorization of the festival institution.

2. *Temporal.* Institutions result from the process of institutionalization that fixes and institutes a social arrangement and infuses it with meaning. The arrangement attains a certain state and property of stability and relative permanence that makes it less vulnerable to intervention. Organized life has a constant and repetitive character. Its institutions are defined by taken-for-granted practices and self-sustaining structures (DiMaggio and Powell 1991, 8–9; Jefferson 1991). Individuals are socialized into norm systems, but they also develop attachments, meanings, and trust through concrete and situated personal relations (Granovetter 1985). The temporal dimension will be explored through historical analysis of the evolution of the club and the festival, including their trajectories from urban scenes into corporate structures, where some practices and mythologies of the past persist.

3. *Organizational.* Each articulation of a performance institution—in the regularized practices at a particular club, festival, concert hall, or community arts center—involves the formal ownership and management of a promoter. Clubs and festivals have historically been synonymous with a single space and organization. In many cases, an individual or a small group of people have created an organization to start a club or festival in their area of residence. Corporate ownership of many clubs or festivals only became a dominant norm in the twenty-first century. This rise of more powerful organizations and organizational fields deserves greater attention in the social study of music.

The promoter is a key actor in the social arrangement of the individual club or festival. The promoter serves functions as a host by coordinating and programming events, maintaining facilities, and selling drinks. It owns the performance space and regulates the space socially through practices such as pricing, admission rules, opening hours, and rules of conduct. The promoter further shapes the symbolic order through music programming, spatial design, and marketing. Independent promoters have occasionally adopted, and been endowed with, the charismatic role of a visionary and champion of the culture, sometimes embodied in the personality of the manager. Corporations, by contrast, operate through the more impersonal and abstract logic of the brand. The larger the market is, the more the scale of production and organization can expand and develop into centralized ownership, and the more bureaucratic the organization becomes. The level of bureaucracy is important because it structures performance culture. The impersonal social relations created by large corporations and markets can contradict and have alienating impacts on the intimate personal setting and on the language of public intimacy and compassion in some forms of performance.

The New Institutionalism that began to transform organizational sociology in the 1970s offers a number of relevant perspectives for popular music's performance institutions. Paul DiMaggio and Walter Powell (1983) reflected on the contemporary relevance of Weber's thinking about bureaucracy, arguing that new dynamics had emerged with the condition of generalized corporate bureaucracy. As organizational life had become increasingly corporate, organizational fields had become more centralized and were now playing a larger role in structuring organizations. New Institutionalists developed this macrolevel perspective on organizations in national and international organizational fields that has since become common. These scholars viewed organizations as units in a population and argued that organizations were increasingly responding to the environment of their field and the behaviors of other organizations. DiMaggio and Powell developed these insights further in a theory of how developments in organizational fields made organizations more similar in both structure and norms. This theory of institutional isomorphism helps explain why the corporatization of musical performance has not just expanded the field but transformed it. Of particular relevance here are the drivers of market-driven isomorphism (DiMaggio and Powell 1983, 154–56). The following drivers inform this book's analysis:

- Growing national and international markets
- Professionalization and the rise of corporate career profiles and trade associations
- Response to uncertainty
- Growing dependency on monopolistic corporations
- Growing dependency on the same vital resources
- Centralized distribution of resources
- Fewer visible alternatives to dominant commercial models

4. *Societal.* As places of collective symbolic value and regulatory power, institutions structure social life. The more an area of social life is institutionalized, the more bureaucratic and integrated with the large engines of society it becomes. In this Weberian perspective, the commercial institutionalization of musical performance makes musical life more organized and musical culture more bureaucratic and integrated with capitalism.

Corporations have come to play a larger role in the societal construction of music—through ownership and influence on the forms of music that are produced, the environments of experience, and the spaces of communication. This book explores how popular music's performance institutions have adapted to the larger bureaucratic environment of the gentrified city and to corporate media and advertising. The investigations highlight how corporations have retooled the institutions around more conformist forms of popular music, while still including stylistic elements of bohemianism, social emancipation, and hedonism.

The Commercial Institutionalization of Leisure

Cultural sociologists have observed a broad international trajectory in modernity from community- to commerce-based forms of leisure (Sassatelli 2010, 5). The drivers of this process include urbanization, the evolution of international systems of media circulation, and growing levels of affluence. The transformation has been particularly striking in musical life in the Nordic countries: local traditions of nonprofit idealism and volunteerism dominated in clubs and festivals until the 2010s, when international corporations quickly expanded. Corporations expanded the market and intensified the competition, forcing nonprofit clubs and festivals to act more like for-profit organizations (chapters 5 and 7; Andersson and Getz 2012).

Roberta Sassatelli's monograph on the fitness gym provides insight into how one leisure institution has evolved through commercial institutionalization (Sassatelli 2010). Based on longitudinal ethnographic research in urban Italy and England, Sassatelli suggests that the rise of fitness culture accompanies a growing interest in body care, refinement, and self-reflexivity in late modernity (Sassatelli 2010, 2). The commercial gym is an institution that frames training in terms of fun and pleasure to create a glamorous and fashionable image of fitness culture for consumers (Sassatelli 2010, 128). Through architectural design, background music, and marketing communications, for instance, the glamour is staged and organized for consumption in a controlled environment. Sassatelli references Foucault's discussions of how institutions put bodies to work through disciplining techniques in a closed environment for a specific purpose (Sassatelli 2010, 20). The focusing of purpose, through spatial design and marketing, limits the space for agency and frames the individual as a consumer. One of Sassatelli's informants describes the gym as a place "where you go to exercise and then you leave again, in and out. Even though you may meet nice people, there aren't many people there who are really interested in making friends"

(Sassatelli 2010, 77–78). Commercial institutionalization transforms leisure into a specialized activity in dedicated environments, illustrating the structural division of modern society into domains (Sassatelli 2010, 187).

The commercialization of the fit body, of self-control, perfection, and endurance, can be further interpreted as an exploitation of values in professional life. Chris Rojek pioneered the argument that leisure is not an entirely autonomous "free time" but is in fact regulated and bound up with labor markets (Rojek 1985). Rojek wrote about body and mind maintenance as a form of unpaid labor shaped by conditions of employment. I argue in chapter 4 that indie concert theaters have developed an aesthetic that resonates with evolving professional subjectivities in the gentrified city, while producing values particular to music.

The Commercial Institutionalization of Musical Performance

Musical performance illustrates general and unique trajectories in the history of the commercial institutionalization of leisure. This book concentrates on two institutions of popular music performance that illustrate this process: the club and the festival. The arena or stadium, by contrast, was a highly commercial institution when it was first adopted in rock music. The arena has a history in settings with a civic dimension, such as the Greek amphitheater, but it had evolved into an entertainment industry of large, for-profit companies when rock music began to be performed there. The commercial potential of the arena's audience capacity was the main motivation for rock stars and promoters, as part of the growing media business of rock music (Frith et al. 2013, 140 and 154). Recording companies created "superstar" series, a key example of which was Atlantic Records' promotion of the album *Déjà Vu* (1970) by Crosby, Stills, Nash, and Young (Edwards, Eyries, and Callahan 2005). The pioneer promoter Bill Graham later recalled that "rock and roll had started in the clubs and the streets and the parks" and evolved into stadiums when some of the artists became stars. Graham described how the business of rock promotion became more narrowly defined by market concerns in the late 1960s. He owned and managed two rock clubs during those years and witnessed how new superstars such as Crosby, Stills, Nash, and Young began to make unusual requests for stage decorations and catering and eventually began performing in Madison Square Garden for the much higher honoraria. Graham detested the idea of rock music in the Garden but adapted to the evolution by closing his clubs and becoming a leading arena tour manager (Graham 1971; Graham and Greenfield 1992/2004, 335 and 354).

The club and the festival have a history in grassroots and DIY cultures, specifically in urban scenes, and their outlook and functions in musical culture have changed considerably through ongoing commercial institutionalization since the 1960s. Unlike the arena, they are dedicated institutions of popular music and do not frequently present events without musical performance as a central component. They have more specialized popular music programming and produce events more frequently, thus enabling them to produce value as institutions of a particular culture and genre.

In rock music, the club evolved from informal performance spaces, such as bars with a stage, and it was a social institution of music scenes and subcultures before the larger and more formal concert club became the dominant model in the 2000s (chapters 4–5). The rock festival evolved from informal countercultural events and festivals in the 1950s and 1960s. It was developed into a music festival by the music industry in 1967 and disrupted in the early 1970s before being commercially institutionalized by the music festival industry that developed in subsequent decades. A growth spiral culminated in the 2000s with the model of the corporate consumer culture festival characterized by glamorous marketing images, constant entertainment on multiple stages, some of the world's best-selling recording artists on the main stage, higher service standards, and more shopping areas for festivalgoers (chapters 7–8).

The commercial institutionalization of the club and the festival thus parallels the fitness gym in several respects. Like the gym, the club and festival have been developed through new marketing images, more consistent and standardized commodities and services, and more commercial regulation of bodies and practices. They, too, have become places focused on specific consumer purposes and not on establishing new friendships or participating in a community or a social scene. This is particularly true in clubs where audiences come for the headliner and leave right after (chapter 4). As in any process of commercialization, the separation between producer and consumer intensifies. Professional aesthetics of craft, perfection, and excellence have a strong market appeal and are easier to institutionalize and corporatize than amateur aesthetics. Furthermore, the functions of these institutions have changed. The club and the festival have evolved from serving urban scenes and distinct culture worlds to serving mass-market consumer demographics and institutions of capitalism.

Commercial institutionalization takes on specific forms in processes of corporatization. The international corporate live music industry has created centralized structures for distributing the same star performers across wide distances to venues owned by the same corporations. The corporatization has resulted in more centralized ownership throughout the entire chain of commerce—from artist management, talent agency, promoter, and venue operator to ticketing. The industrialization of performance institutions has followed well-known strategies in the cultural industries for generating stable and growing profits. They include organizational expansion for market control and the development of commodities with the highest profit margin for larger markets through marketing, formatting, and increased efficiency and consistency (Hesmondhalgh 2003/2019; Frith [1987] 2007). With its particular economy of space and place, the live music industry has expanded the audience capacities and the geographies and intensities of touring. The result is a set of international networks of producers and venues characterized by unprecedented levels of productivity enabled by standardized practices, technologies, and architectural designs. Architectural designs have been optimized for frequent and routinized production and consumption, with more logistic efficiency, bureaucratic control, and consumer safety. Star performers are central to this industry system; it could not be based on amateur performers. The scale of corporatization has had the broader systemic effect of institutionalizing mass-market consumer culture values into the organizational field of popular music performance. I will argue that commercial institutionalization is an industry-driven process, but that the industry exploits rather than creates the conditions for this process. When alternatives to corporate ownership have declined, the reason has not always been corporate competition alone, but also rising real estate prices and changes in lifestyles and labor markets.

Commercial institutionalization has frequently generated tensions and counterreactions in music history. Referring to German music festivals in the 1830s, music critics lamented that amateur soloists were being replaced by professionals in these festivals, and the festival growth spiral in Germany during these decades had implications similar to the recent spiral in pop festivals (chapter 6). In the twentieth century, performance institutions were frequently a refuge from the corporate recording industry. In the 1960s, for instance, bluegrass communities found a refuge from the Nashville music industry in festivals (Rosenberg 1985), and underground jazz and rock musicians found a refuge in abandoned warehouses and factories in the metropolis (Heller 2016; Zukin 1982). The warehouse jazz scene of the 1960s represents an early stage in the history of DIY music scenes that have defined themselves in opposition to commercial institutions (chapter 4).

Another alternative to the commercial institutionalization of popular music performance can be found in television culture. In the 2000s, amateur music contests became a popular form of TV entertainment. Reality TV shows dramatized basic dichotomies that had been tamed by the professionalization of popular music's performance institutions as part of their commercialization, including the dichotomies good versus bad, success versus failure, craft versus emotion, constraint versus spontaneity, and beauty versus ugliness. Professional shortcomings were not filtered out, but rather amplified for amusement, ridicule, and self-identification. These shows integrated into reality television elements from talent contests such as the Amateur Night at the Apollo (since 1934) and from the broader spheres of tabloids, soaps, the lottery, and sports betting. Scholars argued that a new culture of celebrity has evolved in which people of little distinction—people with low-income jobs and no careers or other experiences of social mobility—engage in the fantasy of a different life, but one that is more realistic than professional stardom. By watching people with a story close to their own, audiences can interpret their own life as more glamorous and meaningful and experience a more realistic form of celebrity based on luck (Press and Williams 2015). A key aspect of "lottery celebrity" in a show such as *Big Brother* is the spectacle of mundane ordinariness, often described as a desire to just be famous without talent and skill, thus challenging conventional values of performance (Press and Williams 2015, 179). How well the concept of lottery celebrity applies to reality music shows is a question for future research. Music shows are different from *Big Brother* and *Survivor* in that they focus on an artistic practice (singing) on stage and not on backstage spaces of private life. However, the contestants are generally not members of any social elite, and the ritual has markers of low prestige: performers are contestants in a ready-made competition, not artists with a professionally crafted persona, and they sing cover songs and are evaluated by celebrity judges and anonymous audiences rather than by genre experts. Even so, over the course of their fifteen-plus-year history, reality music shows have themselves become institutionalized within the television industry and shown signs of a professional value system. The shows feature less humiliation of the least talented and more appreciation of skillful talent and virtuosity. The shows have adopted a more general aesthetics of emotional authenticity and intimacy, similar to live concepts such as MTV's "unplugged" and NPR's "Tiny Desk."[9]

Everyday Urban Life and the Summer Season

In many societies, music and other forms of performance culture have distinct dynamics in the domains of everyday life and seasonal festivity. Musical performance institutions typically belong to one or the other domain and have adapted themselves to those specific dynamics and economies. These two domains are not variations of the same thing. They require distinct theories. A theoretical framework of musical performance institutions benefits from analysis of the distinctness of these two domains as opposed to starting from an undifferentiated generalization.

In the Global North, the city has been a primary domain of professional musical performance production throughout modernity. Large modern cities provided the basis for frequent production of musical performances for paying audiences. The concert evolved with the rise of the bourgeois class, music publishing, and music criticism in the city, and the music festival in the summer season evolved as an extension of the urban domain. Music festivals were organized by organizations in the city and held in the city. In several smaller cities, a music festival was the major cultural event of the year and served as a model for creating the types of concerts that only larger cities could support in everyday life (chapter 6). The summer season still has particular significance for small cities.

The two domains and their institutions have coevolved with electronic media since the early twentieth century. The media circulation of sound recordings and motion pictures not only stimulated more touring across wider distances and larger audience capacities; it also contributed to the mediatization of performance culture and the expansion of the festival season. Media culture began to shape the aesthetics, rituals, and curatorial practices in performance culture. An artist's media power, constructed through various forms of media production and circulation, became a major factor in defining the culture and market of the artist's performances. Movies and music journalism coconstructed images and mythologies of clubs and festivals. The evolution of segmented mass-media marketing through genre labels, moreover, shaped curatorial practices.

Performance culture does not simply mirror or contrast media culture, however. Many sound recordings have historically been recordings of performances, and many are still based on performance practices and made for dancing. Sound recordings, videos, and DJ practices are deeply embedded in performance culture and thus challenge dichotomous conceptions of the relationship between media and performance (chapters 2 and 9; Middleton 1990, chapter 3; Rambarran 2017). Clubs and festivals have been a resource for the recording industry and continue to create values that do not exist in media consumption, including in-person experiences of performance, collectivity, place, and architecture. Moreover, media cultures interact differently with performance cultures. Niche media can boost the growth of a small scene or festival and enable artists to develop small audiences in many countries. Mass media, on the other hand, have the capacity to transcend places and leisure seasons, primarily through celebrity power. Superstars can tour arenas throughout the year because of their media fame and without localizing the production. This explains why the arena does not need to present events with a particular frequency or with any consistency in programming in terms of genre; it is a somewhat placeless mass-media space. With respect to music festivals, star performers have had the cultural function of boosting festivity since at least the early nineteenth century, but the growing presence of superstars in popular music festivals indicates that festivals are no longer evolving as much from the urban domain, but increasingly from the mass-media domain.

Diana Crane introduced a distinction in the theory of cultural production that helps explain the evolution of media dynamics in both the everyday urban and summer season domains. She identified a high concentration of performance cultures in the city, which is characterized by a wealth of production for consumption in semipublic spaces. Large cities have a plethora of cultural organizations that are specialized as a result of their differentiation within local markets and among neighborhoods. Crane argues that art and music serve a function within urban class cultures, noting that high-art institutions and for-profit organizations such as Broadway theaters are located in affluent areas, while more experimental art and popular music clubs tend to be found in lower-class neighborhoods (Crane 1992, 141). These class divisions have fundamentally changed with gentrification, but some differentiation still exists among gentrified neighborhoods, even when this is increasingly based on mythologies as opposed to actual economic disparities. Moreover, Crane identifies media production as a more industrial form of production aimed at much larger national and international audiences, cutting across class divisions. This principle generally applies to musical performance culture, as performances for large international audiences tend to be produced by a corporate industry and follow mass-media logics, while performances targeted to smaller and more local audiences are produced by smaller organizations and are less media intense. Productions for small, urban audiences tend to be less celebrity centered and have a smaller budget for videos and other forms of marketing. The performances themselves tend to involve less photography and generate less media activity. Niche media generally plays a key role in stimulating interest in performances of niche music, though.

The conceptualization of the two domains in the following discussion situates them in a historical narrative of evolving culture markets and media cultures. This is particularly relevant with popular cultures that are constantly transformed through evolutions in cities, media, and markets. This book investigates such processes of change and illustrates dynamism between transformations in organizational fields and cultural fields. It therefore does not frame performance institutions within cultural field theory. Bourdieu's field theory, for instance, is primarily a theory of how a cultural field reproduces itself (Calhoun 1995, chapter 5). Its emphasis on reproduction results from a high-art bias that was the object of critique in the 1990s. Crane argued that sociologists had overstated the influence of elites and ignored developments in media cultures and nonelite urban cultures that were broadening the cultural field and challenging the hegemony of high art (Crane 1992).

In the everyday urban domain, a wealth of artistic and economic resources provides the basis of institutions that produce frequent musical performance events. The first major institution in this domain in secular modernity was the bourgeois concert hall that emerged in the eighteenth century. The concert hall expanded on a tradition for organizing concert series outside the church and the court and became a central site of public cultural life throughout the year. It institutionalized the concert ritual for regular consumption, involving new forms of programming and framings of the audience. It provided regular employment for musicians and stimulated the development of the symphonic genre (Rose 2009; Will 2009; Weber 1997). The number and variety of leisure institutions featuring popular music expanded in the nineteenth-century metropolis, as illustrated by the music hall in London, the minstrelsy show in New York, the cabaret in Paris, and popular couple dancing in Vienna (Scott 2008). New institutions of popular music developed from urban transformations in the twentieth century (chapter 3), but the commercial institutionalization of popular music since the late twentieth century has led to a concentration in the concert and the festival, to some extent mirroring the basic structure of these eighteenth-century bourgeois institutions.

The club became the central neighborhood institution of popular music in the twentieth century. In New York City, rock clubs evolved from informal bars with a small stage embedded in a nightlife economy into more formal concert clubs defined by an economy of performers with a larger market. Going to a club has historically been a neighborhood experience, not just because it required one's physical presence in the neighborhood in which the club is located, but also because clubs have adapted to their respective neighborhoods' aesthetics and profited from the neighborhood's social and cultural capital. Like other small nightlife institutions in the city, moreover, the club has been sensitive to neighborhood change. When real estate prices have gone up, the demographics and norms have changed, and certain types of clubs and their networks could no longer subsist. Small and informal club organizations that present experimental artists and have only short-term leases have generally disappeared, while clubs owned by larger for-profit companies that focus on professional entertainment and have capital to invest in real estate have become more common. The latter type of organization is more bureaucratic and designed for continuous commercial growth, with an emphasis on products that are typically considered beautiful and enjoyable by casual consumers (Crane 1992, 129). Examples include commercial art galleries and Broadway musical theaters. The core example among rock clubs in this book is the indie concert theater developed in New York by promoter Michael Swier and the company the Bowery Presents. Clubs thus grow and die like plants in the urban landscape, thriving momentarily in the oasis that is a neighborhood nightlife scene before it is dried out by gentrification and leaves the culture with the task of finding a new home in the city. Clubs are also part of the broader dynamics of neighborhood differentiation, although the differences have lessened with the general gentrification of city centers and with the evolution of clubs into an economy of headliner artists (chapters 4–5).

In the domain of the summer season, musical performance culture takes on distinct dynamics in the larger annual event of the music festival. The music festival has premodern origins in traditional seasonal rituals that celebrated larger existential themes beyond the realm of everyday life. Like other major events of the festive seasons, such as the carnival and the Octoberfest, the music festival involves more extended forms of festivity and a greater suspension of the rules and routines of everyday life. It is a modern invention, however, and it is concentrated in the summer season, which allows for outdoor events and for festival consumption as a vacation activity. The music festival emerged as a distinct type of cultural festival in secular society in the eighteenth century and an extension of growing urban concert markets. The music festival followed a broader process of secularization in which a deeply rooted relationship between festivity and ethics in Christianity was transformed into a narrative of festivity and civic authenticity, specifically in the idea that people could have cultural agency independently of the church and the aristocracy and experience soulful collectivity through musical and cultural festivity. In eighteenth- and nineteenth-century Europe, music festivals were organized by civic associations and involved large amateur choirs. By programming music with a high symbolic value and a large number of concerts, the festival gained power as a major cultural event in musical life and one that attracted artists and audiences from afar.

The annual cycle is central to the festival's functions for musical culture and its capacity to bring music into wider cultural festivity in society (chapter 6).

New forms of music festivals evolved in popular culture in the second half of the twentieth century. While the nineteenth-century music festival was a rather traditional institution of cultural nationalism, the folk and jazz festivals that emerged in the 1950s embodied new postwar worldviews and lifestyles, and the first large-scale popular music festival—the hippie music festival—evolved from exploratory cultural festivity in metropolitan countercultures. This involved new conceptions of the festival as a cultural event and new dynamics of fast-changing popular culture fashions. The rock and electronic dance music festival industries developed the new consumer culture models of the rock festival and the EDM festival around popularized versions of these music genres and a correspondingly smoother festival aesthetic that, again, is more easily accessible and enjoyable for casual consumers. The dominance of these models, resulting from complex processes in new institutional arrangements, has fundamentally changed the popular music festival as an institution (chapters 7–9).

The booming culture of musical events in the early twenty-first century continues to provide pleasure for more people, with few signs of decline, fulfilling strong desires for positive social experiences, for entertainment and love, and for inclusion in spaces of cultural power. But the consumerism and the detachment of performance institutions from civic associations, urban scenes, and social movements raise questions about the deeper social and cultural implications of corporatization.

Ideas about what counts as a better place for music and humanity in performance have changed profoundly, and they are institutionally regulated. An inquiry into this transformation could not be more relevant to the social study of music at this moment.

: 2 :

Conceptualizing Musical Performance Culture

While scholars in specialized subfields of music studies have made major contributions to the study of musical performance, the social study of music still lacks an analytical synthesis of these contributions and a systematic conceptualization of musical performance culture. This chapter provides this synthesis and conceptualization. It expands on the revisionist critiques of textualism in musicology during the 2010s by developing a broader concept of performance culture, drawing from the sociology of the body, ethnomusicology, performance studies, and event studies.

The chapter proposes an integration of three ontologies of musical performance culture and is organized into an exploration of each ontology. It begins with an overview of intellectual histories of performance in music studies to take stock of the current situation and motivate further development. The three ontologies are mapped in table 2.1 and explored in the following sections. The first of these sections explores the ontology of *performing bodies* through the literature on performativity and affect theory in music studies and the sociology of the body. The second explores the ontology of *the musical performance event*, focusing on the relationship between architectural space and ritual. The third explores the ontology of *musical performance within a broader cultural event*, such as a festival or a TV show, highlighting some of the different functions that musical performance can have in cultural events.

Following the book's overall objective, the chapter focuses on performance culture in commercial institutions in which performers and audiences are copresent in the same physical environment. The discussion in the final section of performance in media spaces serves a comparative function. Finally, the chapter points to the impacts of commercial institutionalization on performance culture. Some impacts are examined in later chapters, while others are left for future research.

Intellectual Histories of Performance in Music Studies

Contemporary discourses on performance in music studies can be interpreted in the context of the broader evolution of thinking about performance culture in the humanities. Ideas about performance culture—in the specific forms of theater performance and traditional festive events—emerged in the late 1960s in response to developments in cultural life at the time. Richard Schechner, a pioneer of performance studies, was influenced by various cultural movements in the 1960s. He was particularly influenced by experimental theater and its abandonment of traditional dramatic conventions, which resonated with broader antiauthoritarian sentiments at the time (Schechner 1977/1988; Callaghan 2013). Large public gatherings were central to the Civil Rights movement, the student revolt, and other social movements. At the same time, research literatures on popular culture began to emerge, and some of them drew inspiration from the anthropology of ceremony, performance, and ritual (Mukerji and Schudson 1986, 48–49). This trend in popular culture studies had some impact on popular music studies, but mostly in the form of semiology, not performance theory (e.g., Hebdige 1979; Laing 1985/2015; Walser 1993). Émile Durkheim, Erving Goffman, and John Austin, for instance, received little attention in music studies until the 1990s, and a broader discussion of the potential of social scientific performance theory for music studies is yet to appear. In general, narratives of performance have evolved within literatures on individual music genres and within other, more dominant ontologies of music. Nonetheless, there are developments in music studies that merit more detailed examination.

Western Art Musicology

Cook's 2013 *Beyond the Score* is a foundational contribution to musicology's performative turn, drawing from musical aesthetics and from developments in music psychology (e.g., Clarke 1988). The book is a specialized study of the aesthetics and psychology of performing music—an approach that can also be found in ethnomusicology (Clayton, Dueck, and Leante 2013). Cook's perspective is wide, as he contemplates the implications of his approach for the history and theory of Western art musicology. The book's introduction offers a revisionist argument that performance has a more fundamental role in musical culture than previously recognized. However, the book generally focuses on the role of the performer in interpreting the score, and this, to some extent, reinforces the hegemony of the score.

The book begins with an insightful account of developments in ontologies of music, particularly the influential Platonic conception of music as an abstract entity with a suprasensual reality embodied in the score. This conception evolved with the advent of music notation in the Middle Ages and the idea of writing more generally as an instrument of advanced civilization (Cook 2013, 11–15). In nineteenth-century German idealism, the score became central to the concept of the musical work. The task of the performer was to reproduce the substance of the music, encapsulated in the score, as neutrally as possible. The hegemony of writing was reflected in the objectives of early musicology, which aimed to retrieve, edit, and analyze national cultural canons (Cook 2013, 16). *Beyond the Score* critiques this textualism, arguing that the score is a script and that musicians must therefore employ their experience and creativity in performance. This involves aspects such as emotional expression, phrasing, tempo and timing, dynamics, and timbre. Cook draws on Lydia Goehr's argument that the musical work is a regulatory device as opposed to a fixed essence. This argument is further substantiated by his discussion of the historically informed performance movement, which challenged normative ideas of neutrality and the performer's reproductive function.

Cook's approach, as rigorous and insightful as it is, has a few limitations from which we can learn. First, the book focuses on the artistic activity of musicians and says little about other actors in and ontologies of musical performance. Second, the social dimensions of performance are undertheorized. Although the book recognizes that performance is "an explicitly social activity" (Cook 2013, 231), it lacks a concept of the social body and social space, and it does not situate performance in social life. The chapter on Jimi Hendrix considers issues of race, but its focus remains on the style of the individual performer, and it could have situated this performance at the 1970 Isle of Wight Festival in the evolution of hippie festivals, their concepts of event and festivity, and their commodification. Musicology is insufficient on its own to undertake this type of analysis.

Popular Music Studies

The intellectual history of performance in popular music studies was discussed in the introductory chapter, including its methodological media-centrism and the rise of scene studies in the 1990s. The study of media texts continues to be the modus operandi of popular music studies, though the live music literature has provided one alternative to this. The performative turn in the field has been somewhat limited to the discussion of performance in media texts, beginning with Simon Frith's *Performing Rites* and continuing in work on the pop persona by Philip Auslander and Stan Hawkins (Auslander 2006a, 2006b; Hawkins 2009, 2016). Auslander and Hawkins conceive the pop text as an expression governed by the logic of the pop persona. This work is also relevant to studying musical performance outside media spaces.

Contributions to the study of popular music performance have also appeared in empirical historical research. Dereck Scott and Daniel Cavicchi, for instance, have explored the formative period of commercial popular music performance in the mid-nineteenth century. Scott's history includes a chapter on the emergence of the promenade concert, the music hall, and café concert (Scott 2008, chapter 2). Cavicchi investigates changes in listening and its relationship to consumption (Cavicchi 2011). Cavicchi's revisionist argument about audiences in his earlier book on Bruce Springsteen fans has broad relevance to the study of performance culture and modernity. He critiques modernism's negative view of fans as fanatics and naïve consumers and suggests that fan culture evolved as a new kind of audience culture together with the rise of commercial performances in modernity (Cavicchi 1998).

Ethnomusicology

The concept of performance appeared earlier and has a more central role in ethnomusicology. Studying performance within the life of a community remains a paradigmatic practice in ethnomusicology (Rice 2013, 27). A common underlying narrative is that musical performance is a key site of social sensemaking and serves unique social functions.

Key aspects of ethnomusicological thinking about performance can be found in Steven Feld's seminal *Sound and Sentiment* (1982/1990). The book draws on system-oriented anthropology of myth to analyze the symbolic order of stories among Feld's informants in Papua New Guinea. It also draws on cognitive and interpretative anthropology to understand symbolic systems within "lived activities and events" (Feld 1982/1990, 229). The book is an ethnography of the role of vocal practices in expressing existential myths among the Kaluli. In his analysis of the story about how a boy became a *muni* bird, Feld interprets the sung story in terms of mediation and metaphorization. The community metaphor of the bird mediates between "social sentiments and sound modalities" (Feld 1982/1990, 40–41 and 228).

These ideas about the poetic and mediating functions of the human voice were later developed in Aaron Fox's study of country music in a small town near Austin, Texas. To Fox's informants, "speech and song were inseparable expressive modalities" (Fox 2004, 37). Fox develops a sophisticated narrative of how the human voice mediates across verbal art, song, and everyday conversations (Fox 2004, 45). He additionally explores musical performance as a poetic movement in the context of the ordinary. Country music performance draws from ordinary discourse and experience while also asserting "denaturalizing" poetic movements (Fox 2004, 230). Fox accounts for music as part of this broader cultural performance, thus offering a more complete understanding of the phenomenon than a music-centric conception can provide. His book includes rich ethnographic accounts of the voice as a locus of emotion in the everyday experience of a night at the honky-tonk bar (Fox 2004, 156).

Table 2.1 presents an overview of the three ontologies of musical performance culture that will be explored in the following sections. The mapping of one of them, *the performance event*, deserves a brief explanation: this ontology is organized into three dimensions—the musical, the spatial, and the visual-theatrical—for the purpose of identifying distinct material properties and symbolic systems (in this sense, the conception of the performance event is differentiated into further ontologies). The musical dimension identifies the distinctness of musical sounds, their ordering, and their symbolic and affective dimensions. The visual-theatrical dimension identifies the distinctness of architectural design, costumes, and choreographed movement, for instance. The musical and the visual both have a spatial dimension, which is therefore positioned in the middle.

Ontologies of Musical Performance Culture

Performing Bodies

At the most fundamental ontological level, musical performance involves the phenomenology of bodies that are producing and experiencing musical sound. Musical aesthetics and phenomenology are central to understanding the ontology of musical performance and the role of the body in musical performance. In many forms of performance, bodies have multiple functions: sounds are produced from and by bodies, from the vocal organ in song and from strumming instruments and beating objects; bodily gestures interpret sounds; the clothing and adornment of bodies further defines the symbolic order; and bodies are interacting through listening, movement, and touch. This section focuses on understandings of the

TABLE 2.1 Ontologies of musical performance culture

	Performing bodies	Performance event			Cultural event
		Musical	Spatial	Visual-theatrical	
Material	The biological body	Musical sounds	Acoustics	Visual environment	Event space
	Touch and movement		Proxemics and scale	Gesture	
		Musical "language"		Theatrical "language"	Event narrative
		Musical drama and persona		Theatrical drama roles	and participant
Symbolic	The musical and social body	Music history and genre	Symbolic architecture		Tradition and mythology
			Symbolic place		
			Front stage/backstage		Imagined center in society
Experiential	Affect and meaning				Social function

relationship between performativity and affect in scholarship on cultural and musical performance and provides additional insights from the sociology of the body.

Performativity and Affect

In music studies and other areas of the humanities, interest in the social body appeared in conjunction with feminism and evolved into discourses on performativity and affect. Scholars such as Susan McClary and Marcia Citron pioneered a tradition in music studies of analyzing the construction of gendered bodies in music. This literature offers an alternative to the somewhat mechanistic understandings of the body that can be found in writing about bodily communication in music (Davidson 2005) and in cognitive psychology of gesture and timing (Cook 2013), often driven by interests in using performance as a tool for music analysis (Kozak 2015).

Contemporary social understandings of the body in musical performance have drawn inspiration from work on performativity in performance studies and from affect studies in the 2000s. José Esteban Muñoz's work illustrates key aspects of this development in performance studies. His article "Feeling Brown, Feeling Down" (2006) offers a critical alternative to epistemological, discursive, and universalizing conceptions of the body and affect. The article develops the concept of "brown feeling" to examine the role of feeling in creating a sense of identity and belonging among Latinx populations. Brown feeling is "a modality of minoritarian being or becoming" and "an ethics of self" deployed by "minoritarian subjects who don't feel quite right within the protocols of normative affect and comportment" (Muñoz 2006, 676). Muñoz suggests that we ask not only how minoritized populations speak, but also how they feel, and how they feel each other. He thus conceives the social body as a form of becoming in which the senses play an important role.

One of the best adaptations of affect theory in music studies is Anahid Kassabian's *Ubiquitous Listening* (2013). The book uses affect theory to rethink conventional ideas about music listening in the humanities. Affect is described as "the circuit of bodily responses to stimuli that take place before conscious apprehension. Once apprehended, the responses pass into thoughts and feelings, though they always leave behind a residue" (Kassabian 2013, xiii). Kassabian further elaborates on this idea in a discussion of haptic perception, a concept she adopts from visual studies (Kassabian 2013, xvi–xvii). Haptic listening involves not only hearing but also kinesthetics in immersive experiences of being touched and surrounded by sound. Kassabian notes that the desire for such experiences might be an ideal to which cultures of sound systems and audiophilia aspire.

The relationship between sonic tactility and performing bodies has been explored by Luis-Manuel Garcia (2015a) in a conceptual article in which he draws on the work of Steve Goodman, Pierre Schaeffer, and Eve Sokofsky Sedgwick, among others. The article illuminates the relationship between microlevel material qualities of sound and the performing body. The article first explores how sound touches bodies. The drumbeat—with its attack that is both hard and brief—is the product of beating or hitting a firm or hard object. It is the sound of a body that touches an object or another body and is shaped by their physical properties (Garcia 2015a, 67). In electronic dance music, the dancing body is vibrating, rubbing, striking, and gesturing. These forms of touch are central to erotic feeling and are enhanced sonically through electronic effects. In the interpersonal experience on the dance floor, the repetition of the beat not only sustains movement, it also creates a field of action for dancers, coordinating movements and engendering collective feeling. The music contributes to "an expansive sense of connection in dancing crowds" and creates "spaces of heightened tactility and embodied intimacy" (Garcia 2015a, 60). The music engenders a "social thickening, an intimate world in the making" (Garcia 2015a, 73). Finally, the article provides nuance to the idea of haptic perception in the discussion of bass culture, which is a key element in genres such as techno, rap, reggae, dancehall, reggaetón, and kuduro. Beats and bass at low frequencies and high volumes, moving slowly and in circles, are not fully audible but deliver a felt push on the body from all sides and serve as navigation tools in performance.

The Sociology of the Body in Sports and Music Events

The sociology of the body that developed in the 1980s has been ignored in thinking about musical performance, but it offers crucial perspectives. It encourages critical thinking about who is part of a given performance and how the conditions of the body in everyday life shapes the body in performance. For instance, who has been included and excluded even before a performance begins? How does the construction of identity, sensory being, desire, and health in performance compare to other situations in social life? What images and ideologies are inscribed on performing bodies in their commercial institutionalization?

Bryan Turner's *The Body and Society* (1984/2008) was a pioneering contribution to the sociology of the body. Turner developed ideas for a broad exploration of the body in modern society. He emphasized the politics of the body and its role in relations of power across domains, such as health, government, religion, and science. This included critical analysis of patriarchy. Turner later noted that the body had not really been an issue before second-wave feminism (Turner 1991, 7). Sociology had evolved as the study of urban, industrial society, with a core interest in the conditions of social change, and emphasized its differentiation from biology strongly. The rejection of biologism had been a foundational rationale for the discipline in the nineteenth century (Turner 1984/2008, chapter 3). The modern subject, if not exactly the body, appeared as a common theme in German-language sociology, however. Weber and others imagined that in modern societies humans had grown apart from nature through rationality and institutional regulations of violence and sexuality. They imagined civilization to require the restraint of the body and acknowledged its alienating effects. Bureaucracy was necessary for social stability and justice, but it also transformed people into "cogs in a machine" and "heartless bureaucrats," or, in the words of Nietzsche, "despisers of the body" (Turner 1991, 14). These ideas are echoed in Foucault's argument about how institutions regulated growing urban populations through discipline and surveillance (Foucault [1975] 1995).

The sociology of the body inspired insights in the sociology of sport that have great relevance to the social study of music. For decades, scholarship on sports had taken inspiration from medical science in researching exercise physiology, motor learning, and psychology. While this tradition served a purpose because physical health is a key concern for sports practitioners, it also produced an atomistic, instrumentalist, and mechanistic understanding of the body. Nancy Theberge critiqued these tendencies and drew attention to the social body and issues of domination and exploitation (Theberge 1991). For her, the study of bodies in Western societies "is fundamentally about the control and domination of women under patriarchy" (Theberge 1991, 124). She links the history of excluding women from sports with the wider domination of women in society (Theberge 1991, 128). Theberge also draws on Turner's thinking about the institutional basis of the body to critique assumed "natural" gender differences in physical education programs and in mass media. One example is a study of a TV exercise program called *Twenty Minute Workout*, in which the possibility of resistance through women's embracing of physical activity was reworked into a conventional form of heteronormative exploitation that objectified women's bodies (Theberge 1991, 129).

The exclusion of women and the reproduction of white patriarchy are still major issues in musical performance cultures. How else could women and minoritized people represent such a small percentage of composers and conductors in art music and in popular music festival lineups? Institutions such as the symphony, the club, and the music festival all have a history as patriarchal institutions. Organizations dominated by white men reproduce their own identity in music programming and countless other practices. Claims to white male privilege among audiences at popular music festivals can be painfully registered in the many reports of sexual harassment, rape, and racism.[1] The greenfield is a site of festivity where social rules are relaxed and bodily desires are aroused, but ethical norms are relaxed, too.

A significant moment in the history of white patriarchy in rock festivals can be found in Beyoncé's 2018 performance at Coachella Valley Music and Arts Festival in 2018. Beyoncé situated her performance as a corrective to a national history of white supremacy. She acknowledged on stage that she was the festival's first African American woman headliner, and she quoted Malcom X and sang "Lift Every Voice and Sing." But above all, it was a triumphant celebration of black bodies through music and dance, a performance of brown feeling on the white stage structured around her celebrity persona, and with a large marching band having a prominent musical and theatrical role. The movie that was made out of the performance integrated multiple references to black cultural history (Knowles-Carter 2019).

Commercial institutionalization is central to the construction of the body in popular music festivals. The image of the festival as a sexualized space, conveyed through a preponderance of photographic representations of women, has been exploited since the 1960s (chapter 9). The industrial development of festivals, moreover, has structured larger numbers of social bodies as consumers of celebrity and positioned these bodies in spaces with more organized stimuli and advertising. Commercial motivations have driven the search for symbolic forms with a larger market, particularly mass-market pop music and narratives of fun and pleasure, to attract the largest audiences possible and have them consume more on the ground by developing shopping features and more stages and larger stages filled with a constant stream of concerts.

Commercially motivated self-regulation is widespread, as several festivals have introduced measures to address sexual harassment and made adjustments to their audience capacity. Festivals have responded to sexual harassment as a matter of public relations and consumer safety.[2] Lollapalooza Berlin and Mad Cool in Madrid have responded to the challenges posed by attracting day crowds of about 80,000 by just a few years after they were created. At Mad Cool, the band Massive Attack canceled their performance just five minutes before it was supposed to start because the music from a nearby stage was too loud. Festivals continuously adjust the spatial organization and programming of stages to minimize such problems. At Lollapalooza Berlin, dramatic audience growth has required more than one move to a new location and, like Mad Cool, it has experienced logistical problems, such as overcrowding on public transportation (Navarro 2018; Christine Goebel, email to the author's assistant, November 3, 2017). Fusion Festival in Germany is one example of a festival that has imposed a limit on ticket sales, begun in 2009, to avoid overcrowding. The first limit was 50,000, which was raised to 55,000 and then increased in 2017 to 65,000 (email correspondence with Fusion via the author's assistant, December 14, 2017). The festival industry has learned to gradually expand their audience capacity. Placing a limit on ticket sales close to the highest possible capacity or near the highest expected sales can have a positive marketing effect, as the festival can announce that it is sold out and thus appear to be more desirable and successful. Overall, day crowds have grown considerably since the industry of annually recurring festivals developed in the 1980s (see pp. 23–24).

Institutional theory also helps explain the bureaucratization of bodies and its alienating effects. The industry frames and governs the body through audience capacities based on marketing and safety considerations. The body is constructed through marketing communications to specific demographics and regulated through ticket sales and conditions of consumption, including what the consumer is allowed to do and to bring along. The body is regulated by limiting access to particular areas of a venue or festival, by regulating clothing, behaviors, and drugs, and by the architectural design. Furthermore, the selection and presentation of food, beverages, performances, and other commodities for maximizing consumption simultaneously fills desires and imposes demands on the body. The regulation of commodities shapes the body's relationship to other bodies, to the event, and to music. Because it is profitable, the live music industry encourages alcohol consumption and creates audience areas at stages so large the majority of the audience is watching the artist on screens. Through these marketing, distribution, and design practices, the body is subjected to a process and environment that enable certain bodily activities, interactions, sensations, and crowd densities. In short, attending an arena concert or a large-scale festival involves a bodily experience of an evolving mass-market institution.

The Performance Event

A core example of the musical performance event is the evening concert in a concert hall or a club. In popular music, this often includes one or two opening performances by relatively unknown artists followed by a longer concert by the main act. Another core example is the party event in the electronic dance music club. It often begins around midnight and continues until the early morning or unfolds over an entire weekend. The weekend club event represents a more extended form of festivity, with its longer and more open-ended character and the common occurrence of concurrent performances at the same event. The legendary Berghain club in Berlin, for instance, has continuous DJ sets on two main dance floors, usually more techno-oriented DJs in the larger room and more house-oriented DJs in the bar upstairs.

Institutionalized concert and club party events in the city are typically indoor events in dedicated performance spaces. High ticket prices and restrictive door policies have exclusionary functions and create a distance to everyday public life. If the event is focused on music, ticket prices will generally reflect the market demand for the performers. Central to the musical performance event is the relationship between architectural space and ritual. The following sections highlight key aspects of this relationship.

The Constitutive Role of Architectural Space

The acoustic properties of an architectural space create the conditions of sound and shape how it is experienced. Architectural spaces are in a sense acoustic instruments, as Daniel Libeskind once noted (Till 2016, 176). The architecture shapes how sound waves move from their sources and how they are sculpted. The concert ritual commonly involves the projection of sound from a stage, while the dance ritual in clubs encourages the projection of sound around the crowd on the dance floor. Commercial concert halls and clubs are part of a longer history of perfecting acoustic architecture and amplification for particular types of musical events. The rise of modern engineering and architectural acoustics has historically led to the construction of spaces with standardized acoustics (Thompson 2002). Experiments with amplification systems in the early history of rock music concerts include Pink Floyd's quadrophonic panning in Queen Elizabeth Hall in London in 1967 (Calore 2009) and the Grateful Dead's 1974 "wall of sound" system (Anderson 2015). Some clubs have developed extraordinary sound systems to distinguish themselves, including Berghain in Berlin, Ministry of Sound in London, and the Bowery Ballroom in New York City.

The industrialization of concert and festival production has led to standardized amplification systems developed for the same types of architecture and to continuous building renovations and expansions and more purpose-built performance spaces (chapters 4–5; Kronenburg 2012, 2019). Standardization notwithstanding, the sonic environments of these spaces are very different from domestic spaces. The sonic dimension alone accounts for a major ontological difference between the performance event and media consumption of music. The sound of a performance space cannot be fully captured by recording technology, and the reproduction is limited by the properties of the playback space. In purely physical terms, lower-frequency sound waves, for instance, are longer than many domestic spaces and cannot be reproduced in full by consumer-grade speakers.[3] This means that music has a different materiality in a performance space and is therefore experienced differently.

A key concept for understanding the lived experience of sound in performance is proxemics. The concept was proposed in the 1950s by anthropologist Edward Hall, a pioneer in the anthropology of nonverbal communication and space (he published a book on architecture and social behavior). In his 1959 *The Silent Language*, Hall outlined a typology of the relation between interpersonal distance and forms of speech and socio-emotional categories. This typology identifies the near-field area of up to thirty centimeters between interlocutors as a space of personal, secret, and confidential communication, expressed through whispering and a soft voice. At distances greater than 1.5 meters, conversations become less intimate and private because other people can follow them. At six meters, a loud voice is necessary and typical of a conversation held across a room or addressing a group of people. At the longest audible distances, hailing is required (Hall 1959, 208–9). This typology is still valid, with variations across times and cultures. It helps explain the intimacy of the small jazz club and the folk song café and the generally high emotional registers and loud volumes at mass audience performances. At Simon and Garfunkel's famous 1981 concert in Central Park, quiet ballads, gentle singing, and even some whispering, accompanied by acoustic guitar, were amplified for an estimated five hundred thousand people, and this could not have happened just one or two decades earlier. However, the sound and the experience were less intimate and controlled compared to privately listening to the record at home.

The concept of proxemics also explains how music can be conceived as a scalable practice. Music's ontologies and meanings change with the scale of the event and the sound. This is illustrated by the difference between a performance in a café and a stadium concert, or between playback on the average car stereo and the state-of-the-art high-fidelity system. The scale of performance spaces reflects the local market for a given performance culture and often corresponds with the level of professionalism and industrialization. Going from small performance spaces to larger ones is a career trajectory for musicians, and the live music industry has evolved in an economy of scale. The industry began with superstar touring in arenas and stadiums and later expanded into festivals and clubs. There are still distinct production cultures of small club concerts, arena shows, and festivals, in part because they produce different kinds of experience that require different types of expertise.

While the economy of scale is a high priority for corporations and touring stars in large markets of anonymous consumers, the cultural dimension of architecture is also a matter of importance to a wide range of artists and audiences. Some are drawn to the monumental spaces of arenas and festivals, while others find them too impersonal or experience social anxiety. Bands such as the Eagles, the Rolling Stones, and U2 have cultivated an image as stadium touring bands for decades. Meanwhile, the Beatles, Steely Dan, Joni Mitchell, and Adele have quit or scaled down touring out of frustration with large venues and the concert industry, or simply because they preferred to work in the recording studio (Willman [1993] 2017; Varga 2016; Waddell 2019). Many stars have made rare appearances in small venues and in street performances to experience a break from the industry sphere, and Thom Yorke is one of relatively few who have toured small venues because they preferred their intimacy (Laverne 2019).

Cultural norms for architectural scale and design are further illustrated by responses to the Three Tenors (1990–2003) who moved from institutions of art music into mass culture venues. The Three Tenors stepped outside opera to do two stadium world tours, appeared at the World Cup Final in 1990, and sold incredible numbers of live albums and DVDs. This would normally be perceived as a huge success by mass culture standards, but classical music pundits judge by other standards. The *Seattle Times* music critic, for instance, wrote that audiences were experiencing "some amplified version of the real thing" and that it was "more like a moon landing than a traditional concert" (Bargreen 1996).

The Ritual Logic of Architecture

The ritual logic of performance governs many dimensions of performance culture, including architectural and media practices. In the following, I shall suggest how a basic conception of ritual—tentatively defined as a scripted process with a dramaturgy and mythology that transforms the relationship to the ordinary through techniques of suspension and poeticization—can illuminate the spatial and architectural dimensions of performance culture.

Dedicated performance spaces for music have been adapted to or constructured for specific types of rituals. This includes practical concerns such as sight lines in the concert hall and an elevated stage. It also includes aesthetic and psychological aspects such as the majestic sense of space and the historical aura in many rock concert theaters, or the futuristic design of many dance music clubs. Individual clubs and festivals aspire to create their own ideal version of their respective performance institutions. In a sense, they are creating secular *temples* of a musical culture. Buildings funded by private foundations or city governments are often *monuments* of these organizations, expressing their formal power in terms of magnitude and visual appearance in the urban landscape. A core example is the concept of flagship venues that emerged in the urban regeneration agendas during the 1980s (chapter 5).

The ritual function of spatial boundaries deserves special attention. Performance spaces create boundaries with the outside world. They frame the relationship of performance with everyday life and society. This can be illustrated by comparing outdoor and indoor spaces.

Outdoor spaces have the potential to create a direct relationship with nature and society. The sensory experience of nature, including the colors of the sky, the smell of the air, and the landscape itself, becomes part of the performance. The performance, moreover, can be situated in a public space of high symbolic value to a community. The outdoor setting can thus enhance the material and symbolic dimensions of performance and amplify its difference from media consumption. Furthermore, outdoor spaces are less bounded and controllable than indoor concert venues. There is no protection offered by walls, resulting in less control over sound, weather, and the movement of people. This can empower utopian and subconscious energies and promote hedonism, as illustrated by diverse histories of street parades and outdoor festivals (chapter 6).

Indoor spaces, by contrast, have the potential to achieve greater perfection, control, and intimacy. The concert hall is designed to give the audience the perfect sound and view of the stage performance. In contrast to the Greek amphitheater, which was open and provided a view of the urban landscape, the concert hall is a kind of proscenium theater that directs attention only to the stage and hides the rest of the performance space in darkness. It disciplines and compartmentalizes performance (Schechner 1977/1988, 179; Small 1986).

The crossing of a boundary into a controlled consumer space has long been a defining aspect of the commercial club in genres such as jazz, rock, and electronic dance music. Consider pioneer Bill Graham's conception of the entrance to his Fillmore East rock club:

> I wanted a clean, well-run theater. We fixed the lobby and the concession area. We updated everything. We screwed everything down real tight. I wanted it to look classy. So that when people came in off the street, they would rise up to a higher level. Like when someone walks into a spiffy restaurant. Automatically, their back gets straighter. They change to fit the room. (Graham and Greenfield 1992/2004, 232)

Graham had worked for years as a waiter in a restaurant. His careful attention to customer service and the overall restaurant experience, a ritual of its own, shaped his approach to the concert theater. A similar element of glamour can be found in the bars of the indie club concert theaters in contemporary New York, where patrons enter the club through the bar (chapter 4). Architectural design was only one aspect of Graham's club concept. He also encouraged the artists to think of the concert as a larger entity and to be clear and polite in their communication with the audience. He had a policy on encores and bowing to the audience at the end. This led to tensions with some artists who might not have been comfortable with the ritual that Graham was institutionalizing.

The Musical Ritual versus the Social Ritual with Music

The idea of a ritual centered on musical performance evolved in the eighteenth century. Habermas explains that the evolution of the musical performance event as a commodity created a symbolic order in which music was freed from its representational functions in the church and among the aristocracy. In his somewhat idealist terms, audiences gathered to listen to music as such (Habermas 1962/1989, 39). William Weber nuances this picture by analyzing the social activities that happened around but also during concerts until the cult of silence emerged in the 1830s (Weber 1997). While the concert obviously had social functions in bourgeois life—such as the production of bourgeois identity and cultural capital through bodily experience in an institution of power—it did represent the evolution of musical performance into a distinct form of public consumption. The concert ritual inside the concert hall largely let the music speak for itself, and it was eventually accompanied by a concept of autonomous music, paralleling modernism's "white cube" concept of the arts gallery (Doherty 1986/1999). In the concert hall, music is not an accompaniment to a religious ritual or to another form of entertainment, such as a theatrical performance or dancing. The rituals of drinking and socializing during the concert disappeared in the nineteenth century. The action on stage, moreover, centers on music, not a theatrical representation of bourgeois life. This ritual can therefore be identified as a musical ritual and distinguished from a social ritual with music.[4]

Musical performance in folk, jazz, and popular music, by contrast, frequently has direct social functions and is incorporated into broader social events. At weddings and dance events, for instance, musical performance accompanies a more general social ritual than playing and listening to music. But music-centered rituals have evolved in the aforementioned genres, even as social rituals continue to have an important role. For instance, jazz began as music played at funeral processions and informal social nightlife spaces, and it then evolved into a popular dance culture before later diversifying into various forms of art and popular music. Folk music traditions have similarly given rise to forms of professional music sold on sound recordings and in concert halls. This happened during the urban folk revival in the 1950s and the klezmer revival in the 1970s. Rock music, too, was a type of dance music before the more sophisticated forms emerged, which are now regularly presented in concert venues for audiences who are often not dancing.

The ritual of the extended dance event has remained central in house and techno. For these genres, the club institution originates in semiprivate parties in the late 1960s at which DJs explored the potentials of music to build and maintain a spiritual vibe in a continuous flow (Lawrence 2004). The dance party was developed by commercial clubs into glamorous nightlife clubs with celebrities and spectacle, such as New York's Studio 54 in the 1970s and the house music industry clubs with superstar DJs in England in the late 1990s, such as Home and Fabric in London (Haslam 2001/2002). The large techno raves in the Second Summer of Love 1988–1989, by contrast, explored a more collectivist sensibility in simpler, more tribal rituals held outside commercial institutions in abandoned warehouses and in the rural fields of southeast England (Reynolds 1998).

The Burning Man festival in the Black Rock Desert in Nevada illustrates key aspects of music's relationship with an outdoor environment. It is not a music festival, but music has become a major part of it. Beginning with a small rave camp a mile from the main encampment in 1992, house and techno steadily gained popularity as part of the psychedelic experience in the desert environment. The beats, the bass, and the psychedelic sounds all have particular sensory and symbolic affordances with the panoramic view, the dust, the extreme temperatures, and the geographical distance from cities. By the early 2000s, a growing number of mobile DJ shows were competing for attention, even from those not participating in a performance, since the low frequencies permeate the larger festival area. By 2015, superstar DJs playing at stadium-level volumes had changed the festival's character and made it a customary stop on the DJ tour (St. John 2017b). This evolving musical culture involved the integration of norms and networks of the popular music festival institution and challenged Burning Man's principles of decommodification and gifting (St. John 2017b, 220–21 and 233–36). The mobile sound systems drowned out the drum circles that used to define the soundscape of the concluding ritual, the night when a big sculpture of the Man is burned (St. John 2017b, 237).

Burning Man thus also illustrates core aspects of the third and final ontology in this outline, namely the ontology of musical performance in a cultural event.

The Performance in a Cultural Event

In popular culture, musical performance is frequently part of cultural events, such as festivals, street parades, and song contests. The performance creates a marked moment of musical experience within the event, while the event creates a context to which performers and audiences adapt. The event is defined by an overall theme and symbolic sphere, which involves constructions of space, genre, and identity. In large outdoor events, performers often adapt to audiences who might be distracted and not familiar with their music by playing their most popular repertoire in their most monumental style of expression. Such events thus provide a further case for extending Hall's theory of proxemics to musical performance culture. Moreover, the symbolic power and scale of large cultural events creates the potential for a performance to become a powerful symbolic moment in society. This section addresses general aspects of cultural events, while the festival chapters explore a particular type of event in more detail. The section draws on the literature on events in tourism studies and in media studies.

Events in Tourism Studies

The term "event" gained a distinct presence in the late twentieth century as part of broad transformations in postindustrial societies that stimulated the growth of new forms of leisure, particularly urban cultural tourism. While the musical performance became a distinct commodity in its own right in the eighteenth century, the cultural event emerged as an umbrella term at a time when many forms of culture had developed into commerce-based leisure. The term "cultural event" represents a culmination point in the evolution of commercially institutionalized and mediatized forms of public consumption. In the centuries leading up to the eighteenth century, large festive events had been organized by the church and aristocracy. This began to change with the development of urban culture markets in the eighteenth century, with capitalism providing a system for producing events for anonymous consumers. The growing tourism industry in the decades following World War II further transformed and to some extent replaced traditional rituals and calendars of holidays. This development of leisure events involved a growing emphasis on popular culture fashions and celebrity, reflecting the impact of mass media.

The crisis in the postindustrial economy during the 1970s was a key context for the emergence of the generic event concept, which is an umbrella term for a range of events that were previously conceived in more particular terms. City governments in declining industrial economies began to look to culture-led strategies of economic growth and discovered how events could create positive images of a city and attract tourists (Zukin 1995; Cohen 2007). They began subsidizing events and thus supporting the growth of this leisure industry. This evolution has been chronicled in tourism studies, which for decades focused on the study of the economic impacts of events and inspired the field of event management (Getz and Page 2007/2016). This field introduced unitary frameworks for the production of such diverse events as community celebrations, festivals, sports events, business meetings, industry exhibitions, and mega-events. Typical of the field, Getz and Page situate events in the experience economy (Getz and Page 2007/2016, chapter 1), a discourse that aims to transcend the distinctness of cultural practices and symbolic systems and thus cannot account for the particular affordances of such diverse forms as music, sports, and food. This is further illustrated by the adoption of design discourse from traditions of industrial production in modernity, as an instrument for the systematical exploitation of consumer desires. Elements of theatrical scenography, festival programming, and oral traditions of celebration, for instance, are extracted out of symbolic and historical context and distilled into design parameters on a checklist for the production of any event. Simple psychological models are introduced to maximize the level of entertainment and pleasure throughout the duration of the event (Getz and Page 2007/2016, chapter 7). This discourse of event design is an efficient tool for optimizing and popularizing many events for consumption, but it cannot account for the affordances and deeper historical dimensions of individual cultural forms in society. Participants in this discourse show little interest in culture—in the values and substance of cultural forms, community, history, or in humanity and society. Getz and Page work from an implicit notion of consumer culture. In more than one respect, event design thus shares some of the limitations of the live music discourse, particularly its media-centrism and its disconnect from knowledge interests in culture.

The Media Events Literature

The literature on media events emerged in response to the rise of live broadcasting of major societal events on satellite television in the 1970s. Communication scholars registered the role these transmissions played in the public's interpretation of such events and how the events disrupted everyday media routines. A central argument made by Daniel Dayan and Elihu Katz, the two main pioneering scholars of media event theory, was precisely that live transmissions of events illustrated general aspects of the relationship between media and society. The events showed how television had the power to define society, how it ascribed meanings and emotional values to its objects of mediation, and how it created an imagined center in society.

It was the live broadcast of Anwar el-Sadat's trip to Jerusalem in 1977, during which Sadat prayed at the Al Aqsa mosque, that first caught the attention of Dayan and Katz (1992, 26). The two began by comparing Sadat with the astronauts from the televised moon landings and discovered similar dynamics. Their 1992 book, which laid the foundations for media event theory, also considered events such as the Watergate hearings and the 1989 revolution in Prague (Dayan and Katz 1992, 157–59). Their theory integrated mass communication with perspectives from the anthropology of ceremony. This disciplinary framework has potential for explaining fundamental aspects of the relationship between events and media beyond the culture of broadcast television. Above all, it can account for how media adapt to the ritual dynamics of powerful cultural and social events and coconstruct these events as imagined centers of power (chapter 9).

Much of the book's value lies in its deep understanding of the dynamics between media and events through detailed descriptions and examples. The book's specific typology of events and its specific theoretical framework, on the other hand, have been subject to critiques (Couldry and Hepp 2010, 5). One such criticism concerns the limitations of the typology of contests, conquests, and coronations that Dayan and Katz at one point describe as primordial events (Dayan and Katz 1992, 43). Couldry and Hepp (2010) briefly touch on "popular media events" in "consumer and celebrity culture" but do not explore this further. The media events literature has not yet theorized events in the music field.

A tentative mapping of the differences between two basic forms of popular music events, TV contests and music festivals, can be found in table 2.2.

TABLE 2.2 A typology of popular music events

	Pop contests		Pop festivals		
	Reality concept (*X Factor*, *Idol*, *The Voice*)	Tournament (Eurovision, Intervision, Sanremo)	EDM pop festivals (Tomorrowland, Ultra, Nature One)	Rock festivals (Coachella, Glastonbury, Rock Werchter, Roskilde, Sziget)	Transformational events (Burning Man, Fusion, O.Z.O.R.A.)
Scriptedness	High		Medium		Low
Audience role	"The people"		Consumers Dancers	Concert audiences	Anti-consumers Community/dancers
Live-cast channel	Commercial TV	Public TV	Online	Online and broadcast TV	Generally not televised
Symbolic community	Family and nation		Genre		Subculture
Performer	Amateur	Entertainer	Star		Not star-centered
Process	Evening competition		Days and nights		
Main space of action	TV		Festival area in greenfield or park near a city		Remote nature
	Domestic	Domestic and public			
Role of organizer	Host		Merchant		Collectivist organization
Selection of music	Jury and voters		Professional curation		

Note: Inspired by Dayan and Katz (1992, 34–35).

It draws on Dayan and Katz's conception of the symbolic functions of events to highlight important differences between these events. TV contests are more scripted, as they create a shorter event focused on a narrative in a single channel for heterogenous mass audiences. The outdoor festival, by contrast, is typically a longer event in which participants construct their own journey more freely across the multiple spaces of the festival area. Another core difference is television's power to create official national publics, while music festivals tend to be more specialized, typically focusing on a genre and competing in the music market.

The potential of television to create a kind of public sphere around musical performance is illustrated by Eurovision and the Super Bowl halftime show. Eurovision has been a unique site of international geopolitics since the 2000s, specifically as a cultural arena for negotiating tensions with Putin's Russia (Meerzon and Priven 2013). To think with Dayan and Katz, the broad coalition of nation-states that jointly own Eurovision and provide access to countless national audiences lends the event a transnational authority, and this authority is exploited and contested. Similar dynamics can be found at the Super Bowl, which emerged as a space of race politics in 2016 when Colin Kaepernick led player protests against police brutality during the national anthem and Beyoncé paid homage to the Black Panthers in her halftime show. Repercussions from the subsequent exclusion of Kaepernick could still be registered in the halftime show and the media coverage of the Super Bowl in 2020 (Caramanica 2020).

The forms of ownership also explain important differences among popular music festivals. Large for-profit festivals are organized by bureaucratic organizations and more scripted. They offer a predesigned festival environment and a fixed schedule of entertainment to serve larger numbers of music consumers. Their design and music programming, moreover, is regulated by their transnational corporate owners. Transformational festivals, by contrast, celebrate collectivism and a DIY ethos and therefore tend to be less scripted and bureaucratic (Chen 2009). They also do not present superstars.

Clubs in Everyday Urban Life

: 3 :

The Social Study of Music in Cities

This chapter takes stock of the intellectual history of music in cities to develop the conceptual foundations for studying musical performance institutions in the everyday urban domain. There is no discipline of urban music studies, but instead a diverse range of specialized literatures that cannot meaningfully be subsumed into a single theoretical or disciplinary framework. This chapter reconstructs the intellectual history of music in cities guided by the book's interdisciplinary concept of the social study of music. The reconstruction is developed through a comparative exploration of knowledge interests among literatures that are often considered separately. It will demonstrate how the concept of the social study of music in cities can help grow a field-sensitivity across these literatures. The chapter also provides insight into the cultural history of music in cities across the Global North.

Readers with limited interest in the intellectual history of music in cities and the social study of music can skip this chapter and go straight to the analyses in the chapters that follow.

The chapter conceives its object as "music in cities" and not "urban music" because this terminology more adequately represents the field. Music identified with rural and suburban areas has long been present in cities, and some musical cultures that originate in cities have become less urban over time. The situation reflects diversity and change in urban populations and the deterritorializing effects of media.

Literatures on Music in Cities

While there is no field or discipline of urban music studies, there are rich literatures on individual musical cultures in cities. Knowledge production in the area reflects the plural and divided worlds of cities, but there are also overlapping knowledge interests. This chapter identifies and reviews six literatures.

1. *Cultural elites in European history.* The first literature on music in modern cities emerged as a discourse of the elites and the bourgeoisie in the late nineteenth century. This literature coconstructed the idea of the city as a site of extraordinary cultural achievements, specifically through narratives of Austro-Germanic art music in European civilization and nationalism. In this symbolic order, the city organized its musical life around a national tradition of "great composers" and "classics," with a local organizational basis in bourgeois civic music associations and the city government. The genre of "city music history" ("städtische Musikgeschichte") was a product of this social relation of power. The genre was sponsored by elite bourgeois institutions and chronicled their official history in one city (e.g., Hanslick 1869; Klein 1903). Some scholars constructed a longer history and adopted systematic archival approaches (Sachs 1908; Wustmann 1909). This tradition persists in musicology alongside more interpretative approaches inspired by intellectual developments in the study of bourgeois culture and elite institutions. Carl Schorske's analysis of collective sensibility and cultural consciousness across art forms in fin-de-siècle Vienna (Schorske 1980), for instance, was a source of inspiration in Cook's work on Heinrich Schenker (Cook 2007), while Bourdieu's thinking about national cultural institutions in Paris shaped Born's study of IRCAM (Institut de Recherche et Coordination Acoustique/Musique; Born 1995).

A wave of interest in urban Renaissance Italy in musicology during the 1980s led Tim Carter to propose in 2002 that a field of urban musicology might be emerging. Carter argued that the study of a city provided an opportunity to look beyond individual composers, and he was enthusiastic about Reinhard Strohm's recommendation that scholars study people and soundscapes rather than manuscripts (Carter 2002). However, Carter concludes that research in this area largely remains focused on institutions and their archives, and he does not identify promising alternatives. The concept of urban musicology has not yet been theorized or institutionalized.

2. *Popular leisure in the industrial-era metropolis.* A small literature on public leisure in cities during the industrial era provides insights into the evolution of popular music performance in social and musical institutions. Scholarly interest in this area began in sociology. Pioneering contributions were made by Paul Cressey in his work on the taxi-dance hall and Howard Becker in his work on dance musicians, both of whom were concerned with the social construction of lower-status cultures in the city. Cressey (1932)

found that the reputation of the dance hall affected women's social status negatively throughout their careers as taxi-dancers. Becker (1961) explored how dance musicians were constituted as a deviant group with its own differentiations and tensions between art and commerce, hip and square.

Broader cultural histories of music in the industrial-era metropolis began to appear in the late twentieth century. Lewis Ehrenberg and David Nasaw concentrated on leisure institutions in New York City, such as Fifth Avenue restaurants, Broadway "lobster palaces," vaudeville theaters, and saloons. Ehrenberg (1981) mapped the evolution of these institutions and explored how they created worlds of desire and fantasy outside the spheres of work and domestic life. Nasaw (1993) was more interested in outdoor leisure, such as amusement parks and markets, as sites of convivial sociality and a family-friendly public culture that disappeared with urban development and domestic electronic entertainment. He suggested that urban life had become less authentic, more alienating, and the crowds more homogeneous, but he also did not consider subcultures and New York's large communities of color.

3. *The Great Migration.* Cities of the Global North have a long history of migrations. The Great Migration in the United States from the 1910s until the 1960s is particularly important to the history of Anglophone popular music. Some of the groundwork for this history was done by white authors, partly as a result of the music's exploitation by overwhelmingly white cultural industries, partly because African American intellectuals since the Harlem Renaissance had gravitated toward cultural forms associated with social advancement. Black Renaissance artists found role models in Western art music and not in blues and jazz. Ralph Ellison commented in 1961 that much jazz modernism sprang from "a misplaced shame over the so-called low-class origins of jazz" (Ellison 1961, 8). The first major contribution to African American music history to include postwar popular music, Amiri Baraka's *Blues People* of 1963, had relatively little to say about postwar migration and popular music. Energized by the Civil Rights movement, Baraka's main objective was to provide a critical social history of African American music and the conditions imposed on it in American society. His interests in contemporary culture lay in modernist drama, literature, and avant-garde jazz.

More detailed studies of the popular music that evolved from the Great Migration can be found in Charles Keil's *Urban Blues* (1966/1991) and Charlie Gillett's *The Sound of the City* (1970/1983). *Urban Blues* pioneered research on contemporary popular music in low-income black neighborhoods, noting that this music had been somewhat ignored by the folk revival and

Baraka. The revival's search for authenticity in the past is challenged on ethnographic grounds, with Keil calling for attention to be paid to large and diverse musical cultures among people of color. He reports, for instance, that "there are still at least forty store-front churches for every joint where blues or jazz is played in Chicago" (Keil 1966/1991, 41). The book explores an overall transformation of blues from a rural and religious culture into an urban culture involving touring performers, media industry, and nightlife audiences composed of recent migrants. It analyzes the situation in second-generation urban blues of Memphis origin, arguing that a change had occurred in emotional style and cultural consciousness involving lyrics, style of expression, and ritual behaviors in performance. B. B. King and Bobby Bland, the book's main protagonists, represented a new sense of hope and optimism.[1] The book's primary methodological contribution was the introduction of ethnography into urban popular music research. It demonstrates the value of firsthand field experience and holistic exploration of performances, record production, and touring. It takes media into account without being media-centric. However, the interpretation of ethnography is limited and utilizes a simplistic concept of community.

The Sound of the City (Gillett 1970/1983) is a sweeping account of postwar Anglophone popular music that provides much insight into the musical outcomes of the Great Migration. It demonstrates how local record production became important to musicians and audiences in black neighborhoods across many cities, while also serving a function for the white-dominated corporate cultural industries. The study of musical life following the Great Migration thus cannot be limited to performance culture alone. In particular, Gillett documents the rise of independent recording companies as a social base for black rhythm and blues artists in the 1940s and the long-term stylistic influence of musicians in the large black communities in cities such as Memphis and Chicago. He documents countless recording companies that worked with black artists who were generally excluded from the corporate industry (Gillett 1970/1983, 10 and 39). These recordings were produced for consumption in black neighborhoods but also reached white audiences via radio. Rhythm and blues was eventually co-opted and transformed into white rock 'n' roll for a much larger market. Rock 'n' roll entered the national charts, national television, and Hollywood cinema. When black neighborhoods were hit by the urban economic crisis in the 1960s and 1970s, many independent companies suffered, too, demonstrating again that they existed in the ecosystem of these neighborhoods.

4. *Genre cities and subcultural scenes.* The local independent recording industries of the mid-twentieth century also contributed to local genre dif-

ferentiation and specialization. *The Sound of the City* serves as a locus classicus of the notion of a genre city, which generally identifies a particular city as the center and often the birthplace of one genre of music. This notion has not been theorized, but it has guided literatures on individual genres and cities and been co-opted into tourism, heritage, and city marketing narratives since the late twentieth century. While electronic media played little role in the formative era of jazz in New Orleans, for instance, the recording industry increasingly began to participate in the construction of locality in the mid-twentieth century. This involved not only independent recording companies, but also the corporate industry's development of cities as centers of individual genre production units (Peterson 1997; Negus 1999). In spite of this, the scholarly literature that does register the genre geographies of the recording industry generally pays little attention to the urban social dynamics and sensory environments that shape expressive styles. In music journalism, a city is often assumed to have a spirit that is somehow reflected in its music. There are elements of this in Gillett's account, beginning with the metaphor in the book title. He states that rock music in Los Angeles was shaped by a particular attitude in the city, and he claims that rock 'n' roll "expressed the spontaneous, personal response of singers to city environments" (Gillett 1970/1983, 67 and 99). Gillett's few and brief claims about the music's urban dimension primarily serve a motivational purpose. He does not detail or examine them in the book.

The notion of a genre city has a built-in mythical dimension since it excludes the many other forms of music that exist in a city. Images of small cities have been coconstructed by national media celebrating the assumed uniqueness of the individual city, and smaller cities have tended to subsequently exploit that image. The metropolis, on the other hand, tends to employ narratives of pluralism to celebrate local genre histories as well as the latest trends. With the decline of the broadcast industry monopoly and the rise of the internet, more of the musical diversity of cities has surfaced. At the same time, gentrification has priced artist communities out of city centers, making it more difficult for new genres to develop in an urban environment.

The concept of scene is similarly used to identify a genre of music with a city, but it has other meanings, too, and derives from theory of urbanism as opposed to theory of media production. The concept has been a feature of social theory of urbanism since at least Louis Wirth's "The Urban Society and Civilization" (Wirth 1940). Wirth used the term "scene" as a signifier of a social landscape in a general sense, and this is still a common use of the word. However, in the 1950s "scene" gained new and gendered meanings through its association with jazz and Beat-generation cultures of hip and bohemian masculinity. A strong but mostly implicit ideology of authenticity was thus built into the word's mythology. The word was popular in jazz magazines in the 1950s and adopted in the title of jazz books (Hobsbawm 1960/2014; Charters and Kunstadt 1962). It proliferated further in discourses on Beat-generation scenes in the early 1960s (Rigney and Smith 1961, vii), hippie scenes in San Francisco and Los Angeles (Perry 1984), and urban art worlds (Tomkins 1965).

Sociologists of jazz generally used the concept of community instead, reflecting its central status in postwar sociological thought. Alan Merriam and Raymond Mack's oft-cited article on the topic is primarily concerned with how community was constituted in jazz through symbolic forms such as music genre, language, and ritual. The article explicitly excluded locality from the equation (Merriam and Mack 1960, 211).

The concept of community was also central in the literature on subcultures in British cultural studies of the 1970s and 1980s. This literature can be interpreted as an evolution of sociology's interest in value-orientation and symbol spheres as contexts for explaining order and authority in social groups and institutions (Mills 1959/2000, 36–38). This knowledge interest continues to evolve in studies of popular music in cities, and in close relationship with metaphors of space and place. The literatures on art worlds, culture worlds, scenes, and milieus illustrate complex and diverse conceptions of the relationship between music, community, and urban geography. Some scholars refer to industrially developed scenes and describe them as landscapes of production (Bennett and Peterson 2004, 4–5). Others conceive of cosmopolitan and diasporic scenes as sites of international networks that challenge bounded conceptions of place (Straw 1991; Jackson 2012). Scholars of smaller and more experimental cultures have developed concepts of milieu cultures (Webb 2007) and microscenes (Grazian 2013).

5. *Diaspora, multiculturalism, and migration.* The notion of urban ethnomusicology stimulated an important expansion of the discipline in the 1970s into the domain of modern urban cities. It was one of ethnomusicology's most important scholars, Bruno Nettl, who with his grand vision and international experience pioneered this development (Nettl 1978). He contributed rigorous and insightful local ethnographies that expanded the field of inquiry. It proved harder to establish a theoretical and methodological ground for urban ethnomusicology, however. This would have required a deeper integration with urban social theory. Interest in urban ethnomusicology faded in the 1980s.

Although its theoretical and methodological contributions to the social study of music in cities are limited, ethnomusicology has made substantial contributions to the area. It has broadened the field of inquiry into a broader range of musical cultures in cities in global histories of migration and diaspora, and it has introduced critical understandings of multiculturalism and social justice and given voice to displaced and subaltern populations. The term "urban ethnomusicology" is still occasionally used to identify knowledge interests in individual neighborhoods as sites of diaspora (Toynbee and Dueck 2011; Rollefson 2017) and in public spaces as sites of transcultural encounter (e.g., Bohlman 1994; Turino 2000; Sakakeeny 2010; Klotz, Bohlman, and Koch 2018).

6. Popular music in evolving urban economies. A growing literature on popular music in evolving urban economies is primarily concerned with two questions: How are musical cultures being transformed in gentrification, and how is music being co-opted into the commercial agendas for culture promoted by city governments and cultural industries?

David Grazian's (2003) study of blues in Chicago examined the decline of the South Side scene during the postindustrial crisis and the emergence of blues clubs in a gentrifying white neighborhood on the North Side. This trajectory is somewhat specific to Chicago as a destination for blues tourism, but it has parallels in other cities, including the New York jazz scene (Jackson 2012, 64). Grazian's analysis demonstrated the general theoretical point, inspired by the Chicago School, that urban cultural formations such as music scenes evolve within neighborhood transformations. Moreover, the commercial club is a typical performance institution in the consumer culture environments of gentrified neighborhoods. These environments grow as a result of music tourism, too, even as repeat visitors attempt to consume the city as locals (Gibson and Connell 2005; Garcia 2015b). Grazian later introduced the concept of microscenes into theory of scene transformations, arguing that when experimental and DIY cultures are priced out of the center, they sometimes regroup in the periphery as microscenes (Grazian 2013).

Sara Cohen's response to gentrification involved shifts in her analytical orientations. Her first book, in 1991, was an ethnography of local rock musicians in Liverpool. Her second book, published in 2007, concentrated on the theme of urban renewal and the institutions that were becoming more influential in this process: cultural industries and the city government. The book explored the relationship between local music scenes and the city's cultural economy and the commercialization of musical heritage.

This points to a more general trend of city governments co-opting music into commercial agendas. How are musical cultures transformed by their co-option into culture-led strategies for promoting economic growth and boosting a city's competitiveness? Research on such diverse phenomena as Mozart celebrations in Vienna and the live music branding of Austin has demonstrated that city governments privilege musical cultures of the dominant classes and transform them into regimes of communication and branding (Usner 2011; O'Meara and Tretter 2013). This involves a growing emphasis on large cultural events and commercial performance spaces.

Where Do We Go from Here?

The literatures discussed above are in some ways unfinished intellectual projects, particularly with respect to the unresolved tension between knowledge interests in cultural particulars and in theory for thinking beyond particulars. The latter is necessary for situating a musical culture in broader urban dynamics and for the production and transmission of knowledge across literatures on a variety of musical cultures in the city. The existing literatures either explore some areas of musical life as part of a broad history of leisure or a general urban sociology, or they specialize in one musical culture with limited interest in thinking comparatively about musical cultures in the city. Specialist area literatures serve an important function in the humanities, and it would be both unrealistic and unfruitful to try to subsume all these literatures into a single framework or discipline of urban music studies. Nevertheless, the more specific concept of the social study of music in cities can help strengthen attention to shared conceptual and methodological challenges. It can help further develop concepts and issues within individual area literatures and strengthen knowledge transmission, since it introduces a level of (inter)disciplinary reflexivity. More engagement with urban social theory could be advantageous across the board. Theory of performance institutions can help think about musical cultures in everyday urban life in more general terms. The politics of multiculturalism, feminism, and social justice, moreover, can be addressed more, especially in research on cultures of the dominant classes and their intellectual histories in white patriarchy. The overall methodological thrust of my argument is that area specialization can be balanced with more disciplinary reflexivity—the two are mutually beneficial.

This book's discussion of rock clubs in the following chapters will contribute foundational elements to the social study of popular music's performance institutions in the city, while also contributing to literatures on rock music and urban history, music scenes, and social life in gentrifying cities. The close relationship of the rock club to its urban environment requires that a sociology of its institutionalization must also be an urban sociology. This will enable new interpretations of musical cultures in cities, such as the mapping of developments in music genres that cannot be explained in terms of aesthetics alone but also benefit from sociological analysis of urban conditions that have escaped scholarly attention in music studies. In urban popular culture, musical practices and genres transform in processes in which artists grow professionally, seize career opportunities offered by evolving genre institutions, and adapt to neighborhood change. Managers, venues, and recording companies participate in the transformation of musical aesthetics and performance culture.

: 4 :

The Commercial Institutionalization of the Rock Club in New York

It is of critical importance that we understand the gentrification process—and the art world's crucial role within it—if we are to avoid aligning ourselves with the forces behind this destruction.
DEUTSCHE AND RYAN (1984, 94)

In 2015, I was at a conference at the University of Eastern Finland. This university, located in a historical border region with Russia, is home to a vibrant international research community in the field of border studies. Making the most of their somewhat remote location, local scholars with rather different disciplinary backgrounds participated in the conference, and major methodological differences were exposed. In one session, a distinguished professor of English gave a presentation on ethnicity and nationalism in the fictional character Paddington Bear. The presentation provoked one participant to question the validity of the research. "What can you know about nationalism by analyzing literary fiction?!" This response involved a misunderstanding, but it highlights a fundamental challenge in the humanities: To understand human life and social formations, it is relevant to study cultural practices that matter to people, but how can we account for the role of these practices in social life and their relationship with social structures?

For about one hundred years, cultural research has incorporated ethnography to complement textual analysis, but technological and social changes are challenging conventional ethnographic methods. Evolutions in digital communication, for instance, have prompted the rise of digital humanities and studies of datafied lives that combine ethnography with analysis of technological systems and machine learning. Evolutions in cities, from transportation infrastructure to new economies and population growth, have similarly led to methodological innovations. This chapter is a contribution to the study of music and organized cultural life in the process of gentrification. It demonstrates some of the potential for musical scholarship in integrating sociological analysis more deeply into the study of music in cities. The sociology of gentrification has produced a large literature with ambitious methodologies (e.g., Sassen 1991/2001), while the literature on music in gentrification is much smaller and has focused more on ethnography of local scenes than on broader structural transformations (chapter 3). My fieldwork on rock music in New York City between 2010 and 2013 led me to conclude that the field of rock music performance in this city has been fundamentally transformed by broader changes in the urban condition and illustrates how cultural worlds adapt, transform, and disappear within their urban environments.

I began exploring clubs for rock performance ethnographically in 2008 and soon realized that updating the literature on this topic would require empirical and conceptual groundwork. The performance culture I encountered was strikingly different from the scene culture with which popular music studies had been concerned in the 1990s (Cohen 1991; Shank 1994; Berger 1999). The clubs in my sample of eight cities across Western Europe had gone through a decade or two of building renovations, dramatically increased the number of concerts they produced per year, and presented a growing number of touring artists from the United States and the United Kingdom.[1] Ethnographic dwelling in a few clubs could not explain why these changes were happening. This was not a community culture. It was a consumer culture focused on headliner shows produced by an industry. Some of the clubs were selling more than 300,000 concert tickets per year.

I extended my research in 2010 to New York City, where the industry had developed on a larger scale than in European cities, but where vibrant alternatives to this consumer culture persisted. The core dynamics I had observed in other cities were stronger, so New York became the main case study for analyzing these dynamics. During six one-month field trips from March 2010 to October 2013, concentrating on the Lower East Side and the adjacent neighborhood of Williamsburg, Brooklyn, across the East River, I explored the field of rock performance and its urban environments. On the Lower East Side, the field's historical center, legendary clubs of the 1970s and 1980s were closing, while larger, more polished clubs represented a new trend. This followed the overall change from "gritty" to "cool" in the urban environment (Zukin 2010). Was the visual appearance the only change in the culture? How was the rock club changing as an institution?

The argument of this chapter situates the rock club in gentrification. Changes in real estate prices and labor markets have had a dramatic impact on who and what can exist in individual neighborhoods. Gentrification privileges affluent populations and for-profit cultural organizations. Institutions such as the rock club, fitness gym, and art museum have evolved into corporate forms and been integrated into a consumer culture value system. I argue that the small and informal rock club in bohemian neighborhood scenes of the Lower East Side in the 1970s and 1980s shaped the mythology of the club, but that the contemporary landscape is dominated by another model, the commercial indie concert theater. The latter is governed by a new institutional arrangement of the corporate concert industry, larger media markets, and by the aesthetics and values of a new condition of urban life. Gentrification thus explains fundamental changes to the character and function of leisure institutions and how they adapt to broader changes in the city. The rock club is a core example for the social study of cultural life in gentrification because it was a central part of a neighborhood scene and underwent a profound transformation within the same neighborhood, the Lower East Side. The consequences of gentrification have wider historical significance, however. Gentrification has brought an end, at least temporarily, to more than a century of existence of various cultural scenes that created unique environments of cultural urbanism, artistic creativity, and performance.

The analysis is organized into sections on the rock field's history within neighborhood transformations. This allows for a historically embedded conceptualization, as opposed to a static conception of gentrification and of the institution. Promoters and their performance spaces will serve as focal points for this analysis, since they are central regulatory agents in the network of the institution. The chapter begins in the ethnographic present of the early 2010s with the Brooklyn warehouse scene that articulated the positions of commercial institutionalization and represented an alternative to it. Promoter Todd Patrick is a focal point in this analysis. The second section unpacks the genealogy of the field and analyzes the club's evolution as an institution in the Lower East Side rock scene of the 1970s. The focal point is promoter Hilly Kristal's CBGB in the northern section of the neighborhood—the East Village. The subsequent sections analyze the corporatization of the rock club in the gentrification of the Lower East Side, focusing on the indie rock club concert theater developed by Michael Swier and the company the Bowery Presents.

"I Don't Think You Need a Rock Club": The Brooklyn Warehouse Scene

Media images shaped my construction of the field in the early stages of the research. I have liked rock music since I was a child, later becoming fascinated with New York's jazz history and its downtown experimental scene of the 1980s. When I began this project in 2010, I had little firsthand experience of the city's musical life, but I had been exposed to sounds and images of New York from an early age. My experience was filtered through middle-class media in Scandinavia, where I grew up. In the 2000s, Brooklyn increasingly enjoyed a reputation as a place of cool and authentic popular culture, and rock music was part of this. One of the first things I did was to interview a manager of the bands Beach House and Yeasayer, which were associated with Brooklyn indie rock (Jason Foster, interview with author, January 8, 2010). It turned out that some of the so-called Brooklyn bands had only moved to New York recently, and many of them were touring extensively. There was a scene in Brooklyn, but the musicians were relatively unknown and not the stars featured in mass-market music journalism. The primary media channels of the scene were email lists and simple websites used for concert listings. For scene participants, media spaces were not the primary center of action—performance spaces were. The scene's media culture thus contrasted with the dominant media culture of the city. There was always a film or television team filming somewhere and tourists photographing places made famous by movies.

In one common narrative, the field of rock clubs was characterized by a division between "commercial clubs" in Lower Manhattan and a so-called Brooklyn warehouse scene. This narrative was articulated by Brooklyn scene insiders who partly derived their identity from their opposition to the commercial Manhattan clubs, which did not communicate publicly about the culture apart from promoting their own products. Many talked about a person named Todd Patrick as a pioneer and parent figure of the Brooklyn scene. He was thirty-five and had mentored a handful of other DIY promoters in the mid-2000s, all of them men and about ten years younger. The Patrick circle of promoters lived in Brooklyn and operated almost exclusively in Brooklyn. One anomaly was Ariel Panero, who promoted events in a small basement in Tribeca that he borrowed from celebrity entrepreneur and producer Damon Dash. Panero's motivation was "to prove that it is still possible to do underground rock shows in Manhattan" (Ariel Panero, conversation with the author, April 23, 2010).

It turned out Patrick was not from New York but had moved there from the West Coast to become part of the city's rock mythology. He had arrived in 2001 when a new generation of rock bands began appearing and Williamsburg was becoming a place of bohemian opportunity. Patrick was born in Indiana in 1975 and grew up in Texas. While a student at the University of Texas, Austin, Patrick worked in a coffee shop and found an empty space on the second floor that he used for a couple of shows (Matson 2005). This exploratory approach became a constant throughout his career. The story goes that he found his first performance space in Portland, another city with liberal and countercultural traditions, when he accidentally walked into a dry cleaner the day it was going out of business. He rented the space, removed the machinery, and promoted performances there for about two years (Matson 2005). Patrick called 17 Nautical Miles a "showspace," following a common DIY terminology that distinguishes between "spaces" of its own scene sphere and "venues" of the formal industry sphere. Patrick's success with 17 Nautical Miles motivated him to open a bigger space, but he could not get permission from the city authorities. He continued to promote shows in unauthorized spaces until 2016, a turning point to which I shall return.

In the 2000s, Patrick and his apprentices worked in the area of northwest Brooklyn from Greenpoint down to Williamsburg and into Bushwick. He lived for years in Long Island City, just north of Greenpoint, and in the late 2000s moved to the Richwood neighborhood, which is adjacent to Bushwick and just a few stops on the L train from Williamsburg. When Patrick came to New York in 2001, Williamsburg was in the early stages of gentrification. A few rock clubs had opened in the late 1990s, and by 2001 the neighborhood had an emerging rock scene, with more clubs and with the CMJ showcase festival expanding from Manhattan to Williamsburg (Moser 2001; Anasi 2012). Artist communities were migrating there from Manhattan and elsewhere. Record stores and bars popped up.

The warehouse music scene evolved in the wider ecosystem of the art and cultural scene in Williamsburg. A narrative of a distinct music scene, however, evolved in production culture and in the blogosphere. The Patrick circle of promoters were entrepreneurs of a music scene in close relationship with artists and fans. These young promoters adopted a DIY community narrative in which musical performance was defined as a personal and community-oriented experience. They distanced themselves from the commodity form of musical performance in the concert industry and only charged audiences a small fee for access to their events. They made little profit and had no desire to grow their business (Ariel Panero, interview with the author, April 23, 2010; Edan Wilber, interview with the author, April 26, 2010). These promoters described their performance spaces as their own semiprivate spaces and felt hurt when someone acted disrespectfully. They had no music industry experience, maintained no regular offices or business hours, and did much of the facility maintenance, interior design, and production of performances themselves. Edan Wilber at Dead by Audio, for instance, had for years a daily twelve-to-fourteen-hour routine that involved booking bands in the morning or early afternoon, preparing the performance space in the late afternoon, opening the doors in the early evening, and doing sound production on his small PA system for all performances until three in the morning.

In 2005, the cover for Patrick's shows was usually five or six dollars, and the only form of advertising was a plain-text email providing basic information about the events. These emails were sent to an estimated four thousand people who had signed up (Matson 2005). In 2010, the price was typically eight to twelve dollars. A beer was one dollar, almost the same price as in a corner grocery. This price level posed less of a financial concern to young patrons, many of whom were students or had low-paying jobs and commented on the higher prices in commercial clubs, where tickets were typically fifteen to thirty dollars and a beer cost five dollars. The lower prices in DIY spaces were important to their audience culture. Audiences appreciated being able to enjoy music and socialize all night and have a few drinks at affordable prices.

The unauthorized status of the performance spaces run by the Patrick circle involved uncertainties with respect to safety and taxes. The promoters talked about paying artists fairly, but I am not sure if all financial transactions were reported to the tax authorities. Tickets and drinks were paid in cash, with no visible recording for accounting purposes. The promoters were open about the fact that they did not have permissions from authorities. I now find the ethics of the scene more complicated than when I was in the field. At a pragmatic level, the performance culture could not have existed if the law had been fully followed. The costs would generally have exceeded the expenses significantly. The freedom from institutional regulation generated a certain excitement, moreover—insiders valued the idea of a community that created its own rules—but it also blinded participants to some ethical issues. Such was the atmosphere that it never occurred to me to ask if promoters were paying taxes or putting lives at risk. To be fair, the promoters did pay attention to safety, and serious accidents did not occur. The promoters were considerate and diplomatic hosts and did not simply encourage hedonism. One of Patrick's reasons for bypassing authorization was to allow teenagers entry (Farah 2010; see also Signore 2007). Yet, there was no discussion of the risks and responsibilities involved in allowing, say, a fifteen-year-old into spaces that sold alcohol and had people smoking marijuana.

The Patrick circle took inspiration from the DIY punk scenes of the 1980s, which situated themselves outside the corporate sphere. Local niche magazines and bloggers began referring to "the Brooklyn DIY scene" around 2008 (Piper and Gregorio 2009). The promoters were not part of the corporate industry and did not aspire to become part of it, and they cultivated a community spirit by staging young, talented bands in spaces that embodied the ideal of musical performance as an urban ritual. The promoters organized performances in lofts, basements, and warehouses, under bridges, and in parking lots. They also shared some performance spaces in a collectivist spirit.[2] However, the promoters were not musicians organizing their own performances, and they operated like one-person companies. The more events they organized, the more they were perceived as champions of the scene.

Media exposure helped grow the scene, especially *Brooklyn Vegan* and *Pitchfork*. "The Vegan" was started in 2004 and became known as the city's most popular "live music blog," although it did not promote a discourse of live music. It helped promote small DIY shows by listing them alongside concerts in commercial clubs, and it created a space for simultaneously celebrating and mocking the scene. *Pitchfork*, the most influential indie rock magazine of the late 1990s and the 2000s, had its offices in Chicago, but editor Ryan Schreiber was from Brooklyn and moved back in 2007, and the magazine had a regular reporter in Brooklyn. Edan Wilber said the growing popularity of the scene also led to competition among promoters. He felt forced to stop sharing contact information for bands with colleagues, and he felt increasingly isolated from them (Edan Wilber, interview with the author, April 26, 2010).

The DIY Promoter as a Cultural Hero

Patrick gained status as an auteur promoter for discovering young talent at a time when bloggers generally played a more important role for fans and industry professionals invested in music discovery. "Going to a Todd P show" (he promoted shows under that name) was a thing among fans and bloggers. Patrick helped kick-start the careers of local bands, such as Deerhunter, Dan Deacon, and Dirty Projectors, who eventually grew out of the scene and into the industry orbit. Talent buyers and musicians told me that a band would get attention on blogs if Patrick booked the band a few times within months (Ariel Panero, interview with the author, April 23, 2010; Rami Haykal, interview with the author, April 26, 2010). In 2009, an agent for a major national booking agency said: "Larger venues definitely look at what he's booking and will definitely, definitely move in those directions" (Gleason 2009). Patrick also received attention in middle-class media, such as the *New York Times*, NPR Music, and the *Village Voice*.

Patrick became something of a cultural hero thanks to his charisma and his adventurous rebel approach. He was frequently followed by an entourage, and sometimes by a person with a camera. His language and approach to producing shows implied that the DIY show was an authentic act of community free from alienating industry routines and venues. He and his circle defined themselves against the Manhattan club industry, while benefiting from Williamsburg's proximity to Manhattan. Williamsburg was a hotspot of nightlife tourism, just one stop on the subway from Manhattan. The large crowds of young people on the trains from Manhattan on weeknights were a testament to this. In 2010, there were DIY shows in the neighborhood every night and even more on the weekends. In this context, the Patrick circle appealed to romantic rock myths of raw, untamed performance, uncorrupted by nearby booming consumerism. The scene was fascinated with the imagined authenticity of unknown, unspoiled, young, talented bands, with the mystical, deserted, not-yet-gentrified, and unregulated spaces of the metropolis, and with the spontaneity of one-off events in newly discovered and unique places.

The Patrick circle cultivated an architectural aesthetic of the postindustrial underground. They preferred intimate, esoteric, and decaying architecture. They kept their spaces basic, used cheap secondhand furniture, and put up amateur-style handwritten signs and street art on the walls. At one point an old bed linen was used as a curtain as a backdrop to the stage in Monster Island Basement, lit with lamps made for domestic use. The shadows created by the lamps were evocative and created a quasi-tribal atmosphere. The bar usually had a selection of a few drinks, though these were not always kept in a cooler. Death by Audio had a small secondhand cooler on the floor, with the prices handwritten on a piece of paper. The bartender and door person were volunteer scenesters. Some promoters lived in their performance spaces for periods of time.[3]

Patrick in particular used the city's countercultural legend as a resource. Shortly after his club Llano Estacado was shut down by the police in 2005, he replied to an interviewer's comment about audience demand:

Interviewer: [Llano Estacado] seemed to be doing really well before. Every time I went down there, there were 300–400 people. . . .

Todd: I think it's a testament to how much people are thirsty for something that doesn't operate in the traditional, commercial, seen-it-before, done-it-before-a-million-times kind of way. Shows I did there which brought in 400 people, 500 people, 600 people, if I did them elsewhere, like a bar—less of a community-oriented, exciting place—would bring in 50. It is about who's involved, who's playing, sure, but it's also about what people are getting involved in. They want to be part of something. Bottom line, people move

> to New York because they want to be part of something. Everyone moves here because they want to be in the Factory scene in the '60s, or they want to be watching the Velvet Underground play at Max's Kansas City in 1973, or they want to have seen the Ramones play at CB's in the '70s. They want to have been there for that, or whatever the new version is. Right now the city is doing a really good job of having a stranglehold on any historically significant creative moment that might be taking place in New York. So I think people are really hungry. People are really excited to be part of something that feels like a really free, creative space. (Matson 2005)

Going to Williamsburg and DIY shows was a remarkable social experience for me as an outsider from Scandinavia. I remember the first time I got off the subway and walked down on Bedford Street, the main artery of Williamsburg. There was a vibrant atmosphere that invoked images of San Francisco in the mid-1960s. For periods of time, I was a regular at Death by Audio because of the vibrant atmosphere and the talented performers. I valued how people there were not simply demanding entertainment but engaged in scene sociality with strangers, in some cases bringing perspectives and energies from living a life without a full-time day job. Moreover, I remember the breathtaking experience of entering the large, dark basement at Monster Island, which was basically just one big space, perhaps the size of a soccer field. Its spatial organization felt improvised and did not focus the attention of the entire room on a stage. There was a psychedelic and spiritual atmosphere, stimulated by the lighting and the energetic punk and drone music to which crowds were sometimes dancing wildly. I remember a small stage placed away from the wall in a corner area, somewhat like an ad hoc stage at a large garden party, with groups of people socializing in other parts of the room during the performances.

Monster Island is illustrative of the wider Williamsburg music and arts scene in the 2000s. In 2004, two artist friends had rented the building and made it home to their nonprofit artist organization called Secret Project Robot. They were Erik Zajaceskowski, "an artist, curator and intellectual" with interests "in almost all mediums of art," and Karl LaRocca, a graphic designer and founder of Kayrock Screenprinting. The two developed Monster Island into a party and art space. Patrick's shows were part of this larger ecology. When Monster Island closed in 2010, both Secret Project Robot and Patrick moved their center of activities farther away from Manhattan to Bushwick, and Patrick might have been inspired by Secret Project Robot when he at that time came up with the idea of the Market Hotel project ("Secret Project Robot"; McKinley 2011).

How Did the Patrick Circle Respond to Gentrification?

The story of Death by Audio, a former warehouse, illustrates key aspects of the impact gentrification had on the scene. In 2005, Oliver Ackermann and a few other musicians rented this deserted warehouse at the intersection of Kent Avenue and South Second Street, which was in such poor condition that it could not be rented out legally (Conboy 2016). Ackermann needed a space for his small business making guitar pedals called Death by Audio, and they also created a small recording studio and some bedrooms. A few people lived there and shared the same kitchen, which was also the main common room. The number of individuals who lived there fluctuated for periods of time. To finance the renovations, they decided to organize some parties, and these parties led to the development of a club with frequent shows held in one room with space for about one hundred people and a smaller adjacent room with an ad hoc bar. The club benefited from Ackermann's status as an indie rock star in the band A Place to Bury Strangers and was named after the pedal factory, simply because it was perceived as a space for shows at Death by Audio. The showspace was further developed when Edan Wilber took over the daily productions, improved the sound system, and had visual artists paint street art murals.

In 2013, one of the volunteers at the door commented that an increasing number of new residents in the neighborhood would come in "dressed up as if they were going to a trendy event or a nightclub." She also said that many regulars had moved farther away and therefore traveled long distances to come (Dorie van Dercreek, conversation with the author, October 2013). Many of those I talked to were students or people with low-paid jobs, including experimental rock musicians. Some distanced themselves from thinking about careers and challenged the concept of normality, including through the creative use of informal language characteristic of an oral subculture. I initially felt provincial, but it was easy for me to connect with music nerds like myself and appreciate the passion and idealism in the culture. Edan Wilber, the promoter, felt growing pressures from gentrification and competition but did not want to adapt to the changing environment.

Author: What are your expectations for the future?

Wilber: I have nightmares all the time that something goes wrong. I sometimes have asshole crowds. All it takes is one person to scream on the street and the police come. The place might close, so you gotta do what you can. This place was a warehouse. It was the only thing around here three years ago, and this block now has several things and restaurants. It wasn't a safe neighborhood, and artists moved in here, and they don't bother or look like someone with

> money. Then developers come and people are always in it for their own end. There are plenty of places to eat and plenty of condos already. We don't need more of that. In a few years' time, no one in this neighborhood will know we existed. In any other city, the bubble would go away, but here the process is still running fast. It's a virus in society. Like in science fiction. . . . We are overfarming and destroying the ozone, all that shit, and destroying the earth, but we're also destroying culture. (Edan Wilber, interview with the author, April 16, 2010)

The location of Death by Audio was perfect for Brooklyn DIY promoters in the 2000s. It was a somewhat remote area near the waterfront with a raw, postindustrial atmosphere. However, Williamsburg was being rapidly transformed into a landscape of upscale bars, restaurants, and cafés in the early 2010s. A 2005 rezoning of more than two hundred blocks in Williamsburg and parts of Greenpoint paved the way for the construction of large numbers of luxury apartment towers (Gregor 2014). Williamsburg became the most intensely gentrified neighborhood in New York since 1990 (NYU Furman Center 2016, 6). In the 2000s alone, the white share of the population grew from 34% to 52%, while the Hispanic share declined from 57% to 38%. The black population in Brooklyn as a whole declined by almost 50,000 people during that decade (Center for Urban Research 2011).

Like the other DIY space on Kent and South Second—285 Kent (founded by Patrick)—Death by Audio was forced to close in 2014 because of real estate development. It was particularly painful for the Death by Audio community that its space was taken over by *Vice* magazine. *Vice* had started as a Canadian punk magazine and made a business out of using subculture as an advertising platform for corporations trying to reach younger generations. It was no longer just a symbol of commodification, it was directly eliminating a sacred space of the underground. This story is told in the documentary *Goodnight Brooklyn*, which Matt Conboy of Death by Audio decided to make when it became clear that the club would be closing (Conboy 2016). The movie interprets this moment of crisis in the Brooklyn scene through interviews with numerous key insiders. The closing of Death by Audio is portrayed as a symbol of the scene's death and of the general decline of such scenes in society. The club is interpreted in this context as a place of artistic and social authenticity and an institution of DIY idealism and collectivism. Wilber left New York immediately after and eventually moved to Austin, Texas. Opening a new space in Bushwick was not a viable option for him. Oliver Ackermann summed up the situation: "Something is dying. Something is definitely being destroyed" (Conboy 2016).

Could DIY Performance Be Institutionalized?

By the mid-2010s most of the DIY spaces in Williamsburg had gone, and the mood had changed in the Patrick circle. Panero had tragically died, Wilber had left the city, and Patrick's activities had slowed down. Their imperative "create your own showspace!" of the 2000s had disappeared. The changes were already palpable in 2010. Patrick became a father and decided to convert one of his performance spaces into an authorized one. After fifteen years as a champion of unregulated performance culture in—to paraphrase Marcel Duchamp—"found spaces," he decided to develop the warehouse scene's DIY performance culture into a more institutionalized form.

Patrick introduced his new vision at a public meeting in the performance space he wanted to transform, a deteriorating building in Bushwick called Market Hotel. Patrick had sent out an invitation to a meeting to be held in the showspace on April 27, 2010. Carlos Molina, a passionate scene participant, emailed me the same day to tell me about the meeting in what he described as Patrick's "emblematic venue," which had just been shut down by the police. Molina forwarded the invitation in which Patrick introduced a positive narrative of institutionalization:

> Market Hotel has existed for over two years and in that time has hosted countless legendary events and drawn huge international notice . . . all of this under the constraints of operating completely underground and with no budget. Now the time has come to channel that momentum and create a fully realized space that serves the whole community, that will help define the NYC / Brooklyn scene into the future.
>
> GET INVOLVED IN THE MARKET HOTEL PROJECT!
>
> 1st volunteer orientation meeting: TUESDAY APRIL 27TH 8PM @ MARKET HOTEL—957 Broadway, Brooklyn
>
> ANNOUNCING—a new initiative to create a sustainable, all ages, open-to-the-community, 7-nights-a-week home for independent music and art, in the Market Hotel space.
>
> MARKET HOTEL PROJECT is a new not-for-profit organization dedicated to swiftly reopening and improving the Market Hotel space, by making the venue more viable, comfortable, safe, and better able to weather legal attention. Especially in these days of ever-encroaching commercialism and corporatism in "indie rock," we envision a space that is a non-commercial "spiritual home" for independent rock music and indie art—but also is sustainable and sanctioned enough to expand indie horizons and open our doors to music and art from the rest of our diverse Bushwick community. (Todd

Patrick's email list, quoted from email from Carlos Molina, April 27, 2010; see also Friedlander 2010)

In 2003, Patrick had declared that he did not need a club, just "a room with a door and somebody there stamping hands . . . [and] somebody to work the sound" (Wang 2003). That approach worked in the early 2000s but not in the early 2010s. Patrick responded to the changing conditions by developing a new agenda for the scene that aimed to revitalize an organization with a new form of ownership, legal status, and business model.

The meeting provided a full exposition of Patrick as a DIY auteur in a crucial transitional moment for him and for the scene. He gave a thirty-minute speech that served to mobilize volunteers and sponsors. He assumed the role of an authoritative spokesman for a community and deployed legends about the city's culture worlds[4] to create a sense of tradition and purpose. He also explored the mythology of the building to incorporate its poor condition into a narrative of historical authenticity and mystique. The building was originally a bank in the 1870s, but Patrick highlighted its history as an illegal speakeasy and a location in the 1990 Hollywood movie *Ghost*:

Patrick: I was told that the ghost lives here.

Attendee: I don't know if that's really true.

Patrick: He definitely gets sucked into the ground. It looks like old New York. This is why we love this building. It's old New York. Look around. It's never been renovated. This is a building that looks just like it did when it was built. Except for the fact that it's falling apart. This is ancient.

In a collectivist spirit, Patrick had organized the attendees in a circle around him, with about twenty people sitting on chairs and an equal number of people sitting on the floor. There was a blogger and a reporter from a neighborhood newspaper in attendance, but no representative from major news media or magazines.

Patrick started talking in a relaxed manner but with determination, showing awareness of the challenge involved in turning the building into a legally sanctioned performance space. He introduced the situation and then unfolded his ambitious vision for transforming Market Hotel from a DIY rock space into "a diverse cultural space" for the wider local community. More specifically, the model seemed to be that of a performing arts center:

> So the space we envision . . . is a space that's legal and not for profit, that advertises openly, that's open seven nights a week, that has new bathrooms, you know, obviously fixed up walls and approved electricity, a better sound

> system and stage, nicer entrancing and exiting that doesn't scare people, lots of safety that we can't afford at this moment. . . . Because it's open seven nights a week and because it's legal, we can take more chances. Do events that are smaller or else reach out to elements of the community that we are currently unable to reach out to. Again, we don't wanna be exclusive, we wanna be inclusive. So, yes, even though we will still remain a place that's focused around indie punk, just what I like to think, independent rock music that you guys know, that will still be the focus of what we do, but I will also like the space to be open to the same kind of indie ideas applied to other parts of the community. (Todd Patrick, Market Hotel, April 27, 2010)

Patrick's vision for the organization made it clear that his approach to institutionalization had a strong mythological dimension:

> We also need to put together a series of different governing boards, which is sort of more my area. It's about showing the depth of support from luminaries that define the New York artistic community, as well as getting advice and sharing responsibility among people that are involved in other DIY circles around New York City to try and spread the wealth of the community and make this space a really democratically grounded space. (Todd Patrick, Market Hotel, April 27, 2010)

The broadening of perspective from indie punk to "the New York arts community" involved a strategic decision to shape the political and economic conditions of his organization. Patrick had always been entirely focused on producing musical performance. His new narrative created the possibility of entering the economy of philanthropy and having powerful stakeholders outside the music world. Patrick succeeded in getting a $100,000 grant in 2011 that enabled him to reopen legally in 2016 (Pelly 2011).

One might wonder why a person would embark on such a demanding project with limited and uncertain commercial potential. The building renovations alone took five years. One explanation is that Patrick had altruistic values and relied on other sources of income. In a 2007 interview, he said that he did not make any profit off shows for small audiences and criticized commercial clubs for being "heartless," stating that the commercial exploitation of small shows had a disproportionately high price for the culture (Signore 2007). Patrick's main source of income since 2012 has likely come from his job as curator of Festival NRMAL in Mexico.[5] The festival is small, with an audience of about 5,000, and a ticket price of about fifty dollars as of 2016, but it has corporate sponsors such as Red Bull (Pelly 2013). Patrick is critical of some forms of capitalism and of the corporate music industry. In particular, he has criticized festivals in general for charging prices that are much higher than the operating costs to lower the risk and for concentrating on "a certain brand demographic." These developments made indie rock and festivals "dull" and "classist" (Robbins 2013). In working for Festival NRMAL, Patrick's aim was not just to bring his Brooklyn connections to Mexico. Half of the bands that take part are from around Latin America and the Caribbean. While gentrification brought down the Brooklyn DIY scene and the Patrick circle dissolved, the scene's aesthetics partially survive in festivals like NRMAL and in projects such as Market Hotel.

The East Village Scene in the 1970s and a Century of Poverty

The Brooklyn scene generally did not articulate a cultural history beyond its own. In this respect, it was a popular culture immersed in the here and now. The transformation of the club institution in gentrification can only be fully understood by looking beyond this scene. The social history of the Lower East Side is important in explaining the genealogy of the contemporary field of rock clubs. The field emerged in the neighborhood's northern section, the East Village, in the 1970s and bifurcated in the accelerating gentrification of the 1990s. The commercial club was a product of the neighborhood's gentrification, while the warehouse scene in Williamsburg was an exodus and revival. They had become somewhat separate and contrasting worlds, and they did not articulate their origins in the same neighborhood and the same genre.

A Century of Exploiting the Poor

The performance culture of the Brooklyn scene took inspiration from diverse urban cultures and from music media cultures, from the local punk tradition of the 1970s to national indie and metal scenes of the 1990s, displaying a dynamism between urban performance cultures on the one side and national and international mass-media cultures on the other. A social study of the rock club in gentrification, however, would be insufficient without taking into account the history of white neo-bohemianism on the Lower East Side. From the moment young white people began moving into the East Village in the 1960s, their cultural expressions involved an exoticization of urban decay and ultimately of poverty, and this continued when the influx of white people accelerated in the 1980s. The East Village had been poor long before the low point of the 1960s and 1970s. Most buildings had been constructed in the late nineteenth century by a real estate industry that systematically exploited low-income populations. The industry developed the model of tenement housing in overcrowded buildings of poor quality. In 1890, the Lower East Side was the most densely populated neighborhood in the world, according to Jacob Riis, who described the concentration of epidemic diseases, insurance fraud fires, and class exploitation: "Proprietors frequently urged the filthy habits of the tenants as an excuse for the condition of their property" (Riis 1890, 9). About one hundred years later, Christopher Mele (2000) argued that elites continued to exploit and reinforce social stigmatization.

The peak crisis on the Lower East Side during the 1960s and 1970s followed decades of disinvestment, failed attempts at middle-class renewal, and the construction of low-rent public housing in the 1940s. The population declined from about 550,000 inhabitants in 1910 to a low point of 155,000 in 1980. In the 1970s, the population dropped 27% in the East Village as a whole and 40% in the Loisaida area, now commonly known as Alphabet City.[6] The Lower East Side was the second-poorest neighborhood in Manhattan, only better off than Harlem (Mele 2000, 195; Smith 1996, 21). Real estate developers stopped maintaining buildings, invested in property elsewhere, and in many cases perversely profited by destroying buildings for insurance payouts. This negative spiral added to an atmosphere of despair in a desolate and dirty streetscape of deteriorating houses and high levels of crime, violence, and drug addiction (Smith 1996, 8). The conditions initially limited the development of white bohemian scenes. The hippie scene in the late 1960s declined with a shift to harder drugs (Mele 2000, 177). Merchants catering to hippies on St. Marks closed, as did the rock clubs Electric Circus and Fillmore East in 1971.

CBGB and the Exoticized Frontier

The neo-bohemian East Village scene of the mid-1960s was a scene of experimental art and culture. Small performance events featuring poetry, theater, film screenings, and happenings were important, as was social life in bars, but it was not until 1967 that a few clubs began regularly presenting rock shows. The following year, Fillmore East (1968–1971) began bringing rock stars to the neighborhood. A prominent band of the scene called the Fugs first performed in a small East Village bookstore owned by one of the band members. This was typical of the scene's DIY production, with underground film productions featuring friends and neighbors and neighborhood locations such as streets and lofts.[7] This scene was also not targeting a larger market—the music, poems, and films were generally considered too esoteric and obscene to achieve wider commercial circulation. The rock scene that evolved in the 1970s still had this local dimension, but it also developed a mass-market dimension following the success of the Velvet Underground and others. It was rock music in particular that popularized the neo-bohemian scene, especially certain aspects, such as bodily immediacy, sex, and drugs, that had wide appeal and could reach large media audiences as part of a song with a steady beat.

There were few dedicated rock clubs in Lower Manhattan when CBGB opened in December 1973 (Kozak 1988, 8–9). Manager Hilly Krystal had previously managed the prominent jazz club Village Vanguard and a restaurant and bar called Hilly's on Ninth Street, both in Greenwich Village (Kozak 1988, 35). Kristal said he was attracted to the Bowery because he came down and saw "all this stuff happening with the artists moving and buying lofts there" (Kozak 1988, 35). He had expressed interest in "a growing artists' colony" in the Bowery in 1969 and the influx of bands that had played Mercer Arts Center (Kozak 1988, 3 and 9). David Byrne lived a block from CBGB and later remembered that little else was happening in the area (Kozak 1988, 40). Kristal hoped the Bowery would become the center of a new arts community (Kozak 1988, 3). He initially programmed country music and poetry readings, but this was not in demand, and within a month of opening, CBGB focused on rock music, filling a gap left by the temporary closing in August 1973 of Max's Kansas City in Gramercy Park (1965–1981) and the shuttering of the Mercer Arts Center in Greenwich Village (1971–1973).[8] CBGB entered the growing ecosystem of an emerging punk and neo-bohemian arts scene, but only created musical performance events. It also created an alternative to Max's, which had a cabaret presentation and an arts crowd. In the opinion of Max's new booker Peter Crowley, Max's had more art rock and "hipsters," while CBGB had more punk rock and "hippies" ("Peter Crowley: Max's Man Behind the Music").

CBGB became an institution of a new East Village punk and new wave rock scene, creating a space for many local musicians and audiences. The club created opportunities for musicians participating in this scene to gain performance experience and improve their ability to be discovered by the recording industry, which was the major commercial realm in the rock music economy at the time. Many relatively unknown artists had an opportunity to play several shows in a short time period, sometimes up to six shows in just one weekend (Kozak 1988, 7 and 16). For this reason, many musicians developed a close relationship with the club as an institution of artistic pioneers, of socialization, employment, and career opportunities.

Television played several shows in early 1974, and Blondie got its start as an opening act for Television and the Ramones and played regularly for about seven months, maturing from a band known for its outlandish shows into a headliner (Kozak 1988, 29). Television and Blondie released their first albums in 1977. The first regulars to release an album were Patti Smith in 1975 and the Ramones in 1976. They contributed to the media fame of the club and to its appeal as a showcase for the recording industry, but it did not become a destination for celebrity culture. Incidentally, the Brooklyn warehouse clubs of the 2000s did not serve as industry showcases to the same extent, as this function was now filled by commercial clubs in Manhattan. Kristal also contributed to the scene's development by organizing a festival at the club in 1975 to stimulate media interest in more of the artists (Kozak 1988, 41). Jon Pareles reported in the *New York Times* in January 1976 that CBGB had become "the recognized center" of a "feverishly active New York underground rock scene" (Pareles 1976). CBGB thus extended bohemian SoHo and the East Village eastward and southward, respectively. The club was located on the Bowery, on the fringe of the Lower East Side.

Neighborhood difference was inscribed into the rock scene. In particular, the frontier myth of conquering an urban wasteland, as conceived by Neil Smith (1996), could be found in a bohemian version, characterized by positive but also exoticizing images of the frontier. From the beginnings of the young neo-bohemian social and arts scene in the East Village, which emerged in the early 1960s when Greenwich Village was gentrifying, its freedoms and experimentations were part of the sense of adventure attached to being in an urban space with low rents, informal economies, crime, and poverty. The neighborhood provided a stage and an ecosystem for the everyday performance of these bohemian sensibilities. This is evident in journalist and scenester John Gruen's 1966 book about the scene:

> The rhythm of the Combine Generation is taking over. It can take you to a bottle-party in a $15-a-month loft (records by Bob Dylan only), to an underground poetry reading, to a wild "happening," to a way-out theatrical production. It can lead you to encounters with dope addicts, free-love cultists, Swedenborgians, or white chicks looking for noble savages. . . .
>
> And yet, entering any of the East Village bars, you sense a tension. The music, the drinking, the smoking, the cool, offhand manner notwithstanding, there is always an extra something in the air. It could be fear. It could be guilt. It could be hatred. It could be violence. . . . While rents are cheap, squalor is usually included in the price, and poverty has been an agent for aggressive tensions. (Gruen 1966, 7 and 29)

Clubs were imagined as places to escape and meet other outsiders. For a member of Blondie, for instance, CBGB was "a microcosm no one knew about" in its early years (Waterman 2011, 8). The exoticization of nightlife neighborhoods has been studied in the context of gentrification before (Lloyd 2006), but Smith's frontier metaphor inspires further thinking about these neighborhoods' social utopia. In particular, the club can be situated in a longer history of place-making in social utopias. The word "utopia" means "no place" in Latin and generally refers to imaginary, "unreal" spaces (Foucault [1967] 1998, 178). One of the earliest examples of utopian philosophy was Thomas More's *Utopia* (More [1516] 1997). The book portrayed a society on an imaginary island in the Atlantic Ocean, implicitly positioned as an alternative to Europe. Many spaces in society have a utopian dimension, however. In the folk and popular culture of the French Revolution, celebrations were deliberately organized on open fields at the city limits of Paris because this was a territory without history to the revolutionaries who wanted to create their own history from anew (see p. 171). Later utopias of urban subcultures, nightlife districts, and social movements have sedimented in the mythologies of clubs and festivals. This has generally happened without ethical reflexivity about the exoticized other. White bohemians have paid little attention to how their presence affected the large Latinx population in Alphabet City, for instance. Stephen Amico, then a rock musician and NYU student, lived in Alphabet City circa 1984–1991 and remembered the anxious response among the Latinx population when young whites such as himself began moving into the area. He sensed Latinxs were concerned how this new white demographic might affect their future in the neighborhood (Stephen Amico, conversation with the author, April 26, 2017).

Music scholar Patrick Burke's article on hippie "slumming" in the East Village in the 1960s is helpful in this context. Burke recognizes the history of slums and slumming as a context of cultural production and refers to Robert Park's idea of slums as moral regions defined by deviant behavior. Burke identifies a slum aesthetic in rock music on the Lower East Side in the late 1960s. This aesthetic is characterized by pride in collective neighborhood identity, fascination with literal and metaphorical dirt, and an amateur approach to performance (Burke 2014, 549). Burke's primary case study is the Fugs, a band that arose out of the broader Lower Manhattan literary and hippie scene, influenced by Beat-generation writers who also had a presence in the East Village. Allen Ginsberg was one such key figure in the East Village scene. He was an established author when he lived there in 1958–1961 and made it his permanent home in 1964, having spent years in Morocco and Paris and traveling around India.[9]

While the slum aesthetic was central to the neighborhood's rock scene of the 1970s and 1980s, I should like to point out that there were other aesthetics and that the scene's identity was constructed relationally. This is demonstrated by the small East Village gay scene's opposition to the larger gay scenes in the West Village and Chelsea. The latter scenes were imagined negatively by the East Village scene as spaces of bourgeois and homonormative "white boys with muscles partying all night at places like the Saint, going to circuit parties, summering on Fire Island, wearing Ralph Lauren clothes from Barney's, living in stylish apartments, working for high salaries, etc." (Stephen Amico, letter to the author, June 2, 2017). The East Village scene positioned itself as an authentic alternative through aesthetics of immediacy, nonconformism, imperfection, and anticonsumerism. Informal rock clubs, some of them bars with a stage, were central spaces of this culture, frequently featuring loud soundscapes of distorted guitars, aggressive drumming, and delirious voices of the night. The East Village scene identified with garage rock, punk, and new wave and was opposed to disco and house. Amico recalls that virtually none of the gay rock bands achieved success outside the Lower East Side—RuPaul was the only star—but there were scene personalities, such as John Sex, the Fabulous Pop Tarts, and Dean and the Weenies. Amico played in the latter band alongside Dean Johnson, who had dropped out of NYU, become a doorman, and then had various jobs, including promoter, party host, musician, and sex worker. The band's song "Bourgeois Boys" was a critique of the West Village scene (Buckley 2007; "Bourgeois Boys"; see also "Fuck You").

The exotic frontier is audible in a wide range of recorded music. Burke discusses the recordings by the Fugs from the late 1960s. One of the most influential artists of the 1970s was Lou Reed. Reed cultivated the image of an underground New York rock star and was one of the first to sing about hard drugs in the late 1960s. His music and persona were profoundly shaped by neo-bohemian mythologies of the Lower East Side. "Walk on the Wild Side" on *Transformer* (1972), for instance, is not just a general expression of hedonism, but also references queer culture, prostitution, racial otherness, and specific characters in the Warhol circle who were part of the East Village scene. The song uses images of deviance and otherness as resources of coolness, transforming them by the calm repetition of the sliding bluesy bass motif, the hipster attitude, the jazz-style saxophone solo, and the sexually suggestive female chorus that enters on the hipster syllables "doo doo doo doo doo doo doo doo" at the end of the chorus. "Waves of Fear" on *The Blue Mask* (1982) explores the dark sides of drug addiction in a moment when Reed's health was in critical condition, while "Dirty Blvd" and "Hold On" on

New York (1989) extended his soundtrack to the urban frontier in a brighter and more relaxed manner. His health had improved, he had matured, and he lived a more conventional life in the gentrifying city. Reed's career illustrates how musicians could be heroes of the urban frontier, while exploiting an exoticizing gaze on life in the neighborhood.

CBGB was quickly co-opted into the bohemian version of the frontier myth. The first media reports on CBGB include James Walcott's August 1975 piece in the *Village Voice* that portrays the club as a site of an authentic community undiluted by media culture (Walcott 1975). *Billboard* journalist Roman Kozak's 1988 book about CBGB is more invested in the slum aesthetic. Kozak started going to the club in 1976, by which time it had become a place for music industry showcases. The book begins with a story about Kristal hosting a party for 150 Hells Angels members before the club opened. The introduction goes on to describe the Lower East Side as "sin city," a neighborhood of gang crime and prostitution. This is followed by an account of something repulsive that happened at the club. The book's second chapter has detailed descriptions of the kitchen, the showspace, the toilets, and even a paragraph about mice and rat exterminators coming weekly for years (Kozak 1988).[10]

A resident who moved to the neighborhood in 1984 provides a perspective on rock performance as part of a broader scene experience. Her account below has elements of frontier exoticism, but it is not limited to this myth. She wrote it after she had moved out of the area, presumably in the 2000s:

> My particular corner of the Lower East Side was the thrill of a neighborhood we call Alphabet City—the avenues A, B, C, and D christened, only half-jokingly, Adventurous, Brave, Courageous, and Death. I moved here in the bad old days of drug wars and shootouts, junkies and crackheads, pit bull fights, and walking home with my money in my shoe and a key poking out of my fist in case I had to fight. These were also the glorious days of squatting and cheap rent, streets vivid with graffiti murals and artpolitik posters, Puerto Rican street parties, music pumping from cruising cars and speakers in apartment windows, art in abandoned buildings, hip-hop and punk rock, and after-hours clubs of all types hidden in the storefronts and basements of a neglected neighborhood. . . .
>
> We were spoiled. Here the streets that seemed abandoned and foreboding to most people were our land of opportunity—spaces to be had for a song and transformed into a home or a studio or a club.
>
> My friends and I lived paint-spattered and plaster-dusted, hauling canvases and wood, tools and metals to loft work spaces or minuscule apart-

> ments, coloring the streets with spray paint and stencils, wheat-pasted posters, scrawled wisecracks. We found our furniture on the street. We saw or played in shows at A7, King Tut's, the World, the Pyramid, and 8BC. After-hours we'd go dancing at Save the Robots, subterranean dance hall and den of iniquity, gathering house for every stripe of partygoer—black and white, gay and straight, punks, rastas, rockers, club kids and drag queens, Hells Angels and hustlers. Dancing until noon unless a police raid forced everyone out stumbling and blinking into the daylight. (Wrigley n.d.)

This description illustrates core elements of a cultural scene, including (1) informal spaces of interaction between artists and audiences living in the same neighborhood; (2) intimate relationships between different art scenes with a shared commitment to the neighborhood, in this case rock clubs, dance clubs, and the visual arts scene; and (3) the frequent occurrence of improvised social events and performances in an informal economy and as part of a broader neighborhood experience. These insights into the relationship between social life and the conditions of cultural production in the Lower East Side scenes are important to understanding the performance culture. Jon Pareles has critiqued the simplified exotic images of CBGB, while maintaining that the club once created unique conditions of performance as a particular social and psychological environment:

> With all the legend-mongering that the club [CBGB] has fostered lately, it could use a renewal of what made the place so precious. It wasn't just the club's dumpy physicality. It was the way its squalor once made musicians feel they had nothing to lose by tearing the world apart and starting from scratch. And from squall. And from blare. (Pareles 2005)

Whitening, Suburbanization, and New Cultural Economies of the 2010s

After investment had reached its lowest point in the mid-1970s, real estate prices grew significantly in just a few years. For instance, a five-story building on 270 East Tenth Street that sold for $5,706 in 1976 was bought for $202,600 in 1981. The sixteen-story Christodora House sold for $62,500 in the mid-1970s to then go for $3,000,000 in 1984. Rental prices soared in areas without any rent control (Smith 1996, 22–23). Areas that had been redlined in the 1970s were greenlined by loan officers in the 1980s. The city government supported this development by granting permission for housing construction targeted at the affluent and through systematic evictions (Smith 1996, 25–27). The elites did nothing to help the skyrocketing number of homeless in the 1980s. In 1988, hundreds of policemen evicted three hundred homeless people living in Tompkins Square Park. The president of the policemen's union said the riots were caused by "social parasites, druggies, skinheads and communists," while a real estate developer suggested that homelessness should be illegal (Smith 1996, 5 and 28). The government demolished buildings occupied by squatters and destroyed the tents and belongings of park residents. The entire park population was evicted again on the coldest day of December in 1991 without any alternative housing offered.

Accelerating gentrification led to the growing dominance of white affluent populations in many inner cities during the 1990s and 2000s (Atkinson and Bridge 2005; Keith 2005; Shaw 2007). In New York, black and Hispanic populations grew in the late twentieth century but were pushed out of the center—Manhattan—to the outer boroughs (Abu-Lughod 1999, 299). Gentrification led to a "whitening" of neighborhoods. A condition of generalized gentrification emerged, as many neighborhoods became gentrified (Smith 2002). Like many other cities, New York became increasingly one-dimensional, with declining opposition to gentrification and growing levels of social control and conformity (Tonkiss 2012).

The related phenomenon of inner-city suburbanization materialized to a certain degree on the Lower East Side. At advanced stages of gentrification, inner-city neighborhoods in some cities attract affluent whites from the suburbs, bringing with them norms and lifestyles that have long been associated with suburbs and that intersect with the corporate development of the city. Scholars have pointed to the growing presence of mass-media culture in the cityscape, from corporate advertising to the transformation of Times Square, and to the rise of middle-class-brand stores such as Starbucks, Banana Republic, and Whole Foods. In 2007, two scholars who had spent significant time studying these processes noted: "The Lower East Side does not yet have suburban malls, but it will. They do not yet have Disney, but they have global finance, suburban developers, and international landlords" (Smith and Cohen 2007, 39). By the early 2010s, the situation was changing, but more slowly than in other areas of Manhattan. There were four Starbucks cafés, compared to more than forty in Midtown, and one Whole Foods. The Manhattan-based gourmet coffee minichains of the 2000s were represented by one shop, a Think Coffee on the Bowery near SoHo.[11] Magnolia's gourmet bakery, which first opened in the West Village in 1996, expanded to other affluent neighborhoods and to other cities, but not to the Lower East Side. There were no Banana Republic, Best Buy, Apple, H&M, Hard Rock Café, or Home Depot stores. There were, however, four Duane Reade stores, two 7-Eleven shops, and three McDonald's restaurants.

Census data from the early 2010s shows that the area with the highest level of poverty and lowest education and life expectancy levels south of Central Park was Manhattan Community District 3, to which the Lower East Side belongs, along with Chinatown (King et al. 2015a). Rates of smoking and alcoholism are higher, and the level of violence is high compared to surrounding neighborhoods. The statistics related to these factors for Greenwich Village and SoHo are significantly more positive (King et al. 2015b). The differences between District 2 and 3, however, have narrowed over the past hundred years.[12]

I stayed in Alphabet City during my field trips in 2010–2012, the first three times on East Sixth Street and First Avenue, one block from where Fillmore East used to be. There were still many pre-WWII buildings, and the neighborhood's architecture contrasted with that of the historically affluent neighborhoods of the Upper West and East Sides and with the posh streetscapes of nearby Chelsea and the West Village. Many apartments had undergone utilitarian renovations, however. Stephen Amico said he and his friends had been hopeful when the renovations began in the 1980s. He had vivid memories of how uncomfortable it was to live there, waking up one night and discovering the wall was filled with cockroaches, for example, and how cold the apartment was in the winter. When the renovations began, they had been excited: "Maybe we can have hot water!" (Stephen Amico, conversation with the author, March 31, 2017). The neighborhood I encountered was different, but it was not posh, except for the new high-rises on the Bowery and Houston Street and the luxury stores in their immediate surroundings. I experienced this environment on weekends, when I would sometimes go to Bar Primi to enjoy the food and a break from the crowded nightlife of Alphabet City.

There was no longer a cultural scene in the neighborhood, only a landscape of consumption. There were many rather nondescript bars and fast-food eateries that could have been found in any other neighborhood or city. A popular spot on Avenue B, for instance, was Pommes Frites, which was a walk-in place that served fries and drinks around the clock that would appeal to larger numbers of people nearly anywhere in the United States. Alphabet City was dominated by a nightlife consumer culture. It unfolded in restaurants and bars without musical performances and less in art galleries and music clubs. Some bars would show sports events on a television set. The concentration of nightlife spaces and their central location in the city, along with the atmosphere provided by the buildings and the small streets, contributed to making this one of the most popular nightlife destinations in New York. The East Village had become a center of middle-class nightlife that appeared more local and intimate when contrasted to Midtown, with its many hotels, tourists, and corporate office buildings.

New Cultural Economies in the Ludlow Street Area

A key development in the broad history outlined above occurred in the area of Ludlow Street between Houston and Delancey streets in the late 1980s and early 1990s. Intensifying gentrification of Alphabet City (Abu-Lughod 1995) pushed the cultural scene south to this area. Ludlow Street had once been a place where poor Jewish immigrants worked in sweatshops. A small number of artists began moving there in the 1960s, including John Cale and some of the artists in the Warhol circle (Perler 2013). In the 1980s, it was still a place with poor artists, sex workers, and drug dealers ("This Was Ludlow Street"). A nightlife scene emerged, while the administration under Mayor Rudy Giuliani conducted police drug raids all over the neighborhood (Hae 2012). A new population of college students and recent graduates moved in, and new establishments opened up, several of them rock bars and rock clubs. By the mid-1990s, Ludlow had a reputation as a cool place. Some of the important establishments marking this history include:[13]

Ludlow Street Café: 1987–1996
Brownies: 1989–2002
Max Fish: 1989–2013
Spiral Lounge: 1990–2016
Pink Pony: 1993–2013
Mercury Lounge: 1993–present
Motor City Bar: 1996–2013
Piano's: 2002–present
Cake Shop: 2005–2016

By the early 2010s, Ludlow had become the center of a trendy upscale shopping and nightlife district. There were three prominent small rock clubs within a short distance—Mercury Lounge, Piano's, and Cake Shop. Mercury Lounge had pioneered the ideal of the perfected concert industry club. It exploited the momentum of the area's nightlife boom in the early 1990s and a new generation of bands that would redefine the neighborhood's market of rock music performance from punk and alternative to more polished indie rock and pop. Mercury Lounge was primarily a concert venue with a small bar for the concert audience, while Piano's had a smaller audience capacity, fewer concerts, but a larger bar that was popular in the neighborhood. Cake

Shop was one of the last remnants of bohemian urbanism. A local popular music scholar referred to it as "a place where cool things happen" (Shannon Garland, conversation with the author, April 7, 2010). There were regular shows by young bands playing rock and sometimes jazz with experimental and avant-garde elements. Cake Shop was becoming an island in the urban environment like Death by Audio and eventually lost the battle against rising rents by the end of 2016 (McKinley 2012).

A somewhat suburban development could be identified at Rockwood Music Hall on Allen Street, on the western edge of the same nightlife area, just one parallel street over from Ludlow. Rockwood's model was somewhat similar to Piano's in that the bar served a prominent social and economic function, and the performance space was small, with a capacity that I estimate at below one hundred. The exterior architectural design had a positive and extroverted psychology. This was neither a traditional bar nor a secluded club. Passersby could look through elegant large glass windows into a room with the appearance of a contemporary middle-class wine bar, watch the people standing inside, and walk directly into the integrated bar and performance space. The space felt easily accessible from the street and not sealed off by security and ticketing like a concert venue. The music programming did not compete for recognition among the urban tastemakers in the dedicated spheres of professional popular music. It did not present a series of trendy headliner artists with a heavy touring schedule, but instead included cover bands and more classical rock. I heard young bands inspired by artists such as Neil Young, the Eagles, and Bryan Adams, for instance. One night a small audience was enjoying gentle acoustic music at low volume and drinking red wine in Burgundy glasses, standing closely together in the small space. This was a space of identities and experiences different from those found at the spaces defined more narrowly as rock clubs. I had conversations with a middle-aged married couple and a woman, who were newcomers to the city, for instance, about everyday topics and life experiences, but not specifically music. They said it was "interesting" that someone was researching music. This left me with the sense that I was not in a space of a culture world of expert producers and consumers, and that my understanding of music was shaped more by academic and industry discourse than I commonly realized. Rockwood was not cosmopolitan or transgressive but a hybrid urban-suburban space, epitomized by the elegant but ordinary environment and the rather traditional music programming. The patrons liked the city but did not invest effort in seeking out the city's most unique and specialized cultural milieus.

The Corporate Institutionalization of the Indie Rock Club, 1985–2017

The final sections of this chapter detail the transformation of the club institution in the process of its corporate institutionalization. This is illustrated with reference to the career trajectory of promoter Michael Swier, who pioneered the promotion of a new generation of indie rock artists in the 1990s and who developed and perfected the aesthetic of the ballroom-style club as a state-of-the-art concert theater. I follow Swier's trajectory from his first bar in the East Village in 1985 to his partnership with Live Nation in 2017.

Ethnography of Corporate Power

When I started researching the field of rock clubs in 2010, the dominant company was the Bowery Presents. Its public communications were limited to simple promotion of concerts, primarily in the form of listings on its website and email newsletters, with artist profiles crafted in the style of professional music journalism. The venue staff had fixed roles as security, ticketing, or bartending staff, for instance. I struck up conversations with bartenders a few times, but they were generally too busy selling drinks to large numbers of concertgoers. A person who had worked the door at the company's smallest club for more than a decade was kind when I expressed interest in talking to the management. This person gave me contact information for one of the company's promoters. He was interested in speaking to me but returned the day after to tell me that his boss had firmly told him not to do it and that there was no chance the boss would respond to any inquiries from me. I decided the company's policy should not prevent me from studying its activities. It was an influential organization in the field and should therefore not be exempt from analysis.

The corporate silence extended to the company's business partners. One example is a conversation I had at a concert with the manager of a prominent club on the Lower East Side. We enjoyed the performance and discovered we had a common acquaintance, so the conversation evolved naturally. He told me he was managing a club. When I mentioned I was researching the Bowery Presents, he froze. The conversation became formal and practically fell apart. On another occasion, an industry insider helped me set up a meeting with an artists and repertoire person in his late twenties who worked at a subsidiary of a major recording company. The person looked slightly uncomfortable from the start and requested that he remain anonymous. Although he was going to concerts every night and dealt with the industry all the time, he described everything in superficial and positive terms. He said the live music business was healthy and that he had not observed any changes, for instance. After a while, he confessed that he was scared of getting fired for participating in a research interview about the industry, and he repeated his request for anonymity via email a few days later.

I frequently dismissed my sense of distance from producers and consumers in commercial clubs as a practical barrier that could be overcome through more fieldwork, at times blaming myself for the inability to connect deeply with the community. I now think that I was experiencing the reality of the field, one in which subject positions are constructed through corporately institutionalized conceptions of commodities, consumers, and industry, including a strict separation of the spheres of production and consumption. The commercial club was not a place for a community, but rather for markets of individual artists and genres, and audiences generally experienced the performance as individual consumers. Audiences would typically pick their favorite show once a month or even less frequently and had no expectations for participating in a community.

A person who had been close to some of the managers of the Bowery Presents for many years reacted with skepticism to some of the points I made in a presentation at New York University in 2012. He agreed to discuss his criticisms over a cup of coffee and was helpful, but some differences in interpretation remained. He did not agree that the Bowery Presents was corporate and altogether rejected the idea that live music could be corporatized: "You cannot corporatize live music because live music is about individuals, about personal relationships, and they cannot be corporatized." His understanding of the company was shaped by his history with the managers and with the neighborhood, perhaps not fully realizing how much things had changed. He began working in the music business on the Lower East Side in the 1980s and now had one of the most high-profile jobs in New York's music world.

Michael Swier's Passion for Clubs

Michael Swier is a central figure, but little is known about him. He has only given a handful of interviews, the first in 2007 and the rest between 2014 and 2017. All the interviews are a form of marketing, in which he presents a new club or a business merger. The interviews that include the most details about his life are from the opening of his first club in Los Angeles in May 2015. By that time, he had been in the business for almost forty years, and this was a personal moment. He named the club Teragram Ballroom after his wife Margaret, who died in 2009 (Sisario 2014; Hughes 2015; Kim 2015).

Swier lived in Williamsburg in the 1970s and 1980s and has presented rock performances in Lower Manhattan since the 1980s. In interviews, Swier comes across as a proud craftsman with a passion for the small and intimate concert club. He wears denim in press photos and has a full, trimmed beard, and a friendly but professional, serious attitude. One photo that has been used twice by the *New York Times* constructs this identity of Swier as a backstage professional, as it shows him standing in the bar or the performance space of one of his clubs (Sisario 2014, 2017).

In the personal 2015 interview, Swier describes his clubs as his children because of all the work and attention that has gone into developing each of them, from finding the building to renovating it with his own hands, developing the music profile, and doing the daily management. The interview also reveals Swier's attention to architecture:

> [The building of Teragram Ballroom] revealed every aspect of itself, which is the same feeling I felt with the Bowery Ballroom and the Mercury Lounge and the Music Hall of Williamsburg. You walk into a place, and it almost comes in front of you, what it's going to look like. (Hughes 2015)

In contrast with the social ritual approach to performance architecture in the Brooklyn scene, Swier adopts a concert ritual approach:

> From the beginning, opening the Mercury Lounge, it was all about the stage and the music—for the band, for the people coming to see the bands. (Hughes 2015)

For Swier, acoustics and sight lines are major priorities when choosing architectural spaces for performance, while Patrick has compromised on such aspects and avoided conventional venue models because he is interested in a different kind of performance culture. Patrick has celebrated the tribal energies of "found spaces" in the urban wilderness. By contrast, Swier has concentrated on the club within the frontier of gentrification and later kept developing these clubs within the settlement of gentrification, to use Neil Smith's terminology. Swier has invested in real estate and developed venue profiles through music programming and the perfection of sound systems. Given Swier's ideal of the perfected concert club, structured by the "rationality" of the professional concert commodity, it makes sense to make long-term investments in state-of-the-art amplification, air conditioning, and microperfection of the architecture.

Historical Aura and Musical Authenticity in Accelerated Capitalism

Like Patrick, Swier has a preference for buildings with a historical aura, but he has adopted a somewhat classic and conformist aesthetic in contrast to Patrick's exotic frontier "rubble" aesthetic. This is evident from the clubs that Swier calls his "babies": Mercury Lounge, the Bowery Ballroom, and Music Hall of Williamsburg. During my time in the field, his company also presented concerts in venues with extraordinary historical architecture and a legendary concert history, such as Town Hall and Webster Hall.

Swier's clubs conformed to the values of the gentrifying city, with their legal status, professional rationality, and a product that appeals to the lifestyles of new neighborhood populations. Their outlook and functions have much in common with many for-profit cultural organizations in the city (see pp. 31 and 39). The clubs' music programming provided entertaining and enjoyable experiences every night for casual and semispecialized audiences in a market larger than just a single specialized audience or a subculture. The architectural design was optimized to be comfortable and efficient for the specific purpose of consuming concerts. The interior design was rather neutral and nondescript. There was no graffiti on the walls, and no traces of a specific nightlife imagination. The bars followed the industry standards of many bars in the city, and the cleaning standards were high, higher than at some Starbucks shops, for instance. The air, too, was clean. The schedule and form of performances were punctual and regularized, usually ending before midnight. The generic theater design and perfected interiors were in themselves disciplining; they did not encourage transgressive behaviors or excess.

The venues and the performance culture as a whole were nonetheless distinct from the posh spaces of more gentrified areas and from mass culture. Going to an indie rock performance in a club was a specialized nighttime activity in a space secluded from nearby shopping environments, and in this sense the clubs were not ordinary spaces of everyday life. They created conditions for experiencing more inner values through the hour-long artistic ritual in close proximity to the performer. But Swier's clubs also involved a number of musical, architectural, and visual signifiers of a particular urban intimacy and authenticity that differentiated them further in the urban environment. A key dimension of the indie aesthetic was its differentiation from mass-market popular music, as we shall see, and the interior design of the clubs contrasted with the posh luxury shops and gourmet restaurants in nearby SoHo. The style of interior design was shaped by the history of the rock club in the urban frontier, particularly the image of the club as a dark and somewhat raw space in proximity to the streetscape of the Lower East Side. The frontier myth was embedded in the history of the music and in the neighborhood, all of which had evolved into a more polished form through commercial institutionalization and gentrification. Like the revivalism of the many bands that were inspired by 1970s and 1980s rock music, the frontier myth involved the potential for a nostalgic imagination of an authentic urban past. Swier's fascination with pre-WWII architecture cannot be separated from the mythology of the neighborhood in public consciousness and in rock history in particular.

Entrepreneurialism, a New Condition of Cultural Production

Swier's entrepreneurialism is another aspect of general relevance to the analysis of his role in the commercial institutionalization of the rock club. A basic element in this is Swier's investment in real estate. When he first opened an establishment in 1985, gentrification was already evident in the East Village, and his success in continuously developing clubs that survived and profited from gentrification illustrates how real estate ownership became a necessity for popular music promoters in gentrification. In many cities, rising rents have been the single most important factor in the closing of small and informally managed performance spaces.

Swier bought and renovated the building for every club he opened. He has generally bought buildings when the respective neighborhood was gentrifying and had a vibrant cultural scene but before the prices went up to a level where the cultural scene was commercially institutionalized into a consumer culture in more formal clubs and art galleries, and before the construction of luxury apartment towers accelerated. He created 2A in Alphabet City in 1985, Mercury Lounge one block to the south in 1993, the Bowery Ballroom farther south on the Lower East Side in 1997, and Music Hall of Williamsburg in 2007. In each case, Swier did considerable renovations with his own two hands, together with his wife and architect brother. Upon opening his Williamsburg venue, he said:

> "[It] was nice to see [Williamsburg] finally come around to what it is today . . . It's a perfect spot for what we do because the artistic community that was there, and still is there, [exists] alongside the people who are moving in." (Rathe 2007)

In gentrification, the commercial club has a somewhat parasitic function with respect to DIY scenes because it profits from the ecosystem and the momentum created by smaller organizations. The for-profit promoter tries to secure real estate before competitors and prices increase too much. By owning his buildings, Swier would not be negatively affected by rising rents and could instead profit from the growing consumer culture and from the growing value of his properties.[14] Gentrification thus does not stimulate collectivism or improve the conditions for art worlds as a whole.

Michael Swier's Trajectory in Urban Capitalism

1. *1979–1992: Swier had a bar in the East Village.* Swier began working in East Village nightlife in 1985, possibly as far back as 1979 (Sisario 2017). He likely experienced the East Village rock scene in the late 1970s and early 1980s. At the time, a popular type of rock performance space was the bar with a small stage, reflecting the proximity to the informal nightlife culture of the street. Swier's bar 2A was one of those bars. I assume Swier's interest in rock performance motivated his decision to open a dedicated rock club in 1993. By then he had at least seven years of professional experience in the neighborhood's nightlife and would have been familiar with its rock scene.

2. *1993–1997: Swier opened a small rock club in the Ludlow area and developed relationships with a new generation of indie bands.* Swier opened Mercury Lounge in 1993 when the Ludlow area was gentrifying and voices in the rock world were complaining about the commercialization of indie rock. This skepticism surfaced in fan reactions to Sonic Youth's first albums (Lynskey 2011). The growing market for indie rock would become important to Swier's business, however, and he benefited from the nightlife scene in the Ludlow Street area (see p. 98). Bill Bragin, a music professional who lived in what might be considered Mercury Lounge's backyard for over ten years, remembers how Mercury Lounge built on this momentum and gained a reputation as a place where new, talented bands emerged, similar to what Hilly Kristal had achieved at CBGB two decades earlier (Bill Bragin, personal communication, March 30, 2012). Mercury Lounge thus contributed to the expansion of the rock field from the East Village southward to the Lower East Side.

By the early 2010s, the area had become much more gentrified. Mercury Lounge was dwarfed by a high-rise and surrounded by new luxury stores, bars, and restaurants (figs. 4.1–4.2). There were fewer small music bars and clubs, while Swier had become part of a thriving corporate business of larger concert theaters that featured more famous artists. Moreover, the music programming and the audiences at Mercury Lounge had changed. The programming had a somewhat more general rock and pop profile and was no longer part of a distinct neighborhood scene with a shared sensibility of a

4.1–4.2 The Mercury Lounge and the Ludlow on Houston Street. The photos show how the Mercury Lounge was dwarfed by the Ludlow, which was finished in 2007.

particular cultural moment. The latter was now to be found in the Brooklyn warehouse scene.

Bragin pointed to a particular aspect of Swier's entrepreneurialism that is significant in the history of the rock club. Small bars and music clubs have historically provided opportunities for relatively unknown bands willing to play for a small fee and have kept prices low enough to compete with other nightlife establishments. This business model has allowed club managers to discover new talent and develop relationships with artists. Kristal, Patrick, and Swier all nurtured relationships with young artists who appealed to the cultural moment of a particular neighborhood. Swier became part of the more established Manhattan concert business of the 1990s. He opened larger venues and presented artists that had performed in his smaller venues once they had become more famous. By 1997 Swier had been presenting four to five bands per night for about five years in Mercury Lounge and were now presenting some of these bands in a larger club he opened that same year. Bragin suggests Swier had tested and developed "baby bands" of a new generation to establish himself as a core promoter in this emerging mar-

ket and continued using Mercury Lounge as a "feeder club" for his larger venues.[15] In particular, the club had an important role in the early careers of bands in the so-called class of 2001/2002, such as the White Stripes, the Yeah Yeah Yeahs, the Strokes, and Interpol (Phillips 2007; L. Goodman 2013).

The architectural design of Mercury Lounge was simple, adapted from a former tombstone store. The audience would walk directly into the small bar and on into the performance space with a capacity for two hundred, which was the only other room accessible to patrons apart from the toilets. The performance space had nothing but a stage against the end wall and a sound board at the back wall of the room. The ceilings were low, the stage was low, and the lighting and décor was kept basic.

The dozen times I frequented the club in the period 2010–2013, the professional routines of the club were recognizable. There was experienced staff throughout the small club, from security to bar and stage. The space had received regular maintenance and a few changes might have been made, but it was still basic. There was a small bench along each side of the room where audiences frequently relaxed between performances, and many others would be standing and chatting with a beer in hand. It was easy to strike up conversations and socialize in this somewhat informal and intimate setting, even though many were there only for one concert. The acoustics and amplification were controlled, solid, and of higher quality than at DIY clubs in Brooklyn. A local insider and music professional who had gone to many rock clubs over the years acknowledged that "everything sounds great" at

Mercury Lounge (Richard Zerbo, conversation with the author, November 18, 2010). The Bowery Ballroom had an even more refined sound and a larger soundstage, capable of creating more haptic, immersive sonic experiences.

The micromanagement of the performance schedule regularized the performance culture. It was a small concert factory with two nightly "shows." The early show was around seven o'clock and the late show around ten, later on the weekends. Audiences purchased a ticket specifically for one show and not a night of several performances and informal socializing. Artists were generally ambitious and aware of the club's legacy. They were also appreciative of the attention given to their performance. I vividly remember how even at early shows relatively unknown artists were able to build great intensity and intimacy with their audiences. One evening, an artist gave a solo performance with a repertoire that he had probably developed in bars and perhaps as a street musician, but this club created the conditions for a form of focused listening that is generally not possible in those other spaces.

3. 1997–2004: Swier opens a midsize club and draws more artists and audiences from outside the neighborhood. Swier expanded his business and pushed the rock field farther south in late 1997 with the Bowery Ballroom. This club gave Swier the opportunity to reap the rewards of his talent development at Mercury Lounge and exploit the national market for a new generation of indie rock. The programming of headliner artists attracted audiences increasingly from outside the neighborhood.

The Bowery Ballroom, with a capacity of 575, was the first midsize rock club on the Lower East Side south of the East Village. The largest nearby competitor was the Bottom Line in Greenwich Village, which had a capacity of four hundred. The Bowery Ballroom immediately had greater appeal to younger audiences with its standing presentation and young indie bands. The Bottom Line had a seated cabaret-style presentation. Some of my informants remembered that the Bowery Ballroom was initially "a place for hipsters" and that one of the first artists that played there was P. J. Harvey.[16] Many of those people had since moved to Brooklyn, and the club began to attract more people from other neighborhoods. In the local vernacular, it became more of a "bridge and tunnel" place. This term has a history as a pejorative that can be traced back to at least the bouncers at Studio 54 in the 1970s.

The Bowery Ballroom quickly gained a reputation as a state-of-the-art venue in the historical center of rock music on the Lower East Side. It became the venue of choice for major recording companies when they needed a space to promote an album or start a national tour. By 2010, the larger Irving Plaza near Union Square had been dethroned. Many rock legends had performed in Irving Plaza since its opening in 1978, but it did not have the same purchase in the rock world anymore. Its programming was less focused and lacked the generation of popular indie artists performing at the Bowery Ballroom. In 2013, the Bowery Ballroom was rated "best club in America" in *Rolling Stone* magazine by a panel of twenty-four top-tier industry professionals (Knopper 2013). The club's status was also illustrated by early examples of significant promotional concerts and so-called underplay, where stars perform for a much smaller audience than they normally attract. For instance, Lana Del Rey performed there in December 2011 after "Video Games" and "Blue Jeans" had become viral sensations on YouTube and she was promoting her debut album *Born to Die*. She appeared on the David Letterman show about a month later. Ed Sheeran started his first US headlining tour in this club in June 2012 after he had become a multiplatinum star in the UK. Other examples of underplay include concerts by P. J. Harvey, Robert Plant, and Kanye West, and Patti Smith's New Year's Eve concerts.

The success of the Bowery Ballroom explains why Swier would create more clubs with a similar design. That is precisely what happened in the mid-2000s, resulting in a recognizable model of what we might call the commercial indie rock club concert theater, with a ballroom-style architecture. The performance culture at these venues deserves further analysis, which is presented in a separate section below.

4. *2004–2010: Swier enters the corporate domain with the Bowery Presents, while more culturally diverse clubs are closing.* Swier cofounded the Bowery Presents with a talent buyer named John Moore in 2004. The Bowery Presents created a new organizational platform for Swier and led to his involvement in the corporate market of large concert halls and arenas. The company provided investment capital for Swier to open more clubs. He expanded the Bowery Ballroom concept into other neighborhoods and into New Jersey and Boston. Within a few years, the company had created two midsize clubs with a concert theater design and music programming similar to the Bowery Ballroom (Webster Hall in 2004 and Music Hall of Williamsburg in 2007) and two concert halls (Terminal 5 and United Palace, both in 2007). By the late 2000s, the company promoted a growing number of star concerts in the city's biggest venues, including Beacon Theatre and Madison Square Garden. The company became a monopoly with no real competitors. Even the world's largest concert promoter had only secured a small share of the profitable market for rock concerts. In 2012, Irving Azoff, executive chairman of Live Nation, said his biggest regret was that his company had "lost this city" (Irving Azoff, Roosevelt Hotel, November 7, 2012). Jim Glancy, the president of the company's New York offices, had left in 2007 to become a partner at the Bowery Presents and took with him some of the star performers. A vital

part of Live Nation's most profitable business thus found a new platform at the Bowery Presents.

In the 2000s, legendary rock clubs closed or moved away from Manhattan, including Brownies (2002), CBGB (2006), Knitting Factory (2009), and Tonic (2007), and with their disappearance came a decline in the experimental art, jazz, and noise scene in Manhattan (Lee 2002; Holt 2014). A significant part of the process was the concurrent closing of venues with other cultural profiles, notably the Bottom Line (1974–2004), Wetlands Reserve (1988–2001), and, in the following decade, Santo's Party House (2008–2016).[17] The Bottom Line presented many jazz and world music artists over the years (Pareles 2004), and Wetlands presented a number of African American funk and rock bands (Bill Bragin, conversation with the author, March 30, 2012). Among the few remaining venues for such culturally diverse programming are Le Poisson Rouge and Joe's Pub.

5. 2010–2017: A split between downtown indie and uptown corporate. A boundary between independent clubs downtown and larger corporate venues uptown was reinforced when Swier was bought out of the Bowery Presents in 2010. Swier retained ownership of Mercury Lounge and the Bowery Ballroom but continued to share office space with the Bowery Presents on Ludlow Street and collaborate on marketing (Sisario 2014). Based on Swier's past and the passion with which he talked about clubs in interviews after the split, one might suspect that Swier was not thriving in a corporate setting. The more intimate organizational culture at clubs contrasted with the corporate culture at arenas, and the clubs were relatively insignificant to the business of the Bowery Presents. Swier's "babies" were dwarfed by the company's expansion into larger venues, including Terminal 5 in Midtown Manhattan. There was consensus among the passionate concertgoers that I met in the clubs that Terminal 5 had a sterile feel, poor acoustics, and usually detracted from the overall experience. Yet audiences would go to concerts in that venue if they had a strong interest in a specific artist.

6. 2017–present: Corporate duopoly of the Bowery Presents (AEG) and Mercury Presents (Live Nation). The corporatization of the professional field of rock performance in New York culminated in a duopoly. In 2017, AEG acquired the Bowery Presents and decided to end the collaboration with Swier one month after the acquisition. This might have been a result of AEG implementing a corporate focus on venues with a capacity above 2,500. Another reason could be Swier's unwillingness to accept new requirements. Swier had had his own company for about six months before entering into a partnership with Live Nation, stating that it was impossible for him to remain independent because of corporate dominance in the rock field (Sisario 2017).

Swier's arrangement with Live Nation allowed him to focus on five clubs in the 250-to-1,200-capacity range: Mercury Lounge, Bowery Ballroom, and the legendary Manhattan clubs in nineteenth-century buildings—Irving Plaza and Gramercy Theatre—plus Warsaw in Williamsburg. Swier thus continued to engage his passion for smaller clubs with historical architecture. He named the new company Mercury East Presents, referencing Bill Graham's legendary venues of the 1960s where the rock club concert theater was first institutionalized. One of Swier's legacies might be that the indie concert theater remained a dominant model among midsize clubs in New York City. In many other cities, this domain had been developed under the generic corporate brand House of Blues, which has since 2006 been a subsidiary of Live Nation.

The Indie Rock and Pop Concert Theater: A New Performance Culture?

What did the club concert theaters that Swier created in the late 2000s have in common? Did they transform a performance culture or create a new culture?

One aspect was the systemic shift from a landscape of small rock bars and clubs to a landscape of midsize concert theaters. Small concert theaters had existed for decades but were growing in size and number and thus becoming the norm in rock performance culture. One major difference was the emphasis on more established and famous artists with media power, which shaped audiences' listening practices and relationship with the concert ritual. Audiences in the new indie concert theater would come for the main act of the evening, pay a higher ticket price than smaller clubs charged, be more focused on the performance on stage, and be influenced in their decision and behavior by the performer's celebrity status, even if it was rarely a star celebrity. In smaller clubs, audiences would more often explore an up-and-coming band in a genre context. A person would likely say, "I'm going to Mercury Lounge tomorrow to hear this new singer-songwriter or indie band. Would you like to join? It's only ten dollars. And why don't we ask Jessica if she wants to join us, and we can all go for a drink afterward?" Conversely, it would be common to say, "I'm glad I secured two tickets for me and my girlfriend for Dirty Projectors in the Bowery Ballroom next month because we're big fans and it's our favorite venue. It's well worth the forty dollars, and we'd better do it now before they become more famous and play in bigger places such as Terminal 5."

Most of the performers in Swier's concert theaters during the 2000s represented indie rock and singer-songwriter music with pop sensibilities. The

4.3–4.6 Exterior and interior of the Bowery Ballroom. The Savages performed as a headliner act on March 24, 2013.

music was thus based on established genres and somewhat traditional, but it had a contemporary sensibility, partly through its performance by relatively young but experienced performers, many of them born 1965–1990. Very few artists from the city's rock scene of the 1970s performed there. The artists were mainly recruited from semicorporate agencies such as the Windish Agency and indie labels within major recording companies, such as Rounder

and Canvasback Music. With a handful of commercial clubs in the center of New York City, the Bowery Presents became a more or less exclusive partner for this emerging industry of indie rock and pop. Not only was it indie rock performance that was being commercially institutionalized, but it was also indie rock culture as a whole. This process generally favored the popular versions of indie rock, thus stimulating the evolution of indie pop.

Commercial institutionalization also stimulated aesthetic professionalism. Most headliners excelled in mastering the craft of songwriting and per-

4.7–4.8 The lounge bar and balcony of the Bowery Ballroom. The lighting creates intimacy.

formance with maturity and grace. The performance demonstrated indie pop values of original compositions, band collectivity, stylistic sophistication, tuneful melodies, and dance-friendly grooves, with brighter emotional states, and more pop sentiments and disciplined coolness, than the indie rock of Lower East Side clubs in the 1980s and 1990s. The musical sounds were more beautified and less experimental and aggressive than in the Brooklyn warehouse scene. Some of the core acts in the early 2010s were Animal Collective, Arcade Fire, Beach House, Dirty Projectors, the Joy Formidable, St. Vincent, Yeasayer, and the Yeah Yeah Yeahs. Some of them have since migrated to larger venues. However, during my time in the field, the clubs were increasingly presenting a wider range of rock and pop with little or no relation to indie aesthetics.

Indie pop aesthetics could also be found in other prominent styles of "roots" and singer-songwriter music. Roots music was a significant component in the programming and represented a revival with origins in the urban folk revival in the 1950s. Roots music became a popular revivalist aesthetic in the 2000s in the marketing of music such as country, gospel, and bluegrass, and thus represents a development of these musics into a contemporary consumer culture with urban sophistication (Holt 2007, chapter 2). In Swier's indie rock theater of the early 2010s, folk revivalism was detached from the leftist movement of the 1950s and from exoticized images of the rural past. Audiences reflected the fading intensity of subcultural forms of urbanism, such as slum, punk, and hipster aesthetics. This followed the broader cultural transformation in gentrification discussed above and further suggests the declining relevance of subcultural theory of urbanism (Fischer 1995). The commercial indie rock theater was nonetheless centrally positioned in media images of rock music in New York (e.g., Sisario 2007). A blasé and sophisticated attitude surfaced at some concerts. In March 2012, for instance, a country music artist with a certain small-town simplicity and folkloric aesthetic received a lukewarm reception from the audience in Webster Hall. He was just an opening act, and the audience members neither clapped nor laughed at his jokes. The performance stood out from the more sophisticated performances celebrated in this club.

Media Glamour and Professional Authority

The media bestowed on Swier's club concert theaters an aura of cultural distinction, beauty, and authenticity, including an element of glamour, both directly through coverage of the individual clubs and concerts and indirectly through writing about the music presented in the clubs. Many headliners were featured in popular middle-class media such as *Pitchfork*, *Stereogum*, *Time Out*, NPR, the *New York Times*, and *Rolling Stone*. Animal Collective and Dirty Projectors, for instance, appealed to artistic sophistication and urban coolness in their music and album covers, with extended chords, complex rhythmic patterns, and elements of minimalism. Rock music magazines revered this music and coconstructed its meanings and values, including constructions of gender, sexuality, and race. An article about Animal Collective's *Merriweather Post Pavilion* in the *New York Times*, for instance, reinforced the cultural capital that was building around the band by describing the review of the album at *Pitchfork* that had led to a quickly sold-out tour. The article also reports on a smaller blog that celebrates the evolution of the band's music into a more widely accessible style of music, but one that maintains elements of sophistication and experimentation (Hsu 2009). The article additionally includes a photograph of the three white men aged around thirty surrounded by a mystical, psychedelic halo while sporting a casual, urban look, wearing T-shirts and hoodies. Another photo in the article features the band performing at the Bowery Ballroom two years earlier. A similar narrative can be found in the *Times*'s review of Dirty Projectors' *Bitte Orca* of the same year, which is celebrated for its ambitious "songs that artfully balance catchy melodies with abstract formal experimentation" (Sisario 2009b). The reviewer constructs cultural capital by referencing the band's connections to a number of indie celebrities, including Björk. He is also fascinated with the band's "three young women with otherworldly voices," while celebrating front man David Longhurst as "indie-rock's workaholic mad genius." The album cover shows only the women—or rather, two of them—from the chest up looking at the camera with that contemplative indie gaze that was also typical of Animal Collective and countless other artists in the indie concert theater. In sum, these bands were being positioned as the artistic and popular leaders of a new generation of indie rock, while still being indirectly distinguished from a particular image of mainstream popular music.

The media contributed to the institutionalization of this music as an urban middle-class popular culture, thus coconstructing the performance culture. This could be registered in audience demographics and their styles of clothing. A large part of the audience was made up of groups of friends or couples out on a date night, many of them in their twenties and thirties, dressed casually and conformably, often with aspirations to discreet beauty and sophistication, but rarely with bohemian signifiers. Audiences generally showed appreciation for the music and behaved orderly. Many were casual consumers and tourists who also went to the Metropolitan Museum of Art and Starbucks, but few participated in the Brooklyn warehouse scene. Oftentimes one person in a group of friends, or in a couple, took the initiative to attend the concert, typically inspired by mass-market publications. Members of these audiences were not typically spending hours every day on obscure indie blogs.

This commercial institutionalization was further evident in the operation and interior design of the club, which built on the developments at Mercury Lounge. The performance ritual became more formal, the interior design slightly more glamorous, particularly with the development of lounge bars. The performance space had more grandeur, with the carefully treated acoustics, vintage-style decoration of the ballroom theater, state-of-the-art sound production, and incandescent stage lights of the highest quality with a warm glow, which added to the vintage feel and the theater atmosphere.

Professional authority was a key aspect of both the media and the performance production culture of indie rock and pop. The mastery of musical performance was noted as a factor above, but professional authority was also a product of the wider industry system that institutionalized all these elements into a ritual of perfection. The club concert theater was the product of a larger indie industry that valued professional authority under market conditions: Professional authority was a way of ensuring consistency in quality and sales to urban middle-class audiences seeking pleasure and distinction. Audiences, too, valued professional authority and were thus rather conformist.

A sense of corporate authority developed in marketing and visual identity. The indie aesthetics of Swier's clubs in the 1990s were developed into a somewhat generic and mass-market form during his years at the Bowery Presents (2004–2010). All the concerts were marketed through the Bowery Presents' website and its email marketing tools with the same visual brand and with links to ticket purchases through Ticketmaster. Information was easy to find and available far in advance, and it had the analogue feel and perfection of a printed copy of the *New York Times* with professional photos, which was in contrast to the DIY websites of the Brooklyn warehouse scene, where the editing was raw and last-minute changes frequent. The visual design was characterized by a simple classicism with a roots aesthetic, somewhat similar to the vintage style of Swier's club concert theaters. The design was in the same family as the famous Hatch Show Print posters of Nashville that were made with hand-inked, hand-carved woodblocks, type, and metal plates. The company deployed this retro aura of traditional crafts throughout its communications, including for marketing concerts in Madison Square Garden. By 2019, the company's digital marketing had adopted a more contemporary visual identity but still kept its roots-style logo.

How might the consumer appeal of professional authority be explained? The performance culture can be situated in the broader urban environment in which professional authority has become a more dominant form of symbolic capital. The economic intensification of the city—with rising prices and growing labor markets of advanced services—created a symbolic economy of professional authority. Lower Manhattan was increasingly becoming an environment in which many people produced and consumed high-quality services that they expected to be perfected, reliable, and consistent. The commercial institutionalization of performance culture was thus part of a broader commercial institutionalization of the city and of urban life. This involved greater emphasis on measuring the individual's professional performance, and therefore a culture of greater self-discipline and conformist professional appearances. This was reflected in the culture of the indie club rock theater and its convenient integration into the everyday life of those studying or working in Manhattan. The venues were centrally located, well connected, and the relatively short concert ritual was conveniently scheduled such that it occurred after a day of work and made it easy to go to work the following morning. An experienced insider commented that many consumers at the indie rock theater had a working life that made it too inconvenient to explore late night shows in the more remote Brooklyn DIY clubs (Richard Zerbo, conversation with the author, November 18, 2010). Among the audiences at the Bowery Ballroom, I talked to several young and middle-aged professionals, including architects, bankers, and lawyers, who valued the convenience of going to a high-quality concert environment and did not experience any nostalgia for the gritty clubs of the Lower East Side in earlier decades.

The norms of professionalism that governed the commercial indie club also explain why some insiders of the Brooklyn warehouse scene found the commercial clubs too constraining, while most audiences I talked to in these clubs found them pleasant, well designed for the purpose, and conveniently located. One insider said that the location and design of the bars in the Bowery Ballroom and Music Hall of Williamsburg stimulated audience sociability because the audience entered through the bar in the basement and these bars were designed as a lounge, allowing patrons to look at each other across the bar. A very frequent concertgoer who had come to New York to satisfy his voracious appetite with its "endless buffet of concerts," however, felt that the Bowery Presents was "not as bad as corporate promoters such as Live Nation and House of Blues," but that the venues increasingly felt like distribution centers and that these lounge bars were just like airport lounges, with audiences waiting for the headliner (B. Q. Nguyen, conversations with the author, March and April 2012).

Conclusion: Human Life in Accelerated Capitalism

This chapter brought together ethnography, history, and urban social theory to analyze the commercial institutionalization of the rock club in New York City as part of the broader process of gentrification. The analysis highlighted the transformation of the club institution from the informal bar and club within a neo-bohemian scene into the indie club concert theater within a corporate production system and a national urban middle-class media culture. This transformation followed the commercial institutionalization of indie rock itself, in which elements of urban sophistication were developed into music with a more popular appeal and an emphasis on professional authority, not just in sound recordings and stage performances, but in production and consumption as a whole. The performance culture developed further into media culture as the music and the performance event were increasingly constituted through media and less through regular scene participation.[18] With the growing emphasis on headliners, regular scene participation in performances by local artists died out, while the less frequent, more planned, and formal concert event became a supplement to media consumption. While the professional and commercial aspirations that could be found in leading clubs of the 1970s such as CBGB further evolved in accelerated gentrification, the specifically local neo-bohemian scene and its experimental culture, which had created a socio-artistic ecosystem for the professional clubs, died out in the 1990s. The scene culture migrated elsewhere but eventually died in the 2010s.

Gentrification and commercialization are bound up with questions of value. Fundamental divisions exist between neighborhood scene culture and corporate consumer culture. These value systems have shaped cultural production and human relations in musical life, and they are essential to the history and sociology of the club institution. These value systems, moreover, can be interpreted and contextualized by the more general distinction between public and private value systems in capitalism.

Dominant agents of gentrification and commercialization tend to naturalize their value system, portraying change as inevitable without directly acknowledging the underlying ideologies. As corporations and affluent populations dominate more and more in the condition of generalized gentrification, the value system of private enterprise and corporate consumer culture becomes hegemonic. The products of the corporate concert industry appeal to the dominant population. In its value system, there is little desire for more regulation of gentrification, and the decline of public culture and related conceptions of the city and its cultural life are not perceived as a major problem. The conditions of diversity and history in the city's musical life are left to the market. Neo-bohemian cultural scenes have suffered under this value system and have not been able or willing to confront it on the grounds of public culture. Their positioning outside the spheres of formal power—outside the industry and public institutions—has been a part of their particular culture. Had these local scenes had a stronger grounding in a discourse of public culture values and a closer relationship with public institutions, they could have confronted the challenges of gentrification more directly. They might also have learned from public culture ethics of difference to develop greater compassion for minoritized neighborhood populations and form alliances with other artistic and social communities.

Let me unpack the historical dimension of the city's value systems further. Gentrification was initially accelerated by city governments to overcome the urban economic crisis of the 1970s. The aim was not improvement of living conditions for everyone. Poor populations were stigmatized; they were perceived as a barrier, as the people of the frontier. Eventually middle-class residents also began to leave because of the growing cost of living, and so gentrification continues to eliminate resistance as it evolves. The deaths of music scenes and clubs have not been perceived as a serious public issue. When CBGB was facing imminent closure in 2006, fans and stars rallied, and there were attempts to turn it into a landmark building (Methos 2005), but the city government offered no help, and CBGB survived only as a brand for merchandising and a festival. The Brooklyn warehouse scene of the early 2010s knew the city didn't care.

Humanists need not restrict themselves to analyzing the dominant values of the contemporary city, however. They can expand the perspective to include the city's history of diversity and of exclusion and point to its growing one-dimensionality. The history of difference, in many ways eradicated in the condition of generalized gentrification, becomes a resource for intellectual analysis and social justice. The past is crucial for understanding not only what no longer exists, but also what is no longer possible, and what might be desirable in the future. The corporate promoters who do not communicate about culture but only for marketing purposes are both a methodological and an ethical challenge. They obscure the origins and process of cultural history. Gentrification has created a condition in which the means of production—including the means of producing performance and cultural identity in intimate human relations—are increasingly owned by corporations.

The chapter analysis, moreover, suggests that the commercial rock club illustrates a change in the conditions of urban life. The indie rock club theater appeals to desires for leisure, aesthetic pleasure, sophistication, and intimacy, but it also indicates how the working life ideology of professional authority permeates leisure and imposes constraints on the concert ritual. In the focusing of the performance ritual on the purpose of concert consumption, little space is left for the suspension of everyday order. The potential of the musical ritual to have deep social and existential values is weakened. The Bowery Ballroom can create immersive musical experiences, but it cannot accommodate visceral bodily sensations as part of an existential community experience with elements of scene sociality and social experimentation. Corporate structures have thus constrained the space of individual and collective agency at the microlevel.

In the many performances I attended, there was a low level of ritual intensity, little suspension of self-control, and little departure from the norms and roles that regulate everyday social life. There was little crying or laughter or expressive bodily interaction between strangers. There were few and rather constrained expressions of sexuality and political sentiments. Emotional utopias could be found in song lyrics, in love songs, for instance, but the performance as a whole did not explore those utopias. The desires expressed in songs and sound recordings were not fully realized in the collective experience of bodies. The commercial institutionalization of performance and the mediatization of music do not eliminate the body, but the bodily experience is constrained at deep psychic and social levels. The indie club concert theater is nonetheless a continuation of a now-traditional institution that accommodates intimate collective experiences of music's unique inner values. These values are central to the indie aesthetics of the introverted, contemplative middle-class subject, who values uplifting pop sensibilities and historical authenticity in musical aesthetics, in architecture, and in neighborhood mythology. In some respects, then, the club institution and its musical performance culture have moved closer to the values and aesthetics of the bourgeois concert hall and its institutionalism, even if major differences remain, especially with respect to musical form, sound, and mythology.

Some of these social transformations were put into perspective by the strikingly apolitical culture of indie rock during the Occupy Wall Street protests, which took place right around the corner from these concert clubs. The generation of indie musicians who defined the clubs and who were known as the class of 2000 had no public presence at the Occupy protests and remain disconnected from the critiques of capitalism that later inspired the new progressive wing of the Democratic Party and the climate protest movements. Some of the rock musicians that took part in these protests were in fact musicians who came out of social movements and underground scenes of earlier decades. The 2012 compilation produced by the organization Music for Occupy featured Joan Baez, Yoko Ono, Blondie, and Patti Smith (Pelly 2012). The Manhattan live music industry continued its business as usual.

: 5 :

How Did the Rock Club Evolve in Europe?

How does the history of rock clubs in New York City compare to other cities? The analysis in the previous chapter could be extended to other cities such as Chicago, Austin, and Los Angeles to explore variations of the same process in a national context. Such a study might consider differences in local music histories, geographies, and economies. This could be a book in itself. The objective of the present book, however, is to expand the analysis of transformations in performance institutions into Continental Europe. This chapter examines a variation of the rock club shaped by European public policy.

One might expect the performance culture of rock clubs to be very different in European cities, which are much smaller than New York. There is a growing number of clubs in Western Europe, however, characterized by a design and concert culture similar to the midsize clubs of the Bowery Presents and Mercury East Presents in New York. Many clubs share similar ballroom-style architectural designs, sound and lighting aesthetics, music programming, demographics, and similar concert rituals. The homogeneity partially results from the same processes of professionalization and gentrification, which have had similar structural implications, even in small European cities, analogous to those analyzed in the previous chapter with respect to New York.[1] This chapter therefore does not examine gentrification in general, but rather highlights the role of public policy as a local variable and examines its implications for the development of the rock club institution.

Nevertheless, the differences in scale merit consideration. The chapter examines leading clubs in the capital cities Amsterdam, Brussels, and Copenhagen. They benefit from the prestige and resources that come with being a capital city, which sets them apart from other cities in their respective countries. Artists from the United States and the United Kingdom tend to perform in capital cities when they tour Europe, often skipping cities in the provinces. Still, the populations of Amsterdam, Brussels, and Copenhagen are about ten times smaller than New York's, and the respective national populations are many times smaller than that of the United States. The population in each city is about 600,000 to 1,000,000, and the national populations range from five to seventeen million. The scale of many things in society is smaller, the tempo slower. This includes urban culture worlds and media markets. Global corporations have a smaller presence. The streets and squares of the city centers are quieter and smaller, and many residents walk or bike around town. Moreover, the international flows of people and capital are smaller and simpler than in global cities such as New York and London. All three cities, however, have experienced rising immigration in recent decades, with growing Eastern European and Muslim populations.[2]

The Argument

Amsterdam, Brussels, and Copenhagen are peripheral to Berlin, Paris, and London and had somewhat small and insular national popular music industries until the 2000s. Public policy has played a greater role in the history of the rock club in these three countries than it has in many other countries. City governments helped establish the rock club as a central institution in popular music culture. From the late 1960s and up to the 2000s, the central performance institution in popular music policy was the club, mostly the rock club but also the jazz and the world music club, to a smaller degree. In dedicated policy of popular music, the club is still the performance institution that receives the majority of subsidies, and the dominant model is now by far the club that commonly identifies itself as a rock and pop music club. By only subsidizing nonprofit clubs, public policy helped make the nonprofit club the dominant model in the organizational field. However, city governments in particular stimulated the club's transformation into a form that is somewhat indistinct from for-profit clubs. In the 2000s, city governments began prioritizing other forms of performance culture. They increasingly subsidized large events and the corporate live music industry through departments for tourism and business. This development has challenged the nonprofit value system of popular music performance and the music policies of the departments for the arts.

These evolutions in policy reflect broader changes in society. The subsidizing of rock clubs was initially an outcome of rock music's status in the 1968 student revolt and youth counterculture. The inclusion of popular music in public policy was motivated by arguments about the music's democratic potentials (Kallio and Väkevä 2017). Popular music policy, however, was shaped by the interest of its own elites and developed into a genre discourse. Later, in the 1980s, urban cultural policy was strongly influenced by accelerating gentrification. Cities developed clubs into flagship concert venues before eventually shifting focus to larger events within agendas tied to city marketing. The nonprofit value system of clubs was further challenged by the growing market value of the live music commodity in the 2000s, which attracted a growing number of for-profit entrepreneurs. The nonprofit club's potential as an institution of public culture, engaged with societal ethics, is ever more difficult to realize and has not yet been fully recognized in policy discourse. In short, the policy terrain of rock clubs is a historical amalgam of general principles of popular music policy, the interests of a taste culture, the gentrifying city, and the relationship between nonprofit clubs and the increasingly dominant for-profit organizations in the live music industry.

Similarities with clubs in other countries notwithstanding, local traditions of nonprofit idealism and public policy have created a unique situation in northern Continental Europe:

1. *An independent sector with the nonprofit organization as the norm.* City governments institutionalized the nonprofit model in the 1970s by subsidizing, and in some cases creating and owning, nonprofit clubs with a community value system. Over time, this led to a dominance of the nonprofit model in rock clubs with an audience capacity under 2,000. The systemic effect was that public policy supported the independent sector that had evolved from local traditions of nonprofit idealism. (These traditions also created the foundations for popular music festivals, but festivals have had a smaller role in public policy.)[3] The systemic effect of public policy was amplified by an embracing of the nonprofit value system at the national level and in Denmark by the adoption of this value system into the national government's popular music policy. This development made clubs a less attractive target for business entrepreneurs, aside from the fact that clubs were of little business interest in the first place, since small performance spaces generally have the smallest commercial potential.

2. *More performances of music with a smaller market.* The leading nonprofit clubs have one performance space in the midsize range with a capacity for 1,500 to 2,000, but they also have smaller performance spaces and by a greater proportion than their for-profit counterparts, of which there are a few locally and more internationally in cities such as Berlin, Paris, London, and New York. The nonprofit clubs produce many concerts in these small spaces featuring music with a smaller market. Their programming there-

fore represents a greater diversity of artists within the production system of Anglophone rock and pop music. The clubs provide more opportunities for lesser-known artists, with better rates and facilities to boot. These artists are also promoted in the same media channels as headliners and thus integrated into larger market and industry channels.

3. *Transparency and public engagement*. Although nonprofit and for-profit clubs engage similar styles of marketing communications, the nonprofit organizations feel that subsidies come with a responsibility for transparency and participation in discussions of public interests. These public values are also reinforced by the national associations of nonprofit clubs. Receiving subsidies also encourages a level of self-censorship in that managers are cautious not to express political opinions, knowing that this might provoke local politicians and lead to budget cuts. Some of the managers I interviewed had served on government committees as representatives of popular music. These managers were known in the music industry for their nonprofit values.

Among the dozen managements I interviewed in eight European cities in 2013, the ones in countries with the highest subsidies generally displayed the highest level of public accountability.[4] Nonprofits and for-profits shared basic organizational information, but for-profits shared less information, were less open to discussion of public interests, and had no interest in cultural politics. One manager of a corporately owned club, for instance, dismissed a question by simply stating: "That is a strategic question" (Arnaud Delbarre, interview with the author, September 26, 2013). Corporate managements had less interest in cultural issues because their clubs were either a distribution space for a media corporation or a rental space for external promoters. Managements in Holland, Belgium, and Denmark shared more information and engaged in longer conversations with me about a wider range of questions, especially managers with long-term experience in the independent music industry. They also showed greater personal commitment to public interests in musical culture.

A Note on Methodology and Positioning

The purpose of this chapter is to document and interpret empirical histories within the overall framework of the book. The chapter therefore does not initiate a discussion of new theoretical or methodological issues. The analysis is grounded in general principles of a comparative case study, which serves to highlight variations in conceptions of the nonprofit club within local histories and policies. The chapter uses the individual club management as a focal point for analyzing how interpretations of the club institution have evolved in response to changing value systems of public policy.

The empirical materials comprise interviews with members of the managements, the clubs' policy reports, reportage in national news media, and the record of a debate in the Danish parliament. I met in person with the managements of the two clubs in Copenhagen and Brussels, who also showed me the facilities and offices. The chapter does not attempt an ethnography, nor does it analyze club experiences, but I have some experience of the Copenhagen club and have lived in this city for twenty-eight years. Through informal encounters and participation in two conventions and a seminar for the national club association of Denmark, all between 2007 and 2013, I developed a more critical appreciation for it.[5]

The empirical sample was constructed from an explorative study of clubs in eight cities in Continental Western Europe, from Barcelona in the south to Stockholm in the north.[6] The aim of this preliminary study that I conducted in 2013 was to identify significant cultural and economic developments in fields of Anglophone popular music clubs in cities that are structurally similar. This exploration, using the methods of data collecting and interviewing, led to two general insights. First, clubs in all cities had expanded their productions in the process of gentrification. Second, a unique system of nonprofit clubs had developed in Holland, Belgium, and Denmark under the influence of public policy.

Urban Cultural Policy in Western Europe

The policy situation in these three northern Continental European countries reflects a specific variation of broader developments in European urban cultural policy. The following discussion is guided by the foundational 1993 edited volume *Cultural Policy and Urban Regeneration: The West European Experience*, edited by Franco Bianchini and Michael Parkinson (Bianchini and Parkinson 1993). The book provided the first comprehensive empirical survey of the major international developments up to the early 1990s, and it remains the standard work on the topic. No other book-length publications have offered a survey of equal depth, and later research has confirmed the lasting relevance of the book's analysis of the transition into urban regeneration policies (Sassatelli 2009, chapter 3). The creative city discourse took inspiration from the regeneration discourse and is largely an extension of it.

Bianchini's introductory chapter outlines a history of three value systems (he calls them paradigms) since World War II. The first value system was the bourgeois elite arts policy of the 1950s, which created a system of policies for canonical art forms. In the 1970s, a social and an economic value system evolved outside the domain of arts policy. Their development can be detailed as follows:

1. *Arts policy (1950s–present)*. The arts policy of the 1950s evolved from the nineteenth-century bourgeois elite tradition and was institutionalized in arts councils of the nation-state. These councils effected a shift from regional diversity to national centers of excellence, from amateur participation to professionalism (Bianchini 1993, 18; see also Hewison 1995). The majority of subsidies still go to large national institutions in the capital city, which are dedicated to canonical art forms such as ballet, painting and sculpture, opera, and symphonic music. The subsidy level for classical music and opera performance organizations has in certain cases reached 66% (Deloitte 2015), while the level for popular music clubs is almost without exception below 10%.

The democratization of musical arts policy (music policy within the area of arts policy) has not progressed much in terms of cultural diversity since Anglophone popular music was included in the 1970s and world music, to a lesser extent, in the 1980s. The presence of world music has even declined, both in rock music clubs and in dedicated performance spaces for world music (see p. 139). The new Eastern European and Muslim populations are almost completely ignored, as are lower-income populations. The relative lack of debate about this indicates that little priority is given to issues of social justice and multiculturalism in politics and in society at large. The obvious suspects responsible for this include gentrification, neoliberalism, and the commercial institutionalization of culture, all of which have contributed to depoliticized conceptions of culture as consumer culture. Another important factor is the rise of right-wing populism, which undermines the political autonomy of public arts institutions and makes it riskier for them to take a stance.

2. *Social policy (late 1960s–1990s)*. A social policy of culture emerged in the wake of the student revolt. It introduced a narrative of democratization, and in musical arts policy this led to the inclusion of popular music. In urban cultural policy, youth clubs and neighborhood "community houses" were created. Many of these organizations later developed into more professional consumer culture venues and, in some cases, into dedicated concert venues.

The rise of institutions in the social policy value system and their transformation into consumer culture institutions of the gentrified city can be illustrated through the example of Copenhagen. In 1968, the city government created a number of cultural institutions under the umbrella of

"Copenhagen Youth Centers" (CYC): thirteen neighborhood "community houses," four "culture houses," three "meeting centers," and two "employment centers" ("Københavns Ungdomscentre"). The community and culture houses provided affordable spaces for socializing and cultural participation among lower-income populations. The culture house in particular represented a kind of community arts center for hippie and, later, punk culture, primarily in the form of concerts. In 2002, CYC was folded into the city's department of culture and leisure ("Københavns Ungdomscentre"). Five of the community houses had already been closed, and some turned into more gentrified spaces of consumption.[7] In some cases, the performance space was developed into a professional rock club. The city government still owns and operates rock clubs at Amager Bio, Huset, and Vanløse Kulturstation. During a visit to the latter organization in 2007, I learned that culture houses were distancing themselves from the institution's origins in social policy. The manager, who was also a board member of the national culture house association, talked about "the old culture house" of the 1970s and 1980s as a sleepy place where little happened apart from a few seniors and jobless people having coffee. She was proud of leading her own organization's transformation into a professional cultural institution, with a growing focus on commerce-based leisure. The manager was proud that the organization was no longer competing with the local neighborhood café or bar but with the national gallery and other prestigious places in the city center. Her target audience was a new, more affluent population in the neighborhood (Hannah Haansbæk Rasmussen, conversation with the author, May 11, 2007). The enthusiasm for gentrification was unmistakable, and this was further reflected in the name change in 2010 from "culture house" to "culture station."

3. Economic policy (late 1970s–present). The rise of economic policies of culture was stimulated by the economic crisis in the 1970s and by the decentralization of cultural policy from the national to the city level. This decentralization led to policies guided by local self-interest and to the co-option of culture into agendas of urban regeneration, inspired by developments in the United States (Zukin 1995). City governments began developing flagship institutions, such as museums, opera houses, and large cultural events. Examples include the development of the European Capital of Culture program (since 1985) into an urban regeneration project in the early 1990s, the transformation of Barcelona for the 1992 Olympics, and the transformation of the meatpacking district in Paris's Nineteenth Arrondissement with the construction of Cité de la musique in 1995 (Bianchini 1993, 16–17). In the small countries of northwest Continental Europe, city governments subsidized the renovation and construction of rock clubs as small flagships, before their focus shifted to larger venues and events in the 2000s.

David Throsby notes that economic interests in culture have made culture more central to public policy (Throsby 2010, 7). His work has influenced the creative economy discourse and therefore merits critical scrutiny.[8] Despite Throsby's claim that an economic understanding of culture does not reduce cultural policy to economic policy, this is precisely one of the consequences. He ignores a range of knowledges and interests in the cultural field and lacks a humanist perspective to understand the implications of conceiving of culture in terms of goods and services. Kate Oakley (2009) has argued that the advent of creative industry policies in the 1990s replaced rather than expanded arts policy. Klara Tomson (2011), in her analysis of the institutionalization of the term "experience industry" in Sweden in the 2000s, argues that government spending of about 15 million euros on kick-starting this phantom industry essentially led to nothing aside from promoting a term that many in the cultural field discarded. By the 2010s, the economic value system had become more hegemonic. Many cities, for instance, continued to develop spaces of cultural consumption (e.g., arenas, symphonies, museums, markets, events, and shops) to attract affluent residents and tourists. Nonprofit cultural institutions increasingly adopted economic rationales to improve their standing with sponsors, city administrations, and news media.

The 2017 inauguration concert of the Elbphilharmonie in Hamburg in 2017 illustrated typical aspects of the role of performance institutions as flagship architecture. The concert ritual inside the philharmonic hall followed the tradition of the symphony institution, while a light show outside transformed the event into a visual spectacle for millions of media spectators. The advertising agency that conceived the light show stated that music was central to the visual show ("Grand Opening Elbphilharmonie Hamburg"; "Elbphilharmonie Grand Opening"). The company deployed a visualization software based on a technical measuring of sound, so the music was technologically central to the light show. But the software did not process music as a cultural form, and the show in fact decontextualized the music from its history, performers, and listeners. Many other forms of music would have generated similar visuals with this technology. After two years, the building's viewing platform had hosted many more visitors than the concert hall (Große-Wilde 2019), further suggesting that the general experiential qualities of the building play a larger role than specific politics of music in the public imagination of this concert hall.

In popular music, the economic value system similarly led to the development of flagship venues, but popular music was still largely left to the market, and the competition intensified with the growing market value of the live music commodity and its corporate exploitation. Nonprofit club associations founded in the late 1990s and the 2000s adopted the Anglophone industry discourse of live music. In Germany and Denmark, for instance, the term "venue" to some extent replaced the local-language words for clubs—"Spielstätten" and "spillesteder" ("playing places"; the idiomatic translation is "performance places"). A communications manager at one of the clubs examined in this chapter consistently used the term "cool venue" to describe his ideal of a club. The live music discourse afforded clubs communicative power as they lobbied for subsidies and aspired to grow as an industry. The change in terminology unfolded internationally, with Germany's "Livemusik Kommission" of 2010, Denmark's "Dansk Live" of 2011, and Sweden's "Livemusik Sverige" of 2014. A European umbrella organization called Live Music DMA was established in 2012 with offices in Nantes, France. Some of the members created the network Live Europe in 2014, in which clubs collaborate to create a touring platform for European artists. Live Europe is modeled on and subsidized by the European Union's arts policies of international exchange.

Variations of a Model

The organizational data in table 5.1 shows significant similarities among the three main case studies—Melkweg, Ancienne Belgique, and Vega. They exist in cities with roughly the same age and population size. They produce roughly the same number of concerts and have the same type of concert architecture, audience capacities, budgets, form of ownership, organizational structure, and music programming. A few of the core similarities can be detailed:

- Organizationally, the clubs have full-time administration, with one manager and teams for marketing, music programming, cleaning, and technical staff. In addition, the organizations have about 150–220 part-time workers, most of whom are on the nighttime production teams, including bartenders, coat checkers, and security. The organizational structure shows that while there is cultural labor in programming and marketing, much of the labor is administrative and operational. The organizations do not have the same level of bureaucracy as corporations since most of the full-time staff works in the same offices and with relatively flat

TABLE 5.1 2016 figures for Melkweg, Ancienne Belgique, and Vega

	Melkweg, Amsterdam	Ancienne Belgique, Brussels	Vega, Copenhagen
City population[a]	844,947	1,187,890	591,481
Year of city's founding[b]	1275	979	1167
Organization established	1970	1979	1996
Large hall (capacity)	1,500 + external 1,400	2,000	1,550
Small hall	700	280	500
Smaller spaces, capacity below 250	A cinema, a theater, two art galleries, two bars, a restaurant	Recording studio, a lecture room	A 250-capacity bar
Annual budget	13 million euros	12 million euros	11 million euros
Number of employees	8 full-time, 203 part-time (90 full-time equivalents in total)	46 full-time, 200 part-time, plus 8 full-time in restaurant and bar and 1 full-time for Live Europe (EU project) (113 full-time equivalents in total)	19 full-time, 150 part-time
Subsidies	8%	23%	8%
Number of concert events, usually with an opening act and a headliner		175 in 2006	170 in 2008
	320 (850 performances)	350	340 (750 performances)
Annual audience[c]	160,000 in early 1990s		
	320,000 in 1996–2007		200,000 in 1997
	420,000 in 2008–2015	175,000 in the 2000s	360,000 in 2007
			300,000 in 2011
	435,000 in 2016	350,000 in 2016	250,000 in 2016
		390,000 in 2018	
		50% of the audience is from Belgium outside the Brussels metropolitan region	

TABLE 5.1 *(continued)*

	Melkweg, Amsterdam	Ancienne Belgique, Brussels	Vega, Copenhagen
Audience for musical events (concerts and DJ shows) out of the organization's total audience	90%	90%	90%

Note: The information is from the individual organizations' records and reports: Sherif El Safony, email to the author, December 15, 2016; Dirk De Clippeleir, emails to the author, November 16, 2016, and December 20, 2018; Steen Jørgensen, conversation with the author, February 1, 2017; Cor Schlösser, email to the author, May 26, 2017; "AB Policy Plan: 2017–2021," 29; "Ansøgning om at være regionalt spillsted i perioden 2017–2020: Vega," 15; "Forretningsudvalgets møde den 11. oktober 2011: Bilag 4," 6; "Inspirationskatalog: Oplevelsesøkonomi: 7. Vega"; Jensen (1997b).

[a] The population number for Amsterdam is for 2017. "Population Dynamics; Birth, Death, and Migration Per Region"; "Total Population of Belgium and the Regions"; *Befolkningen i København, Region Hovedstaden og hele landet,1. januar 2016.*

[b] The age of cities is a rough estimate; the key point is that they were founded in the Middle Ages.

[c] The annual audience numbers are in some respects an estimate based on various sources. This was necessary since there were occasionally discrepancies between information presented in management interviews and in policy reports. For Ancienne Belgique, the number of concertgoers was 265,000 in 2016 and 300,000 in 2018. Vega's total audience declined when its nightclub closed in 2010. The number of concerts doubled between 2009 and 2013 and more tickets were sold per concert, with more than ninety sold-out concerts in 2013. Revenue from drinks fell from 48% in 2008 to 32% in 2013, while the share from concert tickets increased from 19% to 26% ("Spillestedsanalyse: Overblik over den rytmiske spillestedsscene i København," 20–21).

hierarchical structures. But the labor is relatively routinized, reflecting the high frequency of concert productions and the organizations' place within an industry of concert tours. The club is to some extent a distribution unit within the music industry, somewhat parallel to the movie theater in the movie industry (Ryan 1992, chapter 3). The club organization is constantly buying a formatted service from musicians—a rehearsed concert performance with a standard duration, one that can be delivered within the technologies and routines of many clubs. The club is not involved in decisions about the outlook and character of the stage performance itself. The practices known from jazz clubs where an artist can have a regular weekly performance or a week-long residency do not exist in these rock clubs. The club's dependence on a steady supply of touring artists leaves little room for other approaches and thus little diversity in performance culture. All clubs in the country buy these standardized performances from a small number of national booking agencies. In this unequal, centralized system of distribution, the individual club has few choices and can barely cover production expenses, while the agencies and headliners generate higher profits. What is more, the structure and function of club organizations explain why they have a building-centered identity. Most of their activities are conducted within a single building that is the site of both performance production and consumption. Much of the organization's labor goes into operating and maintaining this building. Club organizations therefore tend to develop a symbiotic relationship with their buildings to a point at which the distinction between organization and building is nonexistent and the building becomes an indirect agent of organizational passivity. This happens, for instance, when attention is focused on operating the building rather than on the organization's cultural objectives, even as the latter might require a move to a less expensive building as the neighborhood gentrifies.

- Architecturally, the clubs' main concert halls have a similar ballroom-style design, with a rectangular shape and balconies on the sides. These halls have all been renovated in pursuit of the ideal of the state-of-the-art concert venue, which was the term frequently used by the managements at both Ancienne Belgique and Vega. The level of renovations varied considerably, but has in all cases expanded audience capacity, provided better sound systems and acoustic treatment, and modernized the décor. Some of the buildings were constructed before World War II and have been used for public assembly before, but all three now have a contemporary appearance, as opposed to the late nineteenth- or early twentieth-century aura of the Bowery Ballroom, Town Hall, and Webster Hall in New York. These small cities in Europe have historically had fewer spaces with this audience capacity. In Copenhagen, for instance, the largest rock club at the beginning of the 1990s had an audience capacity at around 800 people, and the larger alternatives were buildings designed for sports events. The architecture of popular music clubs in Amsterdam, Brussels, and Copenhagen reflects that the clubs have grown from a situation with limited profits and subsidies. They have generally adapted to architecture designed for other purposes. The clubs in this study have nonetheless achieved recognition as small flagships of popular music. Their architecture stands out from that of the smaller clubs by virtue of the building's size and entrance and the professional standards of the décor, technology, and acoustics.
- Musically, all three clubs started presenting more headliners after the architectural expansions. The number of employees and concerts per year generally doubled in the late 1990s and 2000s. It is of vital importance to the managements that their club is able to develop its own programming and not serve as a mere rental space. The clubs evolve from urban youth cultures of Anglophone rock music in which neo-bohemian images of authenticity and artistic individuality are important. This ideology has governed the evolution of rock clubs into places

for "good" popular music in networks that also regulate popular music in urban media and governments. The clubs have tended to exclude national folkloric and formulaic mass culture forms of music, particularly national-language crooners, "schlager music," and tribute bands. Influential national newspapers, broadcasting corporations, magazines, and arts council members have supported this.[9] In a word, governments have supported a model of cultural sameness. Rock clubs in Amsterdam, Brussels, and Copenhagen commonly included some jazz and world music in the 1970s and 1980s, but this has become rare, and the three clubs in this study identify as clubs for "pop and rock." They present some electronic dance music, but are not dedicated techno and house music clubs and exist in other networks. The music programming in the three clubs, moreover, combines smaller up-and-coming local artists who mostly perform in spaces with a capacity for about three hundred—a so-called "small hall"—with national and international headliners who perform in a "large hall" with a capacity of about 1,500. Many of the headliners are from the United States and United Kingdom on a club tour across Continental Western Europe. These concerts are the bread and butter for these organizations.

Some of the fundamental differences among these three clubs evolved from their conception within different policy value systems:

- Melkweg was conceived in 1970 within the utopian youth culture of the time, as suggested by its name, which means "Milky Way." It still bears the mark of that period's social policy, with elements of a community arts center still evident. Melkweg has a small cinema, a theater, and two art galleries, while the other two clubs are more exclusively music-centered.
- Ancienne Belgique (AB) was conceived within a unique cultural policy of the Flemish region (or Flanders) in 1979 and later, in 2008, promoted to the status as one of the region's eight major cultural institutions. AB is thus defined by a high level of institutionalization in its relationship with the regional government, which for all intents and purposes closely resembles a national government, while the local municipal government has a relatively minor role. This has meant that AB has more autonomy from the market than any other popular music club in the world. The subsidy level is 25%, in contrast to 8% for the two other clubs. AB embodies public culture values that the others do not and has a larger administration.
- Vega was conceived as a professional concert venue and as part of an urban regeneration policy in the mid-1990s. Decisive funding for estab-

lishing the club came from Copenhagen's budget for European Capital of Culture projects in 1996. The club was established in the former community building of the national Workers' Association. The Social Democratic Party constructed the original building in 1895 in a central working-class neighborhood out of the need for an assembly hall for the growing membership body in the city and named it House of the People ("Folkets Hus"). By 1996, the neighborhood was gentrifying and the building's congregations now consisted of a growing "hipster" population in indie rock concerts and DJ nightclub events (Jensen 1996; Sørensen 1996).

Melkweg, Amsterdam

Melkweg is one of the oldest existing rock clubs in the world, along with Paradiso, the other major rock club in Amsterdam. The two were established in 1970 and 1968, respectively, with the help of the city government. The government owned the buildings, which they gave more or less for free to small, nonprofit arts organizations associated with youth culture. It also subsidized these organizations. Paradiso was created in a building occupied by squatters, a former church, and the city gave it temporarily to a group of alternative art and music event organizers who used the name Provadya, which they also used for the events they organized in venues outside Amsterdam. Willem de Ridder, the main organizer, came up with the name "Cosmic Relaxation Center Paradiso." Melkweg had a similar start. A theater company had used a former milk factory for a one-month production in the summer of 1970, and one of the young people in the company, Cor Schlösser, together with three friends, came up with the idea of creating a temporary music and arts venue in the building. The theater company had little interest in the building because it was in poor shape, and there was no electricity and water. Melkweg similarly invested in the idea of Amsterdam as a "cosmic center" of the world (Cor Schlösser, email to the author, May 26, 2017; "About Paradiso"; "About Melkweg").

Music was a big part of youth counterculture and was eventually a medium for transforming the clubs into professionally institutionalized music venues in the 1980s. This involved a move from the youth to the arts department of the city government. Schlösser, manager of Melkweg from 1970 to 2011, recalls:

> During the 1980s, Paradiso and Melkweg had very little respect from the local authorities. The "alternative" spirit of change that also resonated with the authorities in the late 1960s and early 1970s had completely disappeared.

> Also, newspapers began referring to Paradiso and Melkweg as "former hippie temples."
>
> One of my best friends was director of Paradiso from 1975 to 1991 and together we decided to lobby for getting out of the youth department and (back, in case of Melkweg) into the arts department as our agency in the city administration. We succeeded in 1987 and after that Melkweg in particular gained respect because suddenly the city found out we had audiences of all colors and social backgrounds, which fitted the diversity issue that started to come up around 1990.
>
> It is remarkable that Melkweg and Paradiso have survived the ongoing gentrification of the city and are now considered landmarks, although the love of politicians can change like the weather, also when it is only six or seven percent of your budget. (Cor Schlösser, email to the author, May 26, 2017)[10]

The disassociation from the youth department—and from social policy—can be interpreted as a response to gentrification. In a broader perspective, this involved a disassociation from subcultural youths who had felt a sense of belonging in clubs and protested against gentrification, particularly through squatting in buildings designated for demolition.

The city government supported building renovations of both Melkweg and Paradiso during the 1980s to improve the facilities, adapting them to the standards of middle-class populations and to the professional standards of dedicated concert venues. The city government also subsidized the expansion of the clubs' audience capacities. In 1995, Melkweg added to its 700-capacity "Old Hall" a 1,000-capacity hall called the Max. The city's largest club space was still Paradiso's 1,200-capacity hall. The Max enabled Melkweg to double the annual number of concertgoers to an average of about 320,000. This number was increased to 420,000 in 2007 when the audience capacity of the Max was expanded to 1,500 (Cor Schlösser, email to the author, August 13, 2013). In other words, the city government contributed to an increase in the consumption of international headliner artists that appealed to the city's growing affluent population. The city also indirectly contributed to the expansion of the club organizations and the concert industry. This development later helped the clubs survive the budget cuts imposed on spending on culture by right-wing populists in 2013–2017.[11] By the time these cuts took effect, Melkweg had grown revenues from sales (tickets, drinks, and venue rentals) from 65% in the mid-1990s to 92% in 2012. The subsidy percentage from the city's arts department is 6% of the operating budget. Of the audience, 90% attend concerts and DJ-based club nights, and more than 60% attend concerts alone (Jon Heemsbergen, email to the author, September 23, 2013; Cor Schlösser, emails to the author, August 13–14, 2013). The focus on concerts is reflected on the websites of Melkweg and Paradiso, where the culture center dimension has become a secondary priority and is presented in terms of events in the smallest performance spaces.[12]

The development of flagship rock clubs in the capital city also contributed to the national institutionalization of "pop podiums" ("pop music stages") in Holland from the 1990s onward. Twenty-five midsize clubs have been created, most of them in new buildings financed by local city governments (Cor Schlösser, email to the author, May 26, 2017). Several of them struggle to attract the international headliners they hoped for, since many of these artists do only one show per country and prefer the capital city.

Meanwhile, the city's concert industry has developed further with the construction of the 5,500-capacity Heineken Music Hall in 2003 and the 17,500-capacity Ziggo Dome arena in 2012. Both venues are owned and operated by Live Nation and located close to the 53,000-capacity Amsterdam Arena, which is home to the AFC Ajax soccer team. Schlösser says that these bigger venues do not compete with the smaller ones because "they work on a different scale and the public comes from all over the country," adding that it takes two hours at most to get to Amsterdam from anywhere in the country. However, the increased number of big venues have likely shaped attitudes to musical performance and to clubs both in the concert industry and among the public at large. These large venues expand the space of mass culture and corporate industry. Jon Heemsbergen, who was with Melkweg for more than ten years and served as its marketing manager between 2012 and 2016, expressed concerns in 2013 that the live music business boom was a serious challenge to the nonprofit system:

> While Germany, for instance, mostly has rental venues run by promoters, all our pop venues in Holland are nonprofit organizations and most are subsidized by municipalities. We have always been autonomous. We program and promote shows in our own venue. This system might not survive. Record companies now have less influence. Booking agencies and artist managements have more power and do more of the concert promotion. The relationship between booking agencies and [club] venues is becoming more and more tense. These agencies want to rent more often. Also, more artists want to do ticketing themselves and own the customer data. Then there are younger booking agencies that want to promote shows themselves. This has been going on for a couple of years now and poses a risk to our organization. (Jon Heemsbergen, interview with the author, August 9, 2013)

Heemsbergen imagined Melkweg would have to adapt to growing market pressures from the concert industry agencies and increasingly serve more as a rental venue for them. In the process, concerts with smaller artists would be decimated (Jon Heemsbergen, interview with the author, August 9, 2013). Melkweg, in other words, would be co-opted into an organizational field dominated by for-profit values. A major implication of the transition into a rental-based model, he added, would be the loss of the identity and atmosphere that can only be produced by an autonomous in-house staff with a long-term attachment to the building.

Paradiso and Melkweg already developed a "whiter" and culturally more homogeneous programming in the 2000s. It presented more rock, pop, and EDM headliners and less jazz and world music. "We did a lot of world music in the 1980s," said Heemsbergen, "but it has become more difficult now that other theaters in Amsterdam with bigger budgets are doing it" (Jon Heemsbergen, interview with the author, August 9, 2013). Jaïr Tchong, a former curator of world music at Melkweg, who was with the organization for many years, pointed to the aging of world music's traditional white audience demographic and to the decline in subsidies. Some world music clubs closed, while others survived by adopting a more commercial profile. In Tchong's view, this challenged the ideals embodied by organizations such as Melkweg, also because world music acts were rerouted to other types of venues and events. He was particularly concerned about right-wing nationalists' "attack on culture and especially non-Western culture" (Jaïr Tchong, interview with the author, July 9, 2013).[13]

Policies for rock clubs thus cannot be understood in isolation from the changing situation faced by world music and immigrant populations in the country. The situation was particularly complicated in 2012, when as many as four world music venues risked closing. Emiel Barendsen, manager of one of the venues, commented:

> Rasa in Utrecht, World Music and Dance Centre in Rotterdam, The Regent in The Hague, and Tropentheater in Amsterdam are expected to disappear on 1 January 2013. Then you are talking about the four most important world music venues in the Netherlands. And the intermediaries thus fall away. This is because the Netherlands has been withdrawing more and more over the last ten years, becoming whiter. If you see what the Council for Culture still stands for that is white culture. (Verheggen 2012)[14]

Not all of these organizations closed, but the most experienced world music experts in Holland agreed in 2018 that government support for the music had declined. The experts said that the closing of world music venues coincided with a growing presence of world music at festivals. Festival promoters could more easily accommodate diversity, they said, since audiences had more time and willingness to explore new music at festivals. However, they also said that festivals tended to book only popular music forms of world music, the bigger stars and party-oriented music, not traditional music. They also said that festivals could not create the ecosystem infrastructure in everyday life that was important for sustaining the long-term development of audiences for world music. The situation for world music has been further weakened as genre areas in musical arts policy have been merged into one area. Small areas such as world music suffer from this change. Finally, city administrations have introduced quantitative audits that discourage rock music clubs from programming world music. Audience attendance for each concert is being recorded, and concerts with low sales figures are perceived negatively by the city administration (Emiel Barendsen, interview with the author, March 2, 2018; Rob Boonzajer Flaes, interview with the author, March 2, 2018; Sonja Heimann and Stan Rijven, interview with the author, March 21, 2018).

Ancienne Belgique, Brussels

Ancienne Belgique (AB) is perhaps Europe's closest popular music equivalent to a national cultural institution such as an opera house or symphony orchestra. AB was conceived in 1977 as a quasi-national cultural institution: an institution of the Flemish government, which is technically a regional government in Belgium but is also imagined as a national community ("AB History"). When Belgium was divided into three linguistic communities in 1979—Dutch, French, and German—each community became responsible for its own cultural affairs. AB was one of the new Flemish cultural institutions, and the French-speaking community created a local counterpart in Le Botanique, which has more cultural center functions like Melkweg.[15] In their online presence and in conversation, AB's management still describes its purpose and origins in the idea of "a center for Flemish culture in the heart of Brussels" (Dirk De Clippeleir, interview with the author, August 13, 2013). The government requires that 40% of the performers be residents of the Flemish region. In 2008, AB was promoted to one of the eight "great cultural institutions of the Flemish community," a phrase that reflects nationalism ("Ancienne Belgique opgenomen in lijst 'grote Vlaamse Cultuurinstellingen'"). This status provided more access to institutions of formal power, public culture responsibilities, and, from 2017, also more subsidies. In 2017, the subsidy level increased from 23% to 25%, 75% of which comes from the Flemish government. The Brussels Symphony still receives four times more ("Advisering kunstinstellingen en ondersteunende organisaties"; Gatz 2014).[16]

There are mythical layers to AB's evolution into a high-level institution. The building dates back to the Renaissance era and was a concert hall for Francophone popular music in the 1950s and 1960s operating under the same name. Artists such as Jacques Brel, Edith Piaf, and Charles Aznavour performed in Ancienne Belgique during those decades. Brel was Belgian, and the flow of stars from Paris was effected through collaborations with Bruno Coquatrix, who had worked at Ancienne Belgique before he became the manager of Olympia in Paris in 1954 ("AB History"). The closing of the original AB in 1971 reflected the declining popularity of postwar Francophone chansonniers and the rise of new forms of Anglophone popular music. The new AB was developed into a youth culture center by the Dutch-speaking community, but primarily one that organized rock music concerts. The value system at the time was reflected in the choice of a manager with a degree in classics and history.

Jari De Meulemeester managed AB from 1979 to 2011, steering its transition from a youth culture center in a deteriorating building into a state-of-the-art concert venue and major cultural institution with corporate sponsors.[17] De Meulemeester was attracted to the notion of a state-of-the-art concert venue for rock music from the beginning (Garsse 2011). His successor from 2011, Dirk De Clippeleir, has a degree in communications and seventeen years of experience in the corporate music industry, as the manager of EMI, Universal, and the International Federation of the Phonographic Industry in Belgium ("A New General Manager for the AB").

AB has not expanded its audience capacity, but the government has subsidized major renovations of the building in 1982–1986 and again in 1990–1995, when the main hall was demolished and built anew as a concert hall. Both rounds of renovation were motivated by requirements for noise isolation. A major motivation for the second renovation, however, was a 1991 government decision to create a center for "quality popular music" (Dirk De Clippeleir, conversation with the author, August 13, 2013). This mirrored the shift from youth to arts policy in Amsterdam.

Impacts of AB's Promotion

Some of the key impacts of AB's institutional promotion in 2008 can be discerned from the organization's policy plans for the Flemish government. All Flemish institutions with a similar status must deliver a five-year plan detailing how the institution will meet the policy criteria. The criteria are defined in terms of five functions, primarily exhibitionary functions, but there is also an expectation that the individual organization will serve as an institution for the respective art form. The institutions are expected to curate art, host lectures and discussions, and sustain flow and exchange in their respective cultural fields.

AB's thirty-four-page plan for the period 2017–2021 is structured such that it answers to each of the five functions ("AB Policy Plan: 2017–2021"). The section on *presentation* (1) focuses on building facilities, production routines, and the expertise of programmers in diverse local and international musical landscapes. The section on *participation* (2) is about social inclusion and community outreach. This includes a series of free events that are expected to attract 20,000 visitors per year, such as a small festival for Dutch-language music in a public park and a number of concerts and talks. The choice of target groups is formulated in somewhat vague terms. The target groups are identified as "students," "expats," "people with disabilities," and "immigrant communities." Students are already the predominant audience group, and it is not clear if the idea of student discounts targets specific demographics such as students in low-income neighborhoods. AB wants to be more accessible for "people with disabilities," but the plan addresses this in practical terms and not in terms of cultural interests in programming and other activities. The planned outreach initiatives for immigrant communities similarly do not suggest substantial changes in programming.

The section on the *development* (3) function focuses on the nurturing of young talents. AB promises to produce about one hundred concerts annually by artists in this category in the two small spaces AB Club and Huis 23. In addition, AB will develop its artist-in-residence program, through which three artists get various forms of support and exposure for a year via AB's platforms. In response to a function called *production* (4), AB focuses on developing stage productions based on more extensive curatorial work to create unique content to promote the organization's values. The last function is *reflection* (5), which mainly involves talks, debates, and documentaries.

AB's plan is crafted with a bureaucratic purpose in mind, but it should still be read critically. Large parts of the plan describe the organization's history and activities in somewhat superficial and passive terms. There is a positive attitude to public culture values, but the interpretation of these values could be more ambitious. The rationales and strategies for future activities are rather underdeveloped. The plan says little about AB's role as an institution in the music field and in the Flemish region, or about the worldviews of musicians and audiences, or about the situation among musical performance cultures in Brussels. Instead, the plan primarily describes individual activities that meet specific bureaucratic requirements without much sense of an overall direction or reflexivity. The paragraphs on "immigrant communities" indicate that rockism remains unchallenged. On the other hand, the plan seems realistic and honest. The mission statement, for instance, begins by stating that the organization's ambition is "to become the leading concert hall in Belgium" and among the best in Europe, with programming that brings together "the best from a broad range of genres and combines new talent with established performers" ("AB Policy Plan: 2017–2021"). The plan outlines several small projects that a for-profit organization would not undertake, such as the free concerts and the collaborations with minority populations, and they could have impact beyond these specific projects themselves. Nevertheless, the plan has little to say about the intended outcomes.

The plan only reflects part of the organization's interactions with the Flemish government and with other Flemish cultural institutions. This can be seen in the annual reports AB has started to make available on its website since 2013, which serve to promote transparency and accountability to the public. While the 2014 report documents conventional concert venue activities, the 2015 report presents activities such as charity events, a free event for homeless and poor people, and LGBTQ-themed street art on the building's façade ("Annual Report 2014," "Annual Report 2015"). Such explicit commitment to public culture values is rare among rock clubs.

When I asked De Clippeleir in 2016 how AB had evolved since we last spoke three years earlier, he said the increased attention to policy criteria had resulted in "a new mindset" and "mentality" (Dirk De Clippeleir, conversation with the author, October 7, 2016). AB was still primarily a state-of-the-art concert venue that produced concerts for a large audience, but parts of the production were now more conceptual and more culturally diverse.

> Our artistic mind is shifting much more in the direction of our own productions. To give you an example, last year we started a new festival called Broadcast and that is really a development festival not only in terms of the artists we present but also in terms of the formats, the design, and the marketing. It is really a testing ground for new things at all these levels. That costs money, of course, and that's what we see as production and we wouldn't have done that five years ago. We would have launched a new festival, but it would have been about new acts and not all these other elements. We also do a lot more collaborations than in the past. Not only with other rock concert spaces. We have collaborations with all types of arts, even with the opera and with. . . . So we are really looking to expand our horizons in terms of content as well.
>
> Moreover, we have always been booking a lot of jazz artists, but the overall focus and purpose of the programming has not been very clear. So we decided

that next year we will focus on our jazz programming, with a dedicated jazz program, with a dedicated jazz weekend, focus on some of the many young jazz talents in Belgium. We decided to give them a home at AB. So next year you are going to see a lot of young jazz acts at AB, doing a lot of workshops and working at AB, becoming artists-in-residence. We will do collaborations with other partners around jazz. (Dirk De Clippeleir, conversation with the author, October 7, 2016)

The above statements suggest potential avenues for developing a club into a cultural institution with public culture values. De Clippeleir's thinking was maturing from an operational translation of policy criteria to an understanding of how public values can shape the logic of the organization's activities.

The organization's transformation is further illustrated by De Clippeleir's attention to identity politics. He continuously turned to the issue of "diversity" with reference to public policy.

De Clippeleir: The major cultural institutions in Belgium are required to have a diversity policy. We are working on this. Instead of just getting some world music acts . . . we work the other way around. How can we present diversity in our programming from the start? How can we integrate diversity in our real thinking? Instead of going "Oh, there's an opportunity for a nice world music act, let's book them." That's happening for the first time this year actually. Like the opening weekend two weeks ago, which was completely devoted to what we call "global sounds" and had ten–fifteen concerts with artists from all over the world.

Author: Is diversity part of your hiring policy?

De Clippeleir: Yes, it is. It's true that our program team is male, white, and middle-aged, so that's not. . . . If you want to be in sync with what's happening in a diverse city like Brussels you need someone who is part of that diverse scene. On the management level, we have let go of two managers this year. We needed to have a younger management team. Unfortunately, they are all still white, Caucasian. . . . Well, you can't change everything in one go. (Dirk De Clippeleir, conversation with the author, October 7, 2016)

Vega, Copenhagen

Like Melkweg in Amsterdam, Vega is close to having a purely market-based business model and struggles with the pressures of the live music industry boom.

A striking aspect of the situation in Copenhagen is that the city government has shifted its focus to large events. The government put more than 50 million euros into the construction of large venues owned by the multinational corporations Live Nation and CTS Eventim and increased the budgets for large events. Furthermore, Copenhagen and Denmark as a whole have a smaller and less diverse population and constitute a somewhat insular northern periphery. The small-country mentality is revealed in the excitement about large events featuring Anglophone global culture. The news media in Denmark have generally been enthusiastic about the festival boom and the live music business boom. I was interviewed dozens of times by national news media in the late 2000s and early 2010s and witnessed how journalists became less critical of the festival business by the late 2010s. For instance, news stories about events and trends in the cultural field, such as the advent of a new festival and the growth in cultural sponsorship, would increasingly be based on industry sources alone, without any questioning of the industry's narratives. The media have covered budgetary and legal scandals in subsidized events, however. These scandals around the country show that mayors have sometimes been so invested in the idea of large events as tools for reelection that they have rushed decisions and bent rules to make their dreams come true.[18]

Experience Discourse

When asked about the performance culture in their clubs, the managements of Melkweg, AB, and Vega commonly turn to the word "experience." This experience discourse proliferated in all three countries, and I observed its evolution across a number of institutional domains in Denmark during the 2000s. The discourse developed from general corporate marketing interests in emotions and into the cultural field in the early 2000s. It penetrated the organizational field of rock clubs in the late 2000s. In 2009, for instance, the national association Danish Live organized a course for club managements to help them produce better "live music experiences" (I codeveloped and cotaught this course). In 2016, Vega's mission, as stated in its four-year plan for the national government, was to create "a total experience of the highest quality" characterized by "perfect sound, beautiful architecture, and welcoming service staff" ("Ansøgning om at være regionalt spillested i perioden 2017–2020: Vega," 6). This statement reflects an ideal that overlaps with classical music concert hall aesthetics, but the discourse primarily derives from corporate marketing and the tourism events industry (see p. 58). Vega's plan argues that the club fulfills a function in talent development that would not be undertaken by the market, but like AB's plan, there is little sense of this being an institution for a language and network of performance culture. Vega's plan also says little about the artistic and cultural ambitions outlined in the subsidy scheme. It is developed for a specific scheme for "regional clubs," which the national arts council implemented to transform eighteen clubs around the country into flagship platforms of the Culture Department's policy in the area. A core passage defining the scheme says:

> The regional clubs are different and each develops a unique and ambitious profile that challenges artists and audiences and puts the music and the musical experience at the center. ("Ansøgning om at være regionalt spillested i 2017–2020: Vega," 4)

Vega's application does not say how artists and audiences will be challenged. As in AB's plan, the baseline is to develop talent and serve as a leader in the national field of rock clubs ("Ansøgning om at være regionalt spillested i 2017–2020: Vega," 6).

"The Club Law"

The national government introduced a so-called club law (Spillestedsloven) in 2001 that incorporated a specific policy for clubs into national musical arts policy. This was an amendment to the music law, and it was very brief. It simply gave the national Music Council, a unit under the Department of Culture, a budget to subsidize "the production of music at rhythmic music clubs" and only those that receive subsidies for music production from city or regional governments ("Lov om ændring af musikloven," §3g–h). A limited number of clubs could achieve the status of "regional clubs" with fixed annual subsidies, and many of these clubs were in very small cities because the amendment was designed to serve all regions of the country equally. Alternatively, a club could apply for subsidies for individual events, specifically in the form of cofinancing of an individual artist's honorarium. The decision to only subsidize music production and not building maintenance, administration, and marketing contrasted with the situation for art institutions and might have been a means to avoid subsidizing an industry or creating a situation of unfair competition. When the Music Council considered subsidizing festivals in the early 2010s, in the wake of the festival boom, it decided against subsidizing large popular music festivals because they had become highly profitable.[19] By the end of the decade, these festivals were increasingly owned or dominated by international corporations and thus further removed from the sphere of arts policy. All of the subsidized clubs have been independent nonprofit clubs, even though this criterion is not stated in the amendment. The limiting of subsidies to music production means that the government does not subsidize networking activities, production facilities, and communication that could strengthen the ecosystem of music, performance culture, and public culture values.

The nonprofit clubs had lobbied for this amendment to the music law, arguing that clubs were important institutions of popular music. The consensus in the government hearings was that the amendment for clubs was an overdue recognition of popular music, more specifically the kind of popular music that was constructed as "good" popular music by musical arts policy and by nonprofit clubs. The term "rhythmic music" had defined public policy of popular music in Denmark since the 1970s and its urban ideology of "good" music discussed above.[20] For decades, "rhythmic music" was an umbrella term for genres that constituted an alternative to classical music and distinguished themselves from national folkloric and mass culture forms. It is therefore unsurprising that the Danish Folk Party was against the amendment and suggested the money be given to the mentally ill instead (Nødgaard 2000), adding that popular music could easily exist under market conditions.

Minister of Culture Elsebeth Gerner Nielsen stated that various projects and reports during the 1990s had demonstrated the need for creating proper conditions for popular music, and that clubs were central to this development. Clubs, she said, are "the physical setting of the genre's artistic realization" (Nielsen 2000). Nielsen's formulations reveal the influence of lobbyists working on behalf of the nonprofit clubs. They planted the idea that clubs are essential to the vitality of musical culture and to talent development. The idea of the club's role in the ecosystem of musical culture eventually shifted to focus on the ecosystem of the music industry, however. Furthermore, the institutionalization of clubs served a bureaucratic purpose. This surfaced in a 2002 news story about a report commissioned by the city government of Copenhagen:

> The four concert places are, so the report says, in the process of becoming cultural institutions like those one can find elsewhere in cultural life. "From the administration's perspective, the subsidies in the past few years have worked as intended. The attempt at professionalizing rhythmic music clubs is still new. It has happened, however, and the clubs have consolidated in the past couple of years, so they are ready to take the next steps," says Merete Evers, who is head of the city's Department of Culture and Leisure. (Bjerregaard 2002, 6)

The government wanted to institutionalize clubs, and the clubs were playing along. The clubs had an interest in showing that the subsidies had the intended effects, as this increased their chances of receiving more subsidies.

The politicians' limited expertise in the music field surfaced in the minister of culture's summary of the hearings in 2000. Nielsen mentioned the pop band Aqua as an example of what the amendment could sustain in the future (Nielsen 2000). Aqua was a pop sensation that had played in the city's disco clubs and thus represented the antithesis of rhythmic music. The minister had seemingly not understood the basic value systems in the field. The lobbyists may well have introduced a narrative about clubs functioning as the breeding ground for tomorrow's pop stars. Whatever the reason, the government and the amendment did not establish clear criteria for policy in the field.

Another limitation of the amendment was the annual budget of about four million euros for all clubs in the country. This budget has helped the nonprofit model survive, but it has not improved the conditions for realizing the full potential of this model. The amendment gave hope to the national club association, and its leadership in the late 2000s and early 2010s succeeded in developing closer relationships with key politicians in parliament. The association also shaped policy recommendations for the national Music Council, arguing that a larger budget is necessary if the true potential of nonprofit clubs is to be realized (Laursen et al. 2010, 28). The association's momentum has faded, however. It has not been able to convince the parliament that the institution is worthy of more subsidies. Furthermore, the wider public has become more interested in festivals, and austerity policies that cut culture and education spending, with the savings being used to partially funding tax cuts and elderly care, have led to a general stasis in cultural policy.[21]

The challenging situation faced by nonprofit clubs is illustrated by Vega's experiences. The idea of creating Vega emerged in the early 1990s among a small group of managers of local nonprofit cultural and educational institutions. They were not from the recording industry or the corporate live music industry. These managers wanted to create a new platform for the popular music field by integrating a handful of institutions into one building—a concert club, a union, a research institute, a library, and music industry associations. Only the club was established, so the idea of a larger institutional complex for popular music was lost. Vega's first manager assembled a team of six managers who worked together to create "the perfect venue" (Jens Rottbøll, conversation with the author, December 30, 2011). They purchased high-quality audiovisual equipment, optimized the building for the efficient movement of the musicians' equipment, and created an air-conditioning system that was unprecedented in the city's rock clubs. "We wanted clean air and had often been bothered by smoke-filled clubs," said the manager (Jens Rottbøll, conversation with the author, December 30, 2011).

The club was located in the neighborhood of Vesterbro, the most intensely gentrifying neighborhood in the city.[22] I experienced building renovations and changes in demographics and consumption firsthand as a neighborhood resident between 1993 and 1996. Subsidized renovations of apartment buildings began in the early 1990s, and Vega was created in 1996 with six million euros in subsidies (1996 figure), as part of the city's status as a European Capital of Culture (ECOC) that year.[23] The management had six months to prepare the club to meet the ECOC deadline and did not research clubs outside the country (Jens Rottbøll, conversation with the author, December 30, 2011).[24] The project had two major limitations from the outset. First, the building was sold to a private investment firm, which then rented it to the club, and this has led to high rent ever since (the management requested that I not publish the figure). Second, the club was created as an ECOC project without a sustainable, long-term business model. As a consequence, the club had a revolving door of managers in the first decade of its existence. To make the business more sustainable, Vega began in the 2010s to serve more as a rental space for booking agencies, presenting greater numbers of Anglophone headliners (Jens Rottbøll, conversation with the author, December 30, 2011; Trevor Davies, email to the author, October 14, 2011; Torben Schipper, email to the author, October 19, 2011). In several instances, a headliner concert was first scheduled in Vega but moved to a larger venue when a booking agency wanted to capitalize on the potential showed by early ticket sales. This phenomenon demonstrated how the evolving market forces challenged the nonprofit model.

Steen Jørgensen, manager since 2010, has considered various possibilities for improving the Vega's financial situation. He has contemplated moving the club to a place with lower rent farther away from the center, but he is attached to the current building. His main objective has long been to establish a larger performance space. He is convinced that this is necessary for Vega's survival (Steen Jørgensen, interview with the author, October 18, 2016). A larger space could fend off competition from a growing number of for-profit venues with a similar or slightly larger audience capacity, counter growing pressures from booking agencies, and help Vega continue producing a certain number of unprofitable concerts in the organization's smaller spaces. Jørgensen has promoted the idea of having Vega become a national performance institution of popular music similar to AB in Brussels.[25] This plan has been impossible to realize given the general policy situation described above.

However, attempting to replicate the market expansion poses an inherent challenge to the nonprofit model, since it brings the club further into the for-profit domain of the market. If a club regularly produces concerts in the for-profit domain of large concert spaces, it participates in this value system and its organizational network. Indirectly, musical arts policy would also become further embedded in the for-profit value system. In other words, organizing more profitable concerts can help a nonprofit club cover expenses and retain elements of nonprofit idealism, but at what cost?

The commercial institutionalization of popular music is thus a challenge not only to the nonprofit model for club organizations but also to cultural policy. The growing market exploitation reduces the playing field for nonprofit values. Vega illustrates multiple layers of complexity in this transformation, as it was born out of commercial motivations, shaped by gentrification and the development of the concert industry, but also by a local tradition of nonprofit idealism, and it was never profitable enough or recipient of sufficient subsidization to realize its vision of a nonprofit club. The organization was eventually squeezed by for-profit rivals in the market. A nonprofit tradition of popular music was thus challenged by the dominant forces in a growing live music industry and, perhaps more surprisingly, by the city and national governments. In the 2010s, the municipal government increasingly subsidized the live music industry to exploit the forms of prestige and city marketing associated with the notion of live music. The developments in this decade can be detailed further:

- *For-profit growth in the midsize range*: At least two for-profit organizations have entered the field of rock concerts in midsize venues: Bremen (2010–present) and K. B. Hallen (2019–present). The latter is a larger venue that can also be used for concerts in the midsize range. In addition, the historic Tivoli Gardens (1843–present) expanded its pop concert programming beyond the Friday night rock music series that began in 1997.
- *Corporate development of larger venues*: Two large venues have been created, Royal Arena (2017) and K. B. Hallen (2019), that are both operated by international live music corporations. Royal Arena presents concerts with great frequency and is thus commandeering a greater share of the media attention and market at the cost of smaller venues. It presents a large number of superstar concerts because Live Nation, which operates this arena, has a financial interest in filling its own venues around the

world, leading to an expanded touring geography of the superstars with whom the company works. K. B. Hallen is operated by CTS Eventim-FKP Scorpio.

- *City self-interest and the mayor's self-promotion*: The city government and large philanthropic foundations based in the city subsidized the construction of Royal Arena and K. B. Hallen. For the city government, these venues have been given priority at the level of the mayor's office and received considerable subsidies because they generate high levels of media power, consumption, and tourism, as large architectural flagships that present superstar performers. The city government co-owns Royal Arena and took the initiative to create this arena; Live Nation did not. For the mayor, Royal Arena was also a tool for boosting his popularity and shaping his personal legacy.[26] The corporate philanthropists had an interest in creating architectural monuments and showed no particular concern for the city's musical cultures or for musical arts policy.
- *Neighborhood self-interest*: More neighborhood administrations in the city have promoted the development of local flagship venues. This includes a club in the neighborhood of Amager and K. B. Hallen in Frederiksberg.[27]
- *Self-interest among national cultural institutions*: In 2009, the Danish Broadcasting Corporation opened a concert hall with a capacity for 1,800 that is also used as a venue for rock concerts. Midsize nonprofit clubs in the city perceived this venue as a competitor.

Conclusion: Toward a Policy of Musical Performance Culture

The analysis above provides nuance to the argument presented at the beginning of this chapter. While public policy played a key role in establishing the nonprofit model as the dominant model in the organizational field of rock clubs, government support for clubs and in turn nonprofit popular music production has declined during the live music industry boom. The allure of live music, embodied in consumer culture festivals and arena superstar concerts, has put a spell on powerful institutions in society—city governments, the media, and corporate philanthropy. Furthermore, the funding mechanisms for national musical arts policy have been hobbled by austerity. The upshot is that clubs have increasingly been left to the market, with the rare exception of AB in Brussels, which was promoted at the national level and demonstrates some of the potential of a public institution of popular music performance. Melkweg, Vega, and many other nonprofit clubs face the challenges associated with serving more as a rental space for booking agencies, and their programming has become less culturally diverse as a result. The oldest organizations in this study, Melkweg and AB, were conceived within a nonprofit value system, and subsidies helped maintain this value system.

Melkweg and Vega's experiences illustrate how the nonprofit model is challenged. The primary cause is not declining subsidies, but the general commercial institutionalization of the organizational field, involving market growth, the rise of international corporations, and a growing dependency on stars in a distribution system dominated by these corporations. This situation is particularly contradictory in the case of Vega, which was founded from more commercial motivations than Melkweg and AB but is suffering from market competition to a greater degree. As these clubs adapt to their changing environment, they also become less distinct alternatives to for-profit clubs, and they are increasingly reduced to being platforms of consumer culture, as opposed to being platforms of alternatives to this value system and promoting broader conceptions of musical culture. In all three organizations, a growing number of key positions were being filled by people with for-profit backgrounds during the 2010s.

Another general consequence of the political and commercial institutionalization of the rock club is the lack of attention to performance culture. The club has for decades been defined through a policy discourse on music, not a discourse on musical performance. The clubs themselves have lost sight of a broader understanding of musical performance culture in their transition into a speeded-up industry of standardized concert production, defined by a mechanistic language of business models and capacities and by booking rather than curation. Musical arts policy provided a rationale for subsidizing performance organizations as institutions of music genres, but it has not recognized the particulars of performance culture. Why are there policy criteria only for the kinds of music that a club presents, but not for the kinds of performance spaces and rituals that it employs?

A policy of popular music performance could address issues such as architectural design, ritual, and standardization as key elements that define meaning and value in performance. Should the goal of popular music performance, for instance, be limited to the perfected concert hall, or are there other models of performance culture that might be relevant to public culture values? How might a public policy of performance stimulate attention to issues besides the programming of desired forms of music and the perfected concert experience? How might lessons from the social study of music, including the sociology of performing bodies, contribute to higher levels of social justice, specifically with respect to gender and to growing international populations?

Such cultural and political reflexivity could bring long-overdue changes to popular music policy, which has now been dominated for more than a decade by the ideology of talent development in a depoliticized genre system. Current policy narratives are passively conforming to rather than seeking to balance broad changes such as gentrification and the proliferation of Anglophone global consumer culture. These changes explain the shift in aesthetics to contemporary indie rock and pop with pop sensibilities and, to some extent, rap and techno. They also explain the decline of the term "rhythmic music" in Denmark.[28]

A performance culture with a stronger commitment to artistic experimentation and to public values, such as difference and social justice, could be achieved by subsidizing more socially diverse organizations and by focusing more on resources for cultural labor, reducing the subsidy of routine production of standardized commodities. AB in Brussels demonstrates some public culture potential, but other models are relevant, too, including the possible relocation of clubs to lower-income areas, which would also reduce the operating expenses. Finally, it is relevant to consider alternatives to bureaucratic institutionalization. More grassroots-based and collectivist organizations would create other environments for performance and experimentation. All of this can be done at a fraction of the cost of an arena or an opera house.

Music Festivals in the Summer Season

: 6 :

A Worldview History of Music Festivals

The Roman carnival is a festival that is not given to the people but that the People gives to itself.

JOHANN WOLFGANG VON GOETHE, *Das römische Carneval* [1788] 1953, 897

The music festival has become a dominant performance institution across many music genres and a fixture of the broader cultural landscape in the Global North in the early twenty-first century. Music scholars have explored festivals in individual music genres, but a broader discussion of the history and significance of music festivals in musical culture and in society is lacking. Such a discussion might most usefully begin by recognizing that music festivals are part of complex developments in culture and society and that any analysis of the implications for music history therefore requires considerable engagement with social theory. The conception of the festival as an institution and of its commercial institutionalization can provide key insights.

What is known about the growth of popular music festivals and their cultural transformation? Cultural economist Bruno Frey suggested in 1994 that the booms in festivals for classical music and opera were largely due to growing prosperity and leisure time in postwar Western Europe and that festivals represented an alternative to the institutional inertia of the concert hall (Frey 1994). Frey's argument can be expanded to festivals for other music genres and can inform an analysis of changing value systems. Aspects of the commercial institutionalization of the popular music festival have been registered in the literature on popular music festivals. From George McKay's remark about Glastonbury's corporate turn in the mid-1980s to Roxy Robinson's survey of the field as a saturated market of multidimensional experience designs, stars, and vacation packages, the literature suggests that popular music festivals have been developed into mass-market commodities by a cultural industry (McKay 2000, 20; Robinson 2015; St. John 2017a). The evolution of many festivals into mass-market music and celebrity culture in the 2010s has further transformed the field, with headliners, such as Ariana Grande, Beyoncé, Ed Sheeran, and Taylor Swift, who also appear at sports mega-events. The popular music festival field has evolved in international networks governed by the norms of consumers, cultural industries, and cities, while still promoting images of authentic civic festivity.

How might the development of popular music festivals into new forms of consumer culture shape the imagination of festivals in society and their function in musical culture? Have the outlook and functions of seasonal musical festivity fundamentally changed? What kinds of intellectual response, if any at all, might be meaningful if the field of music festivals as a whole is increasingly framed in terms of consumption and commerce?

My objective in this and the following chapters is to analyze the commercial institutionalization of the popular music festival in the context of the longer history of music festivals in modernity. A theoretical and historical understanding of the festival institution is essential to the analysis of transformations in the social imagination and functions of popular music festivals in contemporary life. The longer historical perspective of modernity will provide opportunities for developing the theoretical framework and the conception of the social study of music, as detailed in the introductory chapter.

Music Festivals and the Social Study of Music

A review of knowledge interests in festivals in music studies is relevant to develop the more specific objective of the investigations and how they might advance the social study of music. My argument is that music festivals have been a topic in music studies since the 1980s, when ethnomusicologists took inspiration from the discovery of cultural festivals in history and anthropology during the 1970s, but that music festivals remain a specialist topic. The relevance of music festivals to the study of musical culture is not recognized in discourse on music studies. A discussion of insights across specialized festival literatures can help correct this situation and contribute to a broader field-sensibility among these literatures.

Scholarship on music festivals has generally been driven by the individual scholar's passion for a particular kind of festival and musical culture. Working at the margins of disciplines and institutions, festival scholars have often implicitly assumed the role of the engaged insider and explored narratives of the culture's life cycle, expressing nostalgia for its golden age and concerns about its survival. Such an approach can be an obstacle to critical research, limit the available subject positions, and produce narrow area studies narratives.

Festivals are generally absent in discourse on musicology and the interdisciplinary field of music studies. Textbooks do not have a chapter on festivals, and festivals are not a topic in edited volumes that contemplate the state of the discipline. For instance, the second edition of *The Cultural Study of Music* (Clayton, Herbert, and Middleton 2003/2012) added a chapter on performance but not on festivals. As of 2019, the extensive handbook series produced by publishers such as Oxford, Cambridge, and Bloomsbury had covered numerous topics in musical culture, but not festivals. Music history textbooks usually offer a brief discussion of festivals in a chapter on a broader theme (e.g., Butt 2002; Garofalo and Waksman 2016). This reflects how festivals have only occasionally been a topic of broader cultural interest in society. The prioritization is justifiable from a music-centric perspective, since festivals have had limited direct influence on the development of styles and genres. It does, however, exclude an important dimension of musical culture. The outlook of music festival literatures explains why it has been difficult to create more general narratives of the field in academia and in popular spaces such as Wikipedia. When I checked the Wikipedia entry on "music festivals" in 2017, it simply provided a flimsy definition and a list of names of festivals in different genres and areas ("music festivals"). The entry for "festival" was more substantial but only mentioned music festivals in passing.

Festival scholarship can do more to explain the significance of festivals for musical culture. Scholars have produced valuable accounts of individual music festival traditions, but a broader discourse of music festival studies has not yet emerged. In addition, there is little discussion of the purposes of festival research and its relevance to music studies. In popular music studies, the growing literatures on rock and electronic dance music festivals acknowledge influences from other genres, but this work essentially constitutes a form of area studies that can be identified as genre studies. There is little evidence of attempts to craft inclusive and pluralist narratives in this work. These studies are not individually or collectively building bridges, for instance, to research on festivals of blues, jazz, folk, gospel, polka, tango, metal, and schlager, to name a few examples. Genre studies serve a purpose but can limit conversations about the history and theory of music festivals.

Another challenge is that the growing power of commerce and consumption has discouraged scholars with critical humanist knowledge interests and generated a somewhat uncritical literature. Liana Giorgi and Monica

Sassatelli suggested in 2011 that accelerating consumerism contributed to a decline of humanist interest in cultural festivals in the late twentieth century (Giorgi and Sassatelli 2011, 5). Since then, scholarship on festival consumer culture has emerged in fields such as event management and cultural industry studies. The only field in which festivals have a central place today is the vocational field of event management, and that field generally studies festivals from an events industry perspective. The only Anglophone journal with the word "festival" in its title is the *Journal of Festival and Event Management*. Robinson's (2015) and Anderton's (2018) monographs represent this trend in event management and cultural industry studies. Robinson's extensive personal and professional experience at many festivals shows in her understanding of the field and the tendencies illustrated by Boomtown Fair and Secret Garden Party in the United Kingdom. The book demonstrates the potential gains in combining cultural research with applied interests, but it also betrays some of the limitations. From the outset, the focus is on empirical developments in design, not on broader humanist knowledge interests or conceptual issues. Reflections on consumerism and commercialization pop up here and there in the book, but they are not integrated into the theoretical discussion. As a whole, however, the book is an important contribution to the field, and it represents a new type of festival research that expands the field of inquiry into issues of cultural production.[1]

The Functions of Festivals in Musical Culture

What is the significance of music festivals in musical culture, then? I should like to provisionally identify two functions, a festive and an institutional function. Together the two functions help explain core dynamics of cultural festivals and the specificity of music festivals.

The Festive Function

The festive function is built into the festival concept and derives historically from celebrations during seasonal holidays. A modern cultural festival such as the music festival is a large seasonal event with a program of music that cannot be found in other events. The program is specific to this performance institution and contributes to its particular festive character. The festival, a seasonal cultural event built around a series of musical performances, is the most extensive form of cultural festivity in musical culture. The concentration of people and performances in one place, once a year, creates a sense of extraordinary festivity and attracts broader attention in society. It also creates expectations for an annual restatement of its values and celebration of the past, present, and future of a musical culture.

Many music festivals disrupt everyday routines in their immediate local area and in news media. When a festival assumes a presence in streets, traffic, bars, and restaurants through posters, electronic communications, and moving crowds of festivalgoers dressed for the occasion, festivalgoers might experience the festival as the center of attention of the wider social world, sometimes an entire city. This contributes to a feeling of collective liminality in the sense of a suspension of everyday social order and a transformation of this order into a condition of festivity. The festivity is generally most intense in the festival space itself, enhanced through various ritual and sonic techniques of distancing from the outside world and through the construction of utopian dimensions. The utopianism typically involves the imagination of the music's universalism and a retreat to primordial instincts of nature in the greenfield festival.

The festivity produced through music programming motivates audiences to travel longer distances to attend the festival. The extraordinary programming and scope of the festival, which separate it from events in everyday life, also attract broader audiences and media attention. The combination of musical and social festivity in the festival event not only makes music part of a social experience for participants, but also involves the experience of a musical culture that expresses its own values and worldviews. The festivity involves opportunities for and expectations of extroverted theatrical collectivity. Participants are imagined to be performing for the world—even when only a tiny part of the world is present. The festival space becomes a metonymic space for the culture as a whole, and the festival therefore often becomes a target of debates about the values and ethics of that culture. Even festivals for music with a small audience can surface in mass media such as newspapers, broadcast radio, and television.

The social psychology of festivity was central to the work of Victor Turner. In particular, Turner provides an understanding of the relationship between cultural festivity and everyday social life, although some of his arguments are specific to particular forms of theater. A performance, he says, takes stock of the known world and creates "magic mirrors" through which participants can recognize and experience events and relationships in quotidian life (Turner 1982, 11; Turner 1988, 22). Turner further suggests that performance has a function in collective psychology, stating that "the roots of theatre are in social drama" and that many genres of cultural performance evolve from "the experiential matrix" of social drama (Turner 1982, 11 and 78). One might object that Turner's interpretation is somewhat functionalist and specific to the cultures he studied in African villages in the 1950s. Like the anthropology of traditional rituals and large festive events such as carnivals, Turner's thinking was not developed for the music festival, which through much of its history has been defined by musical performance events and not by the rituals of an entire local community. However, Turner provided a more dynamic understanding of symbols in anthropology that is still widely relevant to the social study of cultural performance. He showed that symbolic systems are not static but instead transform in performance, and this is relevant to understanding the significance of festivals in musical culture.

The Institutional Function

The festival is a self-institutionalizing and self-traditionalizing event with its built-in regularity and continuity. It is expected to happen at the same time every year, in the same place, and to continue indefinitely with a recognizable symbolic order. In this sense, the festival is an institution with a cyclic logic. It mediates tradition by programming both legends and new talents within a genre. Artists and audiences perceive the festival as a seasonal celebration of their music and culture, and the festival is a major source of income for professional artists in many genres. Broader local populations perceive it as a fixture of their city or region and appreciate when a festival organization shows long-term engagement in their community. A sense of collective concern can therefore arise in a culture world and in a city when a festival is in crisis. The music festival, moreover, exists in a dynamic relationship with everyday institutions in a field of cultural production. Music festivals variously complement and compete with each other in a festival field and with everyday institutions. The institutional function of the festival is complex because it is defined not only by the festival itself, but also by the culture it serves and by market structures.

Music festival traditions have often evolved from a cultural moment, an excitement about new music and new sensibilities. The formative stages have often involved amateur organizers and performers. In some traditions, festivals have evolved from loosely structured events that gathered momentum and eventually crystalized into the longer and cyclic festival event. The festival subsequently becomes more regularized, more professionalized, and in some cases co-opted by economic and political institutions as an instrument of cultural and economic power.

Once the identity of a festival has crystalized into a more fixed form, major changes become risky. Typically, the festival will present new artists that play the same kind of music, or it will adapt to changing tastes by co-opting new styles. The architectural environment might be updated, but a festival tends to stay in the exact same location and rarely moves to another city or region. In some festival traditions, music has become an agent of institutionalization, especially as the initial cultural moment fades but interest in the music persists. Festivals have frequently evolved into institutions for individual music genres and are evaluated in terms of how they represent the genre. Are the most important representatives of the genre featured? Debates along these lines can be found in the public spheres of many music genres, from music magazines read by bourgeois Germans in the nineteenth century to bluegrass festivals in the 1960s, Dylan's electric shock at Newport in 1964, and beyond to current social media debates about whether pop festivals have become too commercial and too mainstream. Debates reflect stagnation or change and demonstrate public interest. The authority that comes with being an institution in musical culture bestows prestige on festivals, which is appealing to artists and the recording industry. In the 2010s, stars such as Dolly Parton and Beyoncé have appeared at iconic pop festivals, including Glastonbury and Coachella, not because their careers have evolved from or with that specific festival tradition, but because they bring value to the type of cultural event that the festival has become and benefit from their association with it.

Attention to the two social functions outlined above is relevant to the study of many music cultures. For instance, what forms of music have been institutionalized in festivals and how? How have festivals shaped ideologies of musical experience? What is their role over the course of a lifetime for audiences and artists? How do festivals complement other forms of musical and social life in society?

I would like to conclude this discussion of the music festival's functions in musical culture by outlining some potential avenues of inquiry. The social study of music can usefully consider the role of music festivals in:

- musical and cultural traditions
- ideas about authentic musical festivity and musical experience
- festivalization of music curation and performance culture more generally
- lived musical and social experience
- institutions in musical life
- musical employment and business

A sociological and musicological understanding of institutions can thus help structure different levels of analysis and conceptions of the object of study. One implication is that the individual festival is best analyzed not as an entity in itself, but also in terms of its functions in a culture and as part of the broader history of the festival institution. Another implication is that analysis of individual practices and experiences in the phenomenologically complex microspheres of a festival might usefully consider issues of regulation within the symbolic order and political economy of the institution. Robinson (2015) points out that individual festival models shape the terms of participation and consumption, and an analysis of regulation might consider a wide range of analytical entities, including music programming, marketing, public policy, and genre. The investigations in the following section and in chapter 7 concentrate on the symbolic order in music festival traditions as a focal point in the analysis of the transformation of the institution. The core analytical narrative focuses on the type of symbolic formation that I identify as a cultural worldview.

A Cultural Worldview History

Unlike performance institutions in everyday life, the festival is a cultural event with a symbolic world on a larger scale. Clubs, too, create a symbolic world, but they are generally smaller gatherings with fewer artists. Concert clubs routinely present two concerts per night in one space and promote one artist, while festivals tend to promote an image of a cultural event, not just individual artist names. While analysis of symbolic worlds is relevant to the club institution, it is central to the festival institution.

This book's conception of cultural worldview is grounded in social theory of festive events, specifically symbolic anthropology and sociology. Theoretical work on this topic, explored in more detail below, shares the idea that festive events evolve from social relations and therefore also from value systems and mythologies in everyday life and across a longer cultural history, and that festive events celebrate and institutionalize collective symbolic worlds that I subsume under the general term "worldview." The worldview concept can provisionally include a diverse range of conceptions of the "world," as understood in Victor Turner's sense of "the known world," which is the world that communities construct from experience and probe in performance (Turner 1982, 11). Many festivals have centered on the symbolic sphere of a genre, a city, a cultural class, a social movement, a lifestyle, or a combination thereof. The interpretation of music festival history in this book is to some extent a history of changes in known worlds across the urban Global North.

A cultural worldview furthermore involves the imagination of boundaries between the familiar and the unfamiliar, past and present, insider and outsider, nationalism and internationalism, center and periphery. The festival location is part of this process of imagining and becomes an agent in experiences of belonging to a cultural world. Some festivals have articulated their worldviews more actively and explicitly, especially festivals that participate in major social change. Corporate consumer culture festivals, on the other hand, tend to be less reflexive about their worldviews and how their boundaries are performed. But even the seemingly placeless and escapist culture of the EDM pop festival performs a worldview. It celebrates the sounds, fashions, and brand culture of an Anglophone global consumer culture.

Cultural worldviews are evolving formations and therefore require historical inquiry. This book does not attempt to construct a theory of history, but instead proceeds from empirical explorations of difference and similarity in longer historical processes of change, especially in processes of commercial institutionalization. This approach is inspired by historical sociology, which emerged as a field in the 1970s interested in the relationship between social change and power relations, in "denaturalizing" social conditions by uncovering the paths that shaped them, and in looking beyond the systemic frameworks of functionalism (Calhoun 1998). History is essential to this book's interest in denaturalizing live music and the conditions of performance culture in contemporary society. The chapter approach further follows historical sociology in extending the notion of theory to include narratives of history as a form of knowledge that complements conventional ideals of theory in sociology (Calhoun 1998, 854). In this regard, the chapter is inspired by humanist traditions that work from the exploration of particulars and do not seek to develop a general theory of history. A forceful defense of the latter can be found in Hans-Georg Gadamer's *Truth and Method* (1960/1990), a work that demonstrates the power of knowledge produced from large-scale, longitudinal, empirical engagement with the past. The historical analysis carried out in this book explores the institutional dimensions of festivals in a number of traditions, primarily based on narratives produced by each festival tradition. It draws inspiration from Gadamer's explorative practice, sensibility, and principle of understanding self through the past, but it does not employ Gadamer's comprehensive doctrine.

How might the worldview concept be grounded more specifically in the anthropology and sociology of festive events? In both disciplines, a form of collective self-representation is widely believed to be an important aspect of festive events such as carnivals, celebrations, ceremonies, and festivals.

In anthropology, Turner's writing about "performance reflexivity" provides a useful perspective on thinking about the construction and function of worldviews. He describes this reflexivity as a condition in which participants act as representatives of a social group and "turn, bend, or reflect back upon themselves, upon relations, actions, symbols, meanings, codes, roles, statutes, social structures, ethical and legal rules, and other sociocultural components which make up their public 'selves'" (Turner 1988, 24). Turner adds that performance reflexivity is not a mere reflex or response to a stimulus, but that it is contrived (Turner 1988, 24).

A similar understanding of the psychology of public self is at the center of Robert Cantwell's concept of ethnomimesis, but with greater focus on symbolic space. Cantwell developed this concept in his study of the Festival of American Folklife and how the Smithsonian Institution, the festival's owner and promoter, has staged national self-representations on the National Mall in Washington, DC. One of Cantwell's objectives is to show how the festival "directs its gaze socially outward or downward" and to situate it in a history of powerful institutions incorporating representations of "the lowly" and exotic into their political agendas, a history that he traces back to Renaissance Europe (Cantwell 1993, 1–2). Much of the book explores the symbolic sphere of the Festival of American Folklife as a metonymic microcosm of the nation.

In sociology, Liana Giorgi and Monica Sassatelli have proposed that we think about cultural festivals as cultural public spheres (Giorgi and Sassatelli 2011). The public sphere concept explains important aspects of the symbolic sphere. Festivals, for instance, are spaces not just of exhibited content and scripted roles but also of performative engagements with a plurality of collective sensibilities and agendas. Giorgi and Sassatelli focus more specifically on the cultural festival with cosmopolitan sensibilities, conceiving it as a medium of experience and reflexivity within international cultural flows. This communicative emphasis follows from the public sphere concept, which is tied to a particular narrative in Western modernity. While Giorgi, Sassatelli, and the other contributors to the edited volume *Festivals and the Cultural Public Sphere* that introduced the concept did not follow Habermas closely in explicating their own arguments, they emphasized conventional ideas of public culture at a time when cultural festivals and the cultural field as a whole were being institutionalized as commerce-based leisure in large culture markets. Rising consumerism is acknowledged as a possible factor in the recent history of cultural festivals (Giorgi and Sassatelli 2011, 5), but it is not examined or integrated into the theoretical framework. One of the typical limitations in theorizations of contemporary cultural festivals is precisely this lack of grounding in the longer history of festivals in modernity. Giorgi and Sassatelli gloss over festivals before World War II as "traditional festivals" and thus overlook the formative moment of cultural festivals in the bourgeois public sphere and culture markets in the long nineteenth century.

This book draws on the social theories discussed above, but it adopts a broader historical approach to situate symbolic orders, interpreted as worldviews, within evolving festival traditions. The approaches discussed above illustrate how theory of the symbolic sphere tends to focus on the sphere itself within one culture without examining its evolution through major historical transformations such as industrial revolutions, world wars, and new systems of electronic communications that redefine the geographies and meanings of festive events.

Another key aspect of the analytical discourse adopted here is the contextualization of festivals within a wider range of festive events. The festival is a regularized form of festivity, an institution, and the music festival is a specialized cultural festival. Festivals not only evolve from, but also continue to coexist with other forms of festive events. To study only the regularized and specialized forms would leave one ignorant of the broader dynamics of festivals in society. The most important alternatives to the festival are one-off cultural events, whether in the form of smaller community-based events organized by amateurs, ceremonies organized by formal institutions, or large popular culture events organized by an events industry.

The empirical investigations that follow analyze the music festival institution from the perspective of evolving worldviews in individual festival traditions in modernity. The analysis explores the institution's evolution in national bourgeois traditions in the context of the Enlightenment and the French Revolution. It then explores transformations and the emergence of new worldviews, focusing on the legacy of civic festivity and humanism. Socialist and totalitarian worldviews are examined in this perspective and for comparative purposes. Next, I consider how World War II transformed the institution's trajectories in modernity and shaped the transatlantic flows from which the popular music festival emerged. Thus emerges the central theme of internationalization, which has been explored in scholarship on festive events before (Roche 2000; Giorgi and Sassatelli 2011), but not as a fundamental process in the history of the music festival as an institution. Music plays a unique role in processes of internationalization, and festivals bring music into localized, social experiences. Music festivals continuously track and reflect developments in music genres and thus introduce new fashions and international sensibilities. This perspective is explored in chapter 7, which argues that the music festival has evolved in a broader historical turn in Continental European modernity from national cultures to Anglophone global culture.

National Civic Cultures of the Eighteenth and Nineteenth Centuries

Music festivals first evolved from annual church celebrations in London cathedrals in the late seventeenth century into a tradition that was more independent from the church, with Handel's oratorios playing a central role (Butt 2002). This tradition then evolved into the broader secular music festival that was part of the new bourgeois cultural sphere and its culture markets. The bourgeois music festival tradition in England inspired similar traditions in Continental Europe. The German tradition focused on the most popular German symphonic composers (Porter 1980; Weibel 2006). It began in the 1810s and peaked midcentury. Samuel Weibel's dissertation on this tradition provides an exhaustive empirical account and adds nuance to Cecilia Porter's pioneering argument about the festival's place in bourgeois cultural life. Weibel documents inspiration from the Enlightenment, among other things. I should like to deepen and further contextualize this cultural history by expanding the investigation into conceptions of music and festivity in the Enlightenment and the French Revolution.

Song, Festivity, and Civic Culture in the French Revolution (1789–1799)

The worldviews of the bourgeois music festival and the revolutionary festivity were shaped by broader transformations in society. Feudal society gave way to a modern capitalist and democratic society in which new classes emerged to create their own public cultures. Jean-Jacques Rousseau and Johan Gottfried Herder were central figures in the intellectual history of the worldviews that shaped various forms of cultural festivity in the long nineteenth century. They expressed views later associated with the term Counter-Enlightenment, including a romantic nostalgia for emotional and social authenticity in premodern society. Music, and specifically song, was central to their thinking. Rousseau's and Herder's ideas of culture were not developed in relation to festivals—music festivals and revolutionary festivity emerged in Continental Europe after their deaths—but their cultural poetics, integrating aesthetics and ethics, found their most complete embodiment in civic forms of festivity shortly after their deaths. In festivals, or fests, as they were called in France ("fête") and Germany ("Fest") before "festival" became standard as a result of Anglophone influence in the mid-twentieth century, new publics constituted themselves through these new civic forms of cultural festivity. The civic dimension of music festivals can be identified in their organization (they were organized by civic associations) and in the mode of production, which involved amateurs. A defining characteristic of nineteenth-century music festivals was the large amateur choirs in which people would come into sensory being as a civic public through song.

In his "Essay on the Origin of Languages" of 1761, Rousseau asserts that music was fundamental to authentic communication and being in premodern societies (Rousseau [1761] 1998). He imagined that language was sung rather than spoken and that oral communication had therefore been more organic, intuitive, and musical than in his own time. Rousseau was more interested in music in the context of human communication rather than as a distinct art form. However, he argued that the aesthetic experience of singing had social and ethical potentials. For Rousseau, song communicated "the motion of life from one being to another, a form of contact and connection that relies upon the perception of another sentient being" (Simon 2004, 438–39). His idea of the transcendent powers of music further extended to music's capacity to surpass the realm of sensation and enter the realm of the moral (Simon 2004, 438–39).

Rousseau had direct influence on the culture of the Revolution through his pioneering ideas of musical simplicity and oral transmission of public opinion through song. He preferred unison singing and simple melodies, and he adopted a Parisian tradition of using old popular songs to reach a broad group of people (Geoffroy-Schwinden 2015, 36 and 41). During the Revolution, public opinion was considered a major force in overturning the Ancien Régime in 1788. Communal public singing in the streets and in festivals was perceived as a civic duty to support the Revolution and its ideals of community and nation (Mason 1996). Rousseau was idealized as a father of the Revolution and influenced composers, too. His thoughts on music had been inspired by events early in his life. In a 1758 letter he enthusiastically recounted a childhood experience of a spontaneous form of public festivity on a square in Geneva, where he lived at the time. His account expresses fascination with the conviviality of this occasion marked by improvised music and dance. He also appreciated the diversity of the crowd and female participation, which was not common at the time (Strong 1996, 122–24).

Herder was greatly influenced by Rousseau. In Herder's essays on folk songs of 1778–1779, the essays in which he introduced the concept of folk song, he states that poesy and song originate in premodern societies and in the light, easy language of the masses (Herder [1778–1779] 2017). He adopts the idea, moreover, of a symbiosis of language and music in song. Herder shared Rousseau's romantic appreciation of music's emotional and spiritual capacities, invoked through his use of the words "passion" and "soul." This language builds on a long tradition of Christian thinking about festivity, as illustrated by the following moment in *Paradise* in Dante Alighieri's *Divine Comedy*:

> And I could hear within the smaller circle's
> divinest light a modest voice (perhaps
> much like the angel's voice in speech to Mary)
>
> reply: "As long as the festivity
> of Paradise shall be, so long shall our
> love radiate around us such a garment.
>
> Its brightness takes its measure from our ardor,
> our ardor from our vision, which is measured
> by what grace each receives beyond his merit.
>
> When, glorified and sanctified, the flesh
> is once again our dress, our persons shall,
> in being all complete, please all the more . . ."
>
> (ALIGHIERI [1320] 1984, CANTO 14, LINES 34–45)

Alighieri conceives festivity in Paradise as a unique resource of human completeness. He imagines a sense of connection with God in a transcendental spiritual form, articulated in terms of brightness and warmth. These organic, sensory, and spiritual metaphors were central to Herder, who brought festivity into a secular realm. Consider the core passage in his conception of folk song:

> Song loves the masses, it loves to take shape from the common voice of multitude: song commands the ear of the listener and the chorus of voices and souls. (Herder [1778–1779] 2017, loc. 1253)

Herder's folk song essay draws from his international travels and his teaching experience at Riga's cathedral school between 1764 and 1769. The essay describes singing practices in Estonia and Latvia and anthologizes song lyrics from these countries. Herder's multicultural sensibility was lost on the dominant forms of nationalism that took inspiration from him. By contrast,

Herder's conception of unity in song was influential and gave birth to a new notion of civic festivity. Bohlman writes:

> Identifying the singular Volk was critical for Herder and his generation in the late eighteenth century, because it shifted musical creativity away from divine sources and associated notions of authenticity to a culture constituted of human beings, for whom music could also provide agency. (Herder and Bohlman 2017, loc. 1226–1228)

Festive Events in the Revolution

The historians who in the 1970s began to research the festive events of the French Revolution contributed new understandings of the Revolution and, indirectly, of the wider history of cultural festivity, too. Mona Ozouf pioneered a critique of the conventional focus on political discourse in writing about the Revolution (Ozouf 1976/1988). Ozouf showed that festivals were part and parcel of the affective and ritual character of the Revolution. This explains some of the Revolution's contradictions and why many scholars have found the Revolution mystifying (Hunt 2003, 2–3). The French Revolution gave birth to human rights and democracy, but also to terror and totalitarianism.

In the first years of the Revolution, the forms of festivity changed constantly, each event inventing the form anew. Festive events were improvised at the beginning of the Revolution and became more scripted and regularized out of fear of violence erupting, but they did not become standardized, cyclic cultural festivals. (For this reason, they can be identified specifically as festive events, not festivals.) Festive events emerged as responses and interventions within the larger social movement. Some were large events with long processions and formal rituals. Religious rituals and spaces were used and transformed into secular ones. Churches were turned into "temples of reason," and revolutionary leaders were celebrated instead of religious figures. Not only did revolutionaries remove Catholic rituals, but they also gained an aura of sacredness for their atheist cult (Hunt 2003, 9). These festive events featured costumes, symbols, and ceremonial forms inspired by Antiquity to create a sense of innocence and authenticity, to imagine new beginnings. The intention was not to recreate the past (Ozouf 1975, 381). The desire for new beginnings and freedoms also shaped the choice of event locations. Major events were held in open fields at the city limits. These areas were chosen deliberately as alternatives to places in the center imbued with tradition. They were also chosen because of the unrestricted panoramic views and absence of walls and street paths (Ozouf 1975, 376–77). Pierre-Antoine Demachy's 1794 painting *The Cult of the Supreme Being* provides a romanticized representation of these events.

The German Bourgeois Tradition: The Case of the Lower Rhine Festival

The civic music festival traditions that began in England in the 1760s and in Germany in the 1810s were fundamentally different from the festive events of the French Revolution. Above all, they were focused on concerts, organized within the sphere of musical institutions. They were not staged to coincide with political speeches and parades.

The origins of the music festival can be identified more specifically in the *cathedral festivals* in London during the 1690s. These festivals were choir festivals, expanding on annual celebrations. They combined cathedral and royal choirs into one to amplify the scale. Choirs had been massed before, but this now evolved into a regular phenomenon of its own with a social base in the choral institutions that began to proliferate throughout Europe in the eighteenth century (Butt 2002, 215). The phenomenon spread to other cathedral cities in the British Isles. It was a widespread trend by the 1750s. The Birmingham Music Festival represented the development of cathedral festivals into *civic music festivals*, which included secular music and celebrated individual composers. The Handel Commemorations in London in 1784 stimulated the further growth of music festivals around the country, and the festival movement peaked in popularity in the mid-nineteenth century, the same time as its German counterpart (Drummond [2011] 2016). The Birmingham festival almost exclusively programmed music by Handel from 1768 to 1829 (Weibel 2006, 61).

The small literature on British civic music festivals in the late eighteenth century distinguishes them from earlier celebrations in the church and among the aristocracy. Weibel states that this tradition marked a departure from feudal society, in which cultural festivity was organized by and for the aristocracy. Goethe wrote in 1788 that the Roman carnival was an event that "the People [gave] to itself" (Goethe [1788] 1953, 897), but the music festival that emerged a few decades later in Germany represented a new situation. In the music festival, the bourgeois class constructed its own symbolic order in the geopolitical realms of the city and the nation. Music festivals were organized by city-based civic associations, inspired by ideals of democracy, cultural education, humanism, and solidarity (Weibel 2006, 62). There was more space for these civic ideals in the early era of the 1810s and 1820s when the choirs and orchestras were largely made up of amateurs. As the festivals became commercially institutionalized, their values changed.

The German tradition started in cities of the Lower Rhine region, which had been occupied by Napoleon during the French Revolution. The Revolution intensified nationalism in the subsequent recovery era (Blanning 1989, 127), and music festivals became a site for performing national and bourgeois emancipation. Of particular significance to the bourgeois worldview was the regular programming of large-scale works by German-speaking composers, especially Beethoven and Handel. The evening concert on the first day of the festival was a Handel oratorio featuring a choir with an average of 547 singers (in the 1850s and 1860s). The second day usually concluded with a Beethoven symphony (Porter 1980, 217). The specific local dimension of the worldview can be identified in the organization: The festivals were organized by local associations and subsidized by the local city government. Their bourgeois symbolic order notwithstanding, festivals had the broadest social representation in concert life, incorporating women in mixed choirs and amateur singers from the surrounding region.

The German tradition is the first example in Continental Europe of a major growth spiral and commercial institutionalization. The growth spiral is a self-amplifying process in which the excitement about the growing scale of the event among both audiences and organizers leads to desires for further expansion. For organizers, expanding the festival was variously a strategy of survival and exploitation in the growing market competition. Organizers expanded their festival's audience capacity, programmed bigger stars, and produced more spectacular stage shows. This spiral eventually posed a structural challenge to the institution because the operating costs increased for all festivals in this organizational field. The recent growth spiral in popular music festivals illustrates how this process can be amplified by electronic media and international cultural industries (chapters 8–9).

The commercial institutionalization changed the cultural worldview of the bourgeois festival. Weibel's account shows that more priority was given to popular tastes and star performers, while the humanist aspirations of the Enlightenment weakened. In 1833, the Lower Rhine Festival added a third day with a virtuoso concert, and by the 1850s only a third of the soloists were amateurs and audiences had come to expect star soloists (Porter 1980, 219; Weibel 2006, 68). Moreover, the festival was defined by a perfected and formal concert presentation for larger audiences. Concert halls were renovated and expanded, requiring considerable investments.

Felix Mendelssohn-Bartholdy contributed to the boom in the 1830s as a musical director of the Lower Rhine Festival and of the city of Dusseldorf. Under his leadership, the festival changed from a Biedermeier-style folkloric gathering for passionate music lovers to a series of concert events marked by displays of pomp and high artistic ambitions (Weibel 2006, 68–69). Folkloric elements were eliminated in many festivals, which gained international recognition and began to attract people from the upper classes.[2]

How did the later stages of this growth evolve? Weibel notes that the music festivals remained popular for decades after the boom in the 1840s, but that the culture was exhausted by the high number of festivals. Their relevance started to be questioned. A general growth in concert life around the country further contributed to the decline of music festivals. Following the two world wars, the tradition was revived but has diversified, with many festivals dedicated to different composers, genres, and time periods. Moreover, popular music festivals have generally taken over the role as the dominant type of music festival in many cities, a good number of which have so many music festivals that it is less common in the twenty-first century to name the festival solely after the city in which it is held. Who would start a festival of any kind today and call it simply Hamburg Festival? Barcelona Festival? The proliferation of festivals is such that the need for differentiation exists even in much smaller cities, and many new festivals do not use the word "festival" in their name.

Socialist Festivity and International Humanism in the Twentieth Century

What kinds of cultural worldviews guided music festivals in the twentieth century? The final section of this chapter explores the evolution of international humanist worldviews in the mid-twentieth century in the context of totalitarianism, war, and colonialism. This history will provide a counterpoint to the worldviews explored in subsequent chapters.

The music festival literature excludes cultural festivity in totalitarianism and in times of war. These exclusions leave us with a limited understanding of music festivals in modernity. The history of musical festivity illustrates the extremes of human history, which are not just marked by communitarianism or consumption, but which range from freedom to oppression, colonial conquest, and genocide. Musical festivity has a history in military marching bands, in revolutions, concentration camps, social movements, churches, and schools. Broadening conceptions of musical festivity and its role in human history beyond contemporary popular music festival discourse is vital to the social study of music.

The End of the Lower Rhine Festival in the Holocaust

To that end, let us follow the trajectory of the Lower Rhine Music Festival into the twentieth century. The festival was in financial crisis in the early

1930s, due to growing competition from the city's orchestra and possibly also to the organization's inability to sustain a connection with local audiences. In 1931, the city government took control of the music association, which was on the edge of bankruptcy, and this formally ended the festival's long history of civic ownership (Hill n.d.). The economic depression in the 1930s had consequences, too. The city requested a drastic reduction in expenses for soloists, for instance. Hitler's rise to power in 1933, however, compromised the worldview in fundamental ways. A new city music director, Hugo Balzer, was appointed with the task of developing Dusseldorf as the German capital of music and implementing Nazi policies in all concert programming. The music of Mendelssohn-Bartholdy and other Jewish composers was banned, while musical glorifications of Hitler started to appear. Starting in 1933, Jews, the disabled, and mentally ill people were deported via buses and trains in Dusseldorf to concentration camps, where ceremonial music festivity was exploited by the Nazis (Laks 1979/2000). On Kristallnacht (the Night of Broken Glass) in November 1938, Dusseldorf synagogues were set on fire, Jews were murdered, and hundreds of homes and shops were destroyed (Fleerman and Genger 2008; Fleerman and Jakobs 2015). In 1940, bombings of the city started, the festival was paused, and neither the music association nor the festival ever fully recovered. The festival's last year was 1958. A small number of music festivals in Germany and Austria became instruments of the regime during the war, including the Wagner Fest in Bayreuth, the Mozart Fest in Salzburg, and the Day of German Art in Munich. After the attempted assassination of Hitler in July 1944, Goebbels announced that all festivals would henceforth be banned in the Third Reich ("Salzburg Beneath the Swastika").

Totalitarian and Socialist Festivity

Totalitarianism dominated large parts of Europe in the twentieth century, not just in fascist Germany (1933–1945), Italy (1922–1943), and semifascist Spain (1939–1975), but also in the Soviet Eastern Bloc between 1945 and 1989. Culture was often employed in simple forms of propaganda, but there is also a history of more complex artistic expression and humanist festivity in the socialist East.

German historian Malte Rolf has shown that the regimes in the Soviet Union, Nazi Germany, and fascist Italy all favored mass audience events in public urban spaces with marches and parades that displayed power and control (Rolf 2006/2013). They all used synchronized and choreographed movements for this purpose, as well as massive displays of symbols of power. One basic intent behind these events was honoring the leader. They were designed as monumental statements, in some cases intensified by electronic amplification and broadcasting. Cinema, too, played a role in the international proliferation of totalitarian festivity and the technological manipulation of civic festivity. The most prominent examples are Leni Riefenstahl's films showcasing the 1934 Nazi rally in Nuremberg and the 1936 Olympics in Berlin. These films created a cinematic spectacle of light and advanced a mythical, racist ideal of heroism and beauty. *Olympia* (1938), divided into a "festival of nations" ("Fest der Völker") and a "festival of beauty" ("Fest der Schönheit"), invokes the folk ideal of civic authenticity, particularly in the form of free will to participate and free collectivity.

In terms of cultural events, totalitarian regimes preferred athletic competitions for their capacity to discipline and display physical strength. The arts generally came in second or third and were often approached with the same general political agenda. In the mass events staged at the height of totalitarianism in the Soviet Union, Germany, and Italy, music was reduced to psychological and representational functions as a means to entice masses into "total war" against the perceived "enemies of the regime" (Rolf 2006/2013, 167). The regimes co-opted the folk concept from nineteenth-century national populist movements to forge unity from above and to control and mobilize the masses for regime causes.

In formative moments of Soviet socialism in the late 1910s, in the aftermath of the 1917 October Revolution, some Bolsheviks were inspired by the ceremonial pedagogy of the French Revolution. They adopted the blood-filled "La Marseillaise" before making the socialist "L'Internationale" the official Soviet anthem in 1918 (it was replaced by the "Hymn of the Soviet Union" in 1944). Moreover, ideas of civic festivity were debated, including the potential of the proletariat to express itself freely and become self-aware through celebration (Rolf 2006/2013, 37–38). Civic values began to be suppressed, however, as totalitarianism progressed. The Bolsheviks adopted the Western European working class as a role model, but May 1 celebrations turned into Red Army marches and group saluting of the dictator, like other Soviet celebrations. Celebrations of major holidays eventually became standardized, with a three-part structure. The first part began with the waving of the flag and speeches at a meeting of top party members and state officials. The second part consisted of military formations of the Red Army from morning until afternoon, concluding with a civilian parade in which schoolchildren were first in line. The third part was an evening program of entertainment, which in cities such as Moscow and Leningrad included games, movies, and performances of music, theater, and dance (Rolf 2006/2013, 65–68).[3]

The Postwar Humanist Moment

Festive events moved to the forefront of a new civic moment across East and West in the immediate aftermath of World War II. The scale of destruction and ethical violations together contributed to interests in transnational public order following such extraordinary devastation. A growing interest in transnational alliances for peace led to the formation of the United Nations and the organization that would eventually become the European Union. New worldviews were proposed by intellectuals such as Theodor Adorno, Erich Auerbach, Albert Einstein, and Hannah Arendt. Adorno and Max Horkheimer's *Dialectic of Enlightenment* proposed a rethinking of fundamental beliefs about modern society and particularly the mythology of Enlightenment. They argued that cultural progress had been turned into its opposite and that knowledge had not liberated humans from fear. "[T]he enlightened earth is radiant with triumphant calamity," they claimed (Horkheimer and Adorno 1947/2002, 1). Auerbach wrote one of the most ambitious and influential pieces of literary criticism (Auerbach 1953), one that contemplated Western literature from the position of an exiled European selfhood (Said 1983, 7–8). Einstein wrote several essays about peace, poverty, civilization, and the role of government and science (Einstein [1950/1978] 2011). His call for a new form of global government was echoed in Hannah Arendt's *The Origins of Totalitarianism*, completed in 1950. She wrote it "against the background of both reckless optimism and reckless despair" and challenged narratives of progress and doom as forms of superstition. Arendt felt that the brutality of recent world history called for a fundamental change: "[H]uman dignity needs a new guarantee which can be found only in a new political principle, in a new law on earth" (Arendt 1951/1966, vii and ix).

This international humanism motivated a diverse range of cultural events, from small art festivals to the Eurovision Song Contest. The first international event, and the largest nonmedia event, was the World Festival of Youth and Students. This event developed from Soviet models but also from sensibilities of an emerging global socialism. According to Rolf, the event was part of the general export of Soviet celebration and Stalinism (there was a Stalin celebration on the last night), but it was conceived in a new humanist world image and stands out from the many later events that celebrated Soviet occupation as a form of liberation (Rolf 2006/2013, 183–85). The event was less concerned with celebrating a leader and included a large program of sports, exhibitions, and performing arts. It combined the broad cultural programming of a festival with the global outlook of the Expos and Olympics. The humanist objectives were formulated at the founding meeting of the World Federation of Democratic Youth in London in November 1945. The concluding statement centered on the idea of the peaceful coexistence of all races and cultures:

> We pledge that we shall remember this unity, forged in this month, November 1945
> Not only today, not only this week, this year, but always
> Until we have built the world we have dreamed of and fought for
> We pledge ourselves to build the unity of youths of the world
> All races, all colors, all nationalities, all beliefs
> To eliminate all traces of fascism from the earth
> To build a deep and sincere international friendship among the peoples of the world
> To keep a just lasting peace
> To eliminate want, frustration and enforced idleness
> We have come to confirm the unity of all youths, salute our comrades who have died, and pledge our word that skillful hands, keen brains, and young enthusiasm shall never more be wasted in war
> ("WFDY")[4]

Rolf Schneider, a scholar in the former East Germany, participated in the event held in Berlin in 1951. In 1988, he described the festival as part of the propaganda machine. The official East German position portrayed the festival as a positive combination of political engagement with a festival-like experience of joyous international youth interacting freely with one another (Schneider 1988). Schneider's account indicates that he had an extraordinary experience, from the train ride to the crowds in the city and hanging out with a group of British festivalgoers. He gave up attending theater performances and concerts at night because they were overcrowded, but he remembers that for two weeks the mood in the country was more positive (Schneider 1988).

The festival's worldview was supported and interpreted by Pablo Picasso. He created images for the festival in 1951, 1957, and 1962 that were used for posters, postcards, and a scarf (see fig. 6.1). These images have a peace dove in the center. Two of them depict people of different colors united in a circle formation. In Berlin in 1973 the festival showed some openness to rock music and hippie culture and included appearances by Wolf Biermann, Miriam Makeba, and Angela Davis.

While contemporary, large popular music festivals exist in democracies, their programming gives strikingly less room to worldviews centered around global peace and multiculturalism. The corporate popular music

6.1 Graphic design by Pablo Picasso for the World Festival of Youth and Students for Peace, Berlin, 1951. *Courtesy of the Picasso Administration. Copyright Succession Picasso/ VISDA 2020.*

festival creates an environment of consumption that cannot accommodate social movements and generally does not include explicit political performances. Moreover, the live music industry is generally covered in a positive light; its ethics are generally not questioned by news media and audiences. News media and audiences barely reacted when it became known that industry mogul Philip Anschutz of AEG, the corporation that owns several arenas, the Bowery Presents, and festivals such as Coachella and the New Orleans Jazz and Heritage Festival, for years made donations to Republican politicians in the United States who voted against gun control, same-sex marriage, and a woman's right to abortion (Espinoza 2018; Burks 2019).

Future work might explore how the World Festival of Youth and Students influenced cultural festivity in leftist social movements in the West. The festival was likely an inspiration for the Festival of Britain in 1951, for instance. That festival had similar socialist-humanist aspirations and similarly adopted a multidisciplinary event concept. It was initiated and cosponsored by a Labour-led government and organized as an aggregate of several existing festivals and culture institutions. Churchill and the Conservative Party called it "three-dimensional Socialist propaganda" (Anderson 2007).

Music festivals began to proliferate across Europe in the late 1940s. At least thirty-four festivals in the nineteenth-century art music tradition were created in Europe between 1946 and 1953. Most of them appeared in countries in which this tradition already had a longer history—England, Germany, and France—but also in Central Europe and, in the 1950s, on the Iberian Peninsula and in the Nordic countries (Willnauer 2013). These festivals were all organized by independent promoters. Several of them, including Prague Spring (1946–present), Edinburgh International (1947–present), and Aix-en-Provence (1948–present), were motivated by the idea of art as a healing response to the humanitarian crisis and echoed the Enlightenment idea of musical performance as a means of civic authenticity and ethical collectivity. The nineteenth-century tradition was revived, but not in the prevalent midcentury form of a popular bourgeois culture. In the immediate postwar years, there was little business potential in a music festival.

The humanist moment faded, however. Within a decade, art music festivals had become focused on professional standards and artistic achievements. Edinburgh International is a case in point. The festival was born with the oft-cited goal of "providing a platform for the flowering of the human spirit." One of the inaugural concerts was by the Vienna Philharmonic, conducted by Bruno Walter, a Jew who had fled Germany during the war. They performed Mahler's dark, existential "Das Lied von der Erde" and Beethoven's Pastoral Symphony, an iconic piece of nineteenth-century symphonic art music (Cardus 2016). The festival also nurtured relations with Eastern Europe and brought Shostakovich over in 1962. However, the festival increasingly began to focus on artistic achievements in Western art music. Humanism became an element in the festival's origin narrative, not a central part of its contemporary outlook.

Like the bourgeois model of the nineteenth century, the postwar art music festival evolved into a professional institution. It built on existing professional traditions and institutions of art music, and it was shaped by evolutions in international media cultures. Many art music festivals adopt their music programming to segmented media audiences and to cultural internationalism. They tend to have a program of music from different countries and have adapted themselves to the needs of consumers in larger cities by stretching their programming over weeks, compared to the nineteenth-century length of two to three days and its fixed model of a symphony night and an oratorio night. Choir music thrives in opera festivals or in niche festivals such as the London Handel Festival. The large amateur choir and the idea of a singing national community no longer comprise a common core of art music festivals.[5]

Ethnomusicology and the Promise of Postcolonial Humanism

Another major development in the mid-twentieth century—with implications for cultural worldviews—was the collapse of European empires. This development stimulated a wave of postcolonial reflexivity that is relevant to an analysis of the Anglophone popular music festival and its politics of internationalism. Postcolonial reflexivity became part of the intellectual foundations of North American ethnomusicology, which emerged after World War II. At a fundamental level, ethnomusicology challenges the idea of music history as a history of self (Bohlman 2013). The discipline therefore also expands the social imagination of festival worldviews.

Ethnomusicologists began exploring festivals in the 1980s from the perspectives of tourism and cultural preservation. American ethnomusicologists, along with many Western tourists, attended folklore festivals in Eastern Europe, such as Bulgaria's Koprivshtitsa Festival and Zagreb's International Folklore Festival (MacMillen 2015; Ceribaši 1998). Ethnomusicologists argued that these festivals provided in-person experiences of local musical cultures but also created stereotypes and fictions of folk culture. Judith Cohen's longitudinal study of Festa da Istoria of Ribadavia, Spain, adopted a more critical approach and introduced a diasporic perspective (Cohen 1999). Festa da Istoria began in the late 1980s. Cohen described how the festival imagined the authentic survival of a local Jewish tradition, even though no Jews had lived in the area since the Expulsion in the late fifteenth century. This fiction of the past was created through the reconstruction of music repertoires and costumes and through the sacralization of buildings and reenactment of rituals. Performers appeared as insiders of the imagined tradition. In Cohen's field experience, most audience members were Spaniards with little knowledge of Jewish history. Her study drew attention to an ethical issue of broad relevance, also to klezmer festivals in Germany, for instance. How might the culture of an extinguished people be celebrated? What is there to celebrate? Is postcolonial performance reflexivity possible in music festivals?

Ethnomusicologists have also explored the role of modern institutions in transforming cultural worldviews. For example, Suzel Reily has argued that a festival of the Divine Holy Spirit in a small town in Southeast Brazil was transformed by the growing dominance of urban elites in the area and that this affected the community's relationship with the supernatural (Reily 1994). Thomas Hilder has demonstrated that festivals can create a sense of sovereignty for indigenous populations and that TV song festivals have expanded the presence of indigenous culture in mainstream society (Hilder 2017). Jeff Packman has explored how *sambadores* in the June festival in a poor black neighborhood in Salvador, Bahia, adapted to a new capitalist worldview (Packman 2014).

Finally, ethnomusicologists have pioneered postcolonial reflexivity and multiculturalism as music experts, diplomats, and activists at many festivals around the world. The Festival of American Folklife is an early, important example and a fitting case study on which to end this chapter, since it inspired Cantwell's idea of ethnomimesis as a particular dynamic in the symbolic sphere of festivals. This festival was created in 1967 by the Smithsonian Institution in Washington, DC. While the festival's multiculturalism was mostly developed by general folklorists in the 1970s, ethnomusicologists such as Anthony Seeger played an important role later on in promoting this worldview of the institution. Jeff Titon commented in the late 1990s:

> [The organizers of the Festival of American Folklife have] implemented a cultural policy that involves more than merely a demonstration and preservation theater. Theirs is a vision of a multicultural world living in harmony, celebrating mutuality while learning from one another's different traditions. (Titon 1999, 123)

This type of vision is nowhere to be found in contemporary Anglophone popular music festivals. The next chapter explores the origins and transformation of their worldviews to understand why.

: 7 :

The Evolution of Anglophone Global Culture

I just came from the Old World to here, to the New World.

JERRY RUBIN AT THE HUMAN BE-IN, SAN FRANCISCO, JANUARY 14, 1967

This chapter examines the origins and transformation of dominant worldviews in the Anglophone popular music festival in the process of its international commercial institutionalization, especially within the rock concert industry. The industry of electronic dance music festivals developed later and will be the subject of analysis in chapters 8–9. The chapter highlights the role of corporate cultural industries and the internet in accelerating the transformation of the popular music festival into an institution of Anglophone global culture in Continental Europe.

The chapter is structured chronologically into two large sections. The first half begins by exploring new forms of cultural festivity that were motivated by worldviews of neo-bohemian urban youth cultures in the United Kingdom and the United States in the 1950s and 1960s. It then explores the formative moment of commercial institutionalization in the United States in 1967 when the music industry developed the large hippie gathering into the hippie music festival. The festival declined in the early 1970s and was eventually reinstitutionalized, first in Europe and later in the United States. The second half of the chapter examines this development in Continental Europe, focusing on the festival as an institution of Anglophone global culture, drawing on theory of cultural globalization. This is examined through case studies of festivals primarily from Central and Western Continental Europe, but the analysis also traces Anglophone media flows into festivals in Iceland and Russia.

Festive Events in Neo-Bohemian Worldviews of the 1950s and 1960s

Although popular music festivals took inspiration from music festivals in other genres, particularly jazz and folk music festivals, they evolved out of a variety of festive events in urban cultural scenes and social movements in the 1950s and 1960s, the most influential of which were in London and San Francisco. Within these emerging countercultural and neo-bohemian worldviews of urban youth, festive events were a medium for experiencing and imagining a new world outside institutions of formal power. The evolution up to the commercial institutionalization of the popular music festival in 1967 had a structural similarity with the history of festivity in the French Revolution, in that an ongoing exploration of different forms of festivity was intimately linked with the evolving imagination of a new world. The affective power of rock music in hippie gatherings, its capacity to express collective sensibilities in this particular moment, and its mass-media circulation stimulated the rise of the hippie festival movement. The commercial institutionalization of hippie gatherings into the music festival meant that for-profit music organizations took over and expanded the production that had formerly been done by DIY grassroots organizers. The latter had used festive events to create collectivist social events for a scene and expand its worldview through a large-scale event. To the industry, however, the purpose was to create events that were profitable and to eventually grow a culture of annual festival consumption.

The Evolution of a White Mass Culture

While countercultural scenes were relatively socially inclusive, they were dominated by whites, and whiteness became a defining aspect of the festive events of the counterculture. Insider narratives of universal peace and liberation contrast with the fact that most artists and audiences were white, especially those who occupied roles as informal authorities of the movement. Sly and the Family Stone was a rare example of an interracial band, and Jimi Hendrix was subject to an exoticizing gaze that Bob Dylan and John Lennon were not. No black artists were allowed to assume the role of an authoritative voice of hippie and rock culture. Surely, the boundary between self and other in this worldview was not only between the young and those over thirty, who couldn't be trusted. The particular forms of racial and genre inclusivity notwithstanding, the dominant insider subject was a white subject, and the worldview was constructed from the language, ideas, and emotions of middle-class whites. In particular, the worldview was constructed from and through psychedelic rock music, which had elements of orientalism. Psychedelic rock stimulated the growth of festivals, from the first hippie festival in San Francisco in 1966—the Trips Festival for a few thousand people—to Woodstock, which hosted about half a million people, three years later. The media had a major role in regulating the movement, and they were institutions of white patriarchy. The movement's orientalism had alienating effects on people of color, which perhaps goes some way toward explaining Ravi Shankar's skepticism about Woodstock (Gross 1999).

A small number of popular music festivals organized by and for African Americans emerged in the late 1960s out of a different worldview. The two so-called black Woodstocks were organized in response to the violent events in the Civil Rights movement. The first was the Watts Summer Festival, a celebration of black culture on the anniversary of the 1965 riots in the Watts neighborhood of Los Angeles. This festival, which still exists, became famous for the one-day benefit concert held at the Los Angeles Coliseum in 1972 and the movie of that event released the following year (Stuart 1973; Maycock 2002). The other black Woodstock was the one-off Harlem Cultural Festival, a concert series that ran through two summer months in a public park in Harlem in 1969, the year after the assassination of Dr. Martin Luther King, Jr. The white hegemony of the popular music festival institution might explain why it did not become more popular in minoritized communities, where community festivals and festivals of traditional music have been more common. Since the 1980s, some festivals for urban, black middle-class youths have evolved. Examples include Essence in New Orleans (1994–present) and Afropunk in Brooklyn (2005–present), which was partly motivated by the ignorance in punk subcultures about blacks (Giorgis 2015).[1]

The worldview of white countercultural festivals was only partially shaped by the political culture. Countercultural expressions were a resource for protests against the Vietnam War and for the radical New Left more generally, but hippie gatherings and the subsequent music festivals were cultural events, not political events. Jerry Rubin, an activist of the New Left, appeared briefly at the Human Be-In in San Francisco in January 1967 to declare a boundary between "the new world" and "the old world," but his was not really a political speech. Abbie Hoffman's 1969 idea of a "Woodstock nation" highlighted the synergies between culture and politics that were experienced by many but not integrated into the programming of music festivals.[2] Rubin and Hoffman tried to organize a "Festival of Life" to mobilize antiwar demonstrations during the 1968 national convention of the Democratic Party in Chicago in 1968, but they were unable to get the required permission and the festival production was almost nonexistent. Only one band, the leftist MC5 from Detroit, ended up giving a performance, without a stage and using a power cable from a nearby hot-dog stand, after which the famous clash between protesters and police occurred (Josh Jones 2017). Other music festivals planned for political purposes were canceled because of disputes among organizers or because festivalgoers showed little interest in politics (Peterson 1973, 107).

The Genealogy of the Countercultural Music Festival

George McKay, a specialist in British countercultural history, has traced the evolution of the countercultural festival back to British youth scenes and social movements around London in the 1950s (McKay 2015). McKay shows how leftist (white) youths participated in a variety of festive events, including political marches and festivals, such as the Soho Fair and the Sidmouth Folk Festival in 1955, the 1956 Beaulieu Jazz Festival, the Aldermaston march in 1958, and the Trinidadian carnival in London in 1959. All of the events discussed by McKay are within relatively short driving distance from London, the most remote event being Sidmouth, about 170 miles away. McKay argues that a "new combined practice of music, politics and *festival*" emerged, and that this involved a synergy between grassroots organizers and the anticommercial sentiments of amateur folk and jazz music communities (McKay 2015, 16 and 23; emphasis in the original). McKay uses the word "festival" as a verb for a form of performative doing and sensibility across different kinds of events within a cultural movement. He thus extends the object of study from a type of event, the festival, to a form of cultural performativity, to cultural festivity. McKay suggests that cultural festivity was central to the psychology of these countercultural formations and that the turn to pastoral settings was a utopian practice of imagining a new era through festivals (Gordon 1970; McKay 2000). In this way, he provides substance to this book's comparison drawn between general aspects of the forms and functions of festive events in early countercultural history and in the French Revolution (see p. 171). Peterson's (1973) analysis of American hippie music festivals in 1967–1971 indicates that festival promoters were sometimes more interested in profit than in worldviews and that practical concerns played a role. The choice of a rural location, for instance, was also a way of avoiding practical problems in the city, such as confrontations with the police. Peterson's discussion suggests that the public images of festivals were coconstructed by mass media, which tended to make festivals seem more sensational and exotic.

In the United States, the core developments occurred in San Francisco in a progression of identifiable stages: (1) a series of small hippie gatherings called Acid Tests, which included musical performances in 1965; (2) the first nominal hippie festival, the indoor multiarts Trips Festival in 1966; (3) a number of "love rallies," also known as human be-ins and love-ins, the most prominent of which took place in Golden Gate Park in January 1967; and finally (4) the first concert-based music festivals in June 1967. One key aspect of this development is that the hippie festival—and therefore also the popular music festival—did not only evolve from the Newport jazz and folk festivals (Wein with Chinen 2003), but also from new conceptions of festive events in the counterculture. My argument is that these conceptions emerged from neo-bohemian sensibilities in urban cultural scenes and adopted the happening from experimental arts scenes.

First of all, the *be-ins* and *love-ins* explain the departure from the idea of the festival as a cyclical event. They likely took inspiration from the sit-in, a ritual of nonviolent civil obedience, which had been a powerful instrument for the Civil Rights movement in the first half of the 1960s and which in turn originated in Mahatma Gandhi's Satyagraha movement in India (King 1968, 45; Belafonte 2011, 211). The hippie festival was generally a one-off event and only evolved as a cyclic event in Europe, building on the tradition of countercultural jazz and blues festivals since the 1950s and on the free festival movement of the early 1970s (McKay 2000, 18). In Britain, the Reading Festival, for instance, had begun under a different name as a jazz festival in Richmond in 1961. In Europe, too, however, many hippie festivals ended after just a few years. This is illustrated by the then-small Glastonbury and the huge Isle of Wight festivals, which ended in the early 1970s and returned as regular annual festivals in 1979 and 2002, respectively.

The first "love rally" in October 1966 and the first human be-in in January 1967 were conceived and organized by the same two people, Michael Bowen and Allen Cohen. They were also editors of the newly created San Francisco *Oracle*. Initially, "the sole aim" of their human be-in was to produce "a sense of unity" (Perry 1984, 77). A more ambitious agenda emerged in statements to local magazines and in a press conference two days before the event. The organizers wanted to show that hippies and political radicals could unite in their rejection of "dehumanizing" institutions and in their protest against the Vietnam War. San Francisco's "spiritual generation" and "the emerging revolutionary generation all over California" were going to meet for "a Gathering of the Tribes for a Human Be-In" (Perry 1984, 78). The event was held in Golden Gate Park and featured leading figures of the counterculture. Like the French revolutionaries, they borrowed a sacred aura from religious traditions for their secular rituals. Allen Ginsberg and Gary Snyder did a Hindu blessing ritual, Ginsberg led a chant in honor of the marijuana-smoking god, and Reverend Suzuki of the local Zen temple acted as a kind of master of ceremonies. The poster promised "all of San Francisco's rock bands" (see figs. 7.1–7.2). Other appearances further suggested the production of a

7.1–7.2 Lineup and poster for the Human Be-In, Golden Gate Park, January 14, 1967. Note the order of the lineup: (1) hippie gurus; (2) rock bands; and (3) dressing, props, and social instructions. The art poster was designed by Stanley Mouse and Alton Kelley and shows a mystic guru with three eyes.

cultural worldview, including Timothy Leary's encouragement to "tune in, turn on, drop out" and Jerry Rubin's declaration of the event itself as a new and free world ("Human Be-In Full Program").

The be-in was to a great extent a pop culture development of the *happening* in the experimental arts scene in New York City in the late 1950s. The happening was a one-off event that disrupted conventional performance routines and stimulated metareflexivity of these routines. It was often situated in a gallery or museum, which is to say outside established performance institutions such as theaters and concert halls. The happening was smaller and had a simpler structure than the festival, as it was normally just one performance event. In contrast to the festival's tradition-building annual cycle and the presentation of a theater or music piece, the happening involved the conceptual challenge of reinventing and decentering performance rituals and, in a sense, emancipating the performance from the work and from systems of signification.[3] The inspiration from Antonin Artaud is obvious (Artaud 1958).

The first public happenings were Allan Kaprow's *18 Happenings in Six Parts*, which took place over six days at the Reuben Gallery in the East Village in 1959. Kaprow had experimented with action painting, studied with Cage, coinitiated the Fluxus movement, and introduced the term "happening" in a 1958 essay on Jackson Pollock. The Reuben Gallery event inspired artists around the world to do happenings (Higgins 1976, 268–69).

Happenings proliferated beyond the art world, and many neo-bohemian urban youths attended Fluxus art events. Urban arts scenes were sites of exchange between art and popular culture. John Cage taught at the New School and appeared in a venue called the Club in Greenwich Village that was frequented by young artists such as Jasper Johns and Yoko Ono ("Music Is Everywhere: John Cage at 100"). Greenwich Village booksellers called Cage's 1961 *Silence* an underground bestseller, and scenesters carried this book to happenings (Tomkins 1965, 270). The new avant-garde performance culture additionally reached mass-media audiences thanks to the inclusive programming on popular TV shows in the late 1950s and early 1960s. The avant-garde was not yet restricted to its own slots on PBS, for instance. Cage appeared on one of the most popular TV shows of the time, *I've Got a Secret* on CBS, where he performed a version of "Water Music" that he had developed for television and called "Water Walk" (Mount 2011, 34).

The happening was a fixture of neo-bohemian hippie scenes in the mid-1960s in New York's East Village and in San Francisco (Gruen 1966, 11). These scenes brought the happening into underground popular culture, and in San Francisco it developed into hippie gatherings. Charles Perry, an eyewitness to the San Francisco scene, later remembered:

> The theater was a busy world late in 1965. Satirical comics like Lenny Bruce and the improvisational theater troupes—in San Francisco, the venerable Committee—had been mocking convention since the late fifties and were now in their prime. A new avant-garde sort of theater produced not plays but "events" or "happenings" that required audience participation. This new theater aimed for either Zen spontaneity or the re-creation of primitive ritual from which all the arts were thought to have been born. Beat poets such as Lawrence Ferlinghetti had gotten involved with happenings, and several events had been staged at the Tape Music Center at the eastern fringe of the Haight-Ashbury, a building full of studios used for modern dance and painting as well as avant-garde electronic music. (Perry 1984, 15)

It is not hard to see why the happening resonated with the counterculture, with its dramatized sense of here and now, transgressive blurring of boundaries between art and everyday life, and holistic potential in combining various forms of expression, including theater, visual art, dance, and poetry. Moreover, the happening was associated with the figure of the provocative artist and the informal urban sphere, which appealed to bohemian-countercultural notions of authenticity. Finally, the happening involved the conception of an adventurous and participatory audience: an audience that enters on the premise that they will take part in a transgressive moment and, to some extent, become performers. The happening was a theatrical model that heightened audience agency and intimacy. In the be-ins, which involved thousands of participants, this drama of suspension—fueled by psychedelic rock and drugs—was a vehicle for entering the here and now collectively for a sense of self-empowerment and utopian transcendence.

I should like to conclude this exploration by examining the rapid transformation of hippie events into the hippie music festival in 1966–1967 and how it peaked with Woodstock. The first major cultural event in the San Francisco scene was the Trips Festival held in January 1966. This was an indoor, multiarts festival with a participatory "no spectator" agenda, elements that would later be incorporated into Burning Man (which also originates in San Francisco) and in DIY indie rock scenes. The first hippie *music festival* was the larger outdoor Fantasy Fair and Magic Mountain Music Festival held outside San Francisco in June 1967. Fantasy Fair was promoted as an extension of the Human Be-In in Golden Gate Park in January. Most services were donated, tickets were two dollars, and artists performed for a small fee (Peterson 1973, 100). The lineup included relatively unknown local bands and the experimental Captain Beefheart and the Magic Band. The buses to the site were called Trans-Love Bus Lines, and a famous hippie alchemist flew over the crowd and dropped LSD from the sky (Newman 2014).

Monterey Pop, the second hippie music festival, was held just two weeks later, but involved more famous performers and became a mass-media sensation. There were several international TV crews, and a festival movie was shot. Peterson suggests that the movie inspired millions of young people around the country to dress, behave, and feel like flower children (Peterson 1973, 101). Monterey had a higher-profile lineup and also took inspiration from the Newport Folk Festival, which in the mid-1960s had day crowds of more than 30,000. Peterson and others have rightly observed that Monterey accelerated the business of festivals and led to increasing operating costs as artists and service providers increased their demands. Hendrix got $500 for playing Monterey and $75,000 for Randall's Island three years later (Peterson 1973, 105). This process culminated in Woodstock, which presented many stars who had become established in the late 1960s, paying some of them more for the movie rights than for their stage performance (Laing 2004).

As in earlier festival traditions, stardom shifted the focus from festivalgoers to stage performers. The performances at the Human Be-In in January 1967 were not focused on the professional delivery of musical entertainment. The consumption of musical performance had not yet become institutionalized as the central organizing principle of the festival. Audience members were not yet confined to the role of consumers, but had more sovereignty as performing bodies that defined and performed hippie culture through dressing and behaviors. The Monterey and Woodstock movies show audiences exploring and experimenting in their responses to the music in ways that were and still are distinctly different from the commercially institutionalized forms of this festival culture (Pennebaker 1968/2002; Wadleigh 1970/1999). Audience members experimented with individual self-expression within their own personal psychedelic worlds and in moments of collective affect. They were not uniformly focused on the stage and on listening, indicating that the rituals of rock music performance were not yet fixed. In parts of the Woodstock movie, many audience members seem mildly bored, while in other parts they seem excited and ecstatic. The festival had not yet been industrially developed to present an even flow of familiar entertainment. Monterey and Woodstock had just one concert stage, one major site of gathering, and so this area also served as the singular plenum of the festival and the temporary stage of hippie culture in general. The now-standard practice of shopping around for one's favorite artists at different festival stages did not exist.

The construction of performer and audience subjectivities provided further nuances to the relationship between the festival world and the broader cultural worldview. Performers on stage were endowed with a power to dramatize and comment on contemporary culture through language, behavior, clothing, and music. Moreover, the performance styles of bands such as the Grateful Dead, Hendrix, Joplin, Santana, and the Who were improvisatory and explored psychological states of ecstasy and transgression. Some of the bands had been part of the psychedelic rock dances in San Francisco a few years earlier in which folk-derived amateur bands explored "chiming chords" and simple raga-inspired solos as a kind of mood music for the event (Perry 1984, 46). Psychedelic hippie rock also drew from the electric blues revival in the United Kingdom, using blues narratives for confessional modes of hippie self-expression and for drama and deriving emotional authenticity from myths of blackness. Modal qualities of the blues were used for meditative mental states and ambience.

In this context, we can understand the emerging figure of the rock virtuoso as a performer of and metaphor for the psychedelic journey and the triumph of counterculture. There was a cathartic and heroic dimension to the virtuoso performance of Jimi Hendrix and the Who, for instance. Sound effects and strong amplification contributed to this by creating a new aesthetics and new acoustic environments.

The hippie music festival movement eventually experienced a decline in the United States in the early 1970s. Local governments around the country moved to prevent the staging of festivals. Peterson argued in 1973 that negative mass-media reports were a major factor in this and that a revision of social movement theory was therefore necessary (Peterson 1973). The conventional wisdom at the time was that social movements die when individuals lose interest, but the hippie festival movement showed that mass media could contribute to both the rise and fall of a movement. From the specific perspective of the history of rock music's performance institutions, the negative media reports on festivals indirectly contributed to the arena's status as the primary performance institution of the music industry in the 1970s and 1980s.

Anglophone Global Culture

The Anglophone Turn in Continental Western Europe after World War II

The evolution of Anglophone popular culture in Continental Europe after World War II has been shaped by the region's overall political geography. Deep divisions have existed between the political systems in East and West and between the two superpowers, the Soviet Union and the United States. The division between East and West, originating in the split between the Catholic Church and the Eastern Orthodox Church in the eleventh century, was transformed by the new global order and by the Soviet Union's control of many Eastern European nation-states. Some of the general dynamics of Anglophone popular culture in Continental Europe are illustrated in the example of the divided Germany. Jazz and rock 'n' roll were initially met with skepticism in both countries of the divided Germany, but a narrative emerged in West Germany that positioned these genres as symbols of freedom and economic progress (Poiger 2000). Western European narratives of democracy have long projected positive images of capitalism and of cultural industries and consumer culture. These narratives were central to the evolution of neoliberalism in Western Europe and in postsocialist Central European countries (Szemere 2001).

The aftermath of World War II shaped cultural nationalism and internationalism in West Germany. Uta Poiger argues that the challenged state of nationalism in the 1950s created anxieties about gender and family. From this perspective, the rise of schlager music can be interpreted as a form of postwar recovery, as a positive national culture with idealized images of love, family, and a stable, patriarchal order. For youth, on the other hand, American popular culture provided an alternative to this conformism with its African American aesthetics and more relaxed social and sexual norms.

Other kinds of affective bonds with the United States were created through cosmopolitan and neo-bohemian forms of popular music. Jazz had a history of functioning as a music of multiculturalism in Europe since

World War I (Bohlman 2016). In the second half of the twentieth century, rock music was the most popular genre for expressing liberation from totalitarianism and for coping with the dangers of the Cold War. Examples include the countercultural movement in Spain called La Movida Madrileña after the fall of Franco's regime in 1975. That regime had actively opposed influences of US popular culture. In Germany, Anglophone popular music provided stylistic templates for the New German Wave (Neue Deutsche Welle), which voiced Cold War anxieties, with songs such as Nena's "99 Red Balloons" of 1983. These anxieties were also conveyed through the circulation of Sting's "Russians" of 1985, for example. In the North, Anglophone genres similarly created templates for localized cultural expressions, from Sweden's countercultural rock scene in the 1970s to the contemporary North Atlantic indie rock scenes (Holt 2017a).

Major political and technological developments in the late twentieth century contributed to the further proliferation of Anglophone culture in Continental Europe. The developments include the fall of the Iron Curtain in 1989, the rise of the European Union as a major institution of power and its eastward expansion in the early 2000s, the rise of Anglophone internet corporations, and budget airlines. The penetration of English accelerated considerably in the 2010s with the widespread adoption of new everyday information technologies, especially smartphones and commercial streaming services. National broadcasters and cultural institutions lost considerable territory to corporations, such as Google, Facebook, Netflix, Spotify, Disney, Clear Channel, and Live Nation. By the late 2000s, Live Nation owned more than forty music festivals in Europe and used them as platforms for the company's pop stars from the United Kingdom and North America. Anglophone global popular culture has increasingly become a vernacular for many young Europeans. There are still many artists with a primarily national audience who sing in a national language and use that national language in their social media communications to fans, but Facebook, Instagram, Spotify, and YouTube permeate spheres that were previously more national in focus and accelerate the adoption of Anglophone popular culture. A particular evolution of Anglophone subjectivity in Continental European popular music can be traced through the careers of Nordic artists such as ABBA, A-ha, Roxette, Björk, Röyksopp, Tina Dico, Volbeat, Aviici, Zara Larsson, and Aurora (Holt 2017a).

A Consumer Culture without a Worldview?

The history of the large rock-based music festival in Continental Europe has been shaped by commercial arrangements that will be detailed in chapters 8–9, but let us for now assume that the main priority of the festival industry has not been to promote humanist worldviews. Festival managements commonly ask themselves the following questions: Who are the superstars that can currently attract the largest number of people, and how much do we have to pay them? How can we strengthen the festival's appeal to evolving lifestyle segments? How can we create an aura of novelty and improve consumer convenience? How can we attract more sponsors and sell *all* our tickets?

While for-profit festivals created during the festival boom of the 2000s did not evolve from social movements, formerly hippie festivals tend to show some sympathy toward ethical causes within the limited space of increasingly corporatized structures and consumerist environments. Festivals such as Glastonbury, Sziget, and Roskilde make gestures toward ethics in a number of ways, including charity donations and appearances by activist celebrities. The hippie past of these festivals echoes in their identity after they have fully entered the realm of mass-market consumer culture.

The gestures toward pop culture ethics in former hippie festivals developed into branding strategies during the festival boom in the 2000s. Ethics became a means of creating a sense of authenticity and purpose, and a worldview. Rather than evolving from social movements, the festivals present small elements of such movements in a controlled and compartmentalized form. The festivals do not articulate a worldview explicitly but make discreet and vague gestures that festivalgoers can interpret freely or easily ignore. In the late 2010s, for instance, Roskilde featured a small number of pop icons of internet activism, fourth-wave feminism, and Black Lives Matter. They appeared outside the main schedule of musical entertainment, which did not promote any social movements. Similar gestures toward reflexivity spread in Denmark to a new for-profit festival, owned by Live Nation, that featured a series of talks by popular intellectuals and artists, including avant-garde celebrities Brian Eno and Marina Abramović. These examples border on what Jim McGuigan (2009) calls cool capitalism, the cooption of aesthetic critiques of capitalism into commodities.

Changes in the social imagination of festivals can also be identified in the general consumer culture values of festival environments and media communications. Industry-based festivals generally appeal to consumer ideals of convenience and offer a wider range of commercial services. Festivalgoers are treated to environments designed to provide a range of stimuli, such as art installations, gourmet food, artist talks, and lounge areas (Robinson 2015). These sensory pleasures figure prominently in social media channels belonging to festival companies and festivalgoers. Press releases to news media, on the other hand, tend to make announcements about headliners and ticket sales. It is illustrative that when industry-based festivals began to respond to reports on sexual harassment in the early 2010s, they interpreted the issue to be a matter of public relations and consumer safety (see p. 50). Meanwhile, some festivals continued to use sexualized images of women in their marketing. The festival industry responded to requests for more gender-balanced programming in the late 2010s only *after* this had evidently become a popular interest among festivalgoers.

Corporate Transculturalism and Pop Culture Internationalism

The history of the Anglophone popular music festival in Continental Europe can be usefully informed by theory of cultural globalization. Of particular relevance are Marwan Kraidy's (2005) and Motti Regev's (2013) arguments about how the forces of cultural globalization stimulate the growth of certain types of culture. Kraidy highlights the deregulation of the Anglophone corporate cultural industries and the concept of corporate transculturalism, while Regev focuses on popular music genres as templates of creating international selves, arguing that the same pop culture models are adopted in many cultures out of a desire for international connectivity and recognition in an increasingly global world.

Kraidy's *Hybridity, or the Cultural Logic of Globalization*, published in 2005, provides an overview of the general shift in globalization theory in the 1990s from narratives of cultural imperialism to narratives of hybridity. The imperialism discourse was central to a debate about industry regulation among UNESCO member states in the late 1970s. This debate was motivated by a concern over the perceived dominance of Anglophone communication and media industries. The United States and the United Kingdom adopted a "free flow of information" doctrine. The privileged position of the United States in international trade as a result of the 1945 Bretton Woods agreement had begun deteriorating, and the global economy was becoming more dispersed in terms of production and more centralized in ownership (Sassen 1991/2001, 3). Many countries, including Continental European and African countries, were opposed to the free flow doctrine, arguing that it would lead to continued Anglo-American economic and cultural dominance. The debate also reflected different conceptions of culture. The agenda promoted by the United States and United Kingdom was grounded in consumer culture, while the coalition of countries opposed to it understood culture as a local and national social resource. At one point the United States considered withdrawing from UNESCO (Kraidy 2005, 23–25), but in the 1990s UNESCO generally adopted the consumer culture paradigm, which led to a sweeping deregulation of media markets and subsequent growth of transnational concept products that could be easily localized and cost little to produce (Kraidy 2005, 100). Among the most popular genres was reality television.

Kraidy additionally explores how media industries were shaping the ideologies and formats of media texts. He provides examples of how Hollywood, for instance, rationalized its ethnic-racial biases on economic grounds. Kraidy identifies the "white customer is king" maxim and quotes industry professionals saying that minority actors have limited appeal to foreign audiences (Kraidy 2005, 81–82). This also indicates that the globalization of American popular culture is not simply a matter of free consumer choice, but also involves decisions about what kinds of products are made and distributed by corporations. With the film, music, and information technology industries in the United States, corporate globalization has boosted both mass culture in the United States and its international circulation.

The results of industry deregulation and the advent of American internet corporations have accelerated the circulation of American consumer culture in Continental Europe. These developments have not led to a near-symmetrical situation in which popular culture from Continental Europe circulates at a similar scale and intensity in the United States and United Kingdom. Overall, the flows in popular culture are generally still rather one-directional. The analysis of rock clubs in chapter 5 suggested that the field had become more Anglophone and less multicultural, and the history of popular music festivals presented here will provide further nuance to this argument. This situation challenges the discourse of hybridity, which has dominated since the early 1990s. This discourse imagines cultural globalization as a process of dynamic interactions between cultures, with a continuous transformation and renewal of cultural forms (Kraidy 2005, 16). The situation in Continental Western Europe over the past two decades, by contrast, is characterized by the growing centrality of Anglophone popular culture and by a fading reflexivity about the accompanying power dynamics. For decades, skepticism about the dominance of Anglophone models often referenced the discourse of cultural imperialism. The skepticism has occasionally been voiced in popular music studies (e.g., Fornäs and Ihlemann 1999) and is a defining aspect of the Routledge Global Popular Music Series. I shall argue that the current situation calls for critical thinking about how Anglophone global culture impacts not just national selves, but also immigrant populations in Continental Western Europe.

Another useful theory for explaining the rise of Anglophone global culture can be found in Motti Regev's 2013 *Pop-Rock Music: Aesthetic Cosmopoli-*

tanism in Late Modernity. Regev's objective is to explain the symbolic economy of global pop culture sociologically. He emphasizes the role of generic models as communication models. Regev argues that the same models or schemata in cultural production—including music genres and styles of sound production, and we might add models of musical performance institutions to the list—are used in many societies as a result of intensified media proximity. With the compression of time and space, shared international models become a more powerful form of social capital. "The quest for status, participation, and parity" lies at the core of aesthetic cosmopolitanism (Regev 2013, 10). American or Western models can index not only Anglophone culture, but also internationalism and universalism.

How might this apply to music festivals? In the following section we shall see that a growing media proximity and proliferation of Anglophone models can be registered in the design, music programming, and media productions of festivals. Large popular music festivals in Continental Europe imagine themselves alongside iconic Anglophone festivals. Festival lineups in the 1970s featured many local artists who performed national folkloric styles, but those styles have largely disappeared. Many local artists now aspire to a mastery of Anglophone internationalism, and festival lineups feature many more artists from North America and the United Kingdom.

The further analysis of this transformation of festival worldviews into one of Anglophone internationalism can usefully distinguish between two types of festivals. One is the broad festival that presents a range of stars in the most popular Anglophone media spheres. The other is the niche festival that is an international destination for a particular kind of music and defined by tourist images of its location. The two types thus illustrate different logics and dynamics. This analysis of the worldview transformation focuses on core elements in the symbolic order: music programming, on the one hand, and media distribution and self-image, on the other.

The Broad Pop Festival

This type of festival evolved from the hippie music festival, from hippie culture and its imagination of the festival as a place for restating and experiencing the worldview of contemporary popular music and culture in a greenfield setting. For the festival industry, the broad programming serves to attract local mass audiences. By presenting stars from a range of genres, the festival appeals to audiences in a number of markets. This explains why this festival model is the most common among the largest festivals, and why niche festivals tend to develop a broader program over time to attract larger audiences. Generally speaking, the typical size of the day crowd at the largest festivals in Europe has increased from about 30,000 in the 1980s to 50,000 in the 1990s and 70,000 in the 2000s (see pp. 23–24 and 50–51). This expansion would not have happened if the programming had not been broadened from "hard-core" forms of rock music to "soft-shell" forms of rock and chart-topping pop stars (chapter 8). The broad pop festival has co-opted genres such as metal, rap, house, and techno along the way. The pioneers of this festival type in Continental Europe were influenced by Woodstock and compare themselves to Glastonbury and, since the 2010s, also to Coachella, festivals in relative proximity to London and Los Angeles, respectively. The analysis below focuses on Roskilde in Denmark and compares it to Sziget in Hungary and more recent festivals in Poland, Serbia, and Russia. Future research on variations of this type might also consider festivals such as Lowlands and Pinkpop in Holland, Pukkelpop and Rock Werchter in Belgium, and Festival Internacional de Benicàssim in Spain.

Developments in Programming and Audience Size

Roskilde evolved from the city's small festival that had been held annually since the 1950s and had the support of the city's elite. This small-town festival was influenced by the hippie movement, following local festivals in Thy, Nyborg, and Femern, and the squatter village of Christiania in Copenhagen. In 1972, the local organization committee transferred ownership of the festival to a local philanthropic organization called the Roskilde Foundation and the actual production was organized by two students at a local high school. A music programming team was created in 1973. Leif Skov was a member of this team and became manager of the festival in 1977. He remembers that the first "real" festival was in 1975, at which Procol Harum played. He began networking with managers of other festivals in the late 1970s, but it was still a small organization, and even he was not employed full-time until the late 1980s (Leif Skov, conversation with the author, October 17, 2019).

In its early years, Roskilde presented a mix of local countercultural rock bands along with artists who had performed at hippie festivals in the United States, such as Ravi Shankar and Santana. Interest in world music extended to bookings of Weather Report and Bob Marley. None of these artists figured on the recording industry's list of the top ten best-selling artists in the world, and they generally did not tour regularly in Continental Europe. There were few popular music festivals in Scandinavia in the 1970s and therefore far less market competition than today. Another striking difference was the representation of local artists: A large proportion of the headlining artists were from Denmark and neighboring Scandinavian countries and sang in local languages.

Roskilde's profile transformed gradually through a couple of stages. It first gained an identity as a major international festival in the early 1980s. The Canopy main stage came into place in 1978 and created a more monumental atmosphere, and a wave of new international stars appeared, including Elvis Costello, U2, and Simple Minds, and then in the mid-1980s bigger stars such as the Clash and Eric Clapton. A further transformation occurred in the early 1990s when the average number of headliners largely doubled from three to six, and a new generation of stars began to dominate. The programming incorporated a strong representation of punk and alternative rock, later some metal, combined with an occasional boomer-generation headliner, such as Bob Dylan or Neil Young. The programming was shaped through manager Leif Skov's network with concert agents in London. He was part of an informal network at ILMF circa 1989–1995 and says this was how he was able to book the Cure six times, for instance (see pp. 16–17). It is typical of the current situation in Continental Europe that his successor no longer travels to London to talk to agents but simply receives a package offer from the national Live Nation offices. Meanwhile, the festival management has now traveled for many years to the larger South by Southwest in Austin, Texas, to be informed about international industry trends and explore the many up-and-coming artists that perform there.

The addition of more headliners in the early 1990s contributed to a doubling of audience numbers between 1989 and 1995, with day crowds of about 60,000 by the mid-1990s. In 1995, a limit on ticket sales was imposed for the first time, and that year the festival reached the size that has remained relatively stable since, with about 150 acts, up from twenty in 1971 and sixty-nine in 1990 (Funder 2016; "Roskilde Festival"). Arena stars such as Aerosmith, ZZ Top, and Van Halen appeared 1994–1995. Their music had a large teenage audience, and it had gained wider mainstream circulation through Hollywood blockbuster movies. Aerosmith and ZZ Top had contributed to the soundtracks for *Back to the Future III* and *Mother Goose: Rock 'n' Rhyme* of 1990. Skov says the main stage design was a factor in booking these artists: Some acts had played the main stage with mixed results, and "this simple, pompous, and melodic semi-metal music with a visual spectacle had a long-throw that worked well on this large stage. These acts delivered and their music was easily accessible" (Leif Skov, October 17, 2019). Roskilde's programming continued to reflect new developments in the United Kingdom and the United States, but it also followed a trajectory of mainstreaming, of moving closer to pop. Punk gave way to the lighter Britpop in the late 1990s;

in the 2000s there were more indie pop bands from the United Kingdom and North America, and EDM superstar DJs began appearing more regularly in the 2000s. The Chemical Brothers, Pet Shop Boys, Tiësto, and Deadmau5 have each appeared a couple of times.

The presence of Anglophone pop culminated in the 2010s, when the festival presented artists such as Rihanna, Nicki Minaj, the Weeknd, Dua Lipa, and Bruno Mars. Such a large representation of artists on the American recording industry's list of best-selling artists was a new development at broad, rock-based festivals. In the 1980s, pop royalty such as Michael Jackson, Madonna, and Prince were not part of Glastonbury or Roskilde. Roskilde's then manager says the festival tried to book Madonna and Barry White, for instance, but could not meet the demands of such stars, who toured arenas for higher honoraria and with elaborate productions that would have required shutting down the main stage for several hours (Leif Skov, conversation with the author, October 17, 2019). Yet, there can be little doubt about the "hard-core" profile and rockism of the otherwise broad festivals in Europe in the 1980s. Roskilde stretched to meet the demands of the Rolling Stones, for instance. Prince negotiated with Glastonbury in 2014 and again in 2016 but died before the plans materialized and thus never got to perform there (Shepherd 2016). Beyoncé was the first black female headliner at Coachella. Festivals followed the broader transformation in pop music and cultural life among the urban middle classes. Pop and its genre boundaries were deregulated through digital production and circulation, and female pop celebrities such as Lady Gaga, Beyoncé, and Nicki Minaj were praised by urban middle-class tastemakers for their experimental sensibilities and identity politics. Still, these artists did not commonly appear at the broad pop festival, which generally also did little to actively promote queer artists, although independent post-hippie festivals did more than corporate festivals. Roskilde's programming illustrated the trend of independent broad festivals booking fairly conformist pop stars as level-one headliners.

The advent of pop stars, moreover, signaled the erosion of boundaries between festivals and mega-events. Festivals started to present artists who also performed at events such as the Champions League, the Olympics, and the Super Bowl. Music festivals were not imitating these types of events, but they were becoming a new kind of mega-event of their own, one that is increasingly defined by pop stars and elaborate experience design. Roskilde now routinely presents artists promoted on the landing pages and home screens of the most popular streaming services in the Global North. About half of the artists on the American recording industry's list of "best-selling global artists" of 2017 toured Continental European music festivals in the

7.3–7.4 Roskilde Festival posters from 1975 and 2018. In 1975, there was only local-language marketing, and the festival included several performers with national folkloric styles. The event also featured traditional forms such as theater and circus, and it had a folk and a jazz stage. By the 1980s, the festival had become more exclusively focused on rock music and much bigger. By the 2010s, English had become the standard marketing language on the website and in national news media. The festival brand is only promoted in English.

2010s ("Ed Sheeran Officially Named the Best-Selling Global Recording Artist of 2017"). At the same time, the festival has developed a visual brand identity and a multifaceted experience environment, with many art installations, that follows the boutique festival design trend (Robinson 2015).

Roskilde's lineup for 2018 is a case in point. The poster presents the lineup

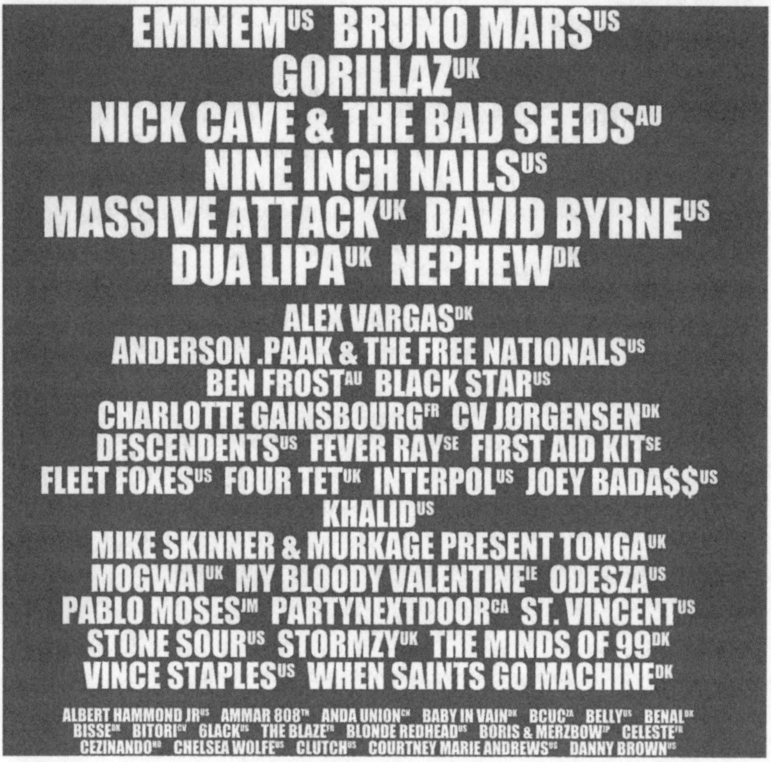

hierarchically on four levels, of which the first two and the beginning of the third can be seen in descending order in figure 7.4.

Levels one and two on the poster show what might be called primary and secondary headliners, respectively. Most of the primary headliners performed on the main stage, while the secondary ones generally appeared on a smaller stage. Of the thirty-five artists on levels one and two, twenty-one were from the UK and North America. Six were local, and three sang in Danish. The majority were white, with a large minority, about 30%, of African Americans. The African American artists were icons of "black" genres, mostly rap. In this respect, the festival has become racially more diverse within an Anglophone white/black framework.

The internationalism is further illustrated by the touring geography of many artists. In 2018, half of the headliners also headlined several other festivals in Central Europe, Western Europe, and North America (table 7.1). Those artists were contracted to Live Nation, so while Roskilde is independently owned, it also serves as a distribution platform for multinational corporations. It is unsurprising that Live Nation has offered to buy Roskilde (Leif Skov, conversation with the author, August 10, 2010).

TABLE 7.1 Examples of primary and secondary headliners at Roskilde 2018 who toured other festivals and venues in Europe and North America during the same season

Level 1	
Eminem	Coachella, Bonnaroo, Firefly, Boston Calling
Dua Lipa	Lollapalooza, Bonnaroo, Panorama NYC, Glasgow Green, Reading, Leeds, Ruisrock Turku, Stavern, Tomorrowland, Lollapalooza Paris, Osheaga, Sziget, Pukkelpop, Lowlands
David Byrne	Coachella and 23 concert halls and festivals in Europe
Massive Attack	14 other European festivals
Level 2	
First Aid Kit	Coachella, Bonnaroo, Bestival, Werchter, Ruisrock Turku, Montreux, Larmer Tree, Cambridge Folk, All Together Now, Rock en Seine
Khalid	Lollapalooza, Bonnaroo, Boston Calling, Governors Ball, Werchter, North Sea Jazz

Note: A comprehensive analysis of the lineups in large popular music festivals over a five-year period would show more examples of shared headliners from the industry's list of best-selling artists.

Figure 7.4 shows the beginning of level three, which has a total of 137 acts. It became common in the 1990s for large music festivals to have such a large number of artists. Festivals began booking more artists to fill the stages with concerts from early afternoon to late at night, offering constant flows of entertainment to their growing audiences. This increase in numbers also explains the large presence of local artists at Roskilde's level three in 2018: They were also cheaper than international touring bands. About half of the level-three artists were local, but they generally aspired to a mastery of Anglophone aesthetics and sang in English. The festival did not represent a broad array of local musical cultures. As a matter of fact, Roskilde cultivated a self-image as an international cultural space through conscious identification with Anglophone indie media and metropolitan music scenes.

It is indicative of the worldview of the broad pop festival that when it presents world music artists, world music tends to appear in the form of somewhat exotic party music on smaller stages and not as part of the core festival identity. World music artists rarely appear on the main stage. In 2018, Roskilde still presented world music programming tailored to an Anglophone popular music taste demographic. One of the first statements in the description of an Argentinian tango ensemble reads: "This seven-member orchestra from Buenos Aires with four dancers approach tango with the intensity of a rock band" ("Rascasuelos"). We are told, moreover, that Yasmine Hamdan of Lebanon "has woven the multi-faceted and vast sounds of the Arabic diaspora into her energised electronic folk pop" and that the audience can expect "a more rocking, explosive energy on stage compared to the recordings" ("Yasmine Hamdan"). I was at a handful of world music concerts at the festival between 2007 and 2013 and witnessed a generally high level of artistry, but also exoticism. Audiences were generally drunk or high, or both, and members of Muslim populations were generally absent. The festival's world music promoter, however, pointed out that the festival has introduced world music genres to local audiences over the decades (Peter Hvalkof, conversation with the author, May 3, 2012).

One of the very few world music concerts on Roskilde's main stage since the 1980s happened in 2016, the year after the immigration of Syrian refugees into Europe peaked.[4] Damon Albarn opened the festival with the Orchestra of Syrian Musicians and implored the world to "keep borders open." The national papers were generally sympathetic to the idea, but none of them asked why this was limited to an opening concert (Gaunt 2016; Skotte 2016). A loyal Roskilde fan and industry insider thought the concert was more of a symbolic statement than a great experience.[5] These comments speak volumes about the cultural worldview at Roskilde. Moreover, the concert illustrates the scale and character of the festival's engagement with ethics. It took place on the main stage and was perceived to be a positive gesture, but it was just one isolated element and did not change the overall outlook and worldview of the festival.

Finally, the artists on the fourth level on the poster appear in a small showcase festival that runs for two days before the main part of the festival begins. The showcase is a great opportunity for up-and-coming bands, who get to perform at the most prestigious festival of this kind in the country. The bands reach larger audiences than usual because thousands of people are already camping there anyway and the main music program has not yet begun. The showcase festival is part of the festival's long-term efforts to create infrastructure and opportunities for local talent, dating back to the 1990s. The showcase festival was developed in collaboration with the national rock music association. In terms of identity politics of performing bodies, of who gets to perform, the showcase festival has largely remained a platform for the white Danish world of rock and pop music. One of the reasons the country's new immigrant populations are not more frequently represented, especially in the context of rising populist nationalism, might in fact be that the white Anglophone self is a big part of the festival culture. It is part of the unwritten social contract of the event. This is evident in the culturally and racially coded programming of the festival's stages. The festival would lose appeal with respect to its core audience demographic in Denmark if it adopted a distinctly multicultural worldview and programmed fewer Anglophone stars. The festival's music programming constructs an international self desired by a dominant subset of the Danish population. The festival celebrates their tastes, their worldview.

Media Distribution and Self-Image

In the 2010s, Roskilde's ticketing and broadcasting shifted hands from local to international corporations. For decades, ticketing had been handled by a Scandinavian company, and broadcasting rights were assigned to the state-owned Danish Broadcasting Corporation (DBC). Interests in growing the business and attracting more international audiences motivated the decision to form a partnership with Ticketmaster in 2014 and with Red Bull TV in 2016 (Østbjerg 2013). The growing market penetration by international ticketing corporations such as CTS Eventim and Ticketmaster, which was purchased by Live Nation in 2010, means that concert and festival promoters are motivated to contract their services because they are already used by more people and thus increase the sales potential (Klemm 2019).

In terms of broadcasting, Roskilde for years tried to get a dedicated live channel on YouTube to attract more international customers and strengthen its general market position during the festival boom (Esben Danielsen, conversation with the author, March 15, 2013). YouTube had provided a live channel to a dozen of the most internationally renowned music festivals in the Global North, including Coachella, the New Orleans Jazz and Heritage Festival, and Tomorrowland (see p. 253). Roskilde's relative inferiority in this symbolic economy might also explain why its partnership with Red Bull lasted only two years. Red Bull TV similarly concentrates on festivals with a stronger international appeal and that are located near larger cities in larger countries. The partnership with Red Bull is nonetheless illustrative of the power of Anglophone global culture and its impact on how festivals and their local audiences imagine themselves.

What characterized Roskilde's media image during the four decades of partnership with DBC? Until the 2000s, DBC primarily covered Roskilde in the form of radio broadcasts of concerts and involved little television coverage. The festival declined access for some small television stations because of incidents of voyeuristic, insensitive photography and because audiences were more anxious about photography before the era of smartphones. Many bands, moreover, declined to have their concerts recorded for television because they preferred to do this under conditions that allowed for higher levels of perfection, including the possibility of sound checks (Leif Skov, October 17, 2019). The main force behind DBC's engagement with the festival in the 1980s and 1990s was not the corporate management but largely a passionate journalist named Jan Sneum.

When the new perception of festivals as pop culture events developed in the 2000s, DBC began sending larger teams to Roskilde and producing more television content. DBC's coverage has generally included broadcasts of many local bands singing in Danish and segments for the evening news, all in Danish and from a Danish perspective. DBC has celebrated the event within the national community that DBC was created to serve. It has been the official media space of the nation throughout its existence, as a state-owned corporation and the only TV broadcaster in the country until 1988. It was also the primary media space for Anglophone "rhythmic" popular music and participated in the general institutionalization of this music as the dominant popular music taste culture of the nation-state, as manifested in the national arts policy of popular music (see pp. 147ff.). Roskilde evolved into the main event of this taste culture. The main reason DBC expanded its Roskilde coverage considerably in the 2000s, however, was the festival's broadened mainstream appeal as a pop culture event. In that decade, the number of press accreditations grew exponentially, but DBC's status was eventually challenged by the growing market competition that motivated the partnership with Red Bull.[6]

In 2016–2017, the transnational online channel Red Bull TV presented Roskilde alongside festivals and sports events in countries such as the United States. All content was in English, and no other Danish festivals were covered or referenced. Red Bull was a prestigious brand in the symbolic economy of Anglophone popular culture, and it brought its visual and narrative brand template into mediations of Roskilde. This is illustrated by the video that introduced Roskilde to Red Bull's audiences in 2016. The video identifies the festival from an international outsider's perspective around a generic image of Copenhagen as yet another frontier of cool consumer culture ("Sound/Sync Roskilde: Copenhagen"). The video is saturated with Red Bull's aesthetics and ideology. The visual narrative creates a particular image of cool around young people in their favorite urban environments, projecting the image of an authentic and pleasant place of possibility, joy, and creativity. Most of the spaces featured in the video are spaces of consumption—an art gallery, a fashion store, and a restaurant. Artists, gallery owners, and chefs are positive about Copenhagen winning more international attention for things that are consistently related to consumption. The video invokes sensations from postulates, such as a local artist saying, "I feel that people are more willing to take chances now," and the narrator's resorting to the cliché of Denmark being the happiest country in the world. Red Bull's presentational video thus builds on narratives in lifestyle magazines and city marketing. It also created an exoticizing gaze, reinforced by locals that feel empowered by their appeal to an international consumer culture sphere. In short, Red Bull's signature style of cool consumer culture, developed by the company's large international marketing apparatus, was projected onto Roskilde. Red Bull created an international coolness for the festival that represented an increasingly powerful form of cultural and economic capital in Continental Europe and that the festival could not get from the national public broadcaster.

Comparisons with Sziget and Nashestvie

Sziget

Sziget emerged from a series of festive events in Hungary after the fall of the Iron Curtain. As the momentum of collectivist possibility faded with the acceleration of the country's market economy, a commercial institution such as the broad popular music festival was likely to survive and grow (Szemere and Nagy 2017). More specifically, it was likely to grow as an institution of Anglophone global culture. Sziget adopted a focus on Anglophone stars after a few years, while still making gestures toward civic freedom and social movements in its romantic self-image as "the Woodstock on the Danube." The festival's image changed, however, with ongoing commercial development, which included corporate sponsorship, more superstars, and the sale in 2017 of a majority stake to a global asset management firm. This acquisition involved a plan to export Sziget internationally as a global brand (Rhian Jones 2017). What began as a festive exploration of the postsocialist moment and the worldview of an idealized New Europe eventually merged into the Anglophone global culture that has transformed Europe. Sziget expanded the territory of large seasonal events for this culture eastward.

Sziget was coconceived by a key figure of the 1980s underground rock scene in Hungary and by a more business-oriented individual. The business side became more dominant with Pepsi's name sponsorship in 1997 that financed the programming of US American rock stars. Countercultural and cosmopolitanism values continue to shape the festival's world music village, its Roma stage, and its queer-friendly Magic Mirror stage. The queer tent in particular frustrated the right-wing populist Budapest government of the

2010s to the extent that the mayor exerted pressure on the festival to abolish the tent. The managers agreed to comply until the LGBTQ movement threatened to boycott the festival (Szemere and Nagy 2017, 21). The management was apparently willing to withdraw from queer activism to ensure business stability, and the mayor likely abandoned his cause for the same reason.

Sziget's cosmopolitanism can be identified in the programming and conception of stages. There is a stage for jazz, a "Europe" stage with a wider representation of Europe than Roskilde's, an "Afro-Latin-Reggae" stage, a World Music stage, a tribute band stage, a stage for retro hit music, and a singer-songwriter stage. The Roma stage creates a space of international modernity for Roma musicians, an alternative to their domestic folk festivals and slick pop shows on national television across Central Europe and the Balkans. One example is the band Shutka Roma Rap from Skopje, North Macedonia, who performed their blend of social commentary, rap, funk, and jazz at Sziget in 2013 ("Shutka Roma Rap Live @ Sziget 2013 [full concert]"). The rockist dimension of the broad popular music festival in Continental Europe can also be found at Sziget, however. For instance, Sziget does not present queer pop stars associated with formulaic mass culture such as Roma chalga star Azis or Eurovision's Conchita Wurst, who have mobilized alternatives to white nationalism.

Sziget opted into global corporate broadcasting around the same time as Roskilde. YouTube provided it with a broader audience without projecting a lifestyle image onto the festival the way that Red Bull does with festivals. Corporate Anglophone online media thus create different conditions for festivals. YouTube has a larger portfolio of broad popular music festivals and is one of the world's most visited websites. Yet Sziget could have benefited from the type of communications expertise that Red Bull has. Sziget's promotional 2017 video, for instance, is a somewhat generic presentational video, full of clichéd situations and crowd responses ("Official Aftermovie—Sziget 2017"). The soundtrack, moreover, is generic EDM pop. The video thus does not convey much of the festival's unique cultural history or identity. It instead gives the festival a vague image as part of a placeless global culture.

Nashestvie

Anglophone global pop expanded farther into Central and Eastern Europe during the 2000s when promoters such as Mikołaj Ziółkowski in Poland and Ivan Milivojev in Serbia created a number of festivals that became part of the circuit of Live Nation tours. The influence of Anglophone popular music and festival culture can be discerned in Russia, too, but more indirectly and without touring Anglophone performers. A case in point is Nashestvie (1999–present), one of the country's largest rock music festivals, located within driving distance of Moscow. The video that ran in the background on the festival's home page in spring 2018 showed a somewhat conformist family-friendly event, similar to many traditional summer events in rural regions of Western Europe.[7] The environment shown in the video is far removed from the multiarts boutique design and semiluxury consumer environment of Roskilde and Sziget. The footage in this video also shows few if any signifiers of rock music's countercultural history. All lyrics are in Russian, and there is none of the hedonist self-expression found in the psychedelic and alcohol-fueled Western festival culture. Other footage, however, shows concert situations that are more similar to open-air rock concerts in Western Europe. Although there are differences in style, there is no question about the event's role models ("Фестиваль Нашествие Главная сцена День Первый" [Festival Invasion Main Stage First Day]). This is also true of the festival's web design and videography, which is inspired by the marketing communications of Western festivals. These mediations indicate that Anglophone popular culture is a source of inspiration but not celebrated openly as a medium of internationalism. The mediations indicate, moreover, that Nashestvie has not adopted the participatory culture of the urban countercultural happening that shaped the hippie festival and the broad popular music festival in Central and Western Europe.

International Niche Festivals

International niche festivals constitute an alternative to the broad festivals by concentrating on a smaller area of popular music and attempting to become the primary international destination for that area or genre. This claim to uniqueness has a geographic dimension: It builds on the mythology tied to a place in popular culture and in the genre more specifically. The niche festival presents music that has an audience in many countries and can be heard at other festivals, but not with the same focus and scale. The Sónar festival in Spain, for instance, was created in 1994 by a few young people who were aware that the local audience for their favorite electronic dance music was small at the time, but who were nevertheless struck by the potential in the music's international online circulation: "One million people all over the world could come together in this one event" (Ventura Barba, public presentation, September 21, 2011). The festival was conceived for an international niche audience from the outset. Another example is the Iceland

Airwaves festival, which was created in 1999 and gained momentum as a core destination of the Anglophone sphere of Icelandic indie rock in Europe's Nordic region, a region that extends into the North Atlantic. In a large country such as Germany, festivals for specific genres, such as Fusion and Wacken Open Air, have become large national niche festivals with a growing international audience. A particular type of niche festival is the showcase festival that highlights local talent. Examples include Eurosonic, Reeperbahn, Tallinn Music Week, and Iceland Airwaves. Like showcase festivals such as Eurosonic and Reeperbahn, Airwaves is a for-profit organization and has developed its profile around the local scene, but it has a more internationally significant profile and focuses less on industry intermediaries. It does not have national showcases curated by external music export agencies, for instance, and it added a conference only in 2015.

With the proliferation of festivals in many genres and the structuration of the organizational field creating increasingly similar models, the ability to develop a unique music profile is diminishing. Some niche festivals have responded with broader and more pop-oriented programming. The desire to grow a larger audience has also motivated many festivals conceived with a somewhat specific genre profile in a national festival field to broaden their programming in a similar fashion. This dynamic can be identified in the trajectories of Primavera in Spain and Southside in Germany, and in American festivals such as Lollapalooza, Coachella, and Bonnaroo, all of which were created between 1991 and 2002 and were transformed during the festival boom of the 2000s.

The following case studies of Sónar and Iceland Airwaves illustrate different models of Anglophone global culture in festivals with a strong element of cultural tourism. One is located in a large city in southern Europe, the other in the remote North Atlantic.

Sónar in the Global Event City of Barcelona

Sónar emerged during Barcelona's transition into a global event city. This process was jump-started by the Olympics in 1992 as part of a local agenda of urban regeneration. About ten billion US dollars were invested in transportation infrastructure and the creation of two miles of beachfront and a marina (Flyvbjerg, Budzier, and Stewart 2016; Taylor 2014). The architectural transformation and the mega-event changed the character of the city, boosting it as a space of global mass tourism. This development was sustained by a number of cultural festivals. Table 7.2 shows a list of festivals created after the Olympics. The list is inspired by a presentation by local event scholar

TABLE 7.2 Festivals in Barcelona created after 1992

1992	Dies de dansa: Festival Internacional de Dansa Contemporània en Paisatges Urbans
1993	Barcelona Acció Musical*
1994	Sónar: International Festival of Advanced Music and Multimedia Art*; L'Alternative Festival*
1995	Barnasants: Festival Internacional del Cantautor*
1996	Festival LEM (Festival de Música Experimental)*
1997	Curt Ficcions
1998	MECAL: Festival de Cortometrajes*
1999	BAFF: Festival de Cinema Asiàtic*
2001	Primavera Sound*
2002	Kosmopolis
2003	IN-EDIT Barcelona*
2004	Festival del Raval
2005	Món Llibre
2006	Summercase*; B-Estival*

Note: The list is developed from Colombo (2015).
*Indicates music and audiovisual festivals.

Alba Colombo (Colombo 2015). Since 1992, one or more festivals have been created every year, several of them music and audiovisual festivals (marked with an asterisk).

Three of the five biggest festivals in Barcelona in the 2010s were music festivals. Sónar was the largest with an estimated number of 121,000 visitors in 2013, 55% of whom were international tourists (Colombo 2015). What kind of cultural worldview did Sónar appeal to? What did it institutionalize? Scholars have argued that Sónar is an international space in cultural flows (Chalcraft and Magaudda 2013), an assertion that deserves additional detail. Sónar evolved as a tourist space of pop culture fashions within Anglophone urban club cultures and within a history of "bird" tourism from the colder North to the warmer South. The festival marketed itself as a space of artistic and technological pop modernism, not just a music festival, through avant-garde audiovisual aesthetics and its location at the Museum of Contemporary Art. The festival channeled a flow of Anglophone cool consumerism into the gentrifying nightlife neighborhood of El Raval, using the museum as a conduit and resource of symbolic capital. Red Bull Music Academy became an obvious partner that further contributed to the festival's image of cool internationalism, an image strategically promoted through the creation of shorter satellite Sónar events in metropolitan centers around the globe, just like Red Bull Music Academy. Like Red Bull, Sónar exploits an aura of experimental art and creativity within a consumer culture value system (Holt 2015). And like Red Bull Music Academy, Sónar appeals to international tastemakers and media such as the BBC and the *Guardian*, who then coconstructed the festival's image (e.g., Dodson 2003).

I experienced the synergy between the various elements of the festival as a participant in 2012. Over the course of a day, many festivalgoers would walk through the center and experience the historical aura and consumer pleasures of the Raval neighborhood and then hang out for hours at the intimate stages in the beautiful yard outside the Museum of Contemporary Art, accompanied by trendy house music and Red Bull vodkas. Later, many festivalgoers would enjoy tapas in a nearby restaurant, go to the first Lana Del Rey show in Europe, or take drugs and dance all night to harder techno in a large postindustrial space outside the city center. Some would wake up the next morning to enjoy the Barcelona sun from a hotel rooftop pool or on the beach. The museum was a remarkable asset for the festival. Similar in style to the Guggenheim in New York, it created a luxurious and spacious ambience. The festival ticket gave the holder access to the museum, so many went inside to experience the art and relax. In 2013, Sónar by Day moved to a larger location to accommodate larger crowds. The new location did not have the same qualities.

Unlike many other festivals, Sónar does not focus its promotion on the lineup or on footage from the festival. The festival instead uses concept videos and posters. Sergio Caballero, one of the festival founders, is a visual artist and is involved in the production (Sotirova 2016). The 2011 promotional video, for instance, stages a fictional sale of the festival ("Sónar Festival Is for Sale: Sónar 2011 Image"). The fictional real estate agent presents the festival in fluent BBC English while walking around what appears to be a commercial art gallery (fig. 7.5). The 2012 video, by contrast, is a two-minute meditative piece with no talking and no footage related to the festival, but it similarly creates an art-world aura. The video highlights the ambience of

7.5 Sónar marketing video, 2011. The space shown in this screenshot appears to be an art gallery. The women wearing burkas in the background create a signifier of difference. The sponsor product is exhibited on a stand to the right.

a former power plant in a remote area of Siberia, with atmospheric sounds and a repetitive, gloomy bass motif in the background ("Sónar 2012: La distancia"). It is made in the style of an independent art movie.

Sónar is no longer using any of its original venues because of its continued expansion, and its music profile has changed from being a niche festival for EDM with underground elements to becoming a broader pop festival with its added layers of more Anglophone pop stars. Stars that drew larger crowds included the Pet Shop Boys in 2002, Björk in 2003, the Chemical Brothers in 2005, the Beastie Boys in 2007, Grace Jones and Deadmau5 in 2009, the Human League in 2011, New Order and Lana Del Rey in 2012, and Massive Attack in 2014. The most popular Brooklyn indie rock bands of the 2000s also appeared. These changes in programming boosted British and North American attendance as well as the attendance of Europeans who embrace this kind of Anglophone global culture.

Iceland Airwaves in the North Atlantic Periphery

Like Sónar, Iceland Airwaves evolved from a tourism agenda, though not mass tourism, and it evolved from a localized form of Anglophone popular music, not a celebration of a somewhat placeless Anglophone culture. Reykjavik is a much smaller city than Barcelona and does not attract the mass audiences necessary for a festival model based on superstar concerts. Instead, the festival has become a seasonal and exotic destination for indie fans in large cities of Western Europe and North America. The festival has built on Iceland's relationship with the London music industry since the 1980s and developed strategic partnerships with the radio station KEXP in Seattle. The festival would not have evolved into its present form if the country's major airline had not invested in the festival to develop tourism in Iceland. Icelandair owned the festival until 2018 and was still involved after it sold the festival to a local event and concert promoter (Demurtas and Rogers 2018).

While the festival itself has not promoted exotic images, such images have been promoted by international media and the wider tourism industry. Ethnomusicologist Kimberly Cannady has uncovered echoes of colonial history in *Rolling Stone* magazine. A 1988 article in the magazine expressed excitement about Iceland as "pop music's final frontier" and described Björk as "an elfin young beauty" (Cannady 2017, 207). The author, David Fricke, found the music "familiar enough for an American to appreciate" but still different. The colonial gaze on Icelandic difference creates a market for local musicians, but it is also a straitjacket. Yet, because Iceland Airwaves is so small, there is space for intimacy and nuance; the crowds are smaller and more personal, and artists experiment musically beyond stereotypes and mass culture formulas. The festival's marketing image is more grounded in the ordinary festival experience than those of megafestivals. A 2012 documentary includes a few elements of global party culture but generally represents local musicians with nuance ("Iceland Airwaves: A Rockumentary").

The localization of Anglophone rock music in Iceland has been shaped by the country's geographic location between Europe and North America, the long history of American military presence after World War II, and the boost in self-esteem from the international successes of Icelandic stars such as Björk and Sigur Rós. Icelandic rock music is based on this Anglophone genre, but the localization is strong enough that the music is perceived as Icelandic. The goal is not a mastery of American or British cultural expression or a placeless international urban subjectivity. This is also reflected in attitudes to language. Many Icelandic musicians gladly speak English with a local accent, while many in Continental Western Europe seek to avoid a local accent in their attempt at mastering the dominant language of Western modernity. The evolution of Anglophone global culture in Continental Europe is thus also an attempt at positioning oneself in the center in a transnational hierarchy of aesthetic cosmopolitanism, to speak with Regev.

Berlin in the Late 2010s

During the year I lived in Berlin from 2017 to 2018, I witnessed the proliferation of Anglophone global culture there. Compared to my experience a decade earlier, English had become more widely spoken on the streets and in organized life. The most visible change was the growing presence of Anglophone corporate brands and advertising culture in places such as Alexanderplatz, the Hauptbahnhof, Potsdamer Platz, and the Kurfürstendamm shopping mile. The latter now had a gigantic Apple store similar to those in Manhattan. In the neighborhoods of Mitte and Prenzlauer Berg, English was spoken frequently on the streets by international tourists, students, and business professionals, most of them young or middle-aged. This demographic frequented gourmet cafés, bakeries, and burger restaurants with Anglophone names, visual identities, and menus. They also patronized budget Italian and Thai restaurants, but more rarely visited traditional German restaurants, which had a more local and older patron demographic. In many shops, clerks had become accustomed to English. A common exception was older, locally owned shops in the lower price range—shops that still sold a cup of coffee for one Euro. However, even the small nonprofit bookstore in my apartment building advertised in the window that they sold English-language books too.

The proliferation of English was a common topic of conversation among locals. In March 2017, a reporter for a national paper complained that none of the four waiters in a Berlin neighborhood restaurant spoke German, and a few months later, a member of Parliament and secretary of state in a federal ministry created a stir with the following statement: "It is increasingly getting on my nerves that in some Berlin restaurants the waiters only speak English" ("Is Too Much English Spoken in Berlin Restaurants?").

The growing presence of Anglophone culture could also be found in festive events and especially in large popular music festivals, which had a growing presence in the city. Fête de la Musique had come to Berlin in 1995, and by 2017 the biggest event was Red Bull's event in Mauerpark, which was almost a festival in itself. For the fourth consecutive year, Red Bull presented concerts from early afternoon to midnight, with constant exposure for its brand on banners and screens by the stage ("RBMA Stage @ Mauerpark Festival"). The main attractions were American rappers and DJs such as Thundercat and Flying Lotus, who were regulars on Red Bull festival stages around the world. During their concerts, I witnessed euphoric excitement in the crowded park. The event left little doubt that this was a music highly desired among young people in Berlin and that it offered the same kind of Anglophone internationalism that Roskilde, Sziget, and Sónar offered, only in more niche form as an all–Red Bull event on one stage and in an increasingly global city. The event did not channel all sensibilities in Berlin at the time, but it channeled a powerful one and illustrated its international corporate dimension.

Another example was the Lollapalooza festival, a clone of the namesake Chicago festival, which came to Berlin in 2015. The festival's introductory video in late 2014 began by proudly highlighting the festival as a global brand:

> Chicago, USA
> Santiago, Chile
> São Paulo, Brazil
> Buenos Aires, Argentina
> Berlin, Germany!
> ("Lollapalooza Is Coming to Berlin!")

The festival introduced itself as global culture, and it delivered on its promise. The majority of headliners were consistently from the United States and United Kingdom, and the music programming was dominated by popular forms of indie rock in combination with more mainstream rock and pop stars such as Macklemore and Ryan Lewis, the Foo Fighters, and Sam Smith. The power of this space of global Anglophone culture in Berlin is illustrated by the appearance of stars from the local EDM scene and by the recruitment of Sziget's music director, Fruzsina Szép, as the festival's director. Furthermore, the festival sold out every year and attracted larger audience numbers: 45,000 in 2015, 70,000 in 2016, 85,000 in 2017 (Christine Goebel, Lollapalooza Berlin, email to the author's assistant, Christin Kleinoth, November 3, 2017). The city government also made a welcoming gesture by giving Lollapalooza permission to use the former Tempelhof airport in Kreuzberg. The festival moved out of the center to expand its audience capacity.

It would be a mistake to consider the Anglophone culture in isolation from the rest of German society. There were other trends in Germany and in Europe during these years relevant to this discussion. One prominent trend was the right-wing populism among populations frustrated with the cultural and economic hegemony of capital cities, including a frustration with inclusive approaches to immigration among more internationally oriented urban populations. A new sense of national pride and of having overcome the legacy of World War II emerged in German politics and popular culture in the 2000s. Prominent right-wing politicians disassociated themselves from extremism and Nazism to claim a place in the center of society, claiming a collective "we" that cared for "the homeland" (Alt 2018). One of the most popular songs in the 2000s was "Wir sind Wir" by Paul van Dyk and Peter Heppner from 2004. The song's chorus validates German identity in the context of World War II. The accompanying music video showed footage of the ruins in Berlin after the war. When Germany won the World Cup in 2010, moreover, the national flag was used in public celebrations for the first time since 1945.

Conclusion: A Better Place for Music Festivals?

This chapter's analysis showed how popular music festivals emerged from a variety of inspirations in large cities such as London and San Francisco and evolved into the dominant model of the large rock-based festival, which proliferated across the Global North. This model has adapted to a dominant form of internationalism in popular culture, and this motivates critical reflection about other forms of internationalism in popular culture and in society at large.

The chapter focused on Europe's strong tradition of independent large post-hippie festivals, a tradition represented by Roskilde and Sziget. The countercultural legacy of these festivals is echoed in gestures toward social inclusivity and humanitarianism. However, they essentially represent an institution of urban white middle classes seeking to position themselves in the center of an evolving international modernity of Anglophone global culture. This is illustrated by the world music programming and by the growing emphasis on Anglophone culture and on the local mastery of this culture. The hippie music festival was not directly engaged in politics, but it was part of a social movement and represented the exploratory spirit of hippie scenes, including their imagination of a new world, peace and love, and the Orient as a spiritual resource. The commercially institutionalized rock festival, by contrast, presents a more standardized and conformist form that is developed for regular consumption among large audiences in many countries.

Like other moments of social change in festival history, the hippie moment was followed by the commercial institutionalization of professional entertainment, reducing the potential of music and of festivals to serve as a resource for social movements. In Continental Europe, the evolving festival industry has gradually adapted to the intensification of media flows of Anglophone global culture, culminating with the growing presence of global pop stars in the 2010s. This transition into Anglophone global culture is particularly striking in the context of the longer history of the music festivals in Continental European modernity. Also striking is the fact that while commercially institutionalized popular music festivals represent a view of a known and desirable world, they have adapted to an internationally hegemonic worldview and not been the site for the exploration of alternatives to it. This involves a particular dynamic in globalization: Many popular music festivals have become more deeply integrated into Anglophone consumer culture flows at a time when Europe's populations have become more diverse and interact more with the Global South.

Commercial institutionalization helps explain the stability and power of a worldview, but it does not justify it. The corporate replacement of local forms of production and ownership in fact increases the risk of a growing disconnection of culture from local social worlds. Future work could further analyze how the European tradition of independent post-hippie festivals has transformed in the process of entering corporate structures and a for-profit value system. One might ask, moreover, if the large Anglophone popular music festival—for more than a decade one of the most popular forms of seasonal festivity among younger generations of Western Europeans—is boosting the white urban dominance of the national cultural sphere. Have popular music festivals thus indirectly contributed to the "spectre of indignation" among older and lower-income rural populations who turned to right-wing populism because they felt left out and let down (Bauman 2014)? This situation suggests a common dynamic in globalization, namely that new international connections can indirectly intensify local divisions.

This analysis of the symbolic sphere thus points to changes in the conditions of production in the festival field and in how the festival is constructed as a place for musical performance culture. Popular music festivals are increasingly constructed not from local and civic communities but by an international industry. With transnational ownership and abstract logics of markets and institutions, the festival has moved further away from Goethe's idealized view of the cultural event that the People gives to itself. To fully understand the implications of this commercial institutionalization, we must look beyond the symbolic sphere to analyze how the festival industry shapes the popular music festival and its place in society. This is the task of the following chapter.

: 8 :

Three Industry Evolutions That Changed Festival Culture

Upon a hill across a blue lake
That's where I had my first heartbreak
I still remember how it all changed
"DON'T YOU WORRY CHILD," SWEDISH HOUSE MAFIA (2012)

This chapter provides further substance to the book's argument that the festival industry has played a major role in transforming festival culture over the past few decades. Consumer demand was stimulated by growing prosperity and leisure time (Frey 1994), but the industry has also transformed the product and induced needs among consumers. The overall profiles and trajectories of individual festivals have increasingly been shaped by the hegemonic logics and structures of international corporations and markets. Festival scholars have frequently pointed to the commercialization of the field, but they have not yet analyzed the systemic and transnational dimensions of this process (see p. 157). This chapter analyzes core systemic changes in the fields of large popular music festivals in the United States and Europe and expands the discussion into electronic dance music festivals. It begins by introducing theory of industry-driven popularization of cultural forms, taking inspiration from Richard Peterson's sociological conception of the relationship between a "hard-core" and a "soft-shell" formation of a popular music genre and the corporate industry's exploitative interests in the soft shell. The argument about industry-driven popularization is detailed in an outline of three distinct evolutions in the industry's conception of the festival and their underlying logics of commercial exploitation. These evolutions have changed the functions of festivals within the cultural industries and in society but also transformed festival culture and its functions in musical culture. The corporate institutionalization of large-scale popular music festivals is not adequately explained as a general pattern in history, but rather benefits from attention to particular historical developments and from differentiated analysis of complex arrangements that are glossed over by seemingly commonsensical ideas of commercialization and mainstreaming. The outline presented here focuses on a few structural transformations and can be nuanced or corrected by future research through more detailed case studies, ethnography, and audience and musician research.

The chapter is based on extensive field research conducted over a ten-year period. Since 2007, I have conducted (1) exploratory fieldwork on general aspects of festival design and experiences at a dozen festivals and (2) systematic readings of scholarly festival literature and festival coverage in trade magazines, especially *Billboard*. Since 2009, I have engaged in (3) formal and informal conversations with industry professionals, chief among them the managements of Roskilde and Tomorrowland, and (4) participated in two major international live music industry conventions in 2012–2013.[1] Of particular importance in gaining knowledge of the industry's inner workings was my experience as a scholar-consultant on four projects between 2010 and 2013 in which festival managements described their situation and challenges to me as an industry advisor, sharing a wealth of information and concerns for the purpose of identifying and solving their most urgent problems. Two projects are confidential and the other two are a report on music festivals in Denmark for the Danish government, for which I served as the chief advisor and main author, and a business project with the Roskilde Festival titled "The Festival as a Platform of Innovation," which I directed. The latter project led to encounters with managers of large independent festivals, including Sziget and Exit. Over the course of these interactions, I learned how festival management in different genres was increasingly operating within similar corporate discourses.

During the field research, I became aware of my sympathy with independent festivals and my discomfort with the incursion of corporate values into these festivals. Above all, I found myself unable to regard impartially the consequences of the concert industry's discovery of the festival as a business opportunity. I participated most actively in the industry sphere at the peak of the commercial boom in the early 2010s, so I could not have chosen a time of more intense turbulence. Over the years, I met members of the managements of a dozen of the largest music festivals in the world and can say with certainty that they have evolved into a corporate culture in which humanist values have all but disappeared. The most profound changes in management value systems occurred in the late 1990s and early 2000s, which is unsurprising given the dramatic change in the economy.

General consequences of the industry's exploitation of festivals are discussed later in this chapter, but there were particular field experiences that shaped my subject position in the field and my analytical perspective. One was an encounter with managers of smaller independent festivals that expressed doubt about their future existence in the face of growing corporate dominance. Another was personal harassment by a for-profit festival organization, partially owned by an international corporation. On two occasions in the mid-2010s, I faced digital harassment from members of management in response to statements I had made in news media interviews. I had encouraged reflexivity about the impact of for-profit ownership on festival culture and about municipal subsidies for for-profit festivals. One manager told me to never participate in interviews about music festivals again, and another vaguely threatened to go nuclear and posted false accusations on his Facebook page, which had thousands of followers. I subsequently learned that the organization had harassed other people and was in serious crisis at the time. The experience nonetheless added to a growing sense of alienation from the industry. A journalist familiar with the local situation commented that the organization was aggressively controlling local discourse, expecting everyone to be their brand ambassadors. My general discomfort with the growing corporatism and consumerism eventually led to my quiet exit from the industry sphere.

A Soft-Shell Formation in a Festival Economy

Peterson's Conception of Industry-Driven Popularization

Richard Peterson was one of the pioneers of the culture of production perspective that emerged in sociology in the 1970s. Central to this direction in sociology was the idea that culture and social structure do not simply mirror each other, but that culture is shaped by the system within which it is created, distributed, and evaluated (Peterson and Anand 2004, 311–12). Peterson's landmark 1997 study of the country music industry develops an argument about industry-driven popularization. The book is a model analysis of the commercial institutionalization of a music genre in the mid-twentieth century. It shows how the corporate music industry started to take interest in country music when the established corporate production system was in crisis and reports on country music's mass-market potentials surfaced regularly in *Billboard* magazine (Peterson 1997, 187–89). One strategy employed by major recording companies was to develop performers into national stars by having them adopt middle-class pop aesthetics and eliminate rural and working-class signifiers (Peterson 1997, chapter 9; Holt 2007, chapter 3). The so-called Nashville Sound was smoother and lusher. Peterson's research showed that many of the performers of this softer form of country music were not positioning themselves in the genre's traditional communities and were not embraced by those communities. To some extent, traditional communities felt that the Nashville Sound was not even country music. To explain these dynamics sociologically, Peterson proposed a dialectic boundary metaphor of a hard core and a soft shell in the genre. His research revealed how the corporate industry was primarily interested in exploiting the latter. Peterson defines the distinction and its political economy as follows:

> The basic justification for hard country is that it represents the authentic tradition of the music called country and that it is by and for those steeped in the tradition. The corresponding justification for soft country is that it melds country with pop music to make it enjoyable to the much larger numbers of those not born into or knowledgeable about country music. The leading hard-core artists have received the most attention from contemporary commentators and later scholars as well. At the same time, the leading soft-shell artists of an era have tended to be more popular with audiences and to make more money than their hard-core counterparts. (Peterson 1997, 150)

This argument can be extended to other music genres and their performance cultures. A key point here is that the development of a soft-shell style of music is shaped by interests beyond the genre itself, and this means that any analysis of this development cannot interpret it solely within the genre. The same principle applies to music festivals: They, too, are increasingly shaped by the adoption of popular culture fashions and by the interests of powerful economic institutions in society. These forces have in fact challenged the autonomy of the popular music festival institution and its historical trajectory. The corporatization of popular music festivals has resulted in a general turn to popularized versions of music genres in festival programming and a general adaptation to mass culture tastes. Moreover, the festival economy has expanded from music and further into general commodity markets, such as advertising, food, and fashion.

EDM Pop

This chapter examines soft-shell developments in rock and EDM festivals to illustrate how they are increasingly governed by the same market logics. Another motivation for bringing the EDM pop festival into the analysis is its broader significance to festival history. The rise of the EDM pop festival in the 2000s represented the peak of the popular music festival's evolution as a commercial institution and a mass-market consumer culture event. The present chapter adds nuance to my earlier work on the industry-driven popularization of EDM pop (Holt 2017b), while the next chapter will explore aspects of EDM pop as a performance and media culture.

EDM pop was the result of the transformation of popular forms of house and techno into a new form of Top 40 pop music in the 2000s. It went on to enjoy mass popularity as a global pop culture novelty. Its growing popularity was signaled by Tiësto's performance at the opening ceremonies of the Olympics in 2004, where he was the first DJ to perform, and by Daft Punk's show at Coachella in 2006. The peak years of EDM pop in the early 2010s are represented by mega hits such as Aviici's "Levels," LMFAO's "Party Rock Anthem," and Martin Garrix's "Animals," the expansions of the Electric Daisy Carnival, Tomorrowland, and Ultra Music festivals, and the Hollywood movie *Spring Breakers* (Bogart 2012; Dargis 2013; Korine 2012). The market declined but did not entirely collapse in the second half of the decade (Smirke 2019). Calvin Harris and Deadmau5 are still very popular, and newer artists have emerged, including Alan Walker, the Chainsmokers, Marshmello, Zedd, and K-pop act Blackpink. Moreover, EDM pop shows are still well attended at large, rock-based music festivals. The music no longer represents a global pop culture moment, but it has transformed the popular music landscape and redefined existing genres.

During its peak years, EDM pop was frequently identified by casual fans and general pop music journalists as "EDM" without being distinguished from other forms of electronic dance music. Many specialist fans and producers discarded the term "EDM," whereas it proliferated in rock and pop music magazines such as *Pitchfork* and *Spin* and in the trade magazine *Billboard* (Yoshitomi 2013; u/Baft_Dastard 2015). Simon Reynolds, an experienced music journalist, pointed out that EDM pop was not entirely new but rather a rebranding of the 1990s rave culture (Reynolds 2012). Nevertheless, the magnitude of changes in aesthetics that accompanied the arrival of a new youth generation and the adoption of new digital production tools should not be underestimated. Evidence of a newly emerging phenomenon can also be identified in the rise of DJ pop celebrities, collaborations with pop star vocalists, and festivals characterized by new styles of architecture and audiovisual digital mediations.

EDM pop has been the subject of little research, but broad arguments about the culture have been proposed by generalist popular music scholars, such as Robin James and myself. In her 2015 book, James discusses "EDM-pop" (with a hyphen) as a trend within broader transformations of popular music in neoliberalism. She conceives it as a crossover formation and identifies core aesthetic elements, such as breaks, the foregrounding of timbre, and modular structures related to computer-based production (James

2015, chapter 1). Some of these elements can also be found in other forms of EDM, but they take on specific forms in EDM pop, and James's comparison with pop rather than hard-core EDM is symptomatic of common experiences among audiences, since many fans have come to EDM from rock and pop. James uncovers the dark side of some EDM pop songs, looking beyond the positive surface being projected, but she does not discuss how the field is constructed or explore its diversity, instead analyzing individual songs in isolation from industry contexts of production, distribution, and consumption. A more representative sample of EDM pop would include the party-oriented house music of David Guetta, Swedish House Mafia, and the abovementioned artists. The centrality of their music to the larger EDM pop culture can be experienced at many large festivals, which are also important sites for artists and audiences and for the broader sensemaking in this cultural field, particularly through dancing. Judy Park's exploration of EDM pop culture at festivals, for instance, provides a more representative account of audience experiences and one that is grounded in field research (Park 2017). A fundamental dimension of EDM pop is its celebration of mass culture aesthetics. Conventional elements of mass culture entertainment can be found in the music, in the visual culture, and in the festivals. Generic models and trivial narratives proliferate in hit songs, theme park designs, and brand culture, and in the mechanical simplicity and light emotions in songs about juvenile love and happiness such as "Don't You Worry Child," quoted above.

How did EDM pop evolve into festivals? It followed an overall trajectory from unauthorized raves to the commercial institutionalization of commercial house music in large clubs and, ultimately, into the large dance floor of the festival. The techno rave, an all-night psychedelic dance event inspired by the hippie events in San Francisco in the mid-1960s, flourished in large, unauthorized warehouse and outdoor raves in the late 1980s, but stricter government regulation in England, France, and Italy, for instance, decimated raves and stimulated the commercial institutionalization of rave culture into clubs for popular forms of house music (St. John 2009, 4–11). The amateur free festival movement of "teknivals" for hard-core techno constituted an alternative across Central and Western Europe. The commercial clubs have been described as "pleasure prisons" that "domesticated" the dance experience (Reynolds 1998, 424). They introduced dress codes, security searches, extensive surveillance, and the enforcement of copyright standards, among other things (St. John 2009, 11). The growing market for these clubs and popular forms of EDM driven by superstar DJs (Haslam 2001/2002) laid the groundwork for the expansion into larger "dance floors" in the 2000s, first into arenas and, in the 2010s, almost exclusively as part of festivals. EDM pop even found its way into a transformational festival such as Burning Man and contributed to its realignment with large popular music festivals (see p. 57). To hard-core ravers, the EDM pop festival challenged the egalitarian community ethos and the "no spectators" principle, introducing a gulf between the headphone-wearing DJ celebrity on a higher and more elaborate main stage and a vast sea of dancers (St. John 2017a, 7). Yet promoters recall an "ur-moment" experience of the liminal vibe and "attempt to recreate the primal rave, augmented by sensory technologies and event design" (St. John 2017a , 8).

In terms of ownership, the organizational field of large EDM pop events and festivals was corporatized and expanded globally in the 2010s, with Ultra Enterprises, Inc., and ID&T expanding considerably in the Global South. Most if not all events with a superstar DJ lineup were owned by SFX and Live Nation, including Creamfields, Electric Daisy Carnival, Sunburn, Stereosonic, Tomorrowland, Nature One, and all the other festivals put on by large national EDM promoters, including Insomniac (1993–present) in the United States, ID&T (1992–present) in Holland, and i-Motion (1994–present) in Germany.[2] After SFX's bankruptcy in 2016, several of the company's festivals were continued by LiveStyle, Inc.

There are reasons to be more cautious in applying the concept of soft shell in the analysis of contemporary popular music compared to mid-twentieth-century country music. At least four factors contribute to the erosion of boundaries between previously more distinct popular music spheres:

1. Gentrification of cities and their club scenes, as illustrated by the rock and techno fields in New York and Berlin, respectively
2. Digitalization of music production and distribution, resulting in deregulation of genres and audiences and their growing media proximity
3. Intensified market competition in festivals, which motivates festivals to program more mass-market music than they might otherwise have done
4. The co-option of underground music in the programming of large festivals, which exploits the festival model's potential for including diverse forms of music but brings underground music into a mass culture setting.

While Peterson's core-boundary conception cannot be adopted wholesale as a framework to structure a theory of contemporary culture, his insights into industry-driven popularization and, specifically, the corporate exploitation of popular forms outside a genre's own networks are central to the analysis of popular music festival history since the formative stages of commercial institutionalization in the 1980s. Peterson's analytical discourse can be expanded by taking into account the new functions of the festival that evolved with popularization. The logics of popularization coevolved with logics of exploitation in a larger economy. In particular, the festival became a business platform for larger commercial institutions in more general commodity markets outside the cultural field. Popular music festivals have increasingly exploited commodity markets, such as advertising, beverage, food, hospitality, media, and transportation. Event management scholars have proposed the concept of mixed industry (Getz and Page 2007/2016), which captures an important aspect. However, music festivals are primarily framed within music markets and the music industry. Their economy involves other industries, but these other industries can be considered supply industries or paraindustries.

The Festival Became a Format for the Music Business (1990s–)

Logic: Music Markets and Headliners

The growing market value of touring star performers in the late 1990s (Krueger 2005) transformed the role of concerts and festivals in the music economy. Large festivals had already begun to present more stars and appealed to music consumers with a combined program of concerts that would cost considerably more if separate. As festivals grew in numbers and scale to form a larger market, meeting growing demands for this type of leisure (see p. 157), festival promoters became more professionalized and interacted more with each other and with the corporate music industry. This resulted in the institutionalization of festivals into a distinct organizational field within the popular music industry. Festivals went from being viewed as idiosyncratic cultural projects outside the main operations of the music business to becoming central to the concert industry and eventually to the music business as a whole. Festivals became one of the main sources of revenue for artist agencies, managers, and booking agencies.

The large-scale festival became such a lucrative format that many event and concert promoters began promoting festivals. To them, the festival functioned as a generic format for selling concerts. This development began in the 1990s and peaked with the boom in the 2000s when festivals gained further cultural and economic centrality and increasingly became owned or dominated by corporate concert promoters. A major implication at the institutional level can be identified in the partial erosion of the large, independent post-hippie festival in Europe. Several of these festivals are no longer fully independent, including Glastonbury (since 2002) and Sziget (since

2017), and they have all become further integrated into international mass markets and become dependent on star performers in a system of corporate ownership.

The limited role of festivals in the music economy of the 1970s and 1980s was reflected in the pricing of performers. Rock festival promoters, for instance, were able to book artists at a discounted "festival rate" compared to arena concerts (Leif Skov, conversation with the author, August 10, 2010). This arrangement eroded when festival headliners became a major source of revenue for concert promoters in the 2000s. The main stage became simply another arena venue.[3] Festival promoters in turn compensated for growing expenses by selling one-day tickets and securing more sponsorship (Anderton 2011; Hampp 2013). The one-day tickets contributed to the rise of an arena concert culture within festivals, as thousands came for one day to hear one headliner and became spectators to the festival culture. At one of Scandinavia's large-scale festivals in 2019, one-day tickets accounted for about 30% of the ticket sales.

One might suspect that the market-driven emphasis on headliners only happened in concert-based festivals of rock and jazz, but it also happened in EDM pop festivals. Electric Daisy Carnival, Tomorrowland, and Ultra Music Festival have marketed themselves as event brands and emphasized the overall party experience rather than the lineup (Sherburne 2013; Mason 2012; Dally 2018), but the lineups continue to feature countless chart-topping DJs, and these DJs are featured prominently in the festivals' live broadcasts. The lineups also reveal that the EDM pop festival model has stabilized. Tomorrowland, for instance, consistently drew from the same pool of DJ superstars every year in the first half of the 2010s and added new ones playing the same kind of music in the second half of the decade.[4] Many rock and pop festivals have featured these DJs to co-opt this pop culture fashion with a broad generational appeal and thus further popularize their own festival. This includes festivals such as Bonnaroo, Coachella, Rock Werchter, and T in the Park.

The evolving headliner economy has had several implications for festival culture. It led to a growing focus on celebrity, main-stage events, and more one-day customers. And because stars operate in a system of corporate ownership, concert industry corporations acquired festivals to use them as platforms for their artists and to control their circulation and reap the full profits. This led to more standardized lineups, with more of the same stars appearing at more festivals. A growing number of festivals are therefore now owned by the same corporations and have similar lineups, architectural designs, hospitality services, and online ticketing services.

The headliner economy, moreover, has resulted in higher prices for tickets, food, and drinks and more sponsorships. The growth in sponsorship was motivated by rising operating costs, but also by an interest in profit maximization. The headliner economy thus contributed to a general commodification of the festival environment. It also shaped the design and location of new festivals, since more festivals have been created based on market research performed on behalf of international corporations, as opposed to evolving from a local community or scene. Festivals of Anglophone popular music have popped up in more countries and in urban parks and former industrial facilities. Many of them have been designed primarily for consumption, with most of the spaces centered around the consumption of music, food, drinks, or around commercial accommodation. Many festivals have developed camping into glamorous "glamping." Many city festivals have no camping, including Lollapalooza (Chicago, Berlin, and Paris), Outside Lands (San Francisco), Governors Ball (New York), Wireless (London), and Sónar (Barcelona).

The large-scale corporatization of the industry began in the 1990s when Robert Sillerman's SFX Entertainment acquired multiple rock music festivals. In addition to serving as a touring circuit, festival identities were developed as product brands to strengthen their appeal to mass-market consumers and sponsors. In 2000, SFX became Clear Channel Entertainment, then in 2005 Live Nation, which expanded internationally. It acquired about forty festivals in Europe, including a majority stake in Britain's Festival Republic. In the 2010s, Live Nation acquired a number of EDM pop festivals in Europe and elsewhere, including Insomniac Events and the Swedish EDM pop festival promoter Stureplansgruppen (Sackllah 2015; "Live Nation's New Groove"; Hanley 2015). The company's development illustrates the overall shift of emphasis in the industry from concert venues and arena concerts to festivals.[5]

Meanwhile, Sillerman embarked on a new corporatization odyssey in the 2010s, this time with EDM pop, still using the name SFX Entertainment. Beginning in 2011, SFX purchased hundreds of EDM pop events and festivals and grew media and advertising infrastructures around them. SFX also acquired Beatport, one of the most popular websites and distributors of EDM, and popularized it by shifting focus to EDM pop and developing partnerships with Shazam and iHeartRadio. Beatport's Top 20 radio show, for instance, was promoted via iHeartRadio's mass-market hit radio stations (Mason 2014).

The corporatization of rock and EDM pop festivals has resulted in more similar organizational cultures and more integration with media and advertising commodities. Yet there are unique aspects to the situation in each genre. Rock festivals, for instance, have not adopted soft-shell rock with mass culture aesthetics. They have presented some EDM pop, but the softer elements in the rock music programming of prestigious rock festivals have focused on urban indie aesthetics, for instance, which represent a popularization of alternative and experimental rock. These artists draw from the softer-rock sounds of singer-songwriters but are far removed from artists that focus on hit song formulas, including teen pop artists such as Justin Bieber, Demi Lovato, Miley Cyrus, or Katy Perry. The commercial institutionalization of indie rock is ongoing, and Ariana Grande's appearance at Coachella in 2019 might signal a further soft-shell orientation, but broad, rock-based festivals generally exclude a range of mass culture to sustain their middle-class, white, patriarchal selves. These festivals reproduce and renew traditional notions of rock authenticity and feature female pop artists that appeal to the male rock fan. Examples include black vocalists such as Beyoncé, Janelle Monáe, Bruno Mars, Nicki Minaj, Rihanna, and Solange, and white vocalists such as Billie Eilish, Kacey Musgraves, and Maggie Rogers.

The Festival Became a Generic Event for Mainstream Society (2000s–)

Logic: Postindustrial Cultural Economy and Celebrity

Through the 1990s, cities, news media, and the mainstream business world generally did not embrace festivals of rock and EDM in enthusiastic terms. Few cities were interested in hosting such festivals. News media ran stories about hedonism, drugs, deviancy, and noise (McKay 2000; St. John 2009). The relationship between popular music festivals and cities was dominated by a perceived need for minimizing negative impacts such as noise and waste. Festival managers were not yet included in the city's elite networks.

The relationship between festivals and cities changed fundamentally in the 2000s when the commercial institutionalization of popular music festivals had diminished their countercultural values and created a "gentrified" consumer culture event that seemed compatible and even appealing to evolving discourses of "the eventful city" and "the festival city" (Richards and Palmer 2010, 2–3). These discourses focused on the impact of festivals on the local economy, building on developments within postindustrial economies of tourism and place marketing. During the 1970s and 1980s, city governments, nudged by private consultancies, started to promote culture as an economic driver (Zukin 1995; Florida 2002). Early culture-led growth strategies typically involved museums, sports facilities, amusement parks, and the development of public spaces for middle-class consumption (Zukin 1995). In the 1980s, the term "festivalization" emerged and cultural events and festivals became a must-have for urban planners seeking to create atmospheres of constant cultural ambience and festivity. Urban planners in cities such as Amsterdam, Barcelona, and Berlin later developed festival strategies for "creative areas" of these cities, thus producing regulated environments of constant festive events (Zherdev 2014, 6 and 14). But popular music became central to eventful city agendas only in the 2000s when the live music industry boom increased the circulation of superstars and appealed to the now-dominant creative economy agenda (see p. 18; Florida 2002). In parts of Continental Western Europe, city elites shared the excitement about the growing number of Anglophone superstar concerts, and this stimulated a trend of arena construction projects that began in the late 1990s and continued into the 2010s. City elites eventually adapted to the popular music festival boom, granting permissions to for-profit music festivals in the city and in some cases also subsidizing them. These festivals were able to attract mass audiences, and EDM pop festivals in particular became recognized by city elites for their production of images of the city as a place filled with large crowds of happy young consumers. Popular music festivals figured prominently among the growing number of large events that were given unprecedented permissions for the use of public space, including closing traffic in parts of the city center.[6]

A few examples of major festive events will help illustrate their changing place in city agendas and the permissions they obtained to use central areas of the city. South by Southwest in Austin is a vehicle for the city's trademarked "Live Music Capital of the World" branding project and closes down part of the city center for about a week (O'Meara and Tretter 2013). The Love Parade went from being announced as a demonstration to getting permission for the use of public space to becoming a mega-event in the late 1990s that created practical challenges for the organizers and the city administration in Berlin. It was eventually adopted into the vision of a "Ruhr Metropolis" to attract young people and boost tourism in the Ruhr region's postindustrial cities, the same vision that shaped Essen's year as European Capital of Culture in 2010 (Hitzler and Nye 2011). The Life Is Beautiful Music & Arts Festival in Las Vegas was created as part of a downtown development project (Kaydo 2014). The CBGB Festival has presented large, free concerts in Central Park and Times Square, with the festival manager commenting in 2013 that Times Square was "the most visited spot on earth," thus indicating the centrality of market logic (Beltrone 2013). When the organizers of

Electric Daisy Carnival decided to move the event from Los Angeles to Las Vegas following the death of a young woman of fifteen, the mayor of Las Vegas brushed aside questions about drugs and safety, in contrast to public attitudes toward raves twenty years earlier:

> We're going to declare June 20–26 Electric Daisy Carnival Week in the City of Las Vegas and ask all of our citizens to support this monumental event. . . . I look forward to it. I may even show up there, who knows. . . . As far as I'm concerned, anything that's going to bring people and money and energy, that's all I care about. (Toplikar 2011)

The economic interests in festivals among city governments and corporate sponsors increasingly became mediated through quantitative discourse on cultural events. The same generic criteria were applied to music festivals, film festivals, fashion weeks, sports events, and other kinds of pop culture events ("Big Brand Sponsors Target Music Festivals"). The quantitative event industry discourse focused on the number of visitors and the volume of spending on hotels and restaurants and accompanied the rise of generic approaches to production. Events in many different cultural fields were increasingly adopting the same mass-market design, communication, and marketing techniques such as theming and visual branding. The specific discourse of economic impacts was adopted from the tourism industry to rationalize public spending and gain access to corporate sponsors and political elites (Getz and Page 2007/2016).[7] Industry-based music festivals, too, began managing their events as a brand and commissioned impact studies to communicate their economic value to stakeholders. Insomniac Events, for instance, has commissioned economic impact studies almost every year since 2010 from the Los Angeles consultancy Beacon Economics, which has many clients in the sports events industry and in the public sector (Shah 2015). ID&T-SFX commissioned a similar study from the same company on the first TomorrowWorld festival in 2013 (Ruggieri 2014). These studies also serve to counter skeptical attitudes related to perceived drug use and situate festival promoters in the top industry tier of culture and sports events (Koen Lemmens and Christophe Van den Branden, ID&T, interview with the author, January 24, 2013).

The role of music festivals as a platform for mainstream society and business[8] was further extended in the 2010s, as fashion and lifestyle industries became involved. This happened at a time when the music industries drew inspiration from the promotional culture of the branded body, defining artists as brand commodities and using them as mediums of branding (Meier 2017). The incursion of fashion culture into festivals happened first and with greatest force at Coachella. This festival became a destination for young Hollywood celebrities and fashion magazines in the 2010s, including "it girls" such as Paris Hilton and Kendall Jenner, but also Cameron Diaz, Clint Eastwood, and Leonardo DiCaprio (McCarthy 2018). In 2016, a reporter for the *New Yorker* wrote that she had never been to Coachella but felt surrounded by the festival all the time. She claimed Coachella had become "a fully formed aesthetic, a lightning rod of inspiration, a way of being," primarily referring to sartorial culture (Battan 2016). *Vogue* started reporting from Coachella around 2010, and H&M launched a Coachella Collection in 2015. Fashion brands continue to produce festival collections. Fashion and celebrity culture even spread to postcountercultural festivals such as Burning Man, which have wealthy patrons and attract some of the same celebrities as Coachella (Robinson 2015, 134; Wmag 2018).

The Festival Became a Social Media Event (2010s–)

Logic: Promotional Culture and Digital Sponsorship

The growing presence of music festivals in popular culture was accompanied by a general media intensification of the individual festival event. Traditional broadcast media expanded their coverage considerably; festival marketers began broadcasting more stage performances to generate digital sponsorship revenues and producing visual mediations of performing bodies for promotional purposes; and festivalgoers with smartphones engaged in self-mediation in their own social media channels to enrich their experience and boost their digital selves. The phone gave the performing body a technology of communication that it had not previously owned, empowering its electronic potentials and challenging its biological sovereignty.

Historically, electronic mediations of music festivals had happened in the form of film productions and broadcasts on radio and television. These forms of media production required considerable resources, and that partially explains the concentration on the largest and most prestigious festivals. National broadcasting corporations, moreover, continue to concentrate on concert broadcasting and on rock festivals in the coverage of popular music festivals, ignoring or giving lower priority to less prestigious rock festivals, EDM festivals, and folk and jazz festivals. The BBC's expansion of festival coverage in the 2000s, for instance, largely happened in the coverage of Glastonbury. When it began producing television broadcasts from Glastonbury in the mid-1990s, about twenty staff produced eight hours of daily broadcasting. Within a few years, the broadcasts had moved to a more popular channel, and by 2015 the BBC had about two hundred people producing livestreams across multiple radio, television, and online channels ("Glastonbury TV"). The BBC covers no other festival with the same intensity (Andrew Rogers, senior producer at the BBC, interview with the author, April 1, 2015).

The popularization of festivals, however, also challenged some of the values espoused by public media. The director of NPR Music felt that the changing outlook of festivals, with the programming of more popular forms of music, reduced the value of festivals to NPR's mission of music discovery (Anya Grundmann, director of NPR, interview with the author, February 4, 2015). The BBC is a larger and more centralized organization that adapted to the popularization as part of its broader populist turn. Even so, the evolution of internet broadcasting challenged the sovereignty of national public media. Boiler Room, Red Bull TV, Yahoo!, and YouTube all became appealing to festivals seeking to attract international audiences and grow their digital sponsorship revenues (Smith 2012; Hampp 2015; see also pp. 206ff.). A large international audience for live broadcasts could generate a substantial source of sponsorship revenue for festivals (Christophe Van den Branden and Koen Lemmens, ID&T, interview with the author, January 24, 2013).

Social media led to the intensification of visual communication in festival culture and more specifically to new visual cultures that participated in the relations of power between performing bodies. At a basic level, social media expanded the agents of mediation from centralized mass media to digital networks, from outsider perspectives of news media to insider perspectives of festival marketers and festivalgoers. Social media practices intensified visual mediations of performing bodies. While in principle all participants had equal access to tools of mediation, dominant psychological and social forces in the seasonal event were empowered in a visual economy that exploited women's bodies in particular (chapter 9). Festivalgoers, press photographers, and festival marketers produced and circulated a growing number of images centered around men's interests in female beauty and sexuality. The boom in social media visual culture thus led to not only a focus on visual appearances, on the exterior of the body, but also exploited and reinforced dominant constructions of gender and sexuality. Festival promoters have used their resources and their authority to privilege a male gaze for commercial gain, and mass media have exploited the same male desires, from CNN to lifestyle magazines such as *Esquire*, *LA Weekly*, *Vogue*, and *W* (March 2018; Saad 2018; Lopes 2017; McCarthy 2018; Wmag 2018).

A combined process of industry popularization and social media exploitation of women can be identified in events promoted by the Dutch-based

EDM promoter ID&T. The company was founded in 1993 and promoted some of Europe's first large commercial EDM events and festivals, specifically the indoor rave Thunderdome (1992–2012) and the Mysteryland festival (1994–present). These were some of the most popular hard-core events in Holland in the 1990s. In 2005, the company created the Tomorrowland festival in Belgium, which represented a change in direction with respect to its EDM pop profile, taking inspiration from the company's flagship EDM pop arena event, Sensation White. Tomorrowland's first headliner was Tiësto, who had just appeared at the Olympics the year before and toured Sensation White events internationally. In 2012, Thunderdome was terminated because ID&T's management felt that the event no longer fit with the company's transition into EDM pop. One of the company's managers had moved to the United States, and the management now "wanted a piece of the EDM pie," like many other promoters of EDM events (Dicker 2018). The decision to end Thunderdome was made less than a year before the company sold a majority stake to SFX.

The most powerful marketing tool for Tomorrowland was online video. Chapter 9 details how the marketers of Tomorrowland developed immersive cinematography of the extroverted performance culture of EDM pop. The marketers, all male, also deliberately used footage of women based on their own perception of female beauty. Young female festivalgoers were presented in high-quality images and with cinematic effects to create glamorous and sensual images for the male gaze. An annual routine was developed in which a video "trailer" was distributed before the event to stimulate consumer desire and an "aftermovie" to strengthen the customer's attachment to the commodity. Some of the videos in the early 2010s became internet sensations with YouTube view counts above one hundred million. For festivalgoers, the videos became folkloric texts that created scripts and interpretative schemes for their festival behaviors and experiences. For wider audiences, the videos were a form of entertainment and voyeurism into a performance culture with which they had little or no experience. Social media video generally contributed to a collapse of contexts between festivals and society and stimulated the growth of festival coverage in mass media.

A range of other social media platforms and applications contributed to the intensified visualization of performing bodies, including Instagram, Facebook, Pinterest, and Snapchat. Instagram was one of the most popular visual applications, and its hashtags are revealing of the functions of these mediations: An Instagram search on one day in October 2017 and again in June 2018 revealed more than one million Instagram posts with the hashtags #festivalstyle, #festivalfashion, #festivalwear, #festivalmakeup, and #festivalhair.[9] The hippies of the 1960s might have been disappointed that there were more posts tagged #festivaljewelry than #festivallove.

The accelerated mediatization of festival culture in the 2010s can be compared to the broadcasting of large sports events on television, which began in the 1960s. A comparison with sports helps identify both similar and unique dynamics in music festivals. General aspects of the evolution of televised sports events can be illustrated by the example of the Olympics. Fees for television broadcast rights replaced ticket sales as the main revenue source for the Olympics in 1972, and since the late 1970s more than half of the income from TV broadcast rights has come from commercial networks in the United States (Real 2014). Corporate sponsorship became a major source of revenue with the 1984 Games in Los Angeles. Television transmissions drove the commercialization of sports, and this became the target of scholarly critiques, the likes of which have not yet been produced to a similar degree in the music festival literature, partly because festivals had already become commercially institutionalized by the time they were being regularly televised, and partly because of a lack of critical music festival scholarship. Scholars of sports argued, for instance, that the growing influence of stars and sponsors challenged the fundamental Olympic values of equality and democracy (Real 1998 and 2014; Roche 2000, 166). Scholars also argued that television broadcasts altered the balance between the ritual elements of the event, placing more emphasis on spectacle. It also boosted the transformation of sports into celebrity culture, beginning with Michael Jordan in the 1980s. Jordan appeared in ads as a glamorous celebrity, not a conventional athlete: He had a line of lifestyle products named after him, and media reported on his lifestyle of a 56,000-square-foot mansion, sports cars, and celebrity friends (Kellner 2002, 64).[10]

Media have stimulated interest in popular music festivals since their beginnings in the 1960s, but media revenues have not become the main element in the business model of music festivals. Media consumption did not evolve into regular consumption of individual performances as bounded commodities, like sports matches and tournaments did. Music festivals, however, are embedded in the media culture of music. The rising headliner economy can be interpreted as an economy of media power and, specifically, celebrity. The media culture of pop stars provided the basis for the commercial institutionalization of festivals. The mediatization of music festivals in broadcasting and in social media, moreover, became commercially institutionalized and contributed to changes in values and behaviors, as demonstrated by the rise of fashion culture and by the mediation of festivalgoers and the remediation of their media content for promotional purposes. The development of regular, annual broadcasts and videos of the individual festival was also accompanied by the intensification of spectacle and celebrity. The superstar DJs of EDM pop brought elements of teenage and tabloid celebrity to the popular music festival. A handful of the highest-earning DJs are on *Forbes*'s Top 100 list and are subjects of tabloid media stories featuring their private jets, parties with Paris Hilton, videos with mostly women pop stars, luxury apartments in celebrity cities such as Miami and Hollywood, residencies in Las Vegas, and paparazzi photos. David Guetta had his name and picture on a series of Coca-Cola bottles in 2012 and met with the United Nations general secretary in 2013 to support World Humanitarian Day. Calvin Harris dated Taylor Swift for about a year and appeared as a model in a global Armani underwear campaign.

Conclusion: A Productivist Argument?

This chapter expanded on Peterson's argument about industry-driven popularization. His conception of the relationship between a genre's core and its shell was adopted into an analysis of contemporary popular music culture and into festivals. I argued that festivals still combine hard-core and soft-shell music in their programming, but that they have shifted emphasis to the latter. Peterson's argument also served to conceptualize the evolution of EDM pop from clubs to festivals and to situate it in the long history of the corporate industry's exploitation of musical formations beyond their own distinct genre spheres. Another key aspect of this chapter's argument is that the soft-shell evolution in rock and EDM pop festivals involved the rise of a media economy of headliners and the broadening of the institutional base from the music and festival industries into mainstream business and society. The latter included alliances with city governments and the integration into general commodity markets, such as fashion and advertising.

How might the social study of popular music festivals add nuance to the old productivist vision of industrial organization as the engine of history? Is the consumer culture music festival merely an effect of the capitalist mode of production? Sociologists have turned away from this vision, which proliferated in the formative era of the discipline (Sassatelli 2007, 1). While the argument presented here highlights the agency of the industry, it goes beyond productivism by combining the analysis of industry and market logics with the analysis of culture and media. The headliner economy and the marketing video, for instance, were analyzed as market-driven developments, but also as an exploitation of consumer desires and the media culture of music. The soft-shell evolution in festival profiles was similarly interpreted as a market-driven development that was also an adaptation to musical tastes in evolving media cultures of rock and EDM. Music programming in the older tradition of commercial rock festivals displays a continuity of neo-bohemian rock ideology, while EDM pop festivals fully embraced mass culture in terms of musical aesthetics and tabloid celebrity.

In conclusion, I hope to have demonstrated why critical approaches to music festivals need not rely on commonsensical ideas of commercialization and mainstreaming, but that they can benefit from analysis of the relationship of festivals to the market and the institutions of capitalism. This chapter's analysis of industry-driven popularization has illuminated changes in the outlook of music festivals *and* in their functions in musical culture and society. The systemic perspective on how festivals act in the market and in changing discourses has helped explain how the festival has evolved into an institution of the corporate music industry and how it has transformed this industry and developed a closer relationship with more general institutions in society, such as cities and corporate advertising. The dominant forms of popular music festivals have reached wider audiences and taken on new functions, but also become further removed from their origins in urban scenes and from the civic values of the festival institution in modernity.

: 9 :

Festival Video and Social Media

Music creates a sense of freedom in my mind and soul. When I am standing in the crowd and feeling the passion, which rises with every beat. . . . That's what excites me and makes me feel alive. . . .

MICHAEL, GERMAN FAN

I love listening to electronic dance music because when I hear the sounds, I feel free! All my stress goes away. Today, I was very stressed about my school stuff, but after school I started to listen to electronic music and felt so much better.

MILLA, FINNISH FAN

I'm not watching the [Tomorrowland] videos to hear specific songs. I'm fully immersed in the experience of these videos and getting excited about the next festival.

ANONYMOUS, GERMAN FAN[1]

The words above come from fans of the Tomorrowland festival in Belgium. The sixty-five fans that completed my online questionnaire in January 2013 demonstrated a strong passion for the music and for experiencing it at this festival. In terms of firsthand experience, 95.6% of them had participated in Tomorrowland 2012 and could not imagine a better place for experiencing their favorite music. Their responses add nuance to the stereotypes of EDM pop festivals as a diluted form of EDM, ridiculed for their superficiality, naïveté, and extroverted visuality.

The visual culture of the EDM pop festival contributed to its proliferation as a global pop culture fashion in the early 2010s. Mass numbers of young people were dancing in broad daylight, visibly communicating euphoria and singing along to hit songs. The festival architecture and pyrotechnics created a spectacular visual setting. The visual culture of performing bodies and event design coevolved with social media marketing. A new form of music video, the music festival marketing video, created glamorous images of a global generation of fans traveling to luxurious festival environments and experiencing pleasure in large crowds to the pulsating beat produced by superstar DJs. Eroticized images of young women, who seemingly took pleasure in the camera's attention, traveled far beyond the spheres of electronic dance music fans. The seminal marketing video in the field was the Tomorrowland "aftermovie" uploaded to YouTube on August 29, 2011. This video had hundreds of millions of views across more than thirty countries within two years and more than 50,000 user comments.[2] The responses from my informants strongly suggest that this video was a defining moment, for some even a major life moment.[3] My informants also witnessed how the video surfaced in broadcast television across the globe, from Scandinavia to Latin America.

I was initially drawn to this internet sensation and to a form of musical festivity that was new to me. I came to the field with stereotypes and expected to feel out of place when I went to Tomorrowland in 2013. Based on my extensive experience of what constitutes a serious and scholarly topic in the humanities, I knew that writing about EDM pop would not strengthen my reputation as a scholar. Even now, in 2020, this music is almost nonexistent as a topic in music studies. The few book chapters and journal articles on festivals dedicated to this music have contributed important insights, but this body of work has not yet matured to include broader cultural analysis and discussions of knowledge interests (e.g., Montano 2009, 2011, and 2017; Park 2017). My motivations were a complex mix of commercial and cultural interests, reflecting my professional experience in academia, which I will discuss in this book's conclusion. I was interested in learning about developments in festivals, media, and cultural production, but I also believed, and still do, that studying mass culture serves a democratic purpose. Mass culture is relevant to understanding the emotions and values of broader population groups that tend to be ignored in favor of the dominant demographic in the humanities, the cosmopolitan middle class.

The friendly attitudes and positivity among festivalgoers at Tomorrowland transformed my perspective. While I did not experience the same level of excitement and could not identify with the dominant macho culture and idealization of the fit body, the default friendliness toward everyone present felt like a gift. I had done nothing to earn this gift, and it reminded me of the complex exclusionary politics and hierarchical nature of many urban music cultures. The juvenile elements in the song lyrics, musical style, and audience behaviors that had appeared naïve in media representations were suddenly more meaningful in the lived experience among festivalgoers in the summer atmosphere on a field near Antwerp. For many of them, this was a coming-of-age experience and a highlight of their youth.

My ethnographic festival experience thus led to an understanding of a culture that cannot be reduced to an image of inauthentic consumerism. This chapter concludes the book's inquiry into festivals by recognizing the ongoing evolution of consumer culture in seasonal festivity, particularly the widespread desires in society for both carefree and conformist experiences. The chapter will not be a blind celebration of this culture, however. The positive attitudes to strangers notwithstanding, Tomorrowland was a social space, defined by ideology and capital. Participating in Tomorrowland meant above all being part of a large crowd of mostly white consumers, half of them international tourists, partying in a Disney-style theme park environment that encourages consumption by preventing festival-goers from bringing food and drinks to the festival, even encouraging luxury consumption in the form of gourmet food, upscale glamping, and VIP packages, expanding from the luxury and excess in the commercial house music club. Park (2017) describes the EDM pop festival as a space of white cool mainstream culture. The whiteness can be registered in audience statistics and in the music programming, which is dominated by white, male, heterosexual DJs, and stands in contrast to the origins of electronic dance music in black and queer communities.[4] Moreover, while my informants did not perceive the festival in political terms, but rather in commonsensical terms of consumer experiences, they nonetheless described their desires and feelings in relation to capital and gender. Several of my respondents said their future dreams included "success" and "a good job." Male respondents also mentioned "money" and "beautiful girls." A greater number of female respondents mentioned "peace" and "unity" as keywords to describe their festival experience.

A Social Study of Music Festival Video

This chapter examines how social media marketing has shaped popular music festival culture in the 2010s and develops a conceptual approach to the social study of festival media culture. The chapter focuses on Tomorrowland, which is one of the largest EDM pop festivals in the world and a pioneer in its field. It is produced by ID&T in Belgium, which has promoted EDM events since the early 1990s. The argument is that the EDM festival industry created a new type of festival cinematography, specifically marketing videos for social media consumption, which transformed the image of EDM pop festivals and the outlook and functions of the festivals themselves. The production of marketing videos led to developments in stage design and in social media storytelling. By developing the production and distribution of video into marketing practices and into commercial media channels, the festival industry commercialized the social media culture of festivals and developed video practices into more professional forms for the purpose of growing consumption and increasing sponsorship revenues. The festival videos created eroticized and glamorous images of EDM pop festivals in a generational worldview of summer festivity. The videos, moreover, were incorporated into the annual cycle of festival consumption, with a ritual function in relation to the festival event. The industry developed a focus on creating consumer desire before the event, boosting excitement during the event, and stimulating interest in further consumption after the event.

Music festival video exposes the media-centrism of audiovisual music studies. The field has studied music as a media culture, ignoring music's history as a performance culture. A foundational discussion of methodology in the field is overdue, as scholars have already recognized the limitations of textual approaches for analyzing music video in contemporary media culture. The literature on song videos developed in relation to MTV broadcasting is still prevalent, however, and has generally failed to integrate the growing array of media practices involved in the construction of the pop persona, including Instagram photo and video selfies, diaries, and travelogues. Carol Vernallis states in *The Oxford Handbook of Audiovisual Aesthetics* that scholars have become uncertain about the definition of music video and that "part of the change has to do with media contexts" (Vernallis 2013a, 438). The term "media contexts" is analytically vague and does not recognize that the dynamics of the object of study have evolved beyond the text itself and into platform technologies and practices of consumption and distribution. Her monograph *Unruly Media* (2013b) convincingly argues that postcinematic aesthetics have emerged, but offers little theory of the evolving dynamics in video culture. These methodological limitations notwithstanding, song videos remain relevant to the cultural analysis of popular music (Railton and Watson 2011, 5).

Valuable alternatives to textualism can be found in Kiri Miller's and Holly Rogers's work on video in performance practices. Miller (2012) points out that video games are performed and analyzes the experiences and meanings that emerge in the course of performance. She also explores how game performance is shaped by online practices such as educational videos on YouTube. Rogers (2013) situates video in a longer history of intermedial practices and takes architectural space into account in a study of music in art gallery video performances. She argues that the advent of videotape technology in the 1960s stimulated audiovisual explorations. The rise of video in festival marketing was similarly stimulated by a new system of digital video production and distribution in the mid-2000s, including a combination of the video-sharing platform YouTube, the Adobe Flash plug-in, smartphones, and faster internet connections and computers. Music festival video also represents the development of video into large cultural events, as compared to the performance cultures analyzed by Miller and Rogers.

I begin this investigation by situating music festival video in the history of festival cinematography, highlighting the relationship between festival culture and style of mediation. The second section of the chapter analyzes the evolution of this video genre at Tomorrowland from an explorative stage into a routine stage in the years 2009–2011. This analysis draws from the production of culture perspective in sociology to explain how the genre was shaped by its system of production and distribution. The third section uses theory of media events to analyze the functions of festival videos in the annual festival cycle.

The empirical data is drawn from interviews with industry players and participant-observation at festivals, the primary case study being ID&T's Tomorrowland festival in Belgium. ID&T's marketing team in Antwerp shared information with me in a meeting in January 2013, including research based on customer surveys with more than one million respondents, which provided insights into audience demographics and the company's self-presentation.[5] My research assistant, Maria Olesen, attended Tomorrowland with two of her friends in 2012, and we subsequently discussed her experience in detail. They danced many hours each day at the main stage and experienced deep trance and euphoria. When we talked about her experience a week later, she was still in a posttrance state and sad the festival was over, describing the transition back into the real world as "cold turkey." This gave me an indication of the strong experiences that fans could have at Tomorrowland, and I decided to attend in 2013. To explore audience perspectives in advance, I conducted an online questionnaire in early 2013 using the SurveyMonkey platform. Informants were recruited from national Facebook groups of Tomorrowland fans in Belgium, Denmark, Germany, and Finland, and from forums where fans were writing about Tomorrowland and EDM. This yielded sixty-five complete responses, most of which were from Germany (German fans account for a substantial portion of the festival's audience, according to ID&T's customer research). I subsequently engaged in correspondence with some of the respondents and received lengthier responses from a handful of them. The latter included a five-page memoir by a Belgian fan, Younes Baghor, who had participated in all of ID&T's events since the early 1990s.

I went to Tomorrowland in July 2013 with fellow scholar and friend Francesco Lapenta. He was in his early forties, like me, and an experienced insider of EDM clubs in Italy in the 1980s and London in the 1990s. He initially reacted with skepticism. He felt the culture was superficial, that the architectural design created a narrow focus on consumption, and that festivalgoers were conformist and unimaginative with their costumes. His reactions highlighted differences in our experiences, social backgrounds, and purposes, representing elite values with which I have a complex relationship. He was a tourist and I was an ethnographer seeking to understand the culture on its own terms, grateful for not feeling out of place among an audience twenty years younger than myself. The field experience helped me understand the festival and how it was being filtered through commercial mediations. It also provided insight into the media production on the ground during the festival.

Festival Cultures and Styles of Mediation

Music festival video is a cinematic mediation of the festival experience and thus belongs to a history of festival cinematography. Before the advent of social media video in the late 2000s, festival cinematography had been limited to the occasional festival film, which integrated elements of a concert film with footage of the festival area. Festival films or documentaries had the length of a full-length feature film and were shown in cinemas or on broadcast television. From the 1980s onward, they also circulated on VHS videotapes and later DVD.

An influential early example was *Jazz on a Summer's Day* (Stern 1960/2001), which featured the Newport Jazz Festival in 1958, by then an established cultural event. The movie was produced by the jazz producer for Columbia Records, George Avakian, who worked with the biggest headliner that year, Louis Armstrong, and also produced a companion album to the movie. The movie was essentially a film of concerts with interspersed footage from the festival grounds and surrounding areas. Footage of audiences and their behaviors made a strong impression on media audiences and was perceived as a distracting factor by modernist jazz critics (Kristin McGee, conversation with the author, April 7, 2014). It demonstrated the potential of moving images to mediate festival performance culture by showing a multitude of micromovements in crowds of performing bodies (Meyrowitz 1985, 93–101) and to tell a story about the festival by showing footage from the various spaces of the festival experience.

Jazz on a Summer's Day has been credited as a template for the movies of Monterey Pop (Pennebaker 1968/2002) and Woodstock (Wadleigh 1970/1999; Micucci 2018). The hippie festivals were extraordinary cultural events of a new generation that became international cultural sensations through live televised footage and other media reporting. The movies had a different function and context of reception. Like *Jazz on a Summer's Day*, the Monterey and Woodstock movies each created a cinematic experience of the individual festival from the assumed perspective of a fan loyal to the event. In spite of limited circulation, they contributed to the international proliferation of hippie music culture. The Woodstock movie, for instance, was premiered in cinemas in Los Angeles and London in spring 1970, about seven months after televised footage appeared in news media during the event. And like *Jazz on a Summer's Day*, the hippie festival movies were integrated into the recording industry business. However, such movies were not a regular part of festival culture, and festivals generally did not pay performers more for the media rights than for their stage performance. The common form of popular music cinematography in subsequent decades was the VHS tape—later the DVD—concert movie made during an arena tour.

In the late 2000s, music festivals began producing short videos for circulation in popular social media, especially Facebook and YouTube. During those transitional years, professional genres of festival cinematography had not yet emerged in social media environments, and festivals initially adopted genres that had been developed for other media environments. Sónar, for instance, simply remediated TV advertising spots in social media until 2008.[6] Tomorrowland made two-to-four-minute videos shortly after the festival for YouTube circulation from 2005 onward but did not develop its distinctive immersive cinematic style until 2011.[7] The videos of the late 2000s show a series of vignettes in a somewhat random sequence without an overall narrative arc. They were shot without professional equipment for camera movements, leaving them with a static character, and the image quality in the first videos is not far from the average amateur production at the time. By 2011, however, Tomorrowland in Europe—and a year later, Ultra Music in the United States—had developed a highly professional style of marketing cinematography in trailers and aftermovies distributed shortly after the festival, with an emphasis on the aftermovies that were about fifteen minutes long. Since 2011, Tomorrowland's aftermovies have been longer than twenty minutes. Around the same time, marketing videos began to be based on footage from the live-cast that festivals had started to produce for distribution on their home pages or on YouTube. The style of the Tomorrowland and Ultra videos soon became common in the marketing of many festivals that were being acquired by the same corporations around this time, including Creamfields in the UK and Nature One in Germany.[8] The genre of music festival video was adopted by countless pop and rock festivals in 2012, albeit with different aesthetics to consciously distinguish themselves from EDM pop festivals. Some festivals avoided the name "aftermovie," for instance. Sziget used the term "official aftermovie" in 2012, Coachella started doing a "thank you" video in 2014, and Glastonbury started using the term "after film" in 2016.[9] Glastonbury also distinguished itself from EDM pop cinematography by fewer images of crowd euphoria, a less sexualized gaze, and a narrator with an urban, college-educated accent.

Burning Man represented a distinct alternative altogether in the 2010s by not producing official promotional videos. The organization also did not endorse or share videos produced by participants on its website. In the late 2010s, the website was still almost video-free.[10] Some of the popular videos of Burning Man on YouTube have the character of aftermovies, however, and a few of them have been produced by a member of the organization who makes a living producing event videos for corporations (Stefan Pildes, interview with the author, October 12, 2013). Moreover, Burning Man did not create a Facebook or YouTube infrastructure for the event the way that many popular music festivals did. Burning Man began livestreaming in 2012, but not in a style typical of music festivals, which would also be against the official principles of the festival. One year, the stream was simply produced from a live cam in a static position that provided a panorama of the playa from a distance, with no close-ups of social situations.[11]

The brief survey above shows that while some forms of promotional video and live-casting have become a fixture of many music festivals, these media practices have been shaped by the systems of production and distribution in which they developed. With the growing frequency of cinematic mediations that evolved with music festival video in social media, the genre became part of the ongoing expression of the individual festival's aesthetics and values and a means of market differentiation. EDM pop festivals suddenly had a mass-media channel, while for iconic rock festivals, such as Glastonbury and Coachella, video was a minor addition to extensive media coverage and concert live-casting in conventional broadcast media. Rock festivals, moreover, were not as visually oriented as EDM pop festivals, which had more visual designers and architects who occupied higher positions at a level equal to that of the director of music programming. Rock festivals have appealed to a sense of magic in their design and marketing, but they have not conceived their symbolic sphere as a fantasy world in the way EDM pop festivals have. They invest less in video marketing and emphasize live-casting of concerts, reflecting their concert-based model of musical performance.

The EDM pop festival is a visual spectacle with an extroverted psychology. The euphoria is produced musically through joyous and sparkling beats and melodies. Visually, euphoria is produced through spectacular stage design and effects and through extroverted crowd expressions of joy and fun. It is a culture that does not cultivate private intimacy but is energized instead by mass excitement and attention from cameras and strangers, perceiving such attention as an extension of the festivity and of universal excitement about the festival in the world. On the festival grounds of Tomorrowland, expressions of excitement occurred only in wide-open spaces with large crowds. There was strikingly little sociability among strangers or liminality on the buses from Antwerp to the festival. The buses were generally quiet, like the sparsely populated areas of the festival grounds.

The EDM pop festival had already found its basic form before social media marketing amplified its extroverted psychology. Tomorrowland began in 2005 and has been held every year in a national park about ten miles outside Antwerp. The park was developed by landscape architects for public leisure activities and has a small lake in the center that patrons cross on bridges to reach the park's assembly areas. These areas are surrounded by trees and can be used for sports or stage performances. When ID&T created Tomorrowland, it had more than ten years of experience as a pioneer in "live concept experiences" of EDM events in twenty countries.[12] The company had also added movies to its event merchandising in the 1990s, but not consistently every year, and with such limited distribution that fans were regularly producing their own extended footage and sharing it in closed online forums.[13]

The Belgium office in Antwerp that produces Tomorrowland was ID&T's first permanent office outside Holland. The Belgian team initially expected to produce Sensation White, one of ID&T's most popular concepts. Sensation White is a large indoor event in which patrons dress in white and the space is bathed in white light and decorations and showered with white confetti. One of the first headliners at Tomorrowland was Tiësto, who had toured Sensation events. The negotiations with the Dutch headquarters resulted in Tomorrowland, however, ID&T's second festival after Mysteryland (1994–present). It began as a one-day event held on a Sunday and evolved into a four-day festival as a result of its growing popularity (Christophe Van den Branden, interview with the author, January 24, 2013).

Tomorrowland is a Disney-style fairytale world, constructed through the naming of the festival and its main areas and through the extensive visual decorations of everything from concessions to the camping area and stages. There are visual decorations in all areas of the festival in the form of gates, walls, arches, and signs with the same color theme. On the path to the main stage in 2013, festivalgoers walked up to higher ground through a long line of arches, like a rite of passage to arrive at a celestial space. On each arch was signage with the words "Yesterday is history. Today is a gift. Tomorrow

9.1 Area near the Ferris wheel at Tomorrowland, Belgium, July 2013. The Ferris wheel was introduced in 2012.

is mystery," which audiences most likely knew from the 2008 Hollywood movie *Kung Fu Panda* (Stevenson and Osborne 2008). Borrowings from children's fantasy and magic genres could be found everywhere (fig. 9.2).

ID&T had the financial resources to quickly develop Tomorrowland through investments in architectural design and world-famous DJs. This festival found its basic form before the 2011 video sensation, and its audience grew from 10,000 in 2005 to 180,000 in 2010. The festival's popular videos of the early 2010s helped boost the festival's popularity further to reach audience numbers of 400,000 by 2014, when it was cloned into two weekends with the same programming. This evolution followed SFX's takeover in 2013, which also led to the export of the concept to the United States and Brazil.

The Evolution of Music Festival Video at Tomorrowland, Belgium

The marketers in ID&T's Antwerp office began to concentrate the marketing of Tomorrowland on Facebook in 2008 and on YouTube in 2009 (see p. 245). The company was exploring the business potential of new media, like many other companies had done in past media evolutions (Frith [1987] 2007). The marketers did not merely find a new channel, they migrated into a new media system. The formative years of music festival video are best understood as a process in which distribution, content, production, and consumption coevolved.

9.2–9.3 Audiences on the festival grounds at Tomorrowland, Belgium, July 2013.

The media system that Tomorrowland migrated into was an aggregate of platform and playback technologies that made video part of everyday media consumption and redefined much televisual content as "online video" (Bondad-Brown, Rice, and Pearce 2012, 472). Large numbers of amateurs could now more easily and cheaply produce and mass-distribute their own videos, and many professional organizations, too, explored the opportunities for self-broadcasting. Mass numbers of media users were remediating diverse forms of content on YouTube, which took on the functions

9.4 Tomorrowland main stage, July 2011. *Courtesy of ID&T, Belgium.*

of a public archive, TV station, amateur playground, and platform for self-education, among other things. YouTube was a metaplatform and the computer a metamedium that together subsumed television, cinema, and diverse physical video archives in the process of their digitalization.

At Tomorrowland the transition was initiated by fans, who began sharing photos and footage in self-organized Facebook groups. ID&T's marketers took notice and decided to adopt Facebook as their primary platform to become directly involved in the media space of the fans. ID&T was thus following the consumer and benefited from the logistical efficiency of Facebook:

> We began [in 2005] by creating our own database of our fans and chat boxes. Everybody was trying to create their own database by e-mails and their own private social media behind their own websites. And there were forums such as Partyflock. . . . The internet wasn't that powerful a media tool. It was there, but not as strong as social media are now. Since 2005, more and more content came on the internet.
>
> The first time we went really social was in 2008. It isn't long ago since it was just flyers and stuff. In the last five years it's just exploded. We created a YouTube channel and didn't know what to expect. With Facebook, we thought everybody is doing it. . . . (Christophe Van den Branden, interview with the author, January 24, 2013)

The team kept some information secret during the interview, but they did not seem to have had an advanced understanding of media when they first approached Facebook. The team had a strong practical sense of communication, however, and developed a marketing strategy tailored to social media in the following years. For instance, the team described to me how they approached Facebook in 2008 not simply as a technology but as a social space that required a certain emotional labor and proactive socializing. They compared it to going to a bar to make new friends and said the skills needed to present a likeable attitude and entertain others in a conversation were the same skills needed to build a Facebook community.

The team's first video project can be interpreted in these terms as a shot of entertaining positivity. It featured Moby's performance on the main stage in 2009. In previous years, the team had received footage from photographers in exchange for press accreditation, but they now adopted a routine of hiring a production company and carefully scripting the photography. ID&T also developed the stage production for the video production in collaboration with Moby. The company invested in massive stage decorations and fireworks. That year, 2009, was the first year the festival had a big mask on the main stage. These large decorations would become a key element of the festival's architectural design. Enthusiastic audience responses to the videos and to the décor prompted a further expansion of the main stage in 2011 and of the video productions. An external event architecture company created a fairytale castle 52 meters wide and 25 meters tall with integrated lighting, laser beams, fireworks, and video walls ("The Fairytale Castle at Tomorrowland 2011"; fig. 9.4). The scale of video production grew with larger teams, more advanced equipment, elaborate scripts, and hundreds of videos on the festival's YouTube channel. In 2013, I observed permanent film teams at the large stages and at least one team filming around the festival grounds equipped with professional movie industry equipment, including Red One 4k cameras that cost about 20,000 dollars each.

The videos from 2009 and 2010 largely conveyed fun and glamorous images of the festival experience. The marketers paid careful attention to visuality, to image quality, and specific symbols:

> We worked really hard with the image. . . . The finest pictures, the finest movies. . . . We could show exactly what we wanted to show people . . . the most beautiful girls and the fireworks. . . . When you show that to people. . . . (Christophe Van den Branden, interview with the author, January 24, 2013)

The team could identify what triggered audience excitement in Facebook comments. In particular, young female festivalgoers became a more frequent object of attention. The 2011 aftermovie opens with an entire sequence of glossy images of women shown as individuals, as singles, expressing joy and pleasure in a paradisiacal setting with light dew on the surrounding flowers. A slow-motion effect creates the sense that the women are in a state of trance, and the camera view creates space for the imagined presence of the male viewer. The aftermovie returns several times to women expressing sensuous pleasure and flirtatiousness. In other words, women are presented as willing erotic objects waiting to be consumed by men. The voyeuristic and glamorous cinematography distinguished these marketing videos from many videos shared by festivalgoers in earlier years.

The 2011 aftermovie also represented a new sense of digital storytelling. The video is not focused on a spectacular stage show, but it instead integrates a series of bodily experiences in idealized social situations over the course of the festival. The cinematography became more immersive through more dynamic photography and close-ups. Much of the footage was shot by cameras on moving cranes that dramatize the waves of excitement across the massive main-stage crowd. Moreover, a white male voiceover in the majestic style of *Lord of the Rings* had been invented. The voiceover framed the video as showing a magical place that emerges out of distant mythical origins once a year, intoning "People of Tomorrowland, the time has come. . . ." The voiceover thus enhanced the cinematic character of the videos and declared the festival to be a tribal community. The voiceover and the tribalist statement were incorporated into the main stage in 2011, at which the voice from the video voiceover introduced the star performer right before each DJ set and appealed to "the people of Tomorrowland." By the mid-2010s, some of these elements—the tribalism and the eroticism—had been toned down in favor of a more generic party cinematography focused on shorter and more general sensations of positivity and spectacle, still focused on a pleasant and magic event experience, and still alternating between moments of serene relaxation and euphoria, between intimacy and monumentalism, and now with an even higher production quality in image and sound ("Tomorrowland Belgium 2019: Official Aftermovie").

The tribalist term "people of Tomorrowland" had emerged in the process of distributing the 2009 or 2010 videos. The person who managed and crafted the communications firsthand, Christophe Van den Branden, felt that it would have been too tame to just say "Hi, friends" or "Hello." At first, the tribalist form of address was just a simple gesture, but enthusiastic responses on Facebook motivated the team to develop it into the digital storytelling and into the presentation at the main stage. The videos were no longer just mediations of the festival. They were constructing a digital narrative for the festival and its audience. Thousands of user comments showed how audiences identified with the tribalist term and would go on to coproduce a party atmosphere through social media.[14] Many fans drew inspiration from national ceremonial festivity by stating their nationality as a way of articulating the global popularity and unity of the festival. This logic could be found at the main stage, too, in the ritual of waving national flags that is still popular at the festival.

ID&T's media productions were shaped by the commercial institutionalization of social media broadcasting of cultural events in the early 2010s. Live transmissions of cultural events were gaining recognition as a form of symbolic capital for internet and TV broadcasters and their advertisers. The growing number of media companies led to intense competition, and it was becoming more difficult for them to secure unique content because content increasingly circulated across channels, platforms, and devices. Above all, the dominance of broadcast television was challenged. The culture of following an evening program organized by a broadcaster (Williams 1974, 92) was being replaced by a more fragmented television culture (Lotz 2007) and later by a more individualized culture of streaming. One response to the loss of power among media companies was to do live transmissions of major cultural events. These types of events have the capacity to break routines and attract audiences from various corners of the otherwise fragmented media landscape. TV broadcasters also expanded the production of their own live events to combat this competition from internet streaming services (Sørensen 2016). Internet broadcasters such as YouTube and Boiler Room benefited from the transnational potentials of the internet, especially in Continental Europe, where much music broadcasting was done by state institutions with national obligations and in national languages other than English. After a few years of serving as a playground for amateurs, YouTube stimulated the professionalization of its content in its guidelines to producers of content, and it developed a "premium content strategy" to compete with the film and television industries. Live-casts of presidential speeches and Olympic ceremonies appeared in the early 2010s, and regular broadcasting of cultural events began in 2012 (Kyncl 2011; Smith 2012; Webster 2012; "Inside the Growing Popularity of Live Streams").

Tomorrowland was among the first music festivals to have a dedicated YouTube live channel. The festival's marketers were excited about YouTube, describing it as "a big, world-wide TV station" that would allow the festival to reach wider audiences and increase sponsorship revenues (Koen Lemmens, interview with the author, January 24, 2013). In one of their standard business presentations, these marketers proudly compared Tomorrowland's social media metrics with the metrics for mega-events. The presentation included a table showing that their festival was in only second or third place after the Olympics and had a larger media audience than all other music festivals. For their first YouTube live-cast, they drew inspirations from the Oscars and Grammys and had celebrity David Guetta flying over the festival in a helicopter to amplify the crowd's excitement.

Tomorrowland's media culture changed with the professional development of the festival's social media marketing in evolving corporate platforms. Festivalgoers became consumers and objects of videography. At the 2013 festival, festivalgoers were excited at the possibility of appearing in the official aftermovie and felt no need to produce their own video documentation of the event. I was unable to identify festivalgoers who were filming the event systematically. A few festivalgoers had a GoPro camera on their forehead, but most were just doing short videos with their mobiles for sharing on their own private channels. They were enriching their own experience in small networks but not creating narratives for the festival or for a larger fan community. The collective narrative of the festival was defined by marketing movies. The 2011 aftermovie had become a folkloric text. Reenactments of its tribalist exclamation of the festival's name created a sense that everyone had watched the video and was using it as a resource for their participation. Festivalgoers were familiar with core symbols and social situations and also reenacted some of the euphoric crowd behaviors shown in this and other marketing videos. The videos had become a resource for expressing and sharing joy among strangers, but they also fixed and narrowed audience behaviors and expectations. Some of the behaviors felt mechanical. This seems to indicate that festival video transforms festival culture from an oral performance culture into a media performance culture scripted by marketing cinematography.

SFX's acquisition of ID&T in 2013 further contributed to this development. First, ID&T's staff in Antwerp was given a key role in exporting Tomorrowland to other continents and thus became more focused on reproducing the formula. The export involved the challenging process of shipping the main stage to Chattahoochee Hills near Atlanta, Georgia, where the clone TomorrowWorld would be held about one month later. TomorrowWorld and the general turbulence experienced by SFX until its bankruptcy in 2016 presented additional challenges for ID&T Belgium and its social media community. One of ID&T's founders, Duncan Stutterheim, left the company in 2015 (Ward 2015), and SFX requested that national Facebook groups run by fans be closed.[15]

The fan-owned groups had promoted forms of self-directed agency and collectivism. They had hosted conversations in their respective languages, enabled fans to coordinate trips to the festival, and encouraged a sense of fan ownership. SFX's corporate control of the media sphere weakened these elements. Most importantly, restricted agency in the festival's social media channels weakened the participatory culture and the dynamism between marketers and fans that had been central to the extraordinary culture of festival video at Tomorrowland in the early 2010s. The communication dynamics became more one-directional and static.

Video in the Annual Festival Cycle

Music festival video has a relationship with the festival event that song video does not. Analysis of this relationship can produce broader insights into the functions and dynamics of media practices in festival culture. Media event theory will be helpful in this regard. Though this theory was developed in relation to television broadcasting of other kinds of events, its basic tenets remain relevant to analysis of the general relationship between media and events (see p. 60). Social media have played a key role in reproducing and transforming interpretations of festivals in the 2010s, bringing images of festivals into wider circulation in society and incorporating media power into festivals. Mediations by promoters and audiences in social media have amplified the charismatic appeal of the festival event and of particular subjects and situations, such as star performers and fans with idealized looks and behaviors. While the development of television broadcasting of major historical events in the 1970s involved an adaptation of the formal and scripted character of ceremonial events, festival promoters and audiences have adopted social media into a seasonal dance party event, forming and conveying the erotic and voyeuristic desires of this club-derived youth culture within a summer experience. The marketing videos situate the EDM pop festival as an imagined center, not of society, but of this generational party culture. They also indirectly imagine the individual festival as the center of the festival field, distinguishing it from competing commodities in the market. The videos, moreover, exploit the visual appearances and affects of performing bodies for marketing purposes. Crowd enthusiasm is presented as an endorsement of the festival.

Media adapt not only to the symbolic order of events, but also to their temporal and ritual dynamics. In major cultural events, the psychological dynamics of media practices in the culture are affected. Dayan and Katz (1992) showed that the television broadcasts followed the ritual process of the event. Media audiences follow the emotional intensities, the language, and the social norms of events. The ritual dynamics of the overall stages in the consumption of the festival event structure media practices, transcending media genres, technologies, and channels. When excitement about a festival builds up, this can be identified in mediations across local news media, national broadcast media, the festival's official announcements, social media conversations, and personal text messages and photos shared among audience members.

Media practices in EDM pop festivals can be conceptualized in terms of the ritual functions of media through three stages in consumption. Media have (1) an anticipatory function before the event; (2) a liminal function during the event; and (3) a memory and re-experiencing function immediately following the event. This process can be interpreted as a variation of a basic ritual structure in many events, but there are aspects unique to the summer experience and the industry's commercial exploitation of the popular music festival and of the EDM pop festival in particular. Unlike rituals in traditional societies, which were obligatory and served to sanction religious and social order, exposing participants to a state of crisis, a "liminoid" ritual of modern society such as the consumer culture music festival is voluntary and offers an escape from conflicts and tensions in social life (Schechner 1977/1988, 186–89). Commercially institutionalized popular music festivals are a form of entertainment for large audiences, attracting broad audiences from the gentrified city and rural areas. These festivals have gravitated toward soft-shell forms of popular music, but nonetheless program dramatic genres to intensify the experience of heightened seasonal festivity. Broad popular music festivals, for instance, typically present hip hop, metal music, and dubstep concerts as a form of dramatic entertainment. The functions of media in the EDM pop festival and, to some extent, the rock-based music festival can be outlined as follows, using music festival videos as the focus:

1. *Anticipatory: Video trailer one to three months before the festival.* The anticipatory function can be identified in mediations that build expectations and stimulate interest in participation. This function appears throughout the year but dominates in the months leading up to the festival. During those months, the level and intensity of mediations accelerate to the point that the festival gains a daily presence among participants and in news media. In the early 2010s, Tomorrowland and Ultra established a routine of releasing a video trailer about a month before the festival. The trailer was released in the official social media channels of the festival. The festival promoter thus used its authority as an organizer of the festival and its media space to announce the return of the festival and invite participants.

In general, festival trailers have been composed of footage from the previous edition of the festival. They serve as a window onto the more intense liminal festivity by showing the idealized atmospheres of summer days and nights at the outdoor event. Trailers thus anticipate the seasonal specificity of festivals through images consumed within the realm of everyday life. In terms of marketing psychology, trailers initiate the consumer journey and induce needs by triggering desires for pleasure and adventure. They often show arrival situations and aerial views of the festival in the beginning, encouraging viewers to imagine their own arrival. Moreover, trailers trigger media participation. Audiences share and talk about the video online and experience a form of commonality through images that stimulate certain interactions and behaviors at the festival.[16]

2. *Liminal: Live reportage and transmissions during the festival.* A liminal function can be identified in mediations of a suspended order and time, characterized by a commitment to an unbroken festive flow condition. This function exists only during the festival and is strong in the collective trance that can build up at the main stage, in the headliner shows on the main stage at night, and in the festival's opening and closing ceremonies. During such moments, mediations are focused on the here and now, on boosting presence in direct response to the unfolding event. Light shows and video mediations on screens positioned on and around stages enhance the experience and sense of immediacy through dynamic cinematography, and announcements between performances are developed to stimulate flow and positivity. Festivalgoers become live reporters of their own experience. They mediate sensations, encounters, and symbols of the festival and of carnivalesque performativity in photos, short videos, and text messages. Even common and seemingly trivial phenomena, such as a T-shirt with a humorous statement or people kissing or spilling beer, can be valuable objects of mediation during the festival because they are signifiers of the unfolding event and serve the construction of presence in the center of action. The same logic can be found in news media, which tend to exhibit a fascination with the extraordinary character of seasonal festivity, with celebrities and mainstage crowds, with drugs and sex, and with scandals such as canceled headliner shows and security incidents. News media follow the ideal of authentic live mediations by doing on-site interviews and reports, no matter the weather conditions. Longer televisual mediations will take the form of live transmissions that reinforce the general sense of collective and valuable, but also transient, time.

A large number of festivals began to broadcast live transmissions from their websites and via online broadcasters in the 2010s, following a period when this had been limited by the lack of standardized copyright arrangements and, to some extent, by slow internet speeds. The copyright issue might have been solved when it became clear that the broadcasts would not be sold like a concert movie but made available for free as a form of promotion.[17] In some cases, more polished, edited versions of concerts at the most prestigious festivals appear later on broadcast television. In the late 2010s, many festivals further enhanced the temporal and ritual dynamics of their media communications by focusing on live content on their websites—switching them into live mode, so to speak—and then a month later clearing their channels of much content. By showing an empty space, the website indicates the festival is gone and thus follows the festival's ontology and the festivalgoers' experience. This also highlights the transience of the festival.

3. Memory: Wristbands and aftermovies after the festival. The memory function can be identified in mediations of the festival in the weeks and months after it has ended. Media content produced before and during the festival is remediated and experienced anew to remember the festival experience. Festivalgoers keep their wristbands on so as not to sever the connection with the experience. The wristband can serve as a status symbol, but to some fans, cutting the wristband would destroy an intimate lifetime experience, provoking emotions similar to those some people might feel when selling their wedding dress or another article of clothing with similar symbolic value. The desire to remember and sustain the affective bond with the festival, however, is also exploited for further consumption and promotion: New products and media content, from merchandising to aftermovies, are distributed after the festival. This framing of desire into consumption and promotion follows the general logics of capitalist cultural industries and consumer culture. The festival industry offers little interpretation of the place of music festival experiences in everyday life and society. Rather, the industry is telling festivalgoers to keep consuming without critical self-reflection. It is aware that consumers are always shopping around for better offers or new trends in pop culture. The aftermovie can thus be interpreted as a commercial exploitation of what Schechner called a "cooling off" ritual (Schechner 1977/1988, 190).

Aftermovies are commonly released a few weeks after the festival, while the memory is still relatively fresh and the festival has news value. Aftermovies are thus essentially extensions of festival consumption. The influential Tomorrowland 2011 aftermovie is, to a great extent, an edited reproduction of an idealized festival experience, an imagined repetition. The aftermovie allows festivalgoers to relive their own festival experience in more glamorous form. It simulates continued immersion, not separation or distance.

Conclusion: Musical Festivals and Mediated Life

Preceded by a situation in which a few festival movies were sold as separate commodities for domestic consumption and a very small percentage of festivals were televised, a new era began in the 2010s in which festival cinematography became a fixture of many festivals in the specific forms produced for social media distribution by festival marketing departments—the trailer, the aftermovie, and the live-cast. The adoption of social media at first expanded the range of mediations, but the industry eventually exploited social media marketing and particularly video through glamorous images and by focusing on specific consumer purposes and desires, integrating marketing video throughout the process of consumption. Immersive mediations in videos and on live screens during the festival coconstructed idealized looks and behaviors of white mainstream coolness and at times targeted male sexual desire, integrating these identities and desires into the festival commodity and encouraging consumption.

Social media could have brought popular music festivals in other directions, as illustrated by the early participatory culture at Tomorrowland. Social media could have created a different place for music festivals in society and therefore also a different place for music. But in the hands of the festival industry, social media became a tool for the further transformation into mass culture, epitomized by the main-stage euphoria, glamour, and spectacle of EDM pop, with audience behaviors scripted by festival marketing video. The growing commodification led to a more commercially regulated environment, at the festival and online, and a disconnection from hard-core musical cultures. But it also led to more spectacular and luxurious experiences for larger numbers of people. The 52-meter-high fairytale castle at the main stage, the extensive visual decorations all around Tomorrowland, and the general quality of services, for instance, could not have happened without the for-profit organization and the marketing that continue to attract large international audiences every year. For my informants and many participants in Tomorrowland's social media channels, this festival was unlike anything they had ever seen and experienced before. Tomorrowland thus also illustrates the potential of its value system and the institutionalization of the EDM pop festival.

The commercial growth in the popular music festival landscape as a whole also rewarded a wide range of industry professionals, from festival marketers to journalists at public media corporations across Europe who appreciated overall improvements in production standards and the growing presence of superstars. The person responsible for all of the BBC's festival coverage, for instance, said in 2015 that he had enjoyed going to Glastonbury twenty years earlier, "but what they're offering now is just phenomenal!" (Andrew Rogers, senior producer of live music at the BBC, interview with the author, April 1, 2015). In short, festivals might not have become a better place for popular music or festival culture as a whole, but they have become a better place for particular classes of consumers and industry professionals.

Another lesson for the social study of music is that music festivals represent the further development of traditional forms of musical performance into media culture, but that music festivals are still capable of disrupting everyday social and media routines through traditional ontologies of musical performance culture—performing bodies, the musical performance event, and the cultural event. Festival performance culture has become mediatized at various levels, from the programming of headliners to social media and the smartphone attached to the performing body. This development challenges the ontological sovereignty of performance culture, but also transforms it into a media-intense event culture that combines powerful in-person experiences of performance with self-mediation and a sense of being in an imagined center of cultural life, enhanced by the media power of the superstars on stage. Media still adapt to the ritual dynamics of the festival, and marketers now highlight elements of performance culture in their promotion of festivals. Seen from the perspective of a media-intense everyday life, the marketing cinematography can be interpreted as a contribution to the general fetishization of festival performance culture in society.

The analyses in chapters 8–9 suggest that the dominant types of popular music festivals in the 2010s increasingly can be characterized as a form of mass-market entertainment. The discourse on these festivals is dominated by marketing communications and consumer journalism, none of which is particularly reflexive about the cultural politics of music and festivity. There is little discussion of the history and future of festivals and their functions in musical culture, but it is relevant to include the most popular festivals in such discussions and encourage more reflexivity. As inclusive as today's large popular music festival might be in terms of gathering large audiences beyond the elites, it might steal attention for the potential of other forms of popular music festivals and naturalize audiences into the role as consumers, especially in areas far from the metropolis in which the corporate festival tends to be more hegemonic and young people are therefore not exposed to more civic alternatives and the experience of festivals that explore new worldviews rather than simply focusing on consumption of the most popular forms of music. The corporate popular music festival is also not particularly inclusive of immigrant populations. The exploration of new worldviews and the experience of more community-based forms of collectivity have historically thrived in grassroots-based, nonprofit organizations and cannot be realized in a corporate industry system. Music festival history has evolved through moments of extraordinary change, with the legacy of humanism on one side and the force of capitalism on the other, and we are currently experiencing the dominance of the latter at an unprecedented level, accelerated by transnational media and cultural industries.

: 10 :
Conclusion

Science explores the course of nature but can never give direction to people. Inclination, love, pleasure, pain, exaltation, exhaustion—science knows nothing of all this. What people live and experience they must interpret *and thereby evaluate.*
FRIEDRICH NIETZSCHE, "THE STRUGGLE OF SCIENCE AND WISDOM" [1875] 1954

The point of departure for this book was the lack of any critical analysis of the new pop culture of live music in the early twenty-first century. The introductory chapter demonstrated the similar lack of comprehensive explorations of the conceptual foundations for the social study of musical performance in modernity. This book has laid some empirical and theoretical groundwork for this and future studies. It has interpreted the live music boom as the result of an industrial exploitation of musical performance within evolving conditions in the urban centers of Anglophone popular music in the Global North.

In epistemological terms, this inquiry is a form of interpretative humanistic scholarship. The centrality of interpretation to the humanities has historically been defined in terms of knowledge interests and the objects of study. The humanities are concerned with human experience and interest and aspire to nuanced, critical, and imaginative understanding, with the wider aim of serving as a resource for thinking about the good society. They are central to a society that guarantees social justice and possibilities for human flourishing. Their knowledge interests have been defined against the ideal of controllable science, which separates its object of study from human experience and interest. The humanities have evolved in response to changes in the conditions of human life, from studies of rhetoric and social order in ancient Greece to biblical exegesis in the Middle Ages, to ideas of secular democracy and art in the Enlightenment and in response to subsequent developments, such as urbanization, media, and the ongoing challenges of war, colonialism, poverty, and the climate crisis (Dilthey [1910] 1970; Habermas 1968/1973; Nussbaum 2013). The humanities are relevant to all areas of science and constitute the core of the liberal model of higher education.

They are also relevant to and not made superfluous by vocational fields, such as communication, design, and culture management, which have become central areas for the study of popular culture.

The theoretical framework outlined in the first two chapters is essentially an interpretative narrative developed from the empirical investigations presented in chapters 3–9 and from existing narratives in music studies and sociology. The framework guided the production of various forms of interpretative knowledge: (1) *empirical facts* through the collection and analysis of data; (2) *interpretations* of more abstract phenomena such as the concept of institutions and their functions and relationships with musical culture, cities, and media; and (3) *critiques* of evolving conditions of musical culture and *imagination* of alternatives to existing narratives and conditions. I made a fundamental interpretative choice by defining the study of object in terms of humanist knowledge interests in performance culture at a time when the object was defined as live music by more dominant interest in business and consumption. As a consequence, this book has analyzed commercial institutions not only in and of themselves but also as agents in music history and in society.

The Framework

The theoretical framework evolved from critical analysis of discourse on live music, which governs the conception of the study object in popular music studies. The term "live music" has become institutionalized through powerful myths of capitalism and now challenges the position held by the term "musical performance." As the British concert industry began to promote itself as a live music industry in the late 1980s, the generic conception of the live music commodity became an instrument of industrial exploitation. The term was adopted by the media, governments, and scholars whose shared enthusiasm for the trend explains a certain ignorance of its cultural and historical dimensions. More than a decade on, popular music scholars are still surfing on the wave of the live music boom without recognizing the commodity form of live music and the historical, ontological, psychological, and political operations of its terminology. The live music literature has found fertile ground in the area studies discourse of popular music studies and in neoliberal research policy.

Explorations of pop culture discourse on live music continue to nuance this discourse and have produced valuable empirical data, but they are unable to offer a genealogy of live music or explain how this discourse structures power relations and promotes particular forms of music, musical experience, and cultural values, and how these changes relate to broader social change. Live music discourse involves a focus on general qualities of consumer experiences and commodities in commercial institutions governed by white patriarchy, and it detracts attention from substantive understandings of music, history, and culture. Because of these considerable limitations, this book has argued against the continued investment in live music as an overarching concept and instead developed a framework of musical performance culture grounded in the social study of music. This ontological reconstruction, with its stronger grounding in the intellectual history of music and performance culture, can produce more adequate analyses of live music and musical performance as part of international music and cultural histories and fields of production in modernity. Sociological thinking about institutions can help scholars overcome some of the limitations of the area studies approaches that dominate the intellectual histories of music and performance and analyze how musical cultures are structured in contemporary societies. Theory of music's performance institutions in modernity has not been developed—mainly due to the long-term hegemony of textualism and media hegemony in music studies, music sociology, and the literatures on clubs and festivals. Thus, an analytical discourse has been lacking for identifying and explaining the bigger picture encompassing the structural transformation of these institutions across the Global North and their increasing power in regulating popular music and its place in society.

The framework developed in three interpretative steps. First was the *reconstruction of the object* summarized above. The reconstruction was grounded in anthropology of performance and ethnomusicology and argued that musical performance culture is defined by a set of distinct ontologies that are historically and socially constituted and therefore require engagement with evolving fields of knowledge production. The ontologies include bodies in performance and in society; the musical performance event with its combination of music, space, and ritual; and the cultural event that shapes the spatial and symbolic context of one or more performances. This theorization addresses the relationship between musical performance and cultural event. The two concepts have evolved separately in different disciplines but are intimately related in contemporary culture, in which musical performance frequently occurs in media events and festivals. This is an important reason for expanding the concept of performance into performance culture. This reconstruction further provides an ontological raison d'être for music studies in discourse on events, and it is essential to interdisciplinary practices involving music, media, and tourism studies.

Second, the concept of *commercial institutionalization* served to frame the overall narrative of the introductory chapter, particularly the analysis of live music as the result of a capitalist process that restructured organizational fields in the popular music business and as a culminating point in a longer history of leisure in modernity. The commodification of popular music performance events follows a trajectory in modernity from civic to commerce-based forms of leisure. Voluntary civic associations played a central role in urban musical life in the eighteenth and nineteenth centuries, and new forms of popular music production evolved with the rise of corporate cultural industries in the twentieth century in the context of wider social and technological changes. For popular music, as for popular sports, television and the internet expanded the international market for large-scale events with touring superstars. The popular music festival evolved in these dynamics and networks, resulting in new types of festival events and in new functions and meanings of the music festival within new institutional arrangements. In short, a new societal construction of music has evolved, one that has parallels in other forms of leisure but nonetheless has its own distinct dynamics.

Roberta Sassatelli's study of the fitness gym provided an illustrative example of the commercial institutionalization of urban leisure places: For-profit venue organizations exploit a growing market by developing a greater focus on general consumer purposes and adapting to the norms of growing affluent demographics in the city. In particular, these organizations serve populations with careers and lives in environments characterized by comfort, individual self-control, and consistency in professional services. As the organizations grow into chains and corporations, they become more bureaucratic and create more standardized, conformist, and glamorous spaces of the culture for wider demographics. Commercial institutionalization tends to be accelerated by growing media markets of the individual form of leisure. This general process explains much of today's pop culture of live music, but area studies expertise on music is needed to account for the deeper cultural and historical implications of this process. The investigations in chapters 3–9 showed that commercial institutionalization is not a single linear process in modernity, but has occurred in cycles and been contingent to the particulars of performance and musical cultures. In addition, the investigations provided an empirically grounded account of musical performance institutions in modernity and integrated organizational and cultural theory.

In the third and final step, the concept of *institutions* was adopted from organizational sociology to explain how musical performance culture is structured. A performance institution is a model of production and consumption in a particular type of performance space that has become socially meaningful through frequent repetition and experience of the rituals and values of a culture. It is a model that makes it possible for promoters to sustain a business and for the social world of a genre to have its own dedicated places, or homes, governed by its traditions and mythologies. Variations of each institution have evolved within differentiations in a genre and in the urban economy. This is illustrated by the analysis of the variations of the rock club, which include the rock bar, the small concert club, the DIY warehouse, and the commercial indie concert theater. Analyzing the symbolic, temporal, organizational, and societal dimensions of performance institutions provides new opportunities for the analysis of cultural forms and social life. This book has analyzed musical performance cultures within musical traditions, organizational fields, and their wider urban and media environments.

Musical performance institutions in modernity have similar seasonal dynamics and functions and are transformed in similar processes, although popular music's institutions have evolved into the corporate bureaucracy of modernity with particular intensity in the past few decades and become an instrument and symbol of this societal order.

Many music cultures have evolved with a central institution in urban everyday life and one in the summer season. In popular music, the central institutions of regular and specialized activity have been the club and the festival, while the arena, governed by the logics of mass-media markets, has not created as regular a cycle of activity for one genre in particular. The arena's programming has been less coherent and frequent, and hence it has not acquired the same institutional functions, such as the production of social capital and the creation of platforms for music worlds and not just stars.

This book has illustrated how the concept of institutions can serve as a resource for developing the social study of music and for critiquing and expanding the historical and cultural imagination, building new narratives and comparisons. The concept guided the integration of musical performance into the social study of music in modern society. It led to the discovery of the longue durée of the everyday and seasonal domains, a more complete understanding of their origins, transformations, and their significance in understanding the conditions of cultural production and human life in the city.

As the inquiry moved into analysis of empirical particulars, the historical dimension became central and to some extent transcended the theoretical framework. History became a resource for explaining social processes and the complex symbolic configuration of performance institutions. It also became a resource for thinking about the social imagination in contemporary popular culture. Examples include the discussions of music and performance in the contexts of urban poverty, cultural festivity, and cultural globalization. This book thus demonstrates the centrality of history to the social study of music. It represents a form of historical sociology of music with a grounding in music studies—a form of inquiry driven by a knowledge interest in how musical culture changes as part of broader shifts in society. It is inspired by but not modeled on the nominal subfield of historical sociology, and it might inspire conversations about its knowledge interests.

In addition, institutional theory provides a means to map and analyze broad changes in value systems. This book has examined values through the narratives and worldviews of each performance institution, drawing from symbolic approaches to performance culture in anthropology and sociology. A recurring theme that deserves further reflection is the relationship between civic and consumer values. While a shift from one system to the other can be identified in processes of commercial institutionalization, a more nuanced account can more fully examine the intimate relationship between them in modernity. The cultural institutions that emerged in the eighteenth century were part of the evolution of consumer society (McKendrick, Brewer, and Plumb 1982). Early ideas of civil society ascribed a positive role to commerce, with Montesquieu, for instance, imagining commerce as a civilizing process. Notions of individual freedom could thus serve narratives of consumer choice and sovereignty. Leisure time could be redefined as consumption time in the interest of capitalism (Slater 1997, 23 and 28–29). Moreover, ideas about personal authenticity in Romanticism were inscribed in consumer culture (Slater 1997, 16). Today's pop culture image of live music is an evolution of this ideology. The current hegemony of consumer culture, moreover, becomes clear through the comparison of past and present festival worldviews and public policies of culture. Since the 1970s, commercial interests in culture have grown unprecedentedly powerful in public policy and research, often without displaying any concern for the social and ethical consequences of accelerating consumerism and capitalism.[1]

Institutions and Domains: Theory, Facts, Critique

Rock Clubs in Everyday Urban Life

The investigations of the rock club (chapters 4–5) highlighted changes in its outlook and functions since the beginnings in the 1960s. Many of the changes were explained by the interpretation of a shift from a neighborhood with neo-bohemian scene clubs in the early stages of gentrification into a landscape of more conformist commercial clubs across a wider territory transformed by generalized gentrification. The investigations showed that this sociological generalization can guide analysis of complex urban formations, but that it also has limitations. It remains a generalization of institutional structure. The analysis of neighborhood transformations of the rock field over the course of six decades has helped clarify the field's history and the social geography of its value systems, but it has also revealed the considerable degree to which the institution has been contingent to particulars in each of the transformations. In addition, chapters 4–5 looked beyond the generic concept of the urban domain and of center-periphery structures to the particularity of individual cities, their societal contexts, and their place in cultural flows in the history of the Global North.

The investigations proceeded on two analytical levels: the microlevel trajectories of individual clubs and the more general level of neighborhood change. Given the limited data available on the contemporary commercial clubs and their audiences—no statistics have been collected, for instance, and the corporations that increasingly dominate the field do not want to share any information—I developed initial hypotheses through ethnographic explorations of clubs and their neighborhood environments, promoters, and audiences. This generated insights into the types of clubs that had declined and emerged over the past couple of decades and into their social geography. It also pointed to the relevance of gentrification theory and, at a later stage, institutional theory, both of which served to further focus the production and collection of a wider range of data in a longer history, drawing from newspapers, magazines, popular books, and documentaries. Changing images and networks of the institution were analyzed in the trajectories of significant promoters and clubs and in the context of neighborhood change, drawing from statistical data on demographics, health, crime, and similar measures. In Europe, I was able to gain access to club management and construct facts about their self-image and their organizational and economic development. This led to the history of how governments in some European countries created a nonprofit system of ownership of clubs, which has gradually transformed into a for-profit value system within gentrification and the corporate live music market. Since the 1990s, midsize clubs in several capital cities across Continental Western Europe have increased their productivity more than 100%.

A further methodological point is that the investigations of the institutions generated insights into the domains. In addition to the longue durée of the urban domain as a basis of institutions in both everyday life and the summer season, the investigations revealed changes in the character and functions of this domain. Clubs have adapted to evolving economies and conditions of human life in the city. The performance culture of the commercial indie rock club illustrates growing professional standards for both artists and services, but it also illustrates the more constrained conditions of human life. Audiences commonly experience a concert before midnight in a more regulated environment, which does not encourage and in some cases does not allow improvised social interactions into the late night. The concert culture itself rarely reaches liminal levels and engages little if any audience reflexively about the relationship between music, self, and everyday life. In addition, the forms of social capital generated by scenes have declined. In many cities, the era of scenes has ended because they cannot exist in the condition of generalized gentrification.

The urban domain is still a cultural and political center in society, but its culture worlds have dissolved and been replaced by landscapes of more formal commercial institutions. The city has fewer of the small performance spaces that have historically allowed for extraordinary creativity and cultural diversity in intimate bodily interactions. Instead, the city has more placeless spaces of global economic and technological networks. In popular music, these developments are illustrated by the growing power of celebrity headliners in clubs and by corporate concert promoters expanding downstream into clubs in the interest of market control and not in small culture worlds of music.

There is little space left for alternatives to the dominant order in the gentrified city, and chapters 4–5 concluded by turning to history as a resource for thinking about the future and to possibilities demonstrated by public policy in northwestern Continental Europe. I argued that conceptions of public culture and performance culture can strengthen reflexivity and dialogue about music and public life in the city and challenge the narrative that the only option left is to adapt to the ever-expanding market. In this respect, the conclusion in chapter 5 questioned the logic that has governed the nonprofit club in Holland, Belgium, and Denmark for the past several decades.

At a more general level, the investigations into clubs provide humanist arguments for transforming the spirits and structures of capitalism in the city. In particular, the negative impacts of gentrification on social justice, public culture, culture worlds, and the constrained life in affluent neighborhoods are striking in the history of the rock club institution. Some of these negative developments can be offset by rolling back local policies that stimulated gentrification and the national policies that deregulated flows of global capital. Cities have increasingly become spatial articulations of global corporate power and its new immigrant workforces (Sassen 1998). A tighter regulation of global capitalism will thus be necessary for creating conditions for the existence of communities with cultural and political agency and a more socially just society.

It will also be necessary for creating more integrated cities. Eric Klinenberg describes the neighborhoods in New York analyzed in this book as "enclaves of affluence" that are cutting themselves off from difference subtly and "perhaps without intent" (Klinenberg 2018, 47). In a more socially just situation, the divisions between the city's affluent enclaves and its three million immigrants will decrease, and broad interdisciplinary approaches to cultural analysis are required to effectively address these divisions. As institutions of musical concerts thrive in the affluent enclave, what kinds of cultural institutions exist in lower-income immigrant communities, and how might these institutions inspire dialogue about music and public culture in the city?

Festivals in the Summer Season

The investigations of the music festival (chapters 6–9) expanded the theorization of this institution and highlighted important shifts in the institution's distinctness and transformations in modernity, particularly in Anglophone popular culture. The investigations focused on how the functions and symbolic order of festivals have transformed in processes of commercial institutionalization and in a wider history of music and cultural festivity. The interpretation of the history prior to World War II was based primarily on literatures on individual music festival traditions. These literatures served as a resource in terms of data and facts, but their genre narratives were also challenged and complemented by this book's institutional approach. The account of the period from the 1690s to 1945 provided general insights that can be further developed in more specialized future studies. The idea of the music festival as a site for the lived experience of the spirits of the Enlightenment, for instance, deserves newly conceived source studies and wider readings in cultural history and philosophy. Another potential task for future work is the further integration of social movement history into the institutional history of the popular music festival.

The theorization in chapter 6 stipulated that festivals have two basic functions for a culture: They celebrate and institutionalize. This involves the regular celebration of a symbolic order in the culture from which the festival emerges. Large festive events following an annual cycle can be found in premodern societies, but the music festival was a particular invention of bourgeois modernity. It was the first festival model focused on musical performance. This was a ritual of bourgeois nationalism and a form of civic becoming through public singing inspired by Enlightenment ideas of cultural citizenship. The cultural aspirations in the formative moment of the pioneering music festival traditions in England and Germany faded in the process of their commercial institutionalization, but elements thereof are still part of the mythology of these traditions. Images of authentic public sociality can be found even in today's corporate popular music festival, but as part of a different symbolic order and system of ownership.

Festivals of popular music emerged from urban youth culture movements in England and the United States following World War II. They began in exploratory gatherings that channeled new cultural and social sensibilities in London and San Francisco, drawing inspiration from neighborhood arts scenes and spreading via mass media. They were developed into distinct music festivals within the realm of the music industry, building on the outdoor concert model and market potential demonstrated in the United States by the Newport festivals. After the decline of the hippie music festival movement in the early 1970s, the popular music industry concentrated on recordings and arena touring. The rock-centered festival developed into a commercial institution—structured by companies organizing an annual event with the aim of long-term economic growth—only in the 1980s and became central to the music industry in the 2000s, when the concert industry expanded into the festival industry. This accelerated the evolution of a densely populated landscape of festivals that is structured by centralized ownership and superstar headliners. This landscape is strongly influenced by corporations governed by mass-market logic and not primarily by broadly conceived cultural interests in music and festivity. This has brought an end to the pop festival's history as an important symbolic place for social movements, scenes, or subcultures.

The analysis of cultural festivity in moments of major social change provided additional nuance to the theorization of the festival institution. In more than one instance, exploratory festivity with music has emerged from a cultural moment and provided alternatives to music's commercial institutions before dying out or developing into more institutionalized forms such as the commercial club or festival. Examples of such moments include the French Revolution, the humanist moment after World War II, the sense of freedom in Berlin after the fall of the Wall, and the Summers of Love in 1967 and 1988–1989. The culture of the happening, which proliferated in neighborhood arts scenes and the hippie gatherings and which defined the formative moment of the pop festival, did not survive the institutionalization of the popular music festival. Another example of transformations in festival culture can be found in the trajectory from the techno rave to the EDM pop festival. While a general sense of hedonism and improvised play in an outdoor area survives, institutionalization has further led to the partition of the festival area into thematic areas for elaborate outdoor bars and restaurants and camping facilities and into continuous entertainment across several stages. This is a hybrid model with elements of a commercial campground, an urban nightlife party district, and an amusement park with a handful of music and dance venues.

The trajectory of the pop festival and its variations can be interpreted in the context of societal changes, such as growing affluence and leisure time from the mid-twentieth century onward, but it is also shaped by industrial exploitation of a media consumer culture of music. This exploitation is epitomized by the development of more large-scale festivals and their changing functions. Mass media thus played an important role in transforming festival culture and putting the smaller club institution of the everyday urban domain under further pressure. The expansion of the season and programming of festivals is shortening the club season and reducing the talent pool for clubs, since more up-and-coming artists are touring festivals instead of clubs for the higher honoraria.

The media culture of music is thus a source of complexity in festival history. Another source of complexity is corporate capitalism. Markets and corporations have their own institutional norms, and they are structuring cultural life. These norms have numerous implications at the microlevel of music programming, architecture, and the management of bodies in space, and ultimately for the ideas about festivity and music. The same institutions of media and commerce that also transformed popular sports events have grown a new culture of festivals that provide powerful bodily experiences and a wealth of entertainment, but no longer serve the same functions as cultural institutions. This is illustrated by the eroding difference between the main stage and the arena concert and between the symbolic order at the festival and in mainstream society.

It follows that the social study of music festivals must rethink and expand its conception of the study object. Festival scholarship developed from individual scholars' passion for individual festival traditions and has tended to disregard newer models and changes related to institutions of modernity. The social study of musical performance institutions allows scholars to consider broader knowledge interests and integrate analysis of media and the institutions that govern the practices of music and cultural festivity.

While festivals have entered the mainstream in the realm of consumption, their presence in the realms of education, research, and journalism leaves much to be desired. Critical and historical thinking about institutions of musical culture is generally nonexistent in school curricula and news media in many societies. The social study of music can provide insight into the rich cultural histories of music's institutions and promote transparency about the role of industry and government in musical life. Is it not true that a person with knowledge of music festival history will have a broader perspective than that provided by the industry and better understand the value of civic forms of cultural festivity and the history of humanity? Is it not a matter of public interest, moreover, that a large share of the profits made from a country's music festivals are wired through a tax haven such as the Bahamas and end up in the pockets of corporate shareholders, while the local production is increasingly regulated by the international headquarters? Why should the music industry be less transparent than other industries, and how could it be regulated better in public interest? What about the donations to anti-LGBTQ and climate science denial groups made by AEG's owner? Have live music corporations created a situation similar to that of Amazon.com, Facebook, and Uber, in which many seem to accept that consumer benefits outweigh ethical concerns? Is it not a matter of public interest, moreover, that governments support critical humanist scholarship now that corporations have become so powerful in cultural life?

A particular challenge to empirical research is that there is little data available on festival organizations, and it has become more difficult for scholars to collect information because of corporatization. Corporatization creates new barriers to public knowledge. I produced data from field explorations in the industry sphere and analysis of reports in trade magazines. While this type of research cannot provide comprehensive statistics on the international industry and leaves gaps to be filled by future research, it can nonetheless provide insight into major patterns and dimensions of change. This is illustrated by the outline in chapter 8 of the festival's evolution into the institutional sphere of corporate capitalism.

Another key point concerns the conception of empirical data: The growing importance of electronic media and marketing communications in popular music festivals makes these forms of data important to cultural analysis. As the social construction of festivals has evolved in modernity, new types of data have become relevant to scholarly analysis. This is reflected in this book's account of dominant festival models in Anglophone global culture. The contemporary pop festival is constructed through the promotor's glamorous images that are integrated into the annual cycle of consumption and circulated in media channels managed by the promoter and by corporate media partners for maximizing sponsorship revenues.

A Better Place for Music and Humanity?

The investigations thus illustrate a theoretical framework, but they also provide insight into a restructuring of places for popular music and social life in the city. The investigations provided several examples of situations structured by a broad change in value systems with implications at the levels of practice, ownership, and institutional functions. The central institutions of popular music performance have become better places for larger numbers of consumers, for mass-market popular music, and for corporate business. They have not become better places for musical culture and society as a whole. They are less dedicated to distinct culture worlds of music and more regulated by corporate interests, and they therefore do not empower audiences with cultural aspirations and social movements. They have become less culturally diverse and thus promote worldviews with narrower conceptions of humanity.

The new models have not simply been added to the existing order, but have largely replaced the older models that evolved in scenes. The challenges to scenes stimulated a series of revivals in more remote neighborhoods and attempts at preserving clubs as landmark buildings or turning them into formal cultural institutions. There is no CBGB, Bottom Line, Wetlands, Cake Shop, or Monster Island in New York anymore, and such neighborhood worlds of music and performance have become virtually extinct. In the festival field, many of today's largest events began as countercultural and independent festivals. Industry exploitation did not lead to the disappearance of these festivals but rather to their transformation into new models in corporate organizational fields. Up until the 2000s, there would typically be few large-scale popular music festivals in a city and its immediate hinterland. These festivals would absorb new developments in music and cultural life. Only in the 2000s did festivals proliferate as a format for commercial events in almost any popular genre, and new festivals were created every year as corporate entrepreneurial projects. The festival was no longer seen as a cultural institution but as a platform of commerce in genre markets.

Young people entering the spheres of popular music in contemporary cities as artists, fans, and promoters are therefore entering a sphere structured by corporations and institutions optimized for consumption. Clubs and festivals are no longer places outside the networks of the corporate music industry: Clubs are conceived as the lower tier of the industry ecosystem and a tool for corporate dominance, and festivals as a core platform of the concert industry. Glastonbury, Sziget, Coachella, and many other festivals capitalize on their legacy as agents of youth culture agendas outside institutions of formal power, but their main form of capital is now produced from more of the same mass-market popular music and the same models of festival design. Festival organizations now exist in an environment of growing competition with other organizations. Many transformational festivals that once provided alternatives to the popular music festival have similarly moved closer to consumer culture, as illustrated by Burning Man and the evolution of for-profit transformational festivals in tourist destinations, such as Morocco and Costa Rica. The emergence of boutique festivals in the 2010s is historically significant in this respect as an example of the commodification of traditions that once presented alternatives to commercial leisure. The utopian gathering is exploited not by the music industry but by the events and tourism industry.

To fully understand this restructuring and how it could change in the future, it is important to recognize that it resulted not only from industry exploitation but also from broader changes in media and society. It began when small organizations exploited the commercial potential of clubs and festivals in the era in which scenes still existed. These organizations adapted to gentrification and media evolutions and began mobilizing as a live music industry. They also adopted the new popular forms of core genres in their programming, such as indie pop and EDM pop, which were themselves products of industry exploitation. All of these forces shaped new models of the club and the festival, which were further developed and institutionalized in the process of corporatization. This means that for conditions to change, the level of corporatization and gentrification would have to change. Popular music's performance institutions have adapted to and exploited evolving conditions in modernity, and they reveal the depth and scale of the cultural consequences of these conditions. The institutions are compromised as playgrounds of humanity and institutions of culture.

The hegemony of the new models is reflected in ideas about pop music performance in media, governments, and the neoliberal public university. These institutions celebrate the new models. Voices of past models, of scenes, grassroots, and independent ownership either appear in nostalgic books and documentaries, as monuments of a lost paradise, or in online microsphere conversations between former participants.

What is the cultural significance of this restructuring for music and society? A common answer is that the new models provide pleasure for more people and boost city marketing. If more people are attending, this evolution cannot be bad, right? This brings us back to the comparison with Amazon.com and Facebook and to the unequal relation between corporations and citizens in societies that privilege the former. A reflexive understanding of music's performance institutions can register the relative lack of historical understanding, the exploitation, and the alienating effects of commerce and mass culture. It can also consider the cultural functions and not just individual products and experiences provided by performance institutions. These institutions have historically served as places for music in that they have sustained a genre and created a home for its social life, a place governed by the worldview and tradition of this music. They provided collectivities with particular forms of ownership, belonging, and intimacy. In this way, places for music could become valuable places of culture, of social experiences with music as a source of cultural aspirations.

How is such cultural life supported by the new models of performance institutions? Not very well. The purpose of corporations is to maximize profits, and this creates more impersonal relationships and structures cultural life around consumption. Cultural forms are separated from their wider social and historical ecosystem. The new models of the commercial indie rock club and the generic festival event do not speak the language of culture worlds of music. They speak the language of live music and consumer culture. The first step toward a better place for music and human experience in performance—a place that is less exclusively defined by corporate interests in narrow conceptions of popular music—is to recognize that these narratives are uncritical and that more reflexive and historically informed understandings can open up new possibilities for popular music culture and the public good. Performance institutions have for centuries existed under market conditions while sustaining social worlds of music, but the recent restructuring has altered this balance. The paradox is that this happened in institutions of popular music that were once fertile ground for cultural collectivities and utopian alternatives to conformism and corporate capitalism.

The critique I have voiced in this book is not that these institutions were once ideal and have now become negative forces. Rather, I have sought to nuance contemporary discourse by showing that their value systems and functions as institutions for culture have been compromised and that they now promote other ideologies of popular music and social life. The corporatization of clubs and festivals is fairly recent and significant to societies in which music, sports, and other forms of leisure were once central institutions of civic society. It is also important to note that musical performance institutions have generally not been idealist cultural institutions in modernity. Their relative lack of political engagement has been striking in moments of major social transformations, as it is today. The existential threat of climate change and the historic growth in global social inequality have led to calls for a restructuring of the relationship between government and market in the Green New Deal proposals and to demonstrations with exploratory and amateur cultural festivity in public places on all continents. Cultural institutions, however, have been strikingly passive and insular. Institutional inertia is part of the explanation, but it would also be naïve to think that cultural institutions merely serve the common good. They are instruments of the economic and cultural elites.

To advance knowledge of these issues, the study of musical performance can expand from area studies of individual genres into the social study of music and further into the more general discourse on the good society. There have been major intellectual achievements in the philosophy of the good life, but their understandings of music have been limited. This is illustrated by the work of Martha Nussbaum. Her extensive writings synthesize perspectives of moral philosophy, development studies, psychology, and aesthetics. Her concept of human development, fashioned in collaboration with economist Amartya Sen, offers an alternative to thinking about development as economic growth and thus to the dominant spirits of capitalism. Nussbaum argues that governments should secure a number of rights, including justice and access to education and health care, but also possibilities for emotional life, of time for family and leisure under conditions of social justice (Nussbaum 2013). She critiques the Kantian tradition for thinking about justice in terms of rationality and highlights the importance of emotions such as compassion for others and trust in common institutions, drawing from Rousseau, Herder, Mills, and others, whose work can bring further nuance to this book's discussion of lived experiences of citizenship in cultural festivity.

Nussbaum's discussions illustrate that philosophical discourse on the good life has taken little interest in popular culture and in the role of commerce and media, and this creates a limited scope for understanding modern life. The social study of music can nuance ideas of emotional life in modernity by providing insight into this cultural form, which is central to formations of self and cultural consciousness for many people. Knowledge of the social life of music is crucial to understanding music's role in the powerful tendencies of narcissism and projective disgust in humans. A major challenge is to balance not just the dualities of pleasure and education, individuality and collectivity, unity and difference, but also of civic and consumer culture, and public and private ownership. Corporations are unlikely to strike this balance, and they have gained more power over the past couple of decades. This leaves the humanist with a tension that cannot be resolved without structural change.

Cultural Aspirations on the Main Stage

Beyoncé's show at Coachella in 2018 showed that the superstar can have agency and voice cultural aspirations at corporate festivals. The show integrated elements of her arena shows and music videos with the performance tradition of the school bands she experienced as a young person in Texas, showcasing large numbers of musicians and dancers on the stage as proud representatives of black culture. Beyoncé expanded on her race- and gender-conscious persona, which had emerged in 2016 in her Super Bowl halftime show, *Lemonade* album, and "Formation" arena tour. At Coachella two years later, she brought her narratives of racial and gender emancipation into the realm of an institution shaped by mythologies of authentic civic becoming but also by white patriarchy. As in her "Formation" arena tour, she presented a number of hit songs suited for the large stage and left out other songs from *Lemonade* (Caramanica 2016). But she did not follow the conventional festival approach of performing only her most popular songs. In addition, she moved further in the direction of performing without song videos in the background and had no elaborate stage decorations, which was also not possible at a festival. The performance had been conceived with inspiration from the performance culture of marching bands that originate outside arena culture and existed before the rise of electronic media. Beyoncé's performance aesthetics thus increasingly moved beyond the logic of imitating televisual media that seemed ever more powerful to scholars in the late twentieth century. Several of the songs were staged explicitly as team performances with an image of collective pride among musicians and dancers, and her selection and presentation of songs conveyed the sense that this performance was a peak moment in her career and in her efforts to promote black emancipation and pride.

Beyoncé's cultural aspirations for black people evolved from a career in arena shows and media culture, not from music festivals, however. She used the festival as part of her storytelling and momentarily transformed and commented on it. The conception of her performance involved the production of a concert movie, which she codirected to complete and control a story that further elaborated on her narrative but said nothing about festival culture or Coachella. In a word, Beyoncé used the festival as a resource for validating her greatness and endowing charisma to her show. The world of the festival beyond the main stage is absent.

Beyoncé's performance illustrates developments in festival culture and festival production by comparison with festivals in the hippie movement, such as Monterey, Woodstock, and the Isle of Wight. It also illustrates a striking disconnection from them. The black performers at these festivals are left out of Beyoncé's narrative, even though the performers—Lou Rawls, Otis Redding, Jimi Hendrix, Richie Havens, Sly and the Family Stone, Marsha Hunt, and Miles Davis—are significant in the broader history on which she draws. Her show integrated iconic elements of black cultural history into her own history, but it did not acknowledge the history of black people in the world of rock music or the history of black popular music festivals. Beyoncé thus put herself in the role of the heroic celebrity that represents the here and now of contemporary black culture, with collectivism in her performance but not in relation to her peers or to festival culture.

Performances with such transformative cultural aspirations are a rare exception and require considerable resources to succeed at the main stage. Damon Albarn's 2016 concert and festival tour with Syrian musicians, another rare exception, ended up being perceived as a sympathetic gesture but not a transformative moment. Unlike Beyoncé's show, it was not developed into an elaborate main-stage production or based on a catalogue of Anglophone hit songs, which was the symbolic capital that allowed Beyoncé to do costly productions with ambitious cultural statements instead of keeping to the conventional industry formats of hits, videos, and touring. Albarn and the orchestra had little time to prepare because of the war and gave a performance of Syrian music, and this was marginal to the symbolic order of the pop festival. The performance therefore had limited resonance in this festival culture.

A Better Place for the Humanities?

The university institution, too, has undergone a certain corporate institutionalization since the 1960s. It has expanded and changed to serve wider populations and more industrial actors. The percentage of each generation entering university in Western Europe increased from 4.5% in the 1950s to 24% in the 1990s and continues to grow. This expansion is accompanied by a growing emphasis on vocational skills and employability (Teichler 2011, 321 and 364; "Graduates by Field of Education").[2] The number of universities in Europe increased from 201 in 1945 to about 800 in 2005. This figure reaches the thousands if vocational schools that have been upgraded to university status are included (Rüegg 2010, 3). In contrast with Enlightenment ideas of the university as a privileged site of academic freedom, the humanities now operate within a larger, more corporate, and sped-up knowledge factory that serves more utilitarian purposes defined by political institutions. In this final section, I analyze some of the elements of this systemic change so as to situate this book in the recent institutional history of the humanities and reflect on the book's possible contribution to thinking about their future. Because of the university's near-monopoly as a knowledge institution, it is important that its history not be excluded from thinking about the future of humanist scholarship.

Two influential books—*The New Production of Knowledge* (Gibbons et al. 1994) and the follow-up *Re-Thinking Science* (Nowotny, Scott, and Gibbons 2001)—explain how systemic changes in research institutions result from the broader transformation of their relationship with society. The term "Mode 2 knowledge production," shortened to "Mode 2 science," was developed to describe a form of knowledge production that is framed by utilitarian agendas of the nation-state and by collaboration with a wider range of societal actors, especially industry. Mode 2 is the ideal of knowledge produced in and for applied industrial contexts, and it thus represents the expansion of the university in its transformation into a vehicle of capitalism. It is in this respect distinctly different from the ideal of the humanities as represented by the so-called "new universities" of the 1960s and 1970s, the ambitions of which included knowledge interests in lower-income populations and collaboration with workers rather than corporations. The limited attention to class and capitalism in Mode 2 discourse contributes to the elimination of political reflexivity in knowledge production. The university is no longer in a position to define its own functions in society. The feeling of "a deep crisis of purpose" that could already be observed at many universities in the 1990s (Nowotny et al. 2001, 80) has been replaced by a culture of technocratic professionalism in areas such as the digital humanities and creative industries, while a critical counternarrative is being produced by tenured professors who are leaving academia out of frustration with the decline of their ideal of the humanities (e.g., Warner 2015; Lee 2015), with the redistribution of power to administrators, and with systems of quantitative evaluation (Sørensen, Bloch, and Young 2016; Watermeyer and Chubb 2018).

The stereotypes of the "ivory tower" university ignore the original meaning of that metaphor, namely the idea of a protected environment. A free and protected environment was essential to university learning and research for Wilhelm von Humboldt, who argued that the role of the nation-state is to guarantee the autonomy of professors (Rüegg 2010, 16 and 28). The declining protection of and trust in professors transform their subjectivities into authoritarian servants. The cocky Adorno and Foucault are being replaced by more docile craftspeople in designated areas, conducting research at the same time as they collect quantitative merits, write grant applications, and serve as industry partners. One may or may not appreciate the cocky humanist, but with the destruction of the ivory tower, society has also lost some of its advantages. A profession of servitude is not conducive to producing wisdom. Intellectual idealists might consider migrating, but where to? They have no protected places, no institutions of autonomy.

The short production cycles of the research project economy detract scholars from longitudinal, large-scale historical and systematic explorations of their field. This form of hypermodernity intensifies fashion dynamics, and longer-term intellectual and cultural histories become unfashionable. In short, universities produce more utilitarian knowledge at faster speeds, but with a reduced depth and scope. To further situate this book in these developments, let us consider how they are articulated by the research funding schemes of the European Union.[3]

European Research Policy

European Union member states began channeling resources into common schemes of research funding in the 2000s. The dominant vision focused on Europe's competitiveness in a global knowledge economy. Europe's future was imagined to depend on technological innovation in a race toward higher productivity (Felt 2014, 387). The humanities were lumped together with the social sciences and integrated into the Horizon 2020 framework to serve as an assistance tool for the technical sciences. This development reflected the hegemony of Mode 2 discourse and its limited understanding of the humanities (Barry, Born, and Weszkalnys 2008, 30; Osborne 2015, 12–13 and 15). The announcement of Horizon 2020 during Helga Nowotny's presidency of the European Research Council (ERC) was met with resistance. This included an international petition demanding a broader concept of innovation and a body of research that critiqued the ERC's conceptions of the social sciences and humanities (Felt 2014; Levidow and Neubauer 2014). These responses indicate that the humanities were redefined in the process of their European centralization.

First, we can discern the political influence on research topics and disciplinarity. The primacy of technoscientific research can be identified in the orientation toward the natural sciences in about half of the music projects funded by the ERC in the period 2007–2024. Many have adopted computational methods and physical-biological conceptions of music.[4] These projects have the potential to make valuable contributions to music studies, but this policy-driven development transforms the ecology of humanist music studies by subjecting the field to the conditions of perpetual competition for funding in "academic capitalism." The system stimulates a culture of "cruel optimism" (Berlant 2011) in which scholars "play along" to receive benefits such as employment security, research time, bonuses, and institutional power (Keskinen and Silius 2006, 78). Such strong incentives are likely to influence decisions about research among professors in an increasingly unprotected environment.

Second, there is an emphasis on current societal challenges and industry partnerships. The EU's dedicated funding program for the humanities since 2009, HERA, has promoted a soft adoption of the Mode 2 agenda. HERA projects have generally operated with a model of transdisciplinarity derived from Mode 2 discourse. The discourse of transdisciplinarity that gained traction after *The New Production of Knowledge* was published can be distinguished from conventional notions of interdisciplinarity by its interest in producing knowledge with and for industries (Nowotny et al. 2001, 89). Applications for HERA funding require industry partners, although the language around this has become softer. The most recent call for applications stipulated that projects develop "links with stakeholders outside [the] academy" to "maximise the societal benefit of the research" ("HERA JRP," 12). The emphasis on societal challenges, moreover, results in a growing reliance on social science discourse in the humanities in order for applicants to convincingly demonstrate societal relevance. This means that humanists are rewarded for cultivating more generalist discourses.

About fifty ERC grants intended to support the development of an individual scholar's career have been awarded to music scholars. This small number of projects represents a circumscribed capacity to strengthen the institutional basis of the field as a whole.[5] What is more troubling is that ERC-funded music projects have had little impact on music studies. Future intellectual histories of music in the early twenty-first century will not draw a distinction between a "before" and an "after" ERC funding. ERC projects have in fact tended to explore topics years after the theoretical groundwork on those topics had been laid by individual scholars. Scholarship on musical performance culture is a case in point. The first HERA project related to musical performance culture was a 2019 project on music festivals.

The intellectual value of ERC funding in music studies is limited by the short production cycle and the growing bureaucratization, which rewards professional craft, not originality. This points to a future in which more innovative knowledge and critiques of powerful institutions will be produced outside the university. This institutional development encourages the evolution of university professors to become more professionalized but also more generic and conformist craftspeople.

A Product of Its Time?

This book is in some ways a product of its time. First, it follows the hegemonic ideal of professional craft. It adopts the language of an investigation with analytical progression, literature review, empirical evidence, and field expertise. Second, this book examines an area of interest to economic and political institutions and involves collaboration with them. It does not question the value of their existence, although the analyses suggest that the race for economic growth has had negative effects on the conditions of music and urban life. After more than a decade, live music scholarship is yet to develop such critical analysis, and this should raise concerns about the impact of current research policies on the quality of research. Is the system that rewards scholars for playing along also promoting uncritical research?

Third, the book's somewhat generalist sociological discourse is shaped by institutional interests. Dominant agendas in society have altered interpretations of the balance between generalist and specialist knowledge in the humanities. Professors in the new transdisciplinary or vocational departments develop more generic skills and knowledge of cultural industries, but they also have less opportunity to develop specialist knowledge of cultural particulars. Such departments tend to generate circumscribed conceptions of art and humanity. As a young music historian and ethnomusicologist, I was fortunate in the mid-2000s to land a tenured job in my home country in a new transdisciplinary and vocational program, but I did not give up music studies or the humanities and continue to experience tension between Mode 1 and 2 regimes.

This leads to the final point, namely that this book draws on Mode 2 experience but is deeply invested in Mode 1, specifically the ideal of noninstrumentalist science and of unfettered academic freedom under the condition of (inter)disciplinary authority.[6] The political agenda for transdisciplinarity in Mode 2 needs to be confronted with critical discussions of knowledge production to secure a system of checks and balances for research quality, knowledge transmission, and interest in the public good. This requires a deep understanding of the history and functions of disciplines. The discipline of musicology that emerged in the late nineteenth century and its development into interdisciplinary music studies provides an immense knowledge resource. It has played a key role in the construction of the study object, the critique of decontextualized live music discourse, and is essential to future transmission of knowledge of music. What is more, this book has not attempted a singular synthesis that erases disciplinary difference, but rather retains the distinctness of music studies and sociology, with their different logics taking leading roles at various stages in the investigation for analyzing different dimensions of the object. Their logics both complement and challenge each other. The sociological narrative of institutions transforms understandings of clubs and festivals in music studies, and music studies expands and transforms the sociological conception of leisure institutions in modernity. Future work in the social study of music can further explore how these different disciplinary logics might productively use competition and friction between them to fully exploit the potential of their combination. This requires specialist knowledge and experience in both disciplines, and that is both a great potential and a challenge of interdisciplinarity scholarship.

Acknowledgments

I would like to thank colleagues and students at Roskilde and two other universities of great importance to this project: Columbia University hosted me as a visiting scholar in 2010–2011, and Humboldt University of Berlin appointed me to the honorable position of full professor in the academic year 2017–2018. I had my first long-term experience in an institution of excellence as a visiting scholar and subsequently as a postdoctoral fellow at the University of Chicago in 2003–2004, and for that I am eternally grateful.

When I started writing this book in early 2016, I was both enthusiastic and insecure about the project. Would it be meaningful to develop an alternative to the live music discourse in popular music studies? Was the empirical scope and interdisciplinary approach too challenging? I needed time to contemplate these difficult questions and did not share any of the arguments in publications or at conferences. Apart from the lectures at Humboldt and one at the Center for World Music in Hildesheim, I pretty much wrote this book in complete isolation. The one exception was a meeting with Philip Bohlman in September 2016, which gave me confidence and helped me write the book I really wanted to write. When a complete draft surfaced in January 2019, Francesco Lapenta offered an in-depth critical reading, for which I am most grateful. He was also an important influence on my research in the early 2010s from which this book derives. Many thanks also to Kristin McGee and Leif Skov for their comments during the final stages of preparation later in 2019. Christopher Geissler and Marianne Tatom provided excellent copyediting assistance. I am delighted and proud that the book found a home in Chicago's Big Issues in Music series. Elizabeth Branch Dyson shepherded the manuscript to publication with great wisdom and care. Editorial associate Mollie McFee and the entire editorial and production team ensured a smooth publication process. Two anonymous reviewers generously took time to read the manuscript carefully and provided brilliant criticisms.

The manuscript was submitted for habilitation in June 2019 under the title "A Better Place for Music? The Social Study of Musical Performance Institutions." The book was finished before I received the committee's report. I nonetheless wish to express sincere gratitude to my committee: Anne Sejten, David Hesmondhalgh, and Thomas Solomon.

This book has benefited from the generosity of a number of culture professionals and fans since the mid-2000s. Those who have been directly involved in this project are named in the relevant chapters, so I shall limit myself to mentioning only a small number of individuals here. I offer my profound thanks to Bill Bragin, B. Q. Nguyen, Cor Schlösser, Dirk De Clippeleir, Dragan Ambrozi, Edan Wilber, Esben Danielsen, Henrik Hatt, Kate Landau, Jakob Brixvold, Jan Sneum, Jon Heemsbergen, Melena Ryzik, Michiel Beers, Sarah Raimann, Simone Hofmann, Sonja Heimann, Spencer Theile, Steen Jørgensen, and Younes Baghor.

In the academic world, I would like to express special gratitude to the following people for their inspiration and encouragement: Alba Colombo, Andrea Bohlman, Anja Lindelof, Anna Lenhof, Arne Stollberg, Arnt Maasø, Bianca Ludewig, Bodo Mrozek, Byron Dueck, Chris Washburne, Christin Kleinoth, Dahlia Borsche, Damon Phillips, Goffredo Plastino, Graham St. John, Hillegonda Rietveld, Jaime Jones, James Deaville, Jedediah Sklower, Jeffers Engelhardt, Jens Papenburg, Jens Skou Olsen, Jim Sykes, Jon Sundbo, Judith Schwarzbart, Kolja Zimmermann, Leah Babb-Rosenfeld, Maria Gable, Maria Olesen, Mark Banks, Martin Tröndle, Matt Stahl, Michael Spanu, Nicola Dibben, Patrick Becker, Rasmus Pedersen, Ron Radano, Safa Canalp, Sebastian Klotz, Shannon Garland, Somar Ashkar, Stan Hawkins, Steffen Just, Stephen Amico, Suzanne Ryan, Tami Gadir, and Thomas Hilder. I would also like to remember Carsten Hatting and Erik Wiedeman, who in the mid-1990s encouraged me to become a scholar.

My deepest personal thanks goes to my family, to my wife, Anja, and our children, Dante, Louisa, and Victor. I feel blessed to have you in my life!

Finally, I should like to remember my paternal grandfather, Jens Holt, and acknowledge his legacy in this work. He died in a car accident in 1954, so I never met him, but I am told he was a critical thinker and ethically engaged—ideals to which I aspire. Jens graduated with a degree in theology in 1936 and became a pastor. Every year, he invited poor people in his community to his house on Christmas Eve, and he risked his life as a member of the resistance movement during World War II. I believe my father's family is a source of my interest in ethics. How does music shape human relations, and what is the role of performance institutions in this? What is being celebrated and protected by those institutions? Are there better alternatives? I hope this book shares some of the pastor's concern with dignity, justice, and soul.

Fabian Holt
Copenhagen
February 2020

Notes

Chapter One

1. DJ performances are still not the norm at the Olympics. Tiësto was the first DJ to perform at the Olympics in 2004, Martin Garrix performed at the Winter Olympics in 2018, and David Guetta performed at the closing ceremony of the UEFA soccer tournament in 2016. Popular wedding blogs suggest that it was common in the late 2010s to discuss whether a band or DJ is better at a wedding, and that the cost of a band is not always the main criterion (e.g., "Band or DJ?"; "DJ or Live Music"). Carol Silverman registered a quick transition in Bulgarian weddings in the 1990s (Silverman 2011, 153).

2. For further discussion of the live music hype in the late 2000s, see Holt (2010).

3. For analysis of general developments in public policy of culture in general and popular music in particular, see Hesmondhalgh et al. (2015); Cloonan (2007); and Homan, Cloonan, and Cattermole (2015).

4. The first statement by Barak has been edited by the author to avoid unintentionally clumsy language.

5. The slogan was coined by a twenty-three-year-old female copywriter inspired by feminism (Komar 2017) and has an element of feminist equality and justice in its rhetoric.

6. The second volume appeared in May 2019, one week before this manuscript was submitted (Frith et al. 2019). This was unfortunately too late for including the book in this discussion.

7. I have observed boredom and chatter at countless concerts and how it became a common topic of conversation in the mid-2010s, often in relationship to conversations about the use of mobile phones. A posting on Reddit in 2016, for instance, generated a lively discussion with more than 300 comments ("I attended a concert last night and not a single person filmed the show, no one talked through the show . . . and it was amazing"). See also Signore (2014) and Zaleski (2018). The live music industry worked with great determination to incorporate mobile phones into consumer practices in the 2010s. The industry recognized the phone as a key communications and commercial platform for many young consumers. The ticket seller Ticketfly experienced a 40% increase in ticket sales via phones from 2013 to 2014. By then, 35% of tickets were sold via phones and 45% of online traffic came from phones. A survey conducted in April 2015 with about 2,000 participants indicated that 31% of concertgoers aged 18–34 were using their phone for half of the concert or

more (Peralta 2015). Penetration of concert operations by mobile phones grew in the following years, certainly in terms of ticket sales.

8. A list of festivals with day crowds of more than 50,000 would include the following:

Denmark: Roskilde, Smukfest
Sweden: Brävalla
Germany: Fusion, Wacken Open Air, Rock am Ring, Hurricane, Southside
Poland: Open'er
Holland: Pinkpop, Lowlands, Laundry Days
Belgium: Pukkelpop, Rock Werchter, Tomorrowland
The UK: Glastonbury, Download, Reading, V (Chelmsford), V (Staffordshire), Leeds, Creamfields, Sonisphere, Bestival
France: Nuits Sonores, Fête de l'Humanité
Austria: Nova Rock
Hungary: Sziget
Serbia: Exit (47,000)
Spain: Benicàssim and Mad Cool
Portugal: Rock in Rio Lisboa

The list is based on extensive research, primarily a combination of information gained from news media, directly from festival managements, and communications with industry professionals (Mikołaj Ziółkowski, email to the author, November 4, 2014; Leif Skov, email to the author, November 7, 2014; Esben Danielsen, email to the author, November 3, 2014; Chris Anderton, email to the author, November 4, 2014; Ivan Milivojev, email to the author, November 4, 2014; Emma Webster, email to the author, November 3, 2014; Webster [2014]; Cor Schlosser, email to the author, November 4, 2014; Fusion festival, email to the author's assistant Christin Kleinoth, circa December 12, 2017). FKP Scorpio declined to provide information on audience size (Jonas Rohde, email to Christin Kleinoth, December 14, 2017).

9. A future discussion might consider arguments that reality music shows serve a purpose for the music industry (Fairchild 2008; Cvetkovski 2015).

Chapter Two

1. Evans (2014); Sanghani (2015); Brown (2017); Davies (2017); Jordan (2017); "Roskilde politi har fået seks anmeldelser om voldtægt" (The police department in Roskilde received six reports of rape); "Swedish Music Festival Is Cancelled in 2018 after Rape and Sexual Assault Claims."

2. See note 1, this chapter.

3. A sound wave at 50 Hz is more than seven meters long.

4. The ritual of the symphonic concert is sometimes interpreted negatively for its perceived lack of social involvement. Such misunderstandings are common when the ritual is interpreted from the perspective of folk and popular music aesthetics. One example is Small's critique of the classical concert (Small 1986). I encounter popular music biases frequently when students familiar with popular music discuss rituals in the classical music concert hall.

Chapter Three

1. Incidentally, they also represented different forms of urbanism. While Bland's style had elements of light forms of popular music and followed hit song formulas more closely, B. B. King's style is more reflective of middle-class culture in the metropolis. This is demonstrated by King's expressive and stylistic range on *Live at the Regal*, recorded in 1964 (King 1965).

Chapter Four

1. The sample of clubs in Europe is detailed in chapter 5, p. 127.

2. In 2008–2010 about five people were booking Glasslands and several people were booking Market Hotel (Edan Wilber, interview with the author, April 26, 2010).

3. The names of specific places are not disclosed here out of privacy concerns.

4. I adopt the term "culture world" from Diana Crane (1992), who defines it as an expansion of Becker's term "art world," which can include popular culture, too.

5. Patrick began talking about a festival as a possible source of income in 2007 and started one in Monterrey, Mexico, two years later. He gave up after one year, and in 2012 he became a curator at its competitor, Festival NRMAL (Pelly 2013).

6. The name Losaida is used by the Puerto Rican community and social activists. The name Alphabet City is derived from the late 1970s arts scene (Mele 2000, xi).

7. The Fugs performed in the Players Theatre in Greenwich Village in 1966–1967 (Burke 2014, 542). For a firsthand account of the scene, see Gruen (1966).

8. It is a myth, however, that Kristal had no idea what he was doing and just gave in to young bands eager to play (Waterman 2011, 3). Max's reopened in 1975, and the Mercer Arts Center reopened later that year but farther away in SoHo.

9. For details on Ginsberg's history in the East Village, see Blechman and Lynn (2013).

10. Other outsider perspectives on CBGB have similarly associated the club with poverty and dirt in the neighborhood. The following statement is by a person who describes her experience of going to the club in the late 1980s. She identifies as middle-aged and suburban. "It was an interesting walk from [South Street Seaport] through China-town and the districts above CBGB. It was also sad. So many poor people walking in the streets. I wondered what stories they had to tell. We approached CBGB about a half hour before show time. . . . How do I even begin to describe this place? Could this gray place with graffiti all over the outside be this famed club? . . . The club's walls looked like the inside of a prehistoric cave—lumpy and scrawled upon. But Kathy and I decided to brave the elements and head to the back and down the stairs to the rest-room (another funny term—if you rested there, heaven knows what you would pick up)" (Haliski 1989, 79–80; see also Goodman 2009, 105).

11. As of 2019, the two prominent minichain gourmet cafés Think Coffee and Joe's Coffee were still concentrated in more affluent neighborhoods.

12. These trends in the Lower East Side could have been analyzed with greater clarity if the dataset did not also include Chinatown.

13. Schoemer (1990); Botton (1996); Carlson (2012); Buckley (2013a, 2013b); J. Goodman (2013).

14. Swier reportedly paid $300,000 for Mercury Lounge's building in 1993 and $1,000,000 for the Bowery Ballroom in 1997 (Sisario 2007).

15. The term "feeder club" is also used in sports in a similar sense for a junior team that serves primarily to grow talented players and feed them directly into the organization's parent club at the top level.

16. I explored accounts of the crowds at the Bowery Ballroom through street ethnography in the immediate area of the venue in March and October 2013.

17. Santo's Party House had a number of different people booking and was infamously closed during a festival with Nazi-leaning punk bands. One of the managers, Alec Reinstein (aka the rapper Despot), claimed on Twitter that he tried to cancel the show once he became aware of the Nazi-leaning bands. The circumstances are unclear, as one of the managers allegedly explained that the club was closing anyway because the ten-year lease had expired and they did not want to renew it (Yoo and Phillips 2016; *Brooklyn Vegan* 2016).

18. This description draws from Hepp's (2013) definition of media culture as a culture that is primarily constituted through media.

Chapter Five

1. I have compared gentrification in European cities before and do not find differences in the fundamental dynamics, and public policy is the most significant difference in terms of music (Holt 2013). For a discussion of homogenization in the cultural industries, see Hesmondhalgh (2003/2019, 424–425).

2. *The Position of Muslims in the Netherlands*; *Belgium 2017 International Religious Freedom Report* (2); Danmarks Statistik (2017, 12); *Befolkningen i København 2017: Orientering fra Velfærdsanalyse: Befolkning i København, Region Hovedstaden og hele landet 2017*.

3. In Denmark, the subsidization of popular music festivals became more common in the 2010s, but dedicated funding schemes for festivals have not yet evolved.

4. In two meetings and email correspondence with the management of SO36 in Berlin in 2007–2009, I experienced a grassroots model of collectivist nonprofit management that is not subsidized. This model is rare.

5. The clubs did not give me their international records of production, sales, and organizational information, but they shared some of this information with me via interviews and email correspondence. I have attended concerts in the Copenhagen club occasionally since it opened in 1996, but not more than three to six concerts annually; I attended one concert in the Brussels club, and none in the Amsterdam club. My research on Amsterdam and the other nine organizations in the original broad sample was based on electronic communications and resources.

6. The clubs were: Sala Apolo, Barcelona; La Cigale and Olympia, Paris; Rockhal, Luxembourg; Melkweg, Amsterdam; Ancienne Belgique, Brussels; Columbiahalle, Berlin; Vega, Copenhagen; and Debaser, Malmö and Stockholm. Estragon in Bologna initially agreed to participate but eventually did not respond to subsequent inquiries.

7. A news report indicated that there were eight community houses in 2000 ("Skandale truer Københavns overborgmester").

8. On the hegemony of creative economy discourse, see Oakley (2009). I met two administrators of the European Commission in November 2016 who said that Throsby's work and this book in particular were a key resource in their field.

9. A person who had a central position in the network of this ideology for decades and who served on the national arts council in Denmark commented on an earlier version of this chapter: "Vega does not include crooners and tribute bands, for instance, because the national arts council does not perceive such forms of music to be quality music" (Leif Skov, conversation with the author, October 17, 2019).

10. This quotation is a slightly edited version of the original to avoid unintentionally clumsy language and typos.

11. According to Schlösser, the overall budget for culture in Holland was cut by 20–30% in this period.

12. This typically includes events such as poetry readings, dance performances, and lectures (e.g., "Paradiso Today"). Many of these events are held in the club's spaces with a capacity below 120, including the cinema, theater, and two art galleries.

13. Since leaving Melkweg, Tchong has promoted world music on an ad hoc basis in smaller clubs such as Podium Mozaïek, Badcuyp, Tolhuistuin, and the jazz-focused Bimhuis and Zaal 100.

14. This passage is quoted from an English translation that the World Music Forum in Holland sent to me. I have made minor language edits.

15. Le Botanique has three small performance spaces (the Orangerie, the Rotonde, and the Witloof Bar) as well as a library, gallery, cinema, and more ("Our Venues"). Its largest performance space has capacity for 700, but Le Botanique also promotes some shows in the nearby 2,000-person-capacity Cirque Royal. Le Botanique managed Cirque Royal in the 2000s, but the two split and Cirque Royal became a rental-based venue ("Cirque Royal").

16. The Flemish government provided a fixed annual base funding of 2,200,000 euros in the mid-2010s plus 90,000 for projects; the Flemish Community Commission in Brussels, 110,000; the city of Brussels, 35,000; and the Brussels region, 60,000 (Dirk De Clippeleir, email to the author, November 16, 2016).

17. In 2013, the sponsors were a bank, the national lottery, a brewery, Coca-Cola, and Samsung (Dirk De Clippeleir, conversation with the author, August 13, 2013).

18. Legal investigations by state authorities took place in the cases of Odense's festival Tinderbox and Copenhagen's hosting of the 2014 Eurovision Song Contest (e.g., "Beretning til Statsrevisorerne om budgetoverskridelsen ved Eurovision Song Contest 2014"). Events have also served as a promotional tool for mayors in cities such as Elsinore, Herning, and Horsens.

19. I met with members of the national Music Council in 2010 in the capacity as chief advisor on a report on music festivals in Denmark.

20. For a history of the term up to 2000, see Michelsen (2001).

21. Since 2016, all educational and cultural institutions have been subject to an annual 2% budget cut to fund tax cuts and reroute money to health care and elderly care (Schmidt, Andersen, and Thobo-Carlsen 2015). The current minister of culture announced from the beginning of her tenure that the budgets for arts and culture would be smaller in the coming years (Kristiansen 2016).

22. By the end of the 1990s, the average income and education levels in the neighborhood had increased more than in any other neighborhood of the city, and there were more families (Henriksen 2002, 9).

23. Funding from the ECOC provided crucial start-up capital that paved the way for contributions from the city government and other sponsors. Once that was established, a

private investor entered the project by buying the building for the purpose of renting it to Vega. The total amount of public funding in the first three years added up to around six million euros (1996 figure). The management had six months to prepare because the club had to open within fiscal year 1996 to get ECOC subsidies (Trevor Davies, email to the author, October 14, 2011; Torben Schipper, email to the author, October 19, 2011; Jørgensen 1996 and 1997; Lindboe 1997). Vega is one of the few surviving projects of the 1996 ECOC in Copenhagen.

24. There were local and European inspirations for the venue complex Vega, which includes the first midsize venue in Copenhagen and the one that is still most central to understanding the gentrification process.

25. Manager Jens Rottbøll proposed the idea in 1997 of developing the club into a national institution, paralleling AB in Brussels, and some of his successors have repeated the suggestion to no avail (Jensen 1997a; Rix 1997; Rix 1998; Strøyer 2008).

26. In the late 2000s and early 2010s, I participated in a couple of event industry conferences in Copenhagen and had firsthand experience of the decision-making processes that led to the funding of large international events and the new arena. I also learned about these processes from two conversations with the CEO of Live Nation who explained, among other things, that the government and not Live Nation was the lead entrepreneur in the arena project. I cannot be more specific about my informants and examples in order to protect my informants' anonymity.

27. In Amager, the club Amager Bio got 3.8 million euros in 2015 for renovating the building and expanding the audience capacity from 1,100 to 1,500 (Veirum 2015). In Frederiksberg, the local government subsidized the construction of K. B. Hallen, for which the total budget was 31.5 million euros (Kierkegaard 2018).

28. The changes in aesthetics can be identified in the music programming of nonprofit clubs around the country, in "rhythmic music" education, and in the music programming of the national broadcasting corporation, for instance. By the 2010s, the term "rhythmic music" was becoming antiquated.

Chapter Six

1. Robinson's book is the first to integrate analysis of festival design into the history of popular music festivals. The book's fundamental distinction between participatory and presentational performance, adopted from Thomas Turino, is employed in a typology of boutique festivals and lineup festivals that is original but somewhat undertheorized. The book at times equates the participant role (participant vs. spectator) with festival design (immersive environment vs. concert-focused design). Moreover, the book could have further explored how a festival can accommodate different cultures of participation, consumption, and production. Many concert industry festivals have co-opted elements of participatory and immersive design. This process does not undermine Robinson's distinctions between different types of design and participation, but it makes them less central to explaining the structure of the popular music festival landscape.

2. Weibel suggests that Mendelssohn-Bartholdy developed special concerts of Handel's music in original instrumentation and performance style to offer something unique since most music festivals played the same repertoire (Weibel 2006, 68–69). Mendelssohn-Bartholdy also worked for the Liverpool and Birmingham festivals on the side, reflect-

ing a passion for Austro-Germanic music that Handel had nurtured (Drummond [2011] 2016, 270).

3. St. Petersburg was named Petrograd in 1914–1924 and Leningrad in 1924–1991.

4. I have been unable to locate the original publication of this statement, but Schneider's German translation (1988, 370–371) supports the validity of this source. The word "youth" has been changed to plural and the final sentence slightly edited for grammatical accuracy.

5. The choir of Edinburgh International, for instance, identifies itself as "a world-class amateur choir" and follows the model of a symphony choir ("Edinburgh Festival Chorus"). Its performance does not represent amateur aesthetics, however. It is generally indistinguishable from a professional choir. Central to the Lower Rhine Festival tradition was the experience of a large local community that sings a national repertoire. The conception of the choir was thus specific to the bourgeois festival institution.

Chapter Seven

1. Afropunk expanded to Atlanta, Johannesburg, London, and Paris in the mid-2010s.

2. Hoffman said that "Woodstock nation" was built on "our energy, music, politics, school, religion, play, battleground and our sensuality" (quoted from Clecak 1971, 610).

3. Some happenings have later been reenacted (Concannon 2008).

4. Like other hippie festivals, Roskilde's history with world music began with Ravi Shankar. The enthusiasm for Bob Marley's appearance in 1978 made the festival management want to book more reggae artists (Leif Skov, conversation with the author, October 17, 2019). Roskilde has embraced the world music industry trends of African, Balkan, and Icelandic artists since the 1980s, leading to headliners such as King Sunny Adé, Youssou N'Dour (who toured arenas with Peter Gabriel), Björk, and Sigur Rós. Apart from the few concerts on the main stage, Roskilde has presented many lesser-known artists on smaller stages. It had a dedicated world music stage circa 1997–2007.

5. I talked to this person a month after the concert. The person shall remain anonymous.

6. When I started doing exploratory field research at Roskilde in 2007, I remember managers of DR saying their team at Roskilde had grown from about twenty in the 1980s to about 150. I unfortunately do not have field notes specifying the exact names of my interlocutors or the dates of these conversations, but the expansion was common knowledge and it paralleled BBC's expansion at Glastonbury.

7. The video was later removed from the home page. Nashestvie, https://nashestvie.ru/, accessed early June 2018.

Chapter Eight

1. *Billboard*'s Touring Conference & Awards in New York City in 2012 and South by Southwest in Austin, Texas, in 2013. At South by Southwest, I was on a panel titled "Music Festivals Powered by Tech Innovation" that included managers of Open'er, Roskilde, Sziget, and Exit. At that event and in a preparatory meeting the day before, I witnessed their enthusiasm about the commercial potentials of information technology and heard their thoughts on festival production more generally.

2. Flanagan (2013); Mason (2013); Montano (2017); "Live Nation Entertainment Acquires Top Electronic Music Company Cream."

3. According to Leif Skov, Live Nation no longer offers headliners at a festival rate. When this company plans a tour in Scandinavia, the company estimates the potential profits from promoting the artist in the largest venue in each country and then demands a price from festivals that would generate at least the same profit margin (Leif Skov, conversation with the author, October 17, 2019).

4. Regulars on the main stage include Carl Cox, David Guetta, Steve Aoki, Swedish House Mafia (with separate performances by the members after the trio split up in 2013), Tiësto, and later Deadmau5, Alan Walker, and the Chainsmokers.

5. Festival Republic emerged from a reorganization of the company Mean Fiddler, which promoted concerts and managed club venues in London. In 2007, two years after Live Nation gained ownership, the venue portfolio was sold and the company was rebranded under the name Festival Republic to concentrate on festivals ("Festival Republic: About Us").

6. I heard stories from two cities at a conference on the event industry in Copenhagen in 2011. The director of Copenhagen's tourism industry association said in 2011 that there had been many objections to closing the square at the city hall for traffic for two days during MTV Europe's Music Awards in 2006, but that it happened every other week in 2011 (Martin Bender, public presentation, September 21, 2011). A representative of Essen's year as the European Capital of Culture in 2010 said in 2011 that their proposal to close 60 kilometers of highway to traffic for an event was met with skepticism, but that they were ultimately granted permission (representative of Essen's European Capital of Culture, public presentation, September 21, 2011).

7. I have witnessed how events use the impact discourse in multiple situations in Denmark through interaction with event organizers and tourism organizations since 2006.

8. This book adopts the phrase "mainstream society and business" from Don Slater's discussions of the sociology of modernity (Slater 1997 and 2011).

9. My research assistant Christin Kleinoth conducted an exploratory search on Instagram in October 2017, which led to insights into self-presentation narratives, and I then subsequently conducted a search shortly afterward and again in June 2018.

10. Jordan was featured in advertisements for Nike's Air shoe model and had clothing and fragrance products named after him.

Chapter Nine

1. These quotations have been slightly edited to avoid unintentionally clumsy language and typos.

2. The exact view count for the 2011 aftermovie is impossible to determine since the festival promoter removed the video at least once and then uploaded it again, and the video has circulated across multiple YouTube channels. The view counts in Tomorrowland's official channel were about 60 million by February 2013, but the video also circulated in other channels.

3. In a top-rated comment on YouTube, a user states that watching this aftermovie the first time was a key moment in his life (Murphy 2017).

4. My research notes from a meeting with ID&T's management in Antwerp on January 24, 2013, suggest that the company's consumer research shows that more than 90% of the audience at Tomorrowland in Belgium was white in the early 2010s, but I do not have documentation to this effect. ID&T's research showed that the average age of the Tomorrowland festivalgoer in 2013 was twenty-four and about half of the audience was from Belgium. The other half came from a relatively even distribution of about thirty other countries. Overall, 40% of attendees were students and 50% were working full-time. There was a slight male dominance (60%), but less than in 1990s hardcore EDM events. ID&T produced the arena event Thunderdome in the 1990s, which was more male dominated.

5. ID&T shared PowerPoint presentations for sponsors, and the company's own customer research was based on email questionnaires sent to all ticket buyers, with a total of more than one million respondents ("Tomorrowland Presentation").

6. Sónar produced TV advertising spots in 1999–2008. They can be found in Sónar's archive on YouTube ("Sónar Festival").

7. Tomorrowland's YouTube channel identifies an annual postfestival video for every year since 2005. However, these videos were posted to YouTube in July 2011 and might retrospectively have been called aftermovies. It is also not certain that the first videos were made specifically for YouTube circulation. The 2009 aftermovie concludes with the announcement that a DVD will soon be available (Robertson 2017).

8. Creamfields was acquired by Live Nation in 2012, and Nature One was acquired by SXF in 2013 ("Live Nation Entertainment Acquires Top Electronic Music Company Cream"; Flanagan 2013). "Relive Ultra Miami 2012 (Official Aftermovie)"; "Creamfields 2013 Official Aftermovie"; "Nature One 2013 Official Aftermovie." The new style of EDM pop marketing videos also influenced independent festivals, including Sea Dance in Montenegro ("EXIT & Sea Dance Festivals 2016—The Magic AFTERMOVIE!").

9. "Official Aftermovie @ Sziget Festival 2012"; "Coachella 2014: Thank You"; "2016 Official After Film."

10. In a separate section on "media coverage," there were for years only three videos: three news features from 2009 to 2013 produced by *Time* magazine, KQED, and PBS, respectively ("Media Coverage").

11. For perspectives on mediations of Burning Man in the early 2010s, see Cohen (2011); Karlin (2013); and Roose (2013).

12. Since at least 2010, ID&T has presented itself as an electronic music experience company, ascribing a central role to the themed concepts, visual-architectural designs, and overall integration of the consumer experience through media storytelling and brand identity from ticket purchase to the live experience. In 2014, the company unveiled a mission statement that included "making a positive impact on human consciousness" and making people aware of their "impact on the world, ecologically, socially, and spiritually." ID&T home page, accessed August 11, 2014, http://www.id-t.com/company/our-company (content altered).

13. In the 1990s, ID&T produced a VHS video of its 1994 Mysteryland festival. A Belgian house music fan since the early 1990s, Younes Baghor remembered that the "aftermovies" succeeded a practice of selling audiotapes of the music played at the club night when audiences were leaving in the morning (Younes Baghor, email to the author, January 4, 2013).

14. The comments I found on the festival's Facebook page in 2014 included statements

such as "YES!," "Nice video!!!!!!," "this is INSANE," "I will be there!," "My next dream!! T.O.P!!," and "I wanna join it absolutely!! I have seen THE video aftermovie sooo manyyy times now and it's still fucking awesome!!!" These quotes were taken from the Tomorrowland Facebook web page in August 2014. The Tomorrowland Facebook pages are constantly changing. The social media marketing department edits and removes user comments. I remember many comments stating the nationality of the festivalgoer and media user with exclamation marks, mirroring the culture of waving national flags at the festival in a celebratory and friendly fashion, and welcoming and often embracing participants with flags from other countries. Tomorrowland's Facebook page is available at https://www.facebook.com/tomorrowland (accessed January 24, 2015).

15. This development was reported to me by the fan administrators of the Facebook groups in Germany and Finland, who helped me distribute my questionnaire in 2013. Unfortunately, I no longer have access to this information on Facebook.

16. A further exploration of this aspect could engage Hesmondhalgh's conception of "mediated communality" (Hesmondhalgh 2013, chapter 5).

17. I talked with Esben Danielsen of the Roskilde Festival about this on a few occasions in 2009–2013.

Chapter Ten

1. See the discussions of public policy in chapters 5 and 7. See also Lipsitz (1999) and Hesmondhalgh et al. (2015).

2. With the introduction of UNESCO's standards for measuring educational attainment in the 1970s, the OECD and other institutions have tended to provide statistics for higher or tertiary education and focus less on universities specifically. The statistics are also complicated by the fact that many vocational institutions have been upgraded to university status (Teichler 2011, 365).

3. National differences will not be discussed in detail. A further discussion could consider the extraordinary situation in Hungary (Foer 2019). Some of the changes in Europe can also be found in the United States (Madrid 2017).

4. This interpretation is based on an analysis of the search results for "music" in the database of ERC-funded projects ("ERC Funded Projects").

5. Five music projects have been funded by HERA in 2009–2022 ("HERA: Projects"). Roughly fifty music-centered projects have been funded through individual excellence grants in 2007–2023 ("ERC Funded Projects").

6. For a discussion of the concept of disciplinary authority, see Post (2009).

Works Cited

"2nd Talent Forum June 1–4." 1976. *Billboard* 88, no. 11 (March 13): 1 and 32.

"2016 Official After Film." 2016. The Common Glastonbury, YouTube video, October 3, https://www.youtube.com/watch?v=Eb1k_gyYVEg, accessed February 8, 2019.

"AB History." Ancienne Belgique, https://www.abconcerts.be/en/about-ab/ab-history/24/, accessed January 2, 2019.

"AB Policy Plan: 2017–2021." Ancienne Belgique. Unpublished report for the Flemish government.

"About Melkweg." Melkweg, https://www.melkweg.nl/en/info/about-melkweg/, accessed October 12, 2016.

"About Paradiso." Paradiso, https://www.paradiso.nl/web/English-Agenda/About-Paradiso.htm, accessed October 12, 2016.

"About the ILMC." http://ilmc.com/index.php/about/about-us, accessed August 29, 2018.

Abu-Lughod, J. 1995. *From Urban Village to East Village: The Battle for New York's Lower East Side*. Oxford: Blackwell.

———. 1999. *New York, Chicago, Los Angeles: America's Global Cities*. Minneapolis: University of Minnesota Press.

"Advisering kunstinstellingen en ondersteunende organisaties." 2016. Departement Cultuur, Jeugd, Sport en Media, Vlaamse overheid, May 18, http://www.kunstenenerfgoed.be/sites/default/files/generated/files/handleiding/160518_Advisering%20kunstinstellingen%20en%20ondersteunende%20organisaties.pdf, accessed October 14, 2016.

Alighieri, D. [1320] 1984. *The Divine Comedy of Dante Alighieri: Paradiso*. Translated by A. Mandelbaum. New York: Bantam.

Alt, M. 2018. *Neurechte Pop-Sounds? Über die Auswirkungen des Rechtsrucks auf die deutschsprachige Popmusik am Beispiel von Frei.Wild*, Unpublished MA thesis, Humboldt University of Berlin.

Anasi, R. 2012. *The Last Bohemia: Scenes from the Life of Williamsburg*. New York: Farrar, Straus & Giroux.

"Ancienne Belgique opgenomen in lijst 'grote Vlaamse Cultuurinstellingen.'" 2008.

Kunstenpunt Muzik, January 9, http://www.muziekcentrum.be/news.php?ID=1037, accessed October 13, 2016.

Anderson, B. 2015. "The Wall of Sound." *Motherboard*, July 5, https://motherboard.vice.com/en_us/article/the-wall-of-sound, accessed March 15, 2017.

Anderson, R. 2007. "Circa 1951: Presenting Science to the British Public." Video recording of lecture, Oregon State University Library, Special Collections, retrieved from the Internet Archive, https://web.archive.org/web/20080706032208/http://osulibrary.oregonstate.edu/specialcollections/events/2007paulingconference/video-s2-3-anderson.html, accessed May 16, 2018.

Andersson, T., and D. Getz. 2012. "Festival Ownership: Differences between Public, Nonprofit and Private Festivals in Sweden." In *Festival and Event Management in the Nordic Countries*, edited by T. Andersson, D. Getz, and R. Mykletun, 87–103. New York: Routledge.

Anderton, C. 2011. "Music Festival Sponsorship: Between Commerce and Carnival." *Arts Marketing: An International Journal* 1, no. 2: 145–58.

———. 2018. *Music Festivals in the UK: Beyond the Carnivalesque*. London: Routledge.

Animal Collective. 2009. *Merriweather Post Pavilion*. Domino Records.

"Annual Report 2014." Ancienne Belgique, https://issuu.com/jotie/docs/jaarverslag_ab2014, accessed October 19, 2016.

"Annual Report 2015." Ancienne Belgique, https://issuu.com/jotie/docs/jaarverslag_final/1?e=1165517/34189710, accessed October 19, 2016.

"Ansøgning om at være regionalt spillested i perioden 2017–2020: Vega." Vega, report for the Department of Culture of the national government in Denmark. Unpublished.

Antek, S. 1957. "Recipe for Children: Young People's Concerts Should Strive to Make Music a Live Experience." *New York Times*, February 3, https://www.nytimes.com/1957/02/03/archives/recipe-for-children-young-peoples-concerts-should-strive-to-make.html, accessed February 24, 2019.

Arendt, H. 1951/1966. *The Origins of Totalitarianism*. San Diego, CA: Harcourt.

Artaud, A. 1958. *The Theater and Its Double*. New York: Grove Press.

Atkinson, R., and G. Bridge, eds. 2005. *Gentrification in a Global Context: The New Urban Colonialism*. London: Routledge.

Auerbach, E. 1953. *Mimesis: The Representation of Reality in Western Literature*. Princeton, NJ: Princeton University Press.

Auslander, P. 1999. *Liveness: Performance in a Mediatized Culture*. London: Routledge.

———. 2004. "Performance Analysis and Popular Music: A Manifesto." *Contemporary Theatre Review* 14, no. 1 (February): 1–14.

———. 2006a. "Musical Personae." *Drama Review* 50, no. 1 (Spring 2006): 100–119.

———. 2006b. *Performing Glam Rock: Gender and Theatricality in Popular Music*. Ann Arbor: University of Michigan Press.

"Band or DJ?" 2019. *Weddingbee.com*, January, https://boards.weddingbee.com/topic/band-or-dj-8/#, accessed February 24, 2019.

Bargreen, M. 1996. "Tenors of The Times: New Year's Eve Show in Vancouver is More an Event Than a Concert." *Seattle Times*, December 27, http://community.seattletimes.nwsource.com/archive/?date=19961227&slug=2367226, accessed May 28, 2019.

Barry, A., G. Born, and G. Weszkalnys. 2008. "Logics of Interdisciplinarity." *Economy and Society* 37, no. 1: 20–49.

Battan, C. 2016. "The Appeal of the Coachella Way of Life." *New Yorker*, April 18, https://www.newyorker.com/culture/cultural-comment/the-appeal-of-the-coachella-way-of-life, accessed April 4, 2019.

Bauman, Z. 2014. "The European Experiment." *Hedgehog Review* 16, no. 1: 18–25.

Baxter-Moore, N., and T. M. Kitts. 2016. "The Live Concert Experience: An Introduction." *Rock Music Studies* 3, no. 1: 1–4.

BBC. 2014. "12 Months of Live Music." YouTube video, December 11, https://www.youtube.com/watch?v=ekgph3GyzEA, accessed August 29, 2018.

Beaster-Jones, J. 2016. *Music Commodities, Markets, and Values: Music as Merchandise*. New York: Routledge.

Becker, H. 1961. *Outsiders: Studies in the Sociology of Deviance*. Chicago: University of Chicago Press.

Befolkningen i København, Region Hovedstaden og hele landet, 1. januar 2016. 2016. Orientering fra Velfærdsanalyse, June 7, https://www.kk.dk/sites/default/files/2016_befolkning_0.pdf, accessed March 21, 2019.

Befolkningen i København 2017: Orientering fra Velfærdsanalyse: Befolkning i København, Region Hovedstaden og hele landet 2017. n.d. The Municipality of Copenhagen, https://www.kk.dk/sites/default/files/2017_befolkning.pdf, accessed March 21, 2019.

Belafonte, H. 2011. *My Song: A Memoir*, with M. Shnayerson. New York: Alfred A. Knopf.

"Belgium 2017 International Religious Freedom Report." US Department of State, Bureau of Democracy, Human Rights, and Labor, https://www.state.gov/documents/organization/281130.pdf, accessed March 22, 2019.

Beltrone, G. 2013. "CBGB Festival Gets Times Square Event Sponsors." *Adweek*, September 16, https://www.adweek.com/brand-marketing/cbgb-festival-gets-times-square-headliners-sponsors-152451/, accessed June 5, 2018.

Bennett, A., and R. Peterson. 2004. *Music Scenes: Local, Translocal, and Virtual*. Nashville: Vanderbilt University Press.

"Beretning til Statsrevisorerne om budgetoverskridelsen ved Eurovision Song Contest 2014." 2015. Rigsrevisionen, June, http://www.rigsrevisionen.dk/media/2042856/budgetoverskridelsen-ved-eurovision-song-contest-2014.pdf, accessed December 30, 2018.

Berger, H. 1999. *Metal, Rock, and Jazz: Perception and the Phenomenology of Musical Experience*. Middletown, CT: Wesleyan University Press.

Berlant, L. 2011. *Cruel Optimism*. Durham, NC: Duke University Press.

Bianchini, F. 1993. "Remaking European Cities: The Role of Cultural Policies." In *Cultural Policy and Urban Regeneration: The West European Experience*, edited by F. Bianchini and M. Parkinson, 1–20. Manchester: Manchester University Press.

Bianchini, F., and M. Parkinson, eds. 1993. *Cultural Policy and Urban Regeneration: The West European Experience*. Manchester: Manchester University Press.

"Big Brand Sponsors Target Music Festivals." 2015. *CNN.com*, April 17, http://edition.cnn.com/videos/tv/2015/04/17/wbt-intv-andrews-music-festivals.cnn, accessed June 17, 2015.

"*Billboard*'s Third International Talent Forum." 1977. *Billboard* 89, no. 18 (May 7): 35.

Bjerregaard, F. 2002. "Spillesteder: Ros til spillesteder." *Jyllands-Posten*, Section 8 (November 15), 6.

Blanning, T. W. 1989. "The French Revolution in Germany and Austria." *Central European History* 22, no. 2 (June): 109–29.

Blechman, E., and A. Lynn. 2013. "Allen Ginsberg in the East Village: A Self-Guided Walking Tour." Grey Art Gallery, New York University, https://greyartgallery.nyu.edu/wp-content/uploads/2017/06/Ginsberg_WalkingTour.pdf, accessed June 1, 2019.

Bogart, J. 2012. "Buy the Hype: Why EDM Could Really Be the New Rock." *The Atlantic* (July 10), http://www.theatlantic.com/entertainment/archive/2012/07/buy-the-hype-why-electronic-dance-music-really-could-be-the-new-rock/259597/, accessed February 25, 2013.

Bohlman, P. 1994. "Music, Modernity, and the Foreign in the New Germany." *Modernism/Modernity* 1, no. 1: 121–52.

———. 2013. "Introduction: World Music's Histories." In *The Cambridge History of World Music*, edited by P. Bohlman, 1–20. Cambridge: Cambridge University Press.

———. 2016. "Jazz at the Edge of Empire." In *Jazz Worlds, World Jazz*, edited by P. Bohlman and G. Plastino, 153–80. Chicago: University of Chicago Press.

Bondad-Brown, B., R. Rice, and K. Pearce. 2012. "Influences on TV Viewing and Online User-Shared Video Use: Demographics, Generations, Contextual Age, Media Use, Motivations, and Audience Activity." *Journal of Broadcasting & Electronic Media* 56, no. 4 (December): 471–93.

Born, G. 1995. *Rationalizing Culture: IRCAM, Boulez, and the Institutionalization of the Musical Avant-Garde*. Berkeley: University of California Press.

———. 2002. "Reflexivity and Ambivalence: Culture, Creativity and Government in the BBC." *Cultural Values* 6 (1–2): 65–90.

———. 2011. "Music and the Materialization of Identities." *Journal of Material Culture* 16, no. 4: 376–88.

———. 2012. "Music and the Social." In *The Cultural Study of Music*, edited by M. Clayton, T. Herbert, and R. Middleton, 261–74. 2nd ed. New York: Routledge.

Born, G., and D. Hesmondhalgh, eds. 2000. *Western Music and Its Others: Difference, Representation, and Appropriation in Music*. Berkeley: University of California Press.

Botton, S. 1996. "Neighborhood Report: Downtown: Ludlow Street Café Changes Hands." *New York Times*, June 2, https://www.nytimes.com/1996/06/02/nyregion/neighborhood-report-downtownludlow-street-cafe-changes-hands-not-to.html, accessed December 15, 2018.

"Bourgeois Boys." 2007. Dean Johnson and the Weenies, YouTube video, October 1, https://www.youtube.com/watch?v=n9vQnh8xM7Q, accessed January 28, 2019.

Brooklyn Vegan Staff. 2016. "Santos Party House Closed for Good?" *Brooklyn Vegan*, May 30, http://www.brooklynvegan.com/santos-party-house-closed-for-good/, accessed August 22, 2016.

Brown, A. 2017. "After Years of Silence, Activists Are Forcing Music Festivals to Take Sexual Assault Seriously." *Los Angeles Times*, May 20, http://www.latimes.com/entertainment/music/la-et-ms-music-festival-20170520-story.html, accessed March 28, 2018.

Buckley, C. 2007. "Disquieting Death Stills the Night Life." *New York Times*, October 14, https://www.nytimes.com/2007/10/14/fashion/14dean.html, accessed January 28, 2019.

———. 2013a. "Another Fixture of Lower East Side Is Gone." *New York Times*, February 11, https://cityroom.blogs.nytimes.com/2013/02/11/another-90s-fixture-of-lower-east-side-is-gone/, accessed December 15, 2018.

———. 2013b. "Max Fish, Celebrated Art Bar, Plans to Cross the River." *New York Times*, April 25, https://www.nytimes.com/2013/04/26/nyregion/max-fish-plans-to-move-to-brooklyn.html, accessed December 15, 2018.

Burke, P. 2014. "The Fugs, the Lower East Side, and the Slum Aesthetic in 1960s Rock." *Journal of the Society for American Music* 8, no. 4: 538–66.

Burks, T. 2019. "Coachella's Owner Donated $134,400 to Republicans in 2018." Spin.com, January 3, https://www.spin.com/2019/01/coachella-owner-philip-anschutz-political-donations/, accessed January 18, 2019.

Burland, K., and S. Pitts, eds. 2014. *Coughing and Clapping: Investigating Audience Experience*. Farnham, UK: Ashgate.

Butt, J. 2002. "Choral Music." In *The Cambridge History of 19th Century Music*, edited by J. Samson, 213–36. Cambridge: Cambridge University Press.

Calhoun, C. 1995. *Critical Social Theory: Culture, History, and the Challenge of Difference*. Malden, MA: Blackwell.

———. 1998. "Explanation in Historical Sociology: Narrative, General Theory, and Historically Specific Theory." *American Journal of Sociology* 4, no. 3: 846–71.

Callaghan, D. 2013. "Ritual Performance and Spirituality in the Work of Living Theatre, Past and Present." *Theatre Symposium* 21: 36–53.

Calore, M. 2009. "May 12, 1967: Pink Floyd Astounds With 'Sound in the Round.'" *Wired.com*, May 12, https://www.wired.com/2009/05/dayintech_0512/, accessed March 15, 2017.

Cannady, K. 2017. "Echoes of the Colonial Past." In *The Oxford Handbook of Popular Music in the Nordic Countries*, edited by F. Holt and A.-V. Kärjä, 203–17. Oxford: Oxford University Press.

Cantwell, R. 1993. *Ethnomimesis: Folklife and the Representation of Culture*. Chapel Hill: University of North Carolina Press.

Caramanica, J. 2016. "Review: 'Formation' World Tour, Beyoncé Through 'Lemonade'-Tinted Glasses." *New York Times*, April 28, https://www.nytimes.com/2016/04/29/arts/music/beyonce-formation-world-tour-lemonade.html, accessed November 14, 2019.

———. 2020. "When Did the Super Bowl Halftime Show Become Political?" *New York Times*, February 1, https://www.nytimes.com/2020/02/01/arts/music/popcast-super-bowl-halftime.html, accessed February 5, 2020.

Cardus, N. 2016. "Conductor Bruno Walter at the Edinburgh Festival: 'Music Moved Visibly on His Face.'" *Guardian*, August 16, https://www.theguardian.com/music/2016/aug/16/from-the-classical-archive-bruno-walter-kathleen-ferrier-edinburgh-festival-1947, accessed May 17, 2018.

Carlson, Jen. 2012. "Watch These Bands Perform at the Old East Village Rock Haunt Brownies." *Gothamist*, October 16, http://gothamist.com/2012/10/16/old_shows_at_brownies.php, accessed December 15, 2018.

Carter, T. 2002. "The Sound of Silence: Models for an Urban Musicology." *Urban History* 29, no. 1: 8–18.

Cavicchi, D. 1998. *Tramps Like Us: Music and Meaning among Springsteen Fans*. Oxford: Oxford University Press.

———. 2011. *Listening and Longing: Music Lovers in the Age of Barnum*. Middletown, CT: Wesleyan University Press.

Center for Urban Research. 2011. "New York City Demographic Shifts, 2000 to 2010." City University of New York, http://www.urbanresearchmaps.org/plurality/, accessed August 11, 2016.

Ceribaši, N. 1998. "Folklore Festivals in Croatia: Contemporary Controversies." *World of Music* 40, no. 3: 25–49.

Chalcraft, J., and P. Magaudda. 2013. "'Space Is the Place': The Global Localities of the Sónar and WOMAD Music Festivals." In *Festivals and the Public Cultural Sphere*, edited by G. Delanty, L. Giorgi, and M. Sassatelli, 173–89. New York: Routledge.

Charters, S., and L. Kunstadt. 1962. *Jazz: A History of the New York Scene*. Garden City, NY: Doubleday.

Chen, K. 2009. *Enabling Creative Chaos: The Organization Behind the Burning Man Event*. Chicago: University of Chicago Press.

"Cirque Royal." Club Belge, http://www.clubbelge.be/VENUES/en/brussel/info/58/Cirque-Royal—-Koninklijk-Circus, accessed October 14, 2016.

Clarke, E. 1988. "Generative Principles in Musical Performance." In *Generative Processes in Music: The Psychology of Performance, Improvisation, and Composition*, edited by J. Sloboda, 1–26. Oxford: Oxford University Press.

Clayton, M., B. Dueck, and L. Leante. 2013. *Experience and Meaning in Music Performance*. Oxford: Oxford University Press.

Clayton, M., T. Herbert, and R. Middleton, eds. 2003/2012. *The Cultural Study of Music*. 2nd ed. London: Routledge.

Clecak, P. 1971. "The Revolution Delayed: The Political and Cultural Revolutionaries in America." *Massachusetts Review* 12, no. 3 (Summer): 590–619.

Cloonan, M. 2007. *Popular Music and the State in the UK*. Aldershot: Ashgate.

"Coachella 2014: Thank You." 2014. Coachella, YouTube video, April 21, https://www.youtube.com/watch?v=sQE9BrHSBuA, accessed February 8, 2019.

Cohen, J. [Joshua]. 2011. "Where to Watch Burning Man Online." *Tubefilter*, August 31, https://www.tubefilter.com/2011/08/31/where-to-watch-burning-man-online-live-stream/, accessed April 6, 2019.

Cohen, J. [Judith]. 1999. "Constructing a Spanish Jewish Festival: Music and the Appropriation of Tradition." *World of Music* 41, no. 3: 85–113.

Cohen, S. 1991. *Rock Music in Liverpool: Popular Music in the Making*. Oxford: Clarendon.

———. 2007. *Decline, Renewal and the City in Popular Music Culture: Beyond the Beatles*. Aldershot: Ashgate.

Colombo, A. 2015. Lecture on the impact of events in Barcelona at Roskilde University, September 23.

Conboy, M., dir. 2016. *Goodnight Brooklyn: The Story of Death by Audio*. Dishwasher Safe Films. Red Bull TV, https://www.redbull.com/int-en/films/goodnight-brooklyn, accessed January 17, 2020.

Concannon, K. 2008. "Yoko Ono's 'Cut Piece': From Text to Performance and Back Again." *PAJ: A Journal of Performance and Art* 30, no. 3: 81–93.

Cook, N. 2007. *The Schenker Project: Culture, Race, and Music Theory in Fin-de-Siècle Vienna*. Oxford: Oxford University Press.

———. 2013. *Beyond the Score: Music as Performance*. Oxford: Oxford University Press.

Couldry, N., and A. Hepp. 2010. "Introduction: Media Events in Globalized Media Cultures." In *Media Events in a Global Age*, edited by N. Couldry, A. Hepp, and F. Krotz, 1–20. London: Routledge.

Crane, D. 1992. *The Production of Culture: Media and the Urban Arts*. London: Sage.

"Creamfields 2013 Official Aftermovie." 2014. Creamfields Festival, YouTube video, November 9, https://www.youtube.com/watch?v=CnRQCjzNrMc, accessed February 8, 2019.

Cressey, P. 1932. *The Taxi-Dance Hall: A Sociological Study in Commercialized Recreation and City Life*. Chicago: University of Chicago Press.

Crosby, Stills, Nash & Young. 1970. *Déjà Vu*. Atlantic Records.

Cvetkovski, T. 2015. *The Pop Music Idol and the Spirit of Charisma*. Basingstoke: Palgrave Macmillan.

Dally, E. 2018. "Magnetic Industry Person of the Year: Ultra Co-Founder Russell Faibisch." *Magnetic Magazine*, January 2, https://www.magneticmag.com/2018/01/magnetic-industry-person-of-the-year-ultra-co-founder-russell-faibisch/, accessed January 15, 2020.

Danmarks Statistik. 2017. *Indvandrere i Danmark 2017*. Copenhagen: Danmarks Statistik, https://www.dst.dk/Site/Dst/Udgivelser/GetPubFile.aspx?id=20705&sid=indv2017, accessed November 22, 2018.

Dargis, M. 2013. "Debauchery and the American Experience (Woo-Hoo!)." *New York Times*, March 14, http://movies.nytimes.com/2013/03/15/movies/spring-breakers-directed-by-harmony-korine.html?pagewanted=all&_r=0, accessed May 16, 2013.

Davidson, J. 2005. "Bodily Communication in Musical Performance." In *Musical Communication*, edited by D. Miell, R. MacDonald, and D. Hargreaves, 215-238. Oxford: Oxford University Press.

Davies, H. 2017. "Are Music Festivals Doing Enough to Tackle Sexual Assault?" *The Guardian*, July 25, https://www.theguardian.com/lifeandstyle/2017/jul/25/music-festivals-sexual-assault-rape-safe, accessed March 29, 2018.

Dayan, D., and E. Katz. 1992. *Media Events: The Live Broadcasting of History*. Cambridge, MA: Harvard University Press.

Deloitte. 2015. *Analyse af Det Kongelige Teater*. Department of Finance and Department of Culture, Danish Government, June, https://kglteater.dk/globalassets/brug-teatret/skoler-og-institutioner/inspirationsmaterialer/kgl-teater-som-virksomhed/deloitte-rapport.pdf, accessed December 28, 2018.

Demurtas, A., and J. Rogers. 2018. "Event Management Company Sena Live Buys Iceland Airwaves." *Reykjavik Grapevine*, February 23, https://grapevine.is/news/2018/02/23/event-managing-company-sena-live-acquires-iceland-airwaves/, accessed April 1, 2019.

DeNora, T. 2000. *Music in Everyday Life*. Cambridge: Cambridge University Press.

———. 2015. "After Adorno." In *The Routledge Reader on the Sociology of Music*, edited by J. Shepherd and K. Devine, 341–48. New York: Routledge.

Deutsche, R., and C. Ryan. 1984. "The Fine Art of Gentrification." *October* 31 (Winter): 91–111.

Dicker, H. 2018. "Thunderdome: 25 Years of Hardcore." *Resident Advisor*, February 19, https://www.residentadvisor.net/features/3149, accessed February 10, 2019.

Dilthey, W. [1910] 1974. *Der Aufbau der geschichtlichen Welt in den Geisteswissenschaften*. Frankfurt am Main: Suhrkamp.

DiMaggio, P., and W. Powell. 1983. "The Iron Cage Revisited: Institutional Isomorphism and Collective Rationality in Organizational Fields." *American Sociological Review* 48, no. 2: 147–60.

———. 1991. "Introduction." In *The New Institutionalism in Organizational Analysis*, edited by W. Powell and P. DiMaggio, 1–38. Chicago: University of Chicago Press.

Dirty Projectors. 2009. *Bitte Orca*. Domino Records.

"DJ or Live Music." 2018. *Weddingwire.com*, January 16, https://www.weddingwire.com/wedding-forums/dj-or-live-music/060e0a9b0b96264d.html, accessed February 24, 2019.

Dodson, S. 2003. "Sónar, so Good." *Guardian*, June 21, https://www.theguardian.com/travel/2003/jun/21/buyingmusic.music.spain, accessed May 31, 2018.

Doherty, B. 1986/1999. *Inside the White Cube: The Ideology of the Gallery Space*. Expanded ed. Berkeley: University of California Press.

Du Gay, P., and G. Morgan. 2013. "Understanding Capitalism: Crises, Legitimacy, and Change Through the Prism of *The New Spirit of Capitalism*." In *New Spirits of Capitalism? Crises, Justifications, and Dynamics*, edited by P. du Gay and G. Morgan, 1–40. Oxford: Oxford University Press.

Drummond, P. [2011] 2016. *The Provincial Music Festival in England, 1784–1914*. Routledge edition. London: Routledge.

Durkheim, É. [1912] 2001. *The Elementary Forms of Religious Life*. Translated by C. Cosman. Oxford: Oxford University Press.

"Ed Sheeran Officially Named the Best-Selling Global Recording Artist of 2017." 2018. International Federation of the Phonographic Industry, February 26, http://www.ifpi.org/news/Ed-Sheeran-officially-named-the-best-selling-global-recording-artist-of-2017, accessed May 29, 2018.

"Edinburgh Festival Chorus." Edinburgh International Festival, https://www.eif.co.uk/about/edinburgh-festival-chorus, accessed February 19, 2019.

Edwards, D., P. Eyries, and M. Callahan. 2005. "Atlantic Album Discography, Part 6: SD-7200 'Superstar' Series (1970–1974)," last updated October 6, http://www.bsnpubs.com/atlantic/atlantic7200.html, accessed June 24, 2016.

Ehrenberg, L. 1981. *Steppin' Out: New York Nightlife and the Transformation of American Culture*. Chicago: University of Chicago Press.

Einstein, A. [1950/1978] 2011. *Essays in Humanism*. New York: Open Road Integrated Media.

"Elbphilharmonie Grand Opening." Jung van Matt, https://www.jvm.com/de/work/elbphilharmonie/, accessed December 31, 2018.

Ellison, R. 1961. "That Same Pain, That Same Pleasure: An Interview." In *Shadow and Act*. New York: Vintage Books, 3–23.

Ellis-Petersen, H. 2015. "Save London's Live Music Venues: City-Wide Campaign Launched." *Guardian*, October 20, https://www.theguardian.com/uk-news/2015/oct/20/save-londons-live-music-venues-city-wide-campaign-launched, accessed August 29, 2018.

"ERC Funded Projects." European Research Council, https://erc.europa.eu/projects-figures/erc-funded-projects/results?search_api_views_fulltext=music&items_per_page=50, accessed May 4, 2019.

Eshbach, R. 2014. "The 31st Lower Rhine Music Festival." Joseph Joachim: Biography and Research, https://josephjoachim.com/2014/09/22/the-31st-lower-rhine-music-festival/, accessed June 5, 2018.

Espinoza, J. 2018. "The Owner of Coachella Is Still Giving His Money to Pro-Gun, Anti-LGBT, Birther Politicians." *Complex*, January 3, https://www.complex.com/music/2018/01/coachella-owner-donated-187-thousand-dollars-republican-party, accessed May 28, 2019.

Evans, L. 2014. "What to Do If You Are Sexually Assaulted at a Festival." *Gothamist*, June 5, http://gothamist.com/2014/06/05/music_fest_sexual_assault.php, accessed March 28, 2018.

"EXIT & Sea Dance Festivals 2016—The Magic AFTERMOVIE!" 2016. Exit Festival, YouTube video, November 10, https://www.youtube.com/watch?v=yF1cDo3iKVk, accessed February 8, 2019.

Fairchild, C. 2008. *Pop Idols and Pirates. Mechanisms of Consumption and the Global Circulation of Popular Music*. Aldershot: Ashgate.

"The Fairytale Castle at Tomorrowland 2011." Phixion, http://www.phixion.be/en/tomorrowland/tomorrowland-2011.html, accessed February 24, 2013.

Farah, A. 2010. "New York Week: A Guide to Brooklyn's DIY Scene." *Drowned in Sound*, October 28, http://drownedinsound.com/in_depth/4141016-new-york-week—a-guide-to-brooklyns-diy-scene, accessed May 28, 2019.

Feld, S. 1982/1990. *Sound and Sentiment: Birds, Weeping, Poetics, and Song in Kaluli Expression*. 2nd ed. Philadelphia: University of Pennsylvania Press.

Felt, U. 2014. "Within, Across and Beyond: Reconsidering the Role of Social Sciences and Humanities in Europe." *Science as Culture* 23, no. 3: 384–96.

"Фестиваль Нашествие Главная сцена День Первый" ("Festival Invasion Main Stage First Day"). 2014. Nashestvie, YouTube video, July 5, https://www.youtube.com/watch?v=QtxvP6J3PGo, accessed January 23, 2019.

"Festival Republic: About Us." http://www.festivalrepublic.co.uk/about-us/, accessed July 24, 2015.

Fischer, C. S. 1995. "The Subcultural Theory of Urbanism: A Twenty-Year Assessment." *American Journal of Sociology* 101, no. 3: 543–77.

Flanagan, A. 2013. "SFX Acquires Major German Promoter i-Motion for $21 Million." *Billboard.com*, November 19, https://www.billboard.com/biz/articles/news/global/5793299/sfx-acquires-major-german-promoter-i-motion-for-21-million, accessed April 6, 2019.

Fleerman, B., and A. Genger. 2008. *Novemberpogrom 1938 in Düsseldorf*. Essen: Klartext.

Fleerman, B., and H. Jakobs. 2015. *Düsseldorfer Deportationen: Massenverschleppungen von 1933 bis zur Befreiung 1945*. Düsseldorf: Droste Verlag.

Florida, R. 2002. *The Rise of the Creative Class: And How It's Transforming Work, Leisure, Community and Everyday Life*. New York: Basic Books.

Flyvbjerg, B., A. Budzier, and A. Stewart. 2016. "The Oxford Olympics Study 2016: Cost and Cost Overrun at the Games." Working Paper, Said School of Business, Oxford University, https://arxiv.org/ftp/arxiv/papers/1607/1607.04484.pdf, accessed January 23, 2019.

Foer, F. 2019. "Viktor Orbán's War on the Intellect." *The Atlantic*, June, https://www.theatlantic.com/magazine/archive/2019/06/george-soros-viktor-orban-ceu/588070/, accessed May 16, 2019.

"Folkets Hus." *Leksikon for det 21. århundrede*, https://www.leksikon.org/art.php?n=842, accessed November 2, 2019.

Fornäs, J., and L. Ihlemann. 1999. "Theme Issue: Place and Meaning in Nordic Popular Music." *Young* 7, no. 2: 2–3.

"Forretningsudvalgets møde den 11. oktober 2011: Bilag 4." Region Hovedstaden, https://www.regionh.dk/politik/nye-moeder/Documents/fu111011_bilag_til_sag_116_v3.pdf, accessed January 2, 2019.

Foucault, M. [1967] 1998. "Different Spaces." In *Aesthetics, Methods, and Epistemology: Essential Works of Michael Foucault 1954–1984, Vol. 2*, edited by J. Faubion, 175–85. New York: Penguin.

———. [1975] 1995. *Discipline and Punish, the Birth of the Prison*. 2nd Vintage ed. New York: Vintage.

Fox, A. 2004. *Real Country: Music and Language in Working-Class Culture*. Durham, NC: Duke University Press.

Frey, B. 1994. "The Economics of Music Festivals." *Journal of Cultural Economics* 18, no. 1: 29–39.

Friedlander, E. 2010. "The Market Hotel Project: Todd P Outlines Plans to Make Market Legit." Visitation Rites, April 28, accessed August 10, 2016.

Frith, S. [1987] 2007. "The Industrialization of Music." In *Taking Popular Music Seriously: Selected Essays*. Farnham: Ashgate, 93–118.

———. 2007. "Live Music Matters," *Scottish Music Review* 1 (1): 1-17.

Frith, S., M. Brennan, M. Cloonan, and E. Webster. 2013. *The History of Live Music in Britain, Vol. 1: 1950–1967: From Dance Hall to the 100 Club*. Farnham: Ashgate.

———. 2019. *The History of Live Music in Britain, Volume 2: 1968–1984: From Hyde Park to the Hacienda*. New York: Routledge.

"From the Archives: The 1993 Interview When Walter Becker Opened Up About Steely Dan's Subversive Intentions." 2017. *Los Angeles Times*, September 3, https://www.latimes.com/entertainment/la-et-ms-walter-becker-steely-dan-archive-interview-20170903-story.html, accessed November 11, 2019.

"Fuck You." 2010. Dean and the Weenies, YouTube video, January 6, https://www.youtube.com/watch?v=Dn4vkSH6Og8, accessed January 28, 2019.

Funder, T. 2016. "Rosikilde Festivalen før og nu," June, https://faktalink.dk/titelliste/roskilde-festivalen, accessed January 22, 2019.

Gadamer, H.-G. 1960/1990. *Wahrheit und Methode: Gründzüge einer philosophischen Hermeneutik*. Gesammelte Werke Band 1. Tübingen: J. C. B. Mohr.

Garcia, L.-M. 2015a. "Beats, Flesh, and Grain: Sonic Tactility and Affect in Electronic Dance Music." *Sound Studies* 1, no. 1: 59–76.

———. 2015b. "At Home I'm a Tourist: Musical Migration and Affective Citizenship." *Journal of Urban Cultural Studies* 2, no. 1/2: 121–34.

Garofalo, R., and S. Waksman. 2016. *Rockin' Out: Popular Music in the U.S.A.* New York: Pearson.

Garsse, S. 2011. "Jari Demeulemeester: 'Mensen zullen elkaar altijd willen ontmoeten.'" *Bruzz*, http://www.bruzz.be/nl/nieuws/jari-demeulemeester-mensen-zullen-elkaar-altijd-willen-ontmoeten, accessed October 13, 2016.

Gatz, S. 2014. "Beleidsnota Cultuur 2014–2019." Vlaamse overheid, October, http://ebl.vlaanderen.be/publications/documents/65569, accessed October 16, 2016.

Gaunt, M. 2016. "Damon Albarn viste os den anden side af Syrien." *Berlingske.dk*, June 29, https://www.berlingske.dk/koncertanmeldelser/damon-albarn-viste-os-den-anden-side-af-syrien, accessed January 22, 2019.

Geoffroy-Schwinden, R. 2015. *Politics, the French Revolution, and Performance: Parisian Musicians as an Emergent Professional Class, 1749–1802*. PhD diss., Duke University.

Getz, D., and S. Page. 2007/2016. *Event Studies: Theory, Research, and Policy for Planned Events*. 3rd ed. New York: Routledge.

Gibbons, M., C. Limoges, H. Nowotny, S. Schwartzman, P. Scott, and M. Trow. 1994. *The New Production of Knowledge: The Dynamics of Science and Research in Contemporary Societies*. London: Sage.

Gibson, C., and J. Connell. 2005. *Music and Tourism: On the Road Again*. Clevedon: Channel View Publications.

Gillett, C. 1970/1983. *The Sound of the City: The Rise of Rock and Roll*. Rev. and expanded ed. New York: Pantheon Books.

Giorgi, L., and M. Sassatelli. 2011. "Introduction." In *Festivals and the Cultural Public Sphere: Cosmopolitanism Between Ethics and Aesthetics*, edited by L. Giorgi, M. Sassatelli, and G. Delanty, 1–11. New York: Routledge.

Giorgis, H. 2015. "Gentrifying Punk." *New Yorker*, August 26, https://www.newyorker.com/culture/culture-desk/gentrifying-afropunk, accessed January 20, 2019.

"Glastonbury TV." Television Company, http://www.the-television-company.co.uk/glastonbury-television/, accessed August 4, 2015.

Gleason, J. 2009. "Promoter Todd P Is Getting His Own Place." NPR Music, http://www.npr.org/templates/story/story.php?storyId=112066997, accessed August 9, 2016.

Goethe, J. W. von. [1788] 1953. "Das römische Karneval." In *Goethes Werke in zwei Bänden*, vol. 2, 897–919. München: Droemersche Verlagsanstalt.

Goldschmitt, K. 2011. "'Joga Bonito Pelo Mundo, Guerreiro': Music, Transmedia Advertising, and Brasilidade in the 2006 World Cup." *Popular Music and Society* 34, no. 4: 417–36.

———. 2019. *Bossa Mundo: Brazilian Music in Transnational Media Industries*. Oxford: Oxford University Press.

Goodman, E. 2009. *Cat Power: A Good Woman*. New York: Random House.

Goodman, J. 2013. "Why Ludlow Street's Last Bastions of Bohemia Are Closing." *Village Voice*, February 13, http://www.villagevoice.com/restaurants/why-ludlow-streets-last-bastions-of-bohemia-are-closing-6517885, accessed August 20, 2016.

Goodman, L. 2013. "Get Yer Yeah Yeah Yeahs Out." *New York Times*, March 29, https://www.nytimes.com/2013/03/31/magazine/get-yer-yeah-yeah-yeahs-out.html, accessed May 28, 2019.

Goodwin, A. 1988. "Sample and Hold: Pop Music in the Digital Age of Reproduction." In *On Record: Rock, Pop and the Written Word*, edited by S. Frith and A. Goodwin, 258–73. London: Routledge.

Gordon, A. 1970. "Satan and the Angels: Paradise Loused." In *Altamont*, edited by J. Eisen, 30–71. New York: Avon Books.

"Graduates by Field of Education." OECD.Stat, https://stats.oecd.org/Index.aspx?DatasetCode=RGRADSTY, accessed May 6, 2019.

Graham, B. 1971. Press communication about the closing of Fillmore West and East, April 29, made available online at Allman Brothers Band forum on November 6, 2009, http://allmanbrothersband.com/modules.php?op=modload&name=XForum&file=viewthread&tid=94382, accessed June 25, 2016.

Graham, B., and R. Greenfield. 1992/2004. *Bill Graham Presents: My Life Inside Rock and Out*. New York: Da Capo.

"Grand Opening Elbphilharmonie Hamburg." schnellebuntebilder, https://schnellebuntebilder.de/projects/grand-opening-elbphilharmonie-hamburg/, accessed May 28, 2019.

Granovetter, M. 1985. "Economic Action and Social Structure: The Problem of Embeddedness." *American Journal of Sociology* 91, no. 3: 481–510.

Grazian, D. 2003. *Blue Chicago: The Search for Authenticity in Urban Blues Clubs*. Chicago: University of Chicago Press.

———. 2013. "Digital Underground: Musical Spaces and Microscenes in the Postindustrial City." In *Musical Performance and the Changing City: Post-Industrial Contexts in Europe and the United States*, 127–51. New York: Routledge.

Gregor, A. 2014. "Brooklyn: New Towers for Williamsburg." *New York Times*, December 19, http://www.nytimes.com/2014/12/21/realestate/brooklyn-new-towers-for-williamsburg.html?_r=0, accessed August 8, 2016.

Gross, T. 1999. "Interview with Ravi Shankar." NPR, *Fresh Air*, transcript on NPR.org, December 13, 2012, https://www.npr.org/2012/12/14/167193821/ravi-shankar-remembering-a-master-of-the-sitar, accessed May 23, 2018.

Große-Wilde, C. 2019. "Von Hassobjekt zum Publikumsliebling," *Welt.de*, January 10, https://www.welt.de/regionales/hamburg/article186856894/Zwei-Jahre-Elbphilharmonie-Vom-Hassobjekt-zum-Publikumsliebling.html, accessed March 20, 2019.

Gruen, J. 1966. *The New Bohemia: The Combine Generation*. New York: Grosset and Dunlap.

Habermas, J. 1962/1989. *The Structural Transformation of the Public Sphere: An Inquiry into a Category of Bourgeois Society*. Translated by Thomas Burger with the assistance of Frederick Lawrence. Cambridge: Polity.

———. 1968/1973. *Erkenntnis und Interesse*. Frankfurt am Main: Suhrkamp.

Hae, L. 2012. *The Gentrification of Nightlife and the Right to the City: Regulating Spaces of Social Dancing in New York*. New York: Routledge.

Haliski, C. 1989. "17-Inch Crash: A Visit to CBGB." *Village Voice* (April 18): 79–80.

Hall, E. 1959. *The Silent Language*. Garden City, NY: Doubleday and Company.

Hampp, A. 2013. "Festival Sponsorship Spending Projected to Set Record in 2013." *Billboardbiz*, May 10, http://www.billboard.com/biz/articles/news/branding/1561337/festival-sponsorship-spending-projected-to-set-record-in-2013, accessed May 28, 2019.

———. 2015. "Yahoo Reveals First-Year Livestream Results, Year-Two Schedule." *Billboard.com*, July 23, http://www.billboard.com/articles/business/6641792/yahoo-reveals-first-year-livestream-results-year-two-schedule, accessed June 30, 2016.

Hanley, J. 2015. "Live Nation Sweden Acquires EDM Promoter." *Music Week*, March 5, http://www.musicweek.com/news/read/live-nation-sweden-acquires-edm-promoter/061069, accessed May 28, 2019.

Hanslick, E. 1869. *Geschichte des Konzertwesens in Wien*. Vienna: Wilhelm Braumüller. Accessed via https://archive.org/details/geschichtedescoo1unkngoog, November 8, 2018.

Haslam, D. 2001/2002. *Adventures on the Wheels of Steel: The Rise of the Superstar DJs*. First paperback ed. London: Fourth Estate.

Hawkins, S. 2009. *The British Pop Dandy: Masculinity, Popular Music and Culture*. Aldershot: Ashgate.

———. 2016. *Queerness in Pop Music: Aesthetics, Gender Norms, and Temporality*. London: Routledge.

Hebdige, D. 1979. *Subculture: The Meaning of Style*. London: Routledge.

Heller, M. 2016. *Loft Jazz: Improvising New York in the 1970s*. Berkeley: University of California Press.

Henriksen, C. 2002. *Den sociale status og udvikling på Indre Vesterbro*. Copenhagen: Center for Alternativ Samfundsanalyse.

Hepp, A. 2013. *Cultures of Mediatization*. Translated by Keith Tribe. Cambridge: Polity.

"HERA JRP: 'Public Spaces in Europe: Culture and Integration in Europe': Guideline for Applicants: Full Proposals." HERA, http://heranet.info/assets/uploads/2018/02/HERA-JRP-PS-Guidelines-for-Applicants-Full-Proposals.pdf, accessed May 2, 2019.

"HERA: Projects." HERA, http://heranet.info/projects/, accessed April 29, 2019.

Herder, J. G. [1778–1779] 2017. "From *Volkslieder* and *Stimmen der Völker in Liedern / Folk Songs* and *Voices of the People in Song*." Translated by P. Bohlman. In J. G. Herder and P. Bohlman, *Song Loves the Masses: Herder on Music and Nationalism*, 50–69. Kindle ed. Berkeley: University of California Press.

Herder, J. G., and P. V. Bohlman. 2017. *Song Loves the Masses: Herder on Music and Nationalism*. Kindle ed. Berkeley: University of California Press.

Hesmondhalgh, D. 2003/2019. *The Cultural Industries*. 4th ed. London: Sage.

———. 2013. *Why Music Matters*. Malden, MA: Wiley-Blackwell.

Hesmondhalgh, D., M. Nisbett, K. Oakley, and D. Lee. 2015. "Were New Labour's Cultural Policies Neo-Liberal?" *International Journal of Cultural Policy* 21, no. 1: 97–114.

Hewison, R. 1995. *Culture and Consensus: England, Art, and Politics Since 1940*. London: Methuen.

Higgins, D. 1976. "The Origin of the Happening." *American Speech* 51, no. 3/4: 268–71.

Hilder, T. 2017. "Sámi Festivals and Indigenous Sovereignty." In *The Oxford Handbook of Popular Music in the Nordic Countries*, edited by F. Holt and A.-V. Kärjä, 363–78. Oxford: Oxford University Press.

Hill, M., ed. n.d. *Städtischer Musikverein zu Düsseldorf e.V—gegr. 1818: Konzertchor der Stadt Düsseldorf: Lebenslauf: Geschichte, Daten, Episoden*, https://web.archive.org/web/20110719085302/http://www.staedtischermusikvereinduesseldorf.de/lebenslauf/lebenslauf_druck.php, accessed May 15, 2018.

"Historique de la Fête de la Musique." Fête de la Musique, https://fetedelamusique.culture.gouv.fr/L-evenement/Historique-de-la-Fete-de-la-Musique, accessed January 24, 2019.

Hitzler, R., and S. Nye. 2011. "Where Is Duisburg? An LP Postscript." *Dancecult: Journal of*

Electronic Dance Music and Culture 2, no. 1, https://dj.dancecult.net/index.php/dancecult/article/view/303/289, accessed January 17, 2020.

Hobsbawm, E. 1960/2014. *The Jazz Scene*. Rev. and expanded ed. [Originally published under the pseudonym Francis Newton]. London: Faber & Faber.

Holt, F. 2007. *Genre in Popular Music*. Chicago: University of Chicago Press.

———. 2010. "The Economy of Live Music in the Digital Age." *European Journal of Cultural Studies* 13, no. 2: 243–61.

———. 2011. "Is Music Becoming More Visual? Online Video Content in the Music Industry." *Visual Studies* 26, no. 1: 50–61.

———. 2013. "The Advent of the Rock Clubs for the Gentry: Berlin, Copenhagen, and New York." In *Musical Performance and the Changing City: Post-Industrial Contexts in Europe and the United States*, edited by F. Holt and C. Wergin, 153–77. New York: Routledge.

———. 2014. "Rock Clubs and Gentrification in New York City: The Case of The Bowery Presents." *IASPM@Journal* 4, no. 1: 21–41, http://www.iaspmjournal.net/index.php/IASPM_Journal/article/view/584/pdf_1, accessed August 22, 2016.

———. 2015. "The Evolution of Corporate Sponsorship in Sensitive Cultural Spheres: Lessons from a Culture-Producing Marketing Unit." In *Prekäre Genres: Zur Ästhetik peripherer, apokrypher und liminaler Gattungen*, edited by H. Berger, F. Döhl, and T. Morsch, 255–88. Bielefeld: Transkript.

———. 2017a. "Introduction: Music in a Globalizing Region." In *The Oxford Handbook of Popular Music in the Nordic Countries*, edited by F. Holt and A.-V. Kärjä, 1–30. Oxford: Oxford University Press.

———. 2017b. "EDM Pop: A Soft Shell Formation in a New Festival Economy." In *Weekend Societies: Electronic Dance Music Festivals and Event-Cultures*, edited by G. St. John, 25–43. New York: Bloomsbury.

Homan, S., M. Cloonan, and J. Cattermole. 2015. "Introduction: Popular Music and Policy." *Popular Music and Cultural Policy*, edited by S. Homan, M. Cloonan, and J. Cattermole, 1–6. New York: Routledge.

Horkheimer, M., and T. Adorno. 1947/2002. *Dialectic of Enlightenment: Philosophical Fragments*, edited by G. Noerr and translated by E. Jephcott. Stanford, CA: Stanford University Press.

Hsu, H. 2009. "Pop Goes the Cult of a Band." *New York Times*, January 16, https://www.nytimes.com/2009/01/18/arts/music/18hsu.html, accessed March 18, 2019.

Hughes, H. 2015. "Michael Swier's Musical Manifest Destiny Reaches from the Bowery to Los Angeles." *Village Voice*, July 8, http://www.villagevoice.com/music/michael-swiers-musical-manifest-destiny-reaches-from-the-bowery-to-los-angeles-7340252, accessed August 22, 2016.

"Human Be-In Full Program." 1967. YouTube video, January 14, https://www.youtube.com/watch?v=HTGyFgyB5Q8, accessed May 18, 2018.

Hunt, L. 2003. "The World We Have Gained: The Future of the French Revolution." *American Historical Review* 108, no. 1: 1–19.

"I attended a concert last night and not a single person filmed the show, no one talked through the show . . . and it was amazing." 2016. *Reddit.com* (exact date not indicated), https://www.reddit.com/r/Music/comments/35qrb7/i_attended_a_concert_last_night_and_not_a_single/, accessed February 10, 2019.

"Iceland Airwaves: A Rockumentary." 2012. YouTube video, February 23, https://www.youtube.com/watch?v=DscddNRltLw, accessed May 31, 2018.

"Inside the Growing Popularity of Live Streams." 2016. IEG Sponsorship Report, June 13, http://www.sponsorship.com/iegsr/2016/06/13/Inside-The-Growing-Popularity-Of-Live-Streams.aspx, accessed January 16, 2020.

"Inspirationskatalog: Oplevelsesøkonomi: 7. Vega." 2007. Kulturministeriet, https://kum.dk/fileadmin/KUM/Documents/Publikationer/2008/Reach_Out/html/chapter05.htm, accessed January 2, 2019.

"Is Too Much English Spoken in Berlin Restaurants?" 2017. The Local, August 14, https://www.thelocal.de/20170814/is-too-much-english-spoken-in-berlin-restaurants, accessed May 30, 2018.

Jackson, T. 2012. *Blowin' the Blues Away: Performance and Meaning on the New York Jazz Scene*. Berkeley: University of California Press.

James, R. 2015. *Resilience and Melancholy: Pop Music, Feminism, Neoliberalism*. Hants, UK: Zero Books.

Jefferson, R. 1991. "Institutions, Institutional Effects, and Institutionalism." In *The New Institutionalism in Organizational Studies*, edited by W. Powell and P. DiMaggio, 143–63. Chicago: University of Chicago Press.

Jensen, E. 1996. "Vegas åbning delte vandende." *Politiken* (September 15), Section PS, 10.

———. 1997a. "Vega vil være national rockscene." *Politiken* (February 22), Section Kultur og Debat, 5.

———. 1997b. "Vegas leder har sagt op." Politiken (November 1), Section Kultur og Debat, 3.

Johnson, B., and S. Homan. 2002. *Vanishing Acts: An Inquiry into the State of Live Popular Music Opportunities in New South Wales*. Sydney: Australia Council and the NSW Ministry for the Arts.

Jones, J. [Josh]. 2017. "The MC5 Performs at the 1968 Chicago Democratic National Convention, Right Before All Hell Breaks Loose." *Open Culture*, May 16, http://www.openculture.com/2017/05/the-mc5-performs-at-the-1968-chicago-democratic-national-convention-right-before-all-hell-breaks-loose.html, accessed March 31, 2019.

Jones, R. [Rhian]. 2017. "Sziget Festival to Launch Globally." *IQ Magazine*, January 16, https://www.iq-mag.net/2017/01/sziget-festival-launch-globally/#.Ww6vyKm-mL5, accessed March 31, 2019.

Jordan, M. 2017. "Burning Man Not Free of Sexual Predators." *Reno Gazette Journal*, September 12, https://www.rgj.com/story/opinion/voices/2017/09/12/burning-man-not-free-sexual-predators-opinion/660266001/, accessed March 29, 2018.

Jørgensen, L. 1996. "Folkets Vega." *Berlingske Tidende* (August 13), Section 2, 1.

———. 1997. "Vega vækker opsigt." *Berlingske Tidende* (January 16), Section 2, 2.

Jurgensen, J. 2010. "The Sound of Summer Festivals." *Wall Street Journal*, Eastern edition, May 7, no. 106, p. W10.

Kallio, A., and L. Väkevä. 2017. "Inclusive Popular Music Education?" In *The Oxford Handbook of Popular Music in the Nordic Countries*, edited by F. Holt and A.-V. Kärjä, 75–89. New York: Oxford University Press.

Karlin, S. 2013. "Drones over Burning Man." *KCRW*, October 11, https://www.kcrw.com/culture/articles/drones-over-burning-man, accessed April 6, 2019.

Kassabian, A. 2013. *Ubiquitous Listening: Affect, Attention, and Distributed Subjectivity*. Kindle ed. Berkeley: University of California Press.

Kaydo, C. 2014. "Cities Create Music, Cultural Festivals to Make Money." *Governing*, January, https://www.governing.com/topics/finance/gov-cities-create-music-festivals.html, accessed April 4, 2019.

Keil, C. 1966/1991. *Urban Blues*. Chicago: University of Chicago Press.

Keith, M. 2005. *After the Cosmopolitan? Multicultural Cities and the Future of Racism*. New York: Routledge.

Kellner, D. 2002. *Media Spectacle*. New York: Routledge.

Keskinen, S., and H. Silius. 2006. "New Trends in Research Funding—Threat or Opportunity for Interdisciplinary Gender Research?" *Nordic Journal of Women's Studies* 14, no. 2: 73–86.

Kierkegaard, F. 2018. "Efter success med del-entrepriser i K.B. Hallen: 'Totalentrepriser tager kvaliteten som gidsel,'" *Politiken*, December 13, https://politikenbyrum.dk/Nyheder/art6913697/Totalentrepriser-tager-kvaliteten-som-gidsel, accessed January 3, 2019.

Kim, J. 2015. "Teragram Ballroom Aiming to Be the Next 'It' Venue in LA." *The Frame: 89.3 KPCC*, July 24, http://www.scpr.org/programs/the-frame/2015/07/23/43801/teragram-ballroom-aiming-to-be-the-next-it-venue-i/, accessed August 22, 2016.

King, B. B. 1965. *Live at the Regal*. ABC Records.

King, L., K. Hinterland, K. Dragan, C. Driver, T. Harris, R. Gwynn, N. Linos, O. Barbot, and M. Bassett. 2015a. *Community Health Profiles 2015, Manhattan Community District 3: Lower East Side and Chinatown*. New York: New York City Department of Health and Hygiene, https://www1.nyc.gov/assets/doh/downloads/pdf/data/2015chp-mn3.pdf, accessed March 17, 2019.

———. 2015b. *Community Health Profiles 2015, Manhattan Community District 2: Greenwich Village and Soho*. New York: New York City Department of Health and Hygiene, https://www1.nyc.gov/assets/doh/downloads/pdf/data/2015chp-mn2.pdf, accessed March 17, 2019.

King, M. Luther, Jr. 1968. *Where Do We Go From Here: Chaos or Community?* Boston: Beacon Press.

Kirshenblatt-Gimblett, B. 2002/2004. "Performance Studies." In *The Performance Studies Reader*, edited by H. Bial, 43–55. New York: Routledge.

Kjus, Y. 2018. *Live and Recorded: Music Experience in the Digital Millennium*. Basingstoke: Palgrave Macmillan.

Kjus, Y., and A. Danielsen. 2014. "Live Islands in the Seas of Recordings: The Music Experience of Visitors at the Øya Festival." *Popular Music and Society* 37, no. 5: 660–79.

Klein, H. 1903. *Thirty Years of Musical Life in London 1870–1900*. London: William Heinemann.

Klemm, T. 2019. "Die kleinste Großmacht an der Börse." *Frankfurter Allgemeine*, January 6, https://www.faz.net/aktuell/finanzen/finanzmarkt/cts-eventim-ist-die-kleinste-grossmacht-an-der-boerse-15974417.html, accessed January 23, 2019.

Klinenberg, E. 2018. *Palaces for the People: How to Build a More Equal and United Society*. London: Bodley Head.

Klotz, S., P. Bohlman, and L.-C. Koch, eds. 2018. *Sounding Cities: Auditory Transformations in Berlin, Chicago, and Kolkata*. Berlin: LIT Verlag.

Knopper, S. 2013. "The Best Clubs in America." *Rolling Stone*, March 28, https://www.rollingstone.com/music/music-lists/the-best-clubs-in-america-143305/brooklyn-bowl-in-new-york-224776/, accessed December 11, 2018.

Knowles-Carter, B., dir. 2019. *HΘMΣCΘMING: A Film by Beyoncé*. Netflix.

"Københavns Ungdomscentre." Københavns Stadsarkiv (Copenhagen City Archive), http://www.starbas.net/arkivskaber.php?id=54&laes_mere=ja, accessed December 31, 2018.

Komar, M. 2017. "L'Oreal's 'Because You're Worth It' Origin Story Is Feminist as Hell." *Bustle*, November 19, https://www.bustle.com/p/loreals-because-youre-worth-it-origin-story-is-feminist-as-hell-73630, accessed January 29, 2019.

Korine, H. 2012, dir. *Spring Breakers*. Muse Productions, Annapurna Pictures, Division Films, and Radar Productions.

Kozak, M. 2015. "Listeners' Bodies in Music Analysis: Gestures, Motor Intentionality, and Models." *Music Theory Online* 21, no. 3 (September), http://www.mtosmt.org/issues/mto.15.21.3/mto.15.21.3.kozak.html, accessed November 1, 2018.

Kozak, R. 1988. *This Ain't No Disco: The Story of CBGB*. Boston: Faber and Faber.

Kraidy, M. 2005. *Hybridity, or the Cultural Logic of Globalization*. Philadelphia: Temple University Press.

Kristiansen, O. 2016. "'Jeg kan lige så godt sige det som det er: Der kommer ikke flere penge på det her område.'" Information.dk, December 30, https://www.information.dk/kultur/2016/12/kan-lige-saa-godt-sige-kommer-flere-penge-paa-omraade, accessed March 24, 2019.

Kronenburg, R. 2012. *Live Architecture: Venues, Stages, and Arenas for Popular Music*. London: Routledge.

———. 2019. *This Must be the Place: An Architectural History of Popular Music Performance Venues*. New York: Bloomsbury.

Krueger, A. B. 2005. "The Economics of Real Superstars: The Market for Rock Concerts in the Material World." *Journal of Labor Economics* 23, no. 1: 1–30.

Kyncl, R. 2011. "More Great Content Creators to YouTube." *The Official YouTube Blog*, October 28, http://youtubeglobal.blogspot.dk/2011/10/more-great-content-creators-coming-to.html, accessed February 26, 2013.

Laing, D. 1985/2015. *One Chord Wonders: Power and Meaning in Punk Rock*. Oakland, CA: PM Press.

———. 2004. "The Three Woodstocks and the Live Music Scene." In *Remembering Woodstock*, edited by Andy Bennett, 1–17. Burlington, VT: Ashgate.

Laks, S. 1979/2000. *Music of Another World*. Translated from the Polish by C. Kisiel. Evanston, IL: Northwestern University Press.

Laursen, A., A. Elbek, J. Brixvold, L. Skov, S. Jørgensen, and J. Traasdahl. 2010. *Styrkelse af den rytmiske music—anbefalinger* [Strengthening rhythmic music—recommendations]. Report for the Arts Council's Music Committee.

Laverne, L. 2019. "Desert Island Discs: Thom Yorke." September 22, BBC, https://www.bbc.co.uk/sounds/play/m0008qg3, accessed November 11, 2019.

Lawrence, T. 2004. *Love Saves the Day: A History of American Dance Music Culture 1970–1979*. Durham, NC: Duke University Press.

Lee, D. 2002. "Neighborhood Report: New York Up Close; Rock Alternatives: A Music Scene Migrates to Brooklyn." *New York Times*, April 8, http://www.nytimes.com/2002/08/04/

nyregion/neighborhood-report-new-york-up-close-rock-alternatives-music-scene-migrates.html, accessed May 28, 2019.

Lee, O. 2015. "I Have One of the Best Jobs in Academia: Here's Why I'm Walking Away." *Vox*, September 8, https://www.vox.com/2015/9/8/9261531/professor-quitting-job, accessed May 5, 2019.

Levidow, L., and C. Neubauer. 2014. "EU Research Agendas: Embedding What Future?" *Science as Culture* 23, no. 3: 397–412.

Lindboe, R. 1997. "Vega overlever." *Aktuelt*, November 6, 16.

Lipsitz, G. 1999. Review of *In Praise of Commercial Culture* (1998) by Tyler Cohen, *Journal of Economic Literature* 37 (December): 1741–1742.

"live, adj. 1, n., and adv. 10a." 1989. *Oxford English Dictionary*. 2nd ed. Oxford: Oxford University Press, http://www.oed.com/view/Entry/109299?rskey=oT6yDO&result=1&isAdvanced=false#eid, accessed May 31, 2016.

"Live Nation Entertainment Acquires Top Electronic Music Company Cream." 2012. Live Nation, May 9, https://www.livenationentertainment.com/2012/05/live-nation-entertainment-acquires-top-electronic-music-company-cream-holdings-limited/, accessed April 6, 2019.

"Live Nation's New Groove: Electronic Dance Music and Scalped Tickets." 2013. *Bloomberg Business*, August 9, http://www.bloomberg.com/bw/articles/2013-08-09/live-nation-jumps-on-electronic-dance-music-scalped-tickets, accessed July 19, 2015.

Lloyd, R. 2006. *Neo-Bohemia: Art and Commerce in the Postindustrial City*. New York: Routledge.

"Lollapalooza Is Coming to Berlin!" 2014. YouTube video, November 13, https://www.youtube.com/watch?v=olIRWkogV1A, accessed May 31, 2018.

Lopes, S. 2017. "The Most Beautiful People of Coachella." *LA Weekly*, April 17, https://www.laweekly.com/slideshow/the-most-beautiful-people-of-coachella-2017-8136691, accessed April 4, 2019.

Lotz, A. 2007. *The Television Will Be Revolutionized*. New York: New York University Press.

"Lov om ændring af musikloven, §3g–h." 2000. Folketinget.dk, May 11, http://webarkiv.ft.dk/?/samling/19991/lovforslag_som_vedtaget/l184.htm, accessed March 24, 2019.

Lynskey, D. 2011. "The Great Rock 'n' Roll Sellout." *The Guardian*, June 30, https://www.theguardian.com/music/2011/jun/30/rocknroll-sellout, accessed December 11, 2018.

MacMillen, I. 2015. "Fascination, Musical Tourism, and the Loss of the Balkan Village (Notes on Bulgaria's Koprivshtitsa Festival)." *Ethnomusicology* 59, no. 2: 227–61.

Madrid, A. 2017. "Diversity, Tokenism, Non-Canonical Musics, and the Crisis of the Humanities in U.S. Academia." *Journal of Music History Pedagogy* 7, no. 2: 124–30.

March, B. 2018. "Some Celebrities Looking Beautiful at Coachella." *Esquire.com*, April 16, https://www.esquire.com/uk/women/g19825520/coachella-2018-beauty-looks/?slide=1, accessed April 4, 2019.

Mason, K. 2012. "Electric Daisy Founder Pasquale Rotella: 'We Don't Want to Book' Superstar DJs Anymore." *Billboard.com*, June 8, http://www.billboard.com/biz/articles/news/touring/1094072/electric-daisy-founder-pasquale-rotella-we-dont-want-to-book, accessed August 2, 2015.

———. 2013. "SFX Purchases 75% Stake in ID&T, Announce U.S. Edition of Tomorrowland at Ultra." *Billboard.com*, March 21, https://www.billboard.com/biz/articles/news/1553846/sfx-purchases-75-stake-in-idt-announce-us-edition-of-tomorrowland-at-ultra, accessed April 6, 2019.

———. 2014. "John Sykes, Robert Sillerman on New Clear Channel, SFX Partnership: 'We Want to Be the Best.'" *Billboard.biz*, January 6, http://www.billboard.com/biz/articles/news/branding/5862290/john-sykes-robert-sillerman-on-new-clear-channel-sfx-partnership, accessed July 27, 2015.

Mason, L. 1996. *Singing the French Revolution: Popular Culture and Politics, 1787–1799*. Ithaca, NY: Cornell University Press.

Matson, J. 2005. "Todd P Interview." *Medium Heat*, April, http://www.mediumheat.com/odds/toddp.htm (site discontinued), accessed via http://web.archive.org/web/20060221203340/http://www.mediumheat.com/odds/toddp.htm, accessed May 29, 2019.

Maycock, J. 2002. "Loud and Proud." *The Guardian*, July 20, https://www.theguardian.com/artanddesign/2002/jul/20/artsfeatures.features1, accessed January 14, 2020.

McCarthy, L. 2018. "A Visual History of Celebrities at Coachella, from Kendall Jenner to Clint Eastwood." *W Magazine*, April 8, https://www.wmagazine.com/gallery/celebrities-at-coachella-kendall-jenner-vanessa-hudgens-clint-eastwood, accessed April 4, 2019.

McGowan, A. 2007. "2007 Review." *IQ* 15: 22–28.

McGuigan, J. 2009. *Cool Capitalism*. London: Pluto.

McKay, G. 2000. *Glastonbury: A Very English Fair*. London: Gollancz.

———. 2015. "'The Pose . . . Is a Stance': Popular Music and the Cultural Politics of Festival in 1950s Britain." In *Pop Festival: History, Music, Media, Culture*, 13–31. New York: Bloomsbury.

McKendrick, N., J. Brewer, and J. Plumb. 1982. *The Birth of a Consumer Society: The Commercialization of Eighteenth-Century England*. London: Europa Publications Limited.

McKinley, J. 2011. "Underground Musicians Lose a Haven." *New York Times*, September 11, http://www.nytimes.com/2011/09/12/arts/music/monster-island-to-close-and-underground-clubs-lose-a-haven.html?_r=1&pagewanted=all, accessed May 29, 2019.

———. 2012. "Crumbs from the Crowd to Pay the Bills." *New York Times*, May 30, https://www.nytimes.com/2012/05/31/arts/music/cake-shop-a-club-for-new-music-is-looking-for-financing.html, accessed December 8, 2018.

"Media Coverage." n.d. Burning Man, https://burningman.org/culture/stories/media-coverage/, accessed April 6, 2019.

Meerzon, Y., and D. Priven. 2013. "Back to the Future: Imagining a New Russia at the Eurovision Song Contest." In *Performing the "New" Europe: Identities, Feelings, and Politics in the Eurovision Song Contest*, edited by K. Fricker and M. Gluhovic, 111–24. Basingstoke: Palgrave Macmillan.

"Meeting of Minds." 2018. *Audience*, no. 217 (February): 24–28.

Meier, L. 2017. *Popular Music as Promotion: Music and Branding in the Digital Age*. Cambridge: Polity Press.

Mele, C. 2000. *Selling the Lower East Side: Culture, Real Estate, and Resistance in New York City*. Minneapolis: University of Minnesota Press.

Meline, G. 2016. "Q&A: Stewart Brand Revisits the Trips Festival, 50 Years Later." *KQED*

Arts, https://www.kqed.org/arts/11263131/qa-stewart-brand-revisits-the-trips-festival-50-years-later, accessed June 5, 2018.

Merriam, A., and R. Mack. 1960. "The Jazz Community." *Social Forces* 38, no. 3: 211–22.

Methos, Z. 2005. "Celebrities and Others Urge NYC to Declare CBGB an Official Landmark." *BC blogcritics*, Music, http://blogcritics.org/music/article/celebrities-and-others-urge-nyc-to, accessed May 4, 2012.

Meyrowitz, J. 1985. *No Sense of Place: The Impact of Electronic Media on Social Behavior*. Oxford: Oxford University Press.

Michelsen, M. 2001. "'Rytmisk musik' mellem høj og lav." *Musik og Forskning* 26: 61–81.

Micucci, M. 2018. "'Jazz on a Summer's Day' 60th Anniversary Edition Out Now." *Jazziz*, October 18, https://www.jazziz.com/jazz-on-a-summers-day-60th-anniversary-edition-out-now/, accessed April 6, 2019.

Middleton, R. 1990. *Studying Popular Music*. Milton Keynes: Open University Press.

Milanovic, B. 2013. "Global Income Inequality in Numbers: In History and Now." *Global Policy* 4, no. 2: 198–208.

Miller, K. 2012. *Playing Along: Digital Games, YouTube, and Virtual Performance*. Oxford: Oxford University Press.

Mills, C. 1959/2000. *The Sociological Imagination*. 40th-anniversary ed. Oxford: Oxford University Press.

Monson, I. 2007. *Freedom Sounds: Civil Rights Call Out to Jazz and Africa*. Oxford: Oxford University Press.

Montano, E. 2009. "DJ Culture in the Commercial Sydney Dance Music Scene." *Dancecult: Journal of Electronic Dance Music Culture* 1, no. 1: 81–93, https://dj.dancecult.net/index.php/dancecult/article/view/272/233, accessed January 17, 2020.

———. 2011. "Festival Fever and International DJs: The Changing Shape of DJ Culture in Sydney's Commercial Electronic Dance Music Scene." *Dancecult: Journal of Electronic Dance Music Culture* 2, no. 1: 63–89. https://dj.dancecult.net/index.php/dancecult/article/view/301/287, accessed January 17, 2020.

———. 2017. "Stereosonic and Australian Commercial EDM Festival Culture." In *Weekend Societies: Electronic Dance Music Festivals and Event-Cultures*, edited by G. St. John, 45–67. New York: Bloomsbury.

Morcom, A. 2015. "Terrains of Bollywood Dance: (Neoliberal) Capitalism and the Transformation of Cultural Economies." *Ethnomusicology* 59, no. 2: 288–314.

More, T. [1516] 1997. *Utopia*. Translated by R. Robinson. Ware: Wordsworth Editions.

Moser, G. 2001. "A Scene Grows in Brooklyn." *FREEwilliamsburg.com*, September, http://freewilliamsburg.com/september_2001/mightymusic.html, accessed August 14, 2016.

Mount, A. 2011. "Testing Art with a Live Studio Audience: John Cage at an Intersection of Popular Television and the Avant-Garde." *Music and the Moving Image* 4, no. 3: 31–56.

Mueller, D. 2012. "Introduction: The Good, the Bad, and the Ugly." In *The Oxford Handbook of Capitalism*, 1–14. Oxford: Oxford University Press.

Mukerji, C., and M. Schudson. 1986. "Popular Culture." *Annual Review of Sociology* 12: 47–66.

Muñoz, J. 2006. "Feeling Brown, Feeling Down: Latina Affect, the Performativity of Race, and the Depressive Position." *Signs* 31, no. 3, New Feminist Theories of Visual Culture (Spring): 675–88.

Murphy, S. 2017. User comment on "Tomorrowland 2011: Official Aftermovie." YouTube video, https://www.youtube.com/watch?v=M7CdTAiaLes, accessed February 2, 2019.

"Music Is Everywhere: John Cage at 100." 2012. NPR Music, September 5, http://www.wrti.org/post/music-everywhere-john-cage-100, accessed January 20, 2019.

Nasaw, D. 1993. *Going Out: The Rise and Fall of Public Amusements*. Cambridge, MA: Harvard University Press.

"Nature One 2013 Official Aftermovie." 2013. Nature One Festival, YouTube video, August 16, https://www.youtube.com/watch?v=l5CR47dpn10, accessed February 8, 2019.

Navarro, F. 2018. "Long Lines and Traffic Jams Infuriate Music Fans at Mad Cool Festival." *El País*, July 16, https://elpais.com/elpais/2018/07/13/inenglish/1531479538_129466.html, accessed November 2, 2018.

Negus, K. 1999. *Music Genres and Corporate Cultures*. London: Routledge.

Nettl, B., ed. 1978. *Eight Urban Musical Cultures*. Urbana: University of Illinois Press.

Newman, J. 2014. "The Untold and Deeply Stoned Story of the First U.S. Rock Festival." *Rolling Stone.com*, June 17, https://www.rollingstone.com/music/news/the-untold-and-deeply-stoned-story-of-the-first-u-s-rock-festival-20140617, accessed May 22, 2018.

"A New General Manager for the AB." 2010. AB Concerts, September 30, https://www.abconcerts.be/en/news/varia/a-new-general-manager-for-the-ab/439/, accessed October 13, 2016.

Nielsen, E. G. 2000. "Tale 56." Folketinget.dk, first hearing of proposal L 184: Proposal to amend the music law, L 184 BEH1, February 29, http://webarkiv.ft.dk/doc.aspx?/samling/arkiv.htm, accessed January 3, 2019.

Nietzsche, F. [1875] 1954. "Wissenschaft und Weisheit im Kampfe." In *Friedrich Nietzsche: Werke in drei Bänden: Vol. 3*, edited by Karl Schlechta, 332–48. München: Carl Hanser Verlag.

Nødgaard, O. 2000. "Tale 2." Folketinget.dk, L 184 BEH1, February 29, http://webarkiv.ft.dk/doc.aspx?/samling/arkiv.htm, accessed January 3, 2019.

Nowotny, H., P. Scott, and M. Gibbons. 2001. *Re-Thinking Science: Knowledge and the Public in an Age of Uncertainty*. Cambridge: Polity.

Nussbaum, M. 2013. *Political Emotions: Why Love Matters for Justice*. Cambridge, MA: Belknap Press of Harvard University Press.

NYU Furman Center. 2016. *State of New York City's Housing and Neighborhoods in 2015*. Report available at http://furmancenter.org/research/sonychan, accessed August 8, 2016.

Oakley, K. 2009. "The Disappearing Arts: Creativity and Innovation After the Creative Industries." *International Journal of Cultural Policy* 15, no. 4: 403–13.

"Official Aftermovie @ Sziget Festival 2012." 2012. Sziget Festival, YouTube video, November 26, https://www.youtube.com/watch?v=WGc-rEscomk, accessed June 25, 2017.

"Official Aftermovie—Sziget 2017." 2017. Sziget Festival, YouTube video, November 3, https://www.youtube.com/watch?v=w6G26rLsryQ, accessed January 14, 2020.

O'Meara, C., and E. Tretter. 2013. "Live Music, Race and the Selling of a City." In *Musical Performance and the Changing City: Post-Industrial Contexts in Europe and the United States*, edited by F. Holt and C. Wergin, 52–76. New York: Routledge.

Osborne, P. 2015. "Problematizing Disciplinarity, Transdisciplinary Problematics." *Theory, Culture & Society* 32, no. 5/6: 3–35.

Østbjerg, S. 2013. "Gør dig klar til næste års festival." *Dagbladet* (October 31), https://sn.dk/Roskilde/Goer-dig-klar-til-naeste-aars-festival/artikel/365068, accessed July 9, 2018.

"Our Venues." Le Botanique, https://www.botanique.be/en/our-venues-en, accessed March 23, 2019.

Ozouf, M. 1975. "Space and Time in the Festivals of the French Revolution." *Comparative Studies in Society and History* 17, no. 3: 372–84.

———. 1976/1988. *Festivals and the French Revolution*. Translated by Alan Sheridan. Cambridge, MA: Harvard University Press.

Packman, J. 2014. "The Other Other Festa: June Samba and the Alternative Spaces of Bahia, Brazil's São João Festival and Industries." *Black Music Research Journal* 34, no. 2: 255–83.

"Paradiso Today." Paradiso, https://www.paradiso.nl/web/English-Agenda/About-Paradiso/Paradiso-today-concert-hall-club-and-cultural-center.htm, accessed October 12, 2016.

Pareles, J. 1976. "CBGB Club Is Hub for Bands Playing Underground Rock." *New York Times*, January 24, 28.

———. 2004. "The Bottom Line, A Place Where the Music Always Came First." *New York Times*, January 24, http://www.nytimes.com/2004/01/26/arts/critic-s-notebook-the-bottom-line-a-place-where-the-music-always-came-first.html, accessed May 29, 2019.

———. 2005. "Punk Rock Doesn't Belong in a Museum." *New York Times*, August 14, http://www.nytimes.com/2005/08/14/arts/music/punk-rock-doesnt-belong-in-a-museum.html, accessed August 18, 2016.

———. 2013. "Selling Stars, Brands, and Baby Bands." *New York Times*, March 17, http://www.nytimes.com/2013/03/18/arts/music/selling-stars-brands-and-baby-bands.html?pagewanted=all, accessed May 29, 2019.

Pareles, J., B. Ratliff, and J. Caramanica. 2016. "Why We're Not Making Plans for Coachella and Bonnaroo." *New York Times*, March 18, https://www.nytimes.com/2016/03/19/arts/music/summer-music-festivals.html, accessed May 29, 2019.

Park, J. 2017. "Searching for a Cultural Home: Asian American Youth in the EDM Festival Scene." In *Weekend Societies: Electronic Dance Music Festivals and Event-Cultures*, edited by G. St. John, 69–90. New York: Bloomsbury.

Pelly, J. 2011. "Todd P Celebrates a Decade." *Village Voice*, October 19, http://www.villagevoice.com/music/todd-p-celebrates-a-decade-6435125, accessed August 10, 2016.

———. 2012. "Mogwai, Yoko Ono, Patti Smith, Yo La Tengo, Thee Oh Sees, Ladytron on Occupy Wall Street Comp." *Pitchfork*, April 18, http://pitchfork.com/news/46204-mogwai-yoko-ono-patti-smith-yo-la-tengo-thee-oh-sees-ladytron-on-occupy-wall-street-comp/, accessed August 23, 2016.

Pelly, L. 2013. "Five Days in Mexico with Todd P and Festival NRMAL." *Stereogum*, March 21, http://www.stereogum.com/1294671/five-days-in-mexico-with-todd-p-and-festival-nrmal/photo/, accessed August 10, 2016.

Pennebaker, D. A., dir. 1968/2002. *Monterey Pop*. Criterion DVD.

Peralta, C. 2015. "Mobile Phones Have a Bright Future at Live Events." Ticketfly.com, May 7, http://start.ticketfly.com/?p=56399, accessed February 10, 2019.

Perler, E. 2013. "The Ludlow Apartment Where Lou Reed and John Cale Formed Velvet Underground." *Bowery Boogie*, October 30, http://www.boweryboogie.com/2013/10/ludlow-apartment-lou-reed-john-cale-formed-velvet-underground/, accessed August 20, 2016.

Perry, C. 1984. *The Haight-Ashbury: A History*. New York: Random House.

"Peter Crowley: Max's Man Behind the Music." 2009. Max's Kansas City, October 7, http://maxskansascity.com/peter-crowley-maxs-man-behind-the-music-part-two/, accessed August 17, 2016.

Peterson, R. 1973. "The Unnatural History of Rock Festivals: An Instance of Media Facilitation." *Popular Music and Society* 2, no. 2: 97–123.

———. 1997. *Creating Country Music: Fabricating Authenticity*. Chicago: University of Chicago Press.

Peterson, R., and N. Anand. 2004. "The Production of Culture Perspective." *Annual Review of Sociology* 30: 311–34.

Phillips, A. 2007. "Lollapalooza Report: Sunday." *Pitchfork*, http://pitchfork.com/news/27360-lollapalooza-report-sunday-amy-phillips, accessed April 11, 2013.

Piper, L., and P. De Gregorio. 2009. "Brooklyn DIY Scene—DIY Generation." *The Deli*, May 13, http://www.thedelimagazine.com/FeatureView.php?artist=diygeneration, accessed August 14, 2016.

Poiger, U. 2000. *Jazz, Rock, and Rebels: Cold War Politics and American Culture in a Divided Germany*. Berkeley: University of California Press.

"POPLIVE." https://www.poplive.nl, accessed January 9, 2020.

"Population Dynamics; Birth, Death and Migration Per Region." 2018. CBS: StatLine, August 20, https://opendata.cbs.nl/statline/#/CBS/en/dataset/37259eng/table?ts=1553166985508, accessed March 21, 2019.

Porter, C. 1980. "The New Public and the Reordering of the Musical Establishment: The Lower Rhine Music Festivals, 1818–67." *19th-Century Music* 3, no. 3 (March): 211–24.

"The Position of Muslims in the Netherlands: Facts and Figures." Utrecht: Forum—Institute for Multicultural Affairs, https://www.eukn.eu/fileadmin/Lib/files/EUKN/2010/o_linkclick.pdf, accessed March 22, 2019.

Post, R. 2009. "Debating Disciplinarity." *Critical Inquiry* 35 (Summer): 749–70.

Powell, W., and P. DiMaggio, eds. 1991. *The New Institutionalism in Organizational Analysis*. Chicago: University of Chicago Press.

Press, A., and B. Williams. 2015. "Fame and Everyday Life: The 'Lottery Celebrities' of Reality TV." In *The Blackwell Companion to the Sociology of Culture*, edited by M. Jacobs and N. Hanrahan, 176–89. Malden, MA: Blackwell.

Railton, D., and P. Watson. 2011. *Music Video and the Politics of Representation*. Edinburgh: Edinburgh University Press.

Rambarran, S. 2017. "'DJ Hit That Button': Amateur Laptop Musicians in Contemporary Music and Society." In *The Oxford Handbook of Music Making and Leisure*, edited by R. Mantie and G. Smith, 585–600. New York: Oxford University Press.

"Rascasuelos." Roskilde Festival, https://www.roskilde-festival.dk/music/2018/rascasuelos?view=grid, accessed May 29, 2018.

Rathe, A. 2007. "Brooklyn on the Bowery." *Brooklyn Paper.com*, August 25, http://www.brooklynpaper.com/stories/30/33/30_33musichall.html, accessed August 22, 2016.

"RBMA Stage @ Mauerpark Festival." Red Bull.com, https://www.redbull.com/de-de/events/rbma-stage-mauerpark, accessed May 31, 2018.

Real, M. 1998. "MediaSport: Technology and the Commodification of Postmodern Sport." In *Media Sport*, edited by L. Wenner, 14–26. London: Routledge.

———. 2014. "Do Media Corrupt the Olympics? The Role of Commerce, Commodification, and Television in the Olympic Games." Blog post on the website of Royal Roads University, School of Communication and Culture, February 13, http://scc.royalroads.ca/do-media-corrupt-olympics-role-commerce-commodification-and-television-olympic-games, accessed February 8, 2019.

Reed, L. 1972. *Transformer*. RCA Records.

———. 1982. *The Blue Mask*. RCA Records.

———. 1989. *New York*. Sire Records.

Regev, M. 2013. *Pop-Rock Music: Aesthetic Cosmopolitanism in Late Modernity*. Cambridge: Polity Press.

Reily, S. 1994. "Musical Performance at a Brazilian Festival." *British Journal of Ethnomusicology* 3: 1–34.

"Relive Ultra Miami 2012 (Official Aftermovie)." 2012. Ultra Music Festival, YouTube video, October 15, https://www.youtube.com/watch?v=3TlJWoM69ww, accessed February 8, 2019.

Reynolds, S. 1998. *Energy Flash: A Journey through Rave Music and Dance Culture*. London: Picador.

———. 2012. "How Rave Music Conquered America." *The Guardian*, August 2, http://www.theguardian.com/music/2012/aug/02/how-rave-music-conquered-america, accessed June 17, 2015.

Rice, T. 2013. *Ethnomusicology: A Very Short Introduction*. Oxford: Oxford University Press.

Richards, G., and R. Palmer. 2010. *Eventful Cities: Cultural Management and Urban Revitalization*. Amsterdam: Elsevier.

Rigney, F., and L. Smith. 1961. *The Real Bohemians*. New York: Basic Books.

Riis, J. 1890. *How the Other Half Lives: Studies of the Tenements of New York*. New York: Charles Scribner's Sons. Original available at Hathi Trust, http://hdl.handle.net/2027/nnc2.ark:/13960/t1dj7qx2q, accessed August 16, 2016.

Rix, L. 1997. "Nationalscene for rytmisk musik." *Aktuelt*, August 8, 15.

———. 1998. "Nej til rytmisk nationalscene." *Aktuelt*, May 1, 19.

Robbins, C. 2013. "Interview: Indie Promoter Todd P Talks Festivals In Mexico, What 'DIY' Means." *Gothamist*, March 5, http://gothamist.com/2013/03/05/chris_so_youve_been_doing.php, accessed August 10, 2016.

Robertson, J. 2017. "Every Tomorrowland Aftermovie—From 2005 to Now." *Festicket.com*, December 20, https://www.festicket.com/magazine/features/every-tomorrowland-aftermovie-2005-now/, accessed April 6, 2019.

Robinson, R. 2015. *Music Festivals and the Politics of Participation*. London: Routledge.

Roche, M. 2000. *Mega-Events and Modernity: Olympics and Expos in the Growth of Global Culture*. London: Routledge.

Rogers, H. 2013. *Sounding the Gallery: Video and the Rise of Art-Music*. Oxford: Oxford University Press.

Rojek, C. 1985. *Capitalism and Leisure Theory*. London: Tavistock.

Rolf, M. 2006/2013. *Soviet Mass Festivals, 1917–1991*. Translated by Cynthia Klohr. Pittsburgh, PA: University of Pittsburgh Press.

Rollefson, G. 2017. *Flip the Script: European Hip Hop and the Politics of Postcoloniality*. Chicago: University of Chicago Press.

Roose, K. 2013. "Burning Man Is Just Like Every Other Social-Media Event Now." *New York Magazine*, August 30, https://nymag.com/intelligencer/2013/08/burning-man-just-a-social-media-event-now.html, accessed April 6, 2019.

Rose, S. 2009. "The Musical Map of Europe c. 1700." In *The Cambridge History of Eighteenth-Century Music*, edited by S. Keefe. Cambridge: Cambridge University Press, 3–25.

Rosenberg, N. 1985. *Bluegrass: A History*. Urbana: University of Illinois Press.

"Roskilde Festival." *Wikipedia.com*, https://da.wikipedia.org/wiki/Roskilde_Festival, accessed January 22, 2019.

"Roskilde politi har fået seks anmeldelser om voldtægt." 2017. *Politiken*, July 1, https://politiken.dk/kultur/musik/roskildefestival/art6018708/Roskilde-politi-har-f%C3%A5et-seks-anmeldelser-om-voldt%C3%A6gt, accessed March 19, 2018.

Rousseau, J.-J. [1761] 1998. "Essay on the Origin of Languages." In *Essay on the Origin of Languages and Writings Related to Music*, edited by J. Scott, 289–332. Hanover, NH: University Press of New England.

Rüegg, W. 2010. "Chapter 1: Themes." In *A History of the European University: Volume 4: Universities Since 1945*, edited by W. Rüegg and H. de Ridder-Symoens, 3–30. Cambridge: Cambridge University Press.

Ruggieri, M. 2014. "Economic Impact of TomorrowWorld: $85.1 Million for the State of Georgia." AJC.com, April 8, http://www.accessatlanta.com/weblogs/atlanta-music-scene/2014/apr/08/economic-impact-tomorrowworld-85-million-state-geo/, accessed January 7, 2015.

Ryan, B. 1992. *Making Capital from Culture: The Corporate Form of Capitalist Cultural Production*. Berlin: Walter de Gruyter.

Saad, S. 2018. "Coachella 2018: Why All Music Festival-Goers Look the Same." *CNN.com*, April 19, https://edition.cnn.com/style/article/festival-fashion-trends-style/index.html, accessed April 4, 2019.

Sachs, C. 1908. *Musikgeschichte der Stadt Berlin bis zum Jahre 1800: Stadtpfeifer, Kantoren und Organisten an den Kirchen städtischen Patronats nebst Beiträgen zur allgemeinen Musikgeschichte Berlins*. Berlin: Gebrüder Paetel.

Sackllah, D. 2015. "Live Nation Takes Bonnaroo: The Ongoing Corporatization of Music Festivals." *Consequence of Sound*, April 29, http://consequenceofsound.net/2015/04/live-nation-takes-bonnaroo-the-ongoing-corporatization-of-music-festivals/, accessed June 17, 2015.

Said, E. 1983. *The World, the Text, and the Critic*. Cambridge, MA: Harvard University Press.

Sakakeeny, M. 2010. "'Under the Bridge': An Orientation to Soundscapes in New Orleans." *Ethnomusicology* 54, no. 1: 1–27.

"Salzburg Beneath the Swastika." The History of the Salzburg Festival, Salzburg Festival, https://www.salzburgerfestspiele.at/en/history/salzburg-beneath-the-swastika, accessed January 17, 2020.

Sanghani, R. 2015. "The Dark Truth About Rape at UK Music Festivals." *The Telegraph*, August 25, https://www.telegraph.co.uk/women/womens-life/11822420/Bestival-UK-music-festivals-have-a-rape-problem-that-needs-action-now.html, accessed March 29, 2018.

Sassatelli, M. 2009. *Becoming Europeans: Cultural Identity and Cultural Policies*. Basingstoke: Palgrave Macmillan.

Sassatelli, R. 2007. *Consumer Culture: History, Theory and Politics*. London: Sage.

———. 2010. *Fitness Culture: Gyms and the Commercialisation of Discipline and Fun*. Basingstoke: Palgrave Macmillan.

Sassen, S. 1991/2001. *The Global City: London, New York, Tokyo*. 2nd ed. Princeton, NJ: Princeton University Press.

———. 1998. *Globalization and Its Discontents: Essays on the New Mobility of People and Money*. New York: New Press.

Schechner, R. 1977/1988. *Performance Theory*. 2nd ed. New York: Routledge.

Schmidt, G., C. Andersen, and J. Thobo-Carlsen. 2015. "Museer og teatre skal på skrump." *Politiken*, September 3, https://politiken.dk/kultur/art5587848/Museer-og-teatre-skal-p%C3%A5-skrump, accessed March 24, 2019.

Schneider, R. 1988. "Morgenröte und Muskelkraft: Die Weltfestspiele der Jugend und Studenten." In *Das Fest: Eine Kulturgeschichte von der Antike zur Gegenwart*, edited by U. Schultz, 369–79. Munich: C. H. Beck.

Schoemer, A. 1990. "In the Nightlife of Houston Street, Some New Kids on the Block." *New York Times*, August 31, https://www.nytimes.com/1990/08/31/arts/in-the-nightlife-of-houston-street-some-new-kids-on-the-block.html, accessed December 15, 2018.

Schorske, C. 1980. *Fin-de-Siècle Vienna: Politics and Culture*. New York: Vintage Books.

Scott, D. 2008. *Sounds of the Metropolis: The 19th-Century Popular Music Revolution in London, New York, Paris, and Vienna*. Oxford: Oxford University Press.

Scott, W. 1995/2014. *Institutions and Organizations: Ideas, Interests, and Identities*. 4th ed. London: Sage.

"Secret Project Robot." https://www.secretprojectrobot.org/about/, accessed December 8, 2018.

Shah, N. 2015. "How Music Festivals Pump Billions into the U.S. Economy." *Wall Street Journal*, July 31, http://blogs.wsj.com/speakeasy/2015/07/31/how-music-festivals-pump-billions-into-the-u-s-economy/, accessed January 7, 2015.

Shank, B. 1994. *Dissonant Identities: The Rock'n'Roll Scene in Austin, Texas*. Middletown, CT: Wesleyan University Press.

Shaw, W. 2007. *Cities of Whiteness*. Malden, MA: Blackwell.

Shepherd, J. 2016. "Glastonbury Festival: Prince Was in Talks to Headline, According to Michael Eavis." *The Independent*, May 31, https://www.independent.co.uk/arts-entertainment/music/news/glastonbury-festival-prince-dead-headline-michael-eavis-a7057366.html, accessed March 29, 2019.

Shepherd, J., and K. Devine. 2015a. "Introduction: Music and the Sociological Imagination—Pasts and Prospects." In *The Routledge Reader on the Sociology of Music*, 1–21. New York: Routledge.

———. 2015b. *The Routledge Reader on the Sociology of Music*. New York: Routledge.

Sherburne, P. 2013. "Electric Daisy Chain: Insomniac and Dick Clark Prod. Plan 2014 EDM Awards." *Spin*, June 21, http://www.spin.com/articles/electric-daisy-carnival-insomniac-dick-clark-productions-edm-awards-2014/, accessed July 19, 2015.

"Shutka Roma Rap Live @ Sziget 2013 [full concert]." 2013. YouTube video, September 3, https://www.youtube.com/watch?v=yCgLog5-fig, accessed May 30, 2018.

Signore, J. 2007. "Todd Patrick, Concert Promoter." *Gothamist*, December 7, http://gothamist.com/2007/12/07/todd_patrick_co.php, accessed May 29, 2019.

———. 2014. "Why Can't You Ever Shut Up During a Concert?" *Gothamist*, July 10, http://gothamist.com/2014/07/10/do_shut_up_during_concerts.php, accessed February 10, 2019.

Silverman, C. 2011. *Romani Routes: Cultural Politics and Balkan Music in Diaspora*. Oxford: Oxford University Press.

Simon, J. 2004. "Singing Democracy: Music and Politics in Jean-Jacques Rousseau's Thought." *Journal of the History of Ideas* 65, no. 3 (July): 433–54.

Sisario, B. 2007. "A Small Strategy for Selling Concerts." *New York Times*, June 7, https://www.nytimes.com/2007/06/07/arts/music/07bowe.html, accessed May 28, 2019.

———. 2008. "It's Been Quite a Pool Party, but the Days Grow Short." *New York Times*, August 1, https://www.nytimes.com/2008/08/01/arts/music/01pool.html, accessed May 28, 2019.

———. 2009a. "Attendance Strong at Coachella Despite the Economy." *New York Times*, April 19, https://www.nytimes.com/2009/04/20/arts/music/20fest.html, accessed March 2, 2019.

———. 2009b. "The Experimental, Led by the Obsessive." *New York Times*, June 3, https://www.nytimes.com/2009/06/07/arts/music/07sisa.html, accessed March 19, 2019.

———. 2014. "A Bowery Titan Puts Down L.A. Roots." *New York Times*, December 31, http://www.nytimes.com/2015/01/01/arts/music/bowery-ballroom-leader-plans-music-club-in-los-angeles.html, accessed August 22, 2016.

———. 2017. "Bowery Ballroom and Mercury Lounge Join with Live Nation." *New York Times*, December 18, https://www.nytimes.com/2017/12/18/business/media/bowery-ballroom-mercury-lounge-live-nation.html, accessed December 11, 2018.

"Skandale truer Københavns overborgmester." 2000. Dr.dk, April 30, https://www.dr.dk/nyheder/indland/skandale-truer-koebenhavns-overborgmester, accessed December 31, 2018.

Skolnick, J. 1978. *House of Cards: The Legalization and Control of Casino Gambling*. Boston: Little, Brown and Company.

Skotte, K. 2016. "Ambassadør Albarn nedbryder grænser." Politiken.dk, June 29, https://politiken.dk/kultur/musik/roskildefestival/roskildeanmeldelser/art5627897/Ambassad%C3%B8r-Albarn-nedbryder-gr%C3%A6nser, accessed January 22, 2019.

Slade, N. 2004. "Ironing Out the Challenges in a Booming Sector." *Music Week* 22 (June 5): 15–17.

Slater, D. 1997. *Consumer Culture and Modernity*. Cambridge: Polity.

———. 2011. "Marketing as Monstrosity: The Impossible Place between Culture and Economy." In *Inside Marketing: Practices, Ideologies, Devices*, edited by D. Zwick and J. Cayla, 23–41. New York: Oxford University Press.

Small, C. 1986. "Performance as Ritual: Sketch for an Enquiry into the True Nature of a Symphony Concert." *Sociological Review* 34, no. 1: 6–32.

Smirke, R. 2019. "Is the Party Over? EDM's Market Share of US Record Market Falls as DJ Earnings Slip to Five-Year Low." *Billboard.com*, May 23, https://www.billboard.com/articles/business/8512892/edm-dance-music-share-us-recorded-music-market-share-ims-report, accessed May 25, 2019.

Smith, C. 2012. "Live Streaming Boosts Festival Boom." *Hypebot.com*, October 16, http://www.hypebot.com/hypebot/2012/10/live-streaming-boosts-music-festival-boom.html, accessed May 28, 2019.

Smith, N. 1996. *The New Urban Frontier: Gentrification and the Revanchist City*. London: Routledge.

———. 2002. "New Globalism, New Urbanism: Gentrification as Global Urban Strategy." *Antipode* 34, no. 3: 440.

Smith, N., and D. Cohen. 2007. "Suburban Manhattan." In *The Suburbanization of New York: Is the World's Greatest City Becoming Just Another Town?*, edited by J. Hammett and K. Hammett, photographs by Martha Cooper, 33–40. New York: Princeton Architectural Press.

Sombart, W. [1913] 1967. *Luxury and Capitalism*. Ann Arbor: University of Michigan Press.

"Sónar 2012: La distancia." 2012. Sónar Festival, March 28, YouTube video, https://www.youtube.com/watch?v=WEaF4Vi9sZ4, accessed May 30, 2018.

"Sónar Festival." YouTube channel, https://www.youtube.com/user/SonarFestival/videos, accessed April 5, 2019.

"Sónar Festival Is for Sale: Sónar 2011 Image." 2011. Sónar Festival, April 19, YouTube video, https://www.youtube.com/watch?v=fSe6AZwbAkY, accessed May 29, 2019.

Sørensen, D. 1996. "Fra dødt sted til in-sted." *Politiken*, I Byen, 14.

Sørensen, I. 2016. "The Revival of Live TV: Liveness in a Multiplatform Context." *Media, Culture & Society* 38, no. 3: 381–99.

Sørensen, M., C. Bloch, and M. Young. 2016. "Excellence in the Knowledge-Based Economy: From Scientific to Research Excellence." *European Journal of Higher Education* 6, no. 3: 217–36.

Sotirova, I. 2016. "Sergio Caballero: 'I'm Interested in the Creative Process. I Couldn't Care Less about the Final Work.'" *Studio International*, May 3, https://www.studiointernational.com/index.php/sergio-caballero-interview-im-interested-in-the-creative-process-could-not-care-less-about-final-work, accessed April 1, 2019.

"Sound/Sync Roskilde: Copenhagen." 2016. Red Bull TV, July 1, https://www.redbull.tv/video/AP-1NCAR6A692111/sound-sync-roskilde-copenhagen, accessed May 30, 2018.

"Spillestedsanalyse: Overblik over den rytmiske spillestedsscene i København." 2015. Copenhagen Municipality, Department of Culture and Leisure, https://www.kk.dk/sites/default/files/edoc/282a198e-2526–46cd-954f-faca8bfa89d6/7973a42d-6f7b-4595-b343-e7a0e4082048/Attachments/12855535–14124908–1.PDF, accessed January 2, 2019.

"Statement of Ralph Ellison." 1966. In *Federal Role in Urban Affairs: Hearings Before the Subcommittee on Executive Reorganization of the Committee of Government Operations: United States Senate: Eighty-Ninth Congress*, Second Session, August 29–30, 1147–170. Washington, DC: US Government Printing Office.

Stern, B., dir. 1960/2001. *Jazz on a Summer's Day*. DVD. Charly Films.

Stevenson, J., and M. Osborne, dirs. 2008. *Kung Fu Panda*. DreamWorks Animation.

St. John, G. 2009. *Technomad: Global Raving Countercultures*. Equinox: London.

St. John, G., ed. 2017a. *Weekend Societies: Electronic Dance Music Festivals and Event-Cultures*. New York: Bloomsbury.

———. 2017b. "Charms War: Dance Camps and Sound Cars at Burning Man." In *Weekend Societies: Electronic Dance Music Festivals and Event-Cultures*, edited by G. St. John, 219–44. New York: Bloomsbury.

Straw, W. 1991. "Systems of Articulation, Logics of Change: Communities and Scenes in Popular Music." *Cultural Studies* 5, no. 3: 368–88.

Strong, T. 1996. "Theatricality, Public Space, and Music in Rousseau." *SubStance* 25, no. 2, issue 80, Special Issue Politics on Stage: 122–24.

Strøyer, R. 2008. "Mega Vega dør inden fødslen." Danmarks Radio, October 17, http://www.dr.dk/Nyheder/Kultur/2008/10/17/111220.htm, accessed October 20, 2011.

Stuart, M. 1973, dir. *Wattstax*. Stax Records and Wolper Productions.

"Swedish Music Festival Is Cancelled in 2018 after Rape and Sexual Assault Claims." 2017. BBC, July 3, http://www.bbc.co.uk/newsbeat/article/40477791/swedish-music-festival-is-cancelled-in-2018-after-rape-and-sexual-assault-claims, accessed March 29, 2018.

Szemere, A. 2001. *Up from the Underground: The Culture of Rock Music in Postsocialist Hungary*. University Park: Pennsylvania State University Press.

Szemere, A., and K. Nagy. 2017. "Setting up a Tent in the 'New Europe': The Sziget Festival of Budapest." In *Made in Hungary: Studies in Popular Music*, edited by E. Barna and T. Tófalvy, 15–25. New York: Routledge.

Taubman, H. 1953. "In the Mill Towns: Steel Workers and Their Families Welcome Symphonies Underwritten by Union." *New York Times*, January 4, https://www.nytimes.com/1953/01/04/archives/in-the-mill-towns-steel-workers-and-their-families-welcome.html, accessed February 24, 2019.

———. 1954. "Standards—at Home: Choice of Hi-Fi Equipment Invokes Factors Bearing on Experience with Live Music." *New York Times*, March 21, https://www.nytimes.com/1954/03/21/archives/standards-at-home-choice-of-hifi-equipment-invokes-factors-bearing.html, accessed March 2, 2019.

———. 1955. "Machines and Men: No Sound Track Can Take Place of Live Performer." *New York Times*, February 6, https://www.nytimes.com/1955/02/06/archives/machines-and-men-no-sound-track-can-take-place-of-live-performer.html, accessed February 24, 2019.

———. 1956. "Projects on Film: Picture Series Designed to Foster Live Music." *New York Times*, June 3, https://www.nytimes.com/1956/06/03/archives/projects-on-film-picture-series-designed-to-foster-live-music.html, accessed February 24, 2019.

Taylor, A. 2014. "Why Sochi Is by Far the Most Expensive Olympics Ever." *Business Insider Australia*, January 18, https://www.businessinsider.com.au/why-sochi-is-by-far-the-most-expensive-olympics-ever-2014-1, accessed January 23, 2019.

Taylor, T. 2016. *Music and Capitalism: A History of the Present*. Chicago: University of Chicago Press.

Teichler, U. 2011. "Chapter 9: Graduation and Careers." In *A History of the European University: Volume 4: Universities Since 1945*, edited by W. Rüegg and H. de Ridder-Symoens, 319–68. Cambridge: Cambridge University Press.

Theberge, N. 1991. "Reflections on the Body in the Sociology of Sport." *Quest* 43, no. 2: 123–34.

"This Was Ludlow Street." 2008. *Lost City*, April 10, https://lostnewyorkcity.blogspot.com/2008/04/this-was-ludlow-street.html, accessed May 29, 2019.

Thompson, E. 2002. *The Soundscape of Modernity: Architectural Acoustics and the Culture of Listening in America, 1900–1933*. Cambridge, MA: MIT Press.

Thornton, S. 1995. *Club Cultures: Music, Media, and Subcultural Capital*. Cambridge: Polity.

Throsby, D. 2010. *The Economics of Cultural Policy*. Cambridge: Cambridge University Press.

Till, N. 2016. "'Sound Houses': Music, Architecture, and the Postmodern Sonic." In *The Oxford Handbook of Sound and Image in Western Art*, edited by Y. Kaduri, 163–91. Oxford: Oxford University Press.

Titon, J. 1999. "'The Real Thing': Tourism, Authenticity, and Pilgrimage among the Old Regular Baptists at the 1997 Smithsonian Folklife Festival." *The World of Music* 41, no. 3: 115–39.

Tomkins, C. 1965. *The Bride and the Bachelors: The Heretical Courtship in Modern Art*. London: Weidenfeld and Nicolson.

"Tomorrowland 2011: Official Aftermovie." 2011. Tomorrowland Festival, YouTube video, August 29, https://www.youtube.com/watch?v=M7CdTAiaLes, accessed February 8, 2019.

"Tomorrowland Belgium 2019: Official Aftermovie." 2019. Tomorrowland Festival, YouTube video, August 9, https://www.youtube.com/watch?v=hvIg3PTJWxs, accessed January 16, 2020.

"Tomorrowland Presentation." 2013. Slideshow presenting the Tomorrowland festival, internal document of ID&T, Belgium, January.

Tomson, K. 2011. "Att skapa en upplevelseindustri." *Nordisk Kulturpolitisk Tidsskrift*, no. 1/2: 71–99.

Tonkiss, F. 2012. "The One-Dimensional City." *City* 16, no. 1/2: 216–19.

Toplikar, D. 2011. "Goodman Raves about Electric Daisy Carnival's Move to Las Vegas." *Las Vegas Sun*, June 17, https://lasvegassun.com/news/2011/jun/17/goodman-raves-about-electric-daisy-carnivals-move-/, accessed April 4, 2019.

"Total Population of Belgium and the Regions." n.d. StatBel: Belgium in Figures, https://statbel.fgov.be/en/themes/population/structure-population#panel-12, accessed March 21, 2019.

Toynbee, J., and B. Dueck, eds. 2011. *Migrating Music*. London: Routledge.

Tröndle, M., ed. 2009/2011. *Das Konzert: Neue Aufführungskonzepte für eine klassische Form*. 2nd expanded ed. Bielefeld: Transcript.

Turino, T. 2000. *Nationalists, Cosmopolitans, and Popular Music in Zimbabwe*. Chicago: University of Chicago Press.

Turner, B. 1984/2008. *The Body and Society: Explorations in Social Theory*. 3rd ed. London: Sage.

———. 1991. "Recent Developments in the Theory of the Body." In *The Body: Social Process and Cultural Theory*, edited by M. Featherstone, M. Hepworth, and B. Turner, 1–35. London: Sage.

Turner, V. 1982. *From Ritual to Theatre: The Human Seriousness of Play*. New York: PAJ Publications.

———. 1988. *The Anthropology of Performance*. New York: PAJ Publications.

u/Baft_Dastard. 2015. "How Do You Feel About the Term EDM?" *Reddit.com*, https://www.reddit.com/r/EDM/comments/20sck1/how_do_you_feel_about_the_term_edm/, accessed April 2, 2019.

Usner, E. 2011. "'The Condition of Mozart': Mozart Year 2006 and the New Vienna." *Ethnomusicology Forum* 20, no. 3: 413–42.

Varga, G. 2016. "Robin Adler, Dave Blackburn to Salute Joni Mitchell's More Political Songs." *San Diego Union Tribune*, November 4, https://jonimitchell.com/library/view.cfm?id=3378, accessed November 11, 2019.

Veirum, K. 2015. "Amager Bio bliver ombygget for millioner." *Gaffa*, March 29, https://gaffa.dk/nyhed/93990/amager-bio-bliver-ombygget-for-millioner, accessed January 3, 2019.

Verheggen, A. 2012. "Interview with Emiel Barendsen." *World Music Forum*, October 14, https://www.worldmusicforum.nl/interview-met-emiel-barendsen-in-muziekwereld/, accessed March 21, 2019.

Vernallis, C. 2013a. "Music Video's Second Aesthetic." In *The Oxford Handbook of New Audiovisual Aesthetics*, edited by J. Richardson, C. Gorbman, and C. Vernallis, 437–65. Oxford: Oxford University Press.

———. 2013b. *Unruly Media: YouTube, Music Video, and the New Digital Cinema*. Oxford: Oxford University Press.

Waddell, L. 2019. "Adele 'CLOSES Her Touring Firm' Leading to Fear among Fans over Live Show Future . . . Two Years after Multi-Million Pound 123 Date Tour." *Daily Mail*, https://www.dailymail.co.uk/tvshowbiz/article-6560057/Adele-NEVER-tour-closed-touring-firm.html, accessed November 11, 2019.

Waddell, R. 2000. "Concert Industry Marks Big Year." *Billboard* 112, no. 2 (January 8): 1.

———. 2001a. "Rock Touring Sees Renaissance." *Billboard* 113, no. 10 (March 10): 1.

———. 2001b. "Concert Biz Is on the Road to Success." *Billboard* 113, no. 20 (May 19): 22.

———. 2006a. "Smart Money: Live Music Deals Ramp Up." *Billboard* 118, no. 19 (May 13): 15.

———. 2006b. "Burning Up the Road." *Billboard* 118, no. 51 (December 23): YE-8, YE-12, YE-16, and YE-18.

———. 2007. "Festival Fever." *Billboard* 119, no. 2 (January 13): 14.

———. 2008a. "The Rules of the Road." *Billboard* 120, no. 51 (December 20): 50–56.

———. 2008b. "From Labels to Live." *Billboard* 120, no. 32 (August 9): 17.

———. 2009. "The Great Escape." *Billboard* 121, no. 51 (December 19): 50–56.

Wadleigh, M., dir. 1970/1999. *Woodstock: The Director's Cut*. Warner DVD.

Walcott, J. 1975. "A Conservative Impulse in the New Rock Underground." *Village Voice*, August 18, 6.

Wald, E. 2009. *How The Beatles Destroyed Rock 'n' Roll: An Alternative History of Popular Music*. Oxford: Oxford University Press.

Walser, R. 1993. *Running with the Devil: Power, Gender, and Madness in Heavy Metal*. Middletown, CT: Wesleyan University Press.

Wang, A. 2003. "Todd Patrick: The City's Hardest-Working Club Promoter Has a Vision." *Straus News*, March 4, http://www.nypress.com/todd-patrick-the-citys-hardest-working-club-promoter-has-a-vision/, accessed December 7, 2018.

Ward, N. 2015. "Duncan Stutterheim, Founder of ID&T, Quits after 23 Years." *YourEDM*.

com, April 11, https://www.youredm.com/2015/04/11/duncan-stutterheim-founder-of-idt-quits-after-23-years/, accessed February 8, 2019.

Warner, M. 2015. "Learning My Lesson." *London Review of Books* 37, no. 6 (March 19): 8–14, https://www.lrb.co.uk/v37/n06/marina-warner/learning-my-lesson, accessed May 5, 2019.

Waterman, B. 2011. *Television's* Marquee Moon. New York: Bloomsbury.

Watermeyer, R., and J. Chubb. 2018. "Evaluating 'Impact' in the UK's Research Excellence Framework (REF): Liminality, Looseness and New Modalities of Scholarly Distinction." *Studies in Higher Education*: 1–13.

Webb, P. 2007. *Exploring the Networked Worlds of Popular Music: Milieu Cultures*. London: Routledge.

Weber, M. [1922] 1978. "Bureaucracy." In *Economy and Society*, edited by G. Roth and C. Wittich, 956–1005. Berkeley: University of California Press.

Weber, W. 1997. "Did People Listen in the 18th Century?" *Early Music* 25, no. 4 (November): 678–91.

Webster, A. 2012. "New Orleans Jazz Fest Streaming on YouTube for Free All Weekend." *The Verge*, May 5, https://www.theverge.com/2012/5/5/3001264/new-orleans-jazz-fest-youtube-stream, accessed February 9, 2019.

Webster, E. 2014. "Association of Independent Festivals Six-Year Report." Association of Independent Festivals, October, http://aiforg.com/wp-content/uploads/AIF-Six-Year-Report-2014.pdf, accessed January 27, 2016.

Weibel, S. 2006. *Die deutschen Musikfeste des 19. Jahrhunderts im Spiegel der zeitgenössischen musikalischen Fachpresse*. Kassel: Merseburger.

Wein, G., with N. Chinen. 2003. *Myself among Others: A Life in Music*. New York: Da Capo Press.

"WFDY." Young Communist League of Britain, https://ycl.org.uk/wfdy/, accessed January 18, 2019.

Will, R. 2009. "Eighteenth-Century Symphonies: An Unfinished Dialogue." In *The Cambridge History of Eighteenth-Century Music*, edited by S. Keefe, 613–47. Cambridge: Cambridge University Press.

Williams, R. 1974. *Television: Technology and Cultural Form*. London: Fontana.

Willman, C. [1993] 2017. "From the Archives: The 1993 interview when Walter Becker opened up about Steely Dan's subversive intentions," *Los Angeles Times*, September 3, 2017, https://www.latimes.com/entertainment/la-et-ms-walter-becker-steely-dan-archive-interview-20170903-story.html, accessed January 10, 2020.

Willnauer, F. 2013. "Musikfestivals und Festspiele in Deutschland." Deutsche Musikinformationszentrum Bonn, http://www.miz.org/static_de/themenportale/einfuehrungstexte_pdf/03_KonzerteMusiktheater/willnauer.pdf, accessed May 16, 2018.

Wirth, L. 1940. "The Urban Society and Civilization." *American Journal of Sociology* 45, no. 5 (March): 743–55.

Wmag. 2018. "Celebrities at Burning Man: A Visual History of Susan Sarandon, Cara Delevingne, Katy Perry, and More Glamping." *W Magazine*, August 25, https://www.wmagazine.com/gallery/burning-man-celebrity-photos, accessed April 4, 2019.

Wrigley, M. n.d. "Lower East Side Blues." *Designer / Builder: A Journal of the Human Environ-*

ment, http://www.designerbuildermagazine.org/designerbuilder_les.html, accessed August 18, 2016. [The article was written circa 2006.]

Wustmann, R. 1909. *Musikgeschichte Leipzigs, Bd. 1: Bis zur Mitte des 17. Jahrhunderts*. Berlin and Leipzig: B. G. Teubner.

"Yasmine Hamdan." Roskilde Festival, https://www.roskilde-festival.dk/music/2018/yasmine-hamdan?view=grid, accessed May 29, 2018.

Yoo, N., and A. Phillips. 2016. "Andrew W.K.'s NYC Club Santos Party House Closed Amid Neo-Nazi Controversy." *Pitchfork*, May 30, http://pitchfork.com/news/65830-andrew-wks-nyc-club-santos-party-house-closed-amid-neo-nazi-controversy/, accessed August 22, 2016.

Yoshitomi, D. 2013. "EDM Editorial: Do You Hate the Term EDM?" *Magnetic Magazine*, July 1, https://www.magneticmag.com/2013/07/edm-editorial-do-you-hate-the-term-edm/, accessed April 2, 2019.

Zaleski, A. 2018. "The Loudmouth at the Concert: Why Can't People Stop Talking and Listen to the Music?" *Salon*, June 25, https://www.salon.com/2018/06/25/a-loudmouth-at-every-concert-why-cant-people-stop-talking-and-listen-to-the-music/, accessed January 29, 2019.

Zherdev, N. 2014. "Festivalization as a Creative City Strategy." Doctoral Working Paper, Open University of Barcelona, https://cercles.diba.cat/documentsdigitals/pdf/E140137.pdf, accessed April 4, 2019.

Zukin, S. 1982. *Loft-Living: Culture and Capital in Urban Change*. Baltimore, MD: John Hopkins University Press.

———. 1995. *The Cultures of Cities*. Cambridge, MA: Blackwell.

———. 2010. *Naked City: The Death and Life of Authentic Urban Places*. Oxford: Oxford University Press.

Index of Names

Page numbers followed by "f" or "t" refer to figures or tables, respectively.

Ackerman, Oliver, 83–84
Adorno, Theodor, 25, 177, 281
AEG: corporatization of the concert industry, 23, 110; owner's politics, 179, 273
Aerosmith, 200
Albarn, Damon, 205, 279
Amateur Night at the Apollo, 35
Amico, Stephen, 92–93, 97
Amsterdam: in international context, 123–24, 151–53; gentrification and cultural policy, 136–37; and Melkweg, 132–33t, 135, 136–40
Ancienne Belgique (Brussels), 131–36, 140–44
Animal Collective, 115–16
Anschutz, Philip, 179, 273
Antwerp (Belgium), 240, 243, 247
Arendt, Hannah, 177
Auerbach, Erich, 177
Auslander, Philip: liveness, 14; persona, 44
Austin, Texas: live music branding of, 18, 72; South by Southwest, 200, 231

Baraka, Amiri, 67–68
Barcelona, 127, 129, 211–14, 231
Barendsen, Emiel, 139
Bartak, Karel, 18–19
Bayreuth, 175
BBC: festival coverage, 233–34; Live Lounge and Music Awards, 15; live music discourse, 15–16
Becker, Howard, 66–67
Beethoven, Ludwig van, 173
Berghain, 52
Beyond the Score (2013), 42–43
Bianchini, Franco, 127–29
Billboard: concert and live music industry coverage, 17; EDM, 224; International Talent Forum, 16; Live Music Summit, 16; source of festival industry research, 221
Birmingham Music Festival, 172
Bitte Orca (2009), 116
Björk, 116, 194, 215
Black Lives Matter, 195. *See also* Beyoncé Knowles
Blackpink, 5, 224
Blues People (1963), 67
Body and Society, The (1984), 48–49
Bolsheviks, 176
Born, Georgina, 25, 66
Bottom Line, 108, 110, 274
Bowen, Michael, 187
Bowery Ballroom, 52, 102–18, 121

Bowery Presents, 39, 76, 100–101, 109–11, 113, 117, 179
Bragin, Bill, 105–6
Brel, Jaques, 141
Brooklyn Vegan, 16, 80
Brussels: and Ancienne Belgique, 131–36, 140–44; in international context, 123–24, 151–53
Burke, Patrick, 92–93
Burning Man, 57–58, 61t, 191, 226, 233, 246, 275

Cage, John, 189–90
Cake Shop, 98–99, 274
Cannady, Kimberly, 215
Cantwell, Robert, 166, 182
Carter, Tim, 66
Cavicchi, Daniel, 44
CBGB, 90–92, 94–95, 110, 119–20, 274
CBGB Festival, 231
Clippeleir, Dirk De, 141, 143–44
Coachella Valley Music and Arts Festival, 50, 61t, 163, 179, 199, 201, 206, 211, 224, 228, 230, 233, 275, 278–79
Cohen, Allen, 187
Cohen, Judith, 181
Cohen, Sara, 71
Colombo, Alba
Conboy, Matt, 84
Cook, Nicholas, 42–43, 47, 66
Copenhagen: and Vega, 132–33t, 144–51; author's experience, 127; in international context, 123–24, 151–53; gentrification and cultural policy, 128–29
Coquatrix, Bruno, 141
Couldry, Nick, 60
Crane, Diana, 37–39
Crosby, Stills, Nash, and Young, 32
Cult of the Supreme Being, The (1794), 172
Cultural Study of Music, The (2003/2012), 24, 159

Danish Broadcasting Corporation (DBC), 206–8
Dante Alighieri, v, 170
Dayan, Daniel, 60–62, 255
Death by Audio, 82–84, 99
DiMaggio, Paul, 27–30
Dirty Projectors, 80, 111, 115–16
Divine Comedy, The (1320), v, 170
Durkheim, Émile, 28
Dusseldorf, 173, 175

Edinburgh International Festival, 180
Ehrenberg, Lewis, 67
Einstein, Albert, 177
Elbphilharmonie, 130
Electric Daisy Carnival, 224, 226, 228, 231–32
Ellison, Ralph, 5–6, 67
European Capital of Culture: Copenhagen 1996, 136, 149; Essen 2010, 231; and gentrification, 129
European Union: and globalization, 194; live music policy, 18–19, 131; and postwar recovery, 177; research policy, 281–83
Eurovision, 61t, 62, 177

Fantasy Fair and Magic Mountain Music Festival, 191
Feld, Steven, 44
Festa da Istoria of Ribadavia, 181
Festival NRMAL, 87–88
Festival of American Folklife, 166, 182
Festival of Britain (1951), 179–80
Festivals and the French Revolution (1976/1988), 171
Festivals and the Public Cultural Sphere (2011), 159–60, 166–67
Fête de la Musique, 13, 216
Fillmore East and West, 55–56, 89
Fitness Culture: Gyms and the Commercialisation of Discipline and Fun (2010), 31–32
Fox, Aaron, 45
Francis Newton (Eric Hobsbawm)
French Revolution, 92, 168, 171–73, 176, 186, 271
Frey, Bruno, 23, 157
Fricke, David, 215

Frith, Simon, 1, 19–20, 44
Fusion (festival), 51, 61t, 211

Gadamer, Hans-Georg, 165
Garcia, Luis-Manuel, 48, 71
Gillett, Charlie, 67–69
Ginsberg, Allen, 92, 187
Glancy, Jim, 109–10
Glastonbury, 61t, 163, 187, 195, 199, 201, 227, 233, 234, 246, 260, 275
Goethe, Johan Wolfgang von, 157, 172
Goodnight Brooklyn (2016), 84
Goodwin, Andrew, 14
Graham, Bill, 32, 55–56, 111
Grande, Ariana, 158, 230
Grazian, David, 70, 71
Gruen, John, 91, 190
Guetta, David, 225, 237, 254

Habermas, Jürgen: bourgeois concert life, 56; cultural public sphere, 166; humanities, 262
Hall, Edward, 53
Handel, Georg Friedrich, 168, 172, 173
Harris, Calvin, 15, 224, 237
Heemsbergen, Jon, 138–39
Herder, Johan Gottfried, 168–71, 277
Hesmondhalgh, David, 25
History of Live Music in Britain, The, Vol. 1: 1950–1967: From Dance Hall to the 100 Club (2013), 19–20
Human Be-In (1967), 185, 186–89, 191
Hybridity, or the Cultural Logic of Globalization (2005), 196–97

ID&T, 234–35
"Iron Cage Revisited: Institutional Isomorphism and Collective Rationality in Organizational Fields, The" (1983), 28, 30
Irving Plaza, 108, 111

James, Robin, 224–25
Jazz on a Summer's Day (1960), 244–45
Jørgensen, Steen, 149–50
Journal of Festival and Event Management, 160

Kaprow, Allan, 189
Kassabian, Anahid, 47
Katz, Elihu, 60–62, 255
K. B. Hallen (Copenhagen), 150, 151
Keil, Charles, 67–68
Klinenberg, Eric, 270
Knowles, Beyoncé, 50, 62, 158, 163, 201, 278–79
Kozak, Roman, 94
Kraidy, Marwan, 196–97
Kristal, Hilly, 76, 90, 91, 94, 105–6

La Movida Madrileña, 194
Lang, Jack, 13
Last Night of the Proms, 16
Lemonade (2016), 278
Live Nation: EDM, 226, 229; Europe, 138, 145, 150, 206, 209; and festival programming, 200, 203; globalization, 194; New York City, 109, 110–11; origin and development, 17, 23, 229
Liveness: Performance in a Mediatized Culture (1999), 14
LiveStyle, Inc., 23, 226
Llano Estacado (club), 81–82
Lollapalooza, 211, 229; Berlin, 50–51, 217
Love Parade, 231
Lower Rhine Festival, 172–75

Mad Cool, 50–51
Madison Square Garden, 32, 109, 117
Market Hotel, 82, 85–88
Marley, Bob, 5, 199
Mauerpark, 216
McKay, George, 157, 186
Media Events: The Live Broadcasting of History (1992), 60–62, 255–56
Melkweg (Amsterdam), 131–40, 151–53
Mendelssohn-Bartholdy, Felix, 173, 175
Mercury Lounge, 98, 102–8, 110–11
Merriweather Post Pavilion (2009), 116
Meulemeester, Jari De, 141

Milivojev, Ivan, 24, 209
Miller, Kiri, 242–43
Monster Island Basement, 81–82, 274
Monterey Pop Festival, 191–92, 244–45
Muñoz, José Esteban, 47
Music and Capitalism: A History of the Present (2016)
Music Hall of Williamsburg, 102–4, 109, 118
Mysteryland, 235, 247

Nasaw, David, 67
Nettl, Bruno, 70
New Institutionalism in Organizational Analysis, The (1991), 27–31
Newport festivals, 163, 187, 191, 244, 271
New Production of Knowledge, The (1994), 280
New York City: bohemianism in, 76, 77, 89, 91–93, 99, 116, 119–20, 134, 183–93, 238, 268; and the Bowery Presents, 109, 113; center of Anglophone popular music, 5; corporatization of clubs in, 110–11; cultural and social transformation of, 119–22; experimental arts scene in the 1950s and 1960s, 92, 187–88; field site, 75–76; gentrification of Manhattan, 96, 119–22; history of clubs in, 38–39; history of leisure institutions in, 67; jazz scene, 71; Live Nation, 109; motivations for moving to, 77–78, 81–82, 118; "old New York," 86; rock mythology, 77, 82, 86–87. *See also* gentrification *in Index of Subjects; and names of individual artists, clubs, neighborhoods, and promoters*
Nielsen, Elsebeth Gerner, 147–48
Nietzsche, Friedrich, 262
1917 October Revolution, 176
NPR: Brooklyn indie rock, 80, 115–16; and the live music industry boom, 234; Tiny Desk, 15
Nussbaum, Martha, 262, 277

Occupy Wall Street, 121–22
Olympia (club), 141, 292n6
Olympics: Barcelona 1992, 129, 211–12; Berlin 1936, 176; and television, 236; DJs, 13, 224
Oxford Handbook of Audiovisual Aesthetics, The (2013)
Ozouf, Mona, 171–72

Paradiso, 136–39
Park, Judy, 225, 241
Parkinson, Michael, 127
Patrick, Todd: biography, 77–78, 85–88; career trajectory, 76–88; Patrick circle, 77–85
Perry, Charles, 190
Peterson, Richard: hard core and soft shell, 220, 222–27; hippie festival movement, 185–86, 191–93; industry-driven popularization theory, 220, 222–27, 237; Nashville Sound, 222–23
Picasso, Pablo, 178–79
Pitchfork: Brooklyn indie rock, 80, 115–16; EDM, 224; festival, 15
Political Emotions (2013), 262, 277
Pop-Rock Music: Aesthetic Cosmopolitanism in Late Modernity (2013), 197–98
Powell, Walter, 27–30

Red Bull: broadcasting, 2, 206–9, 234; festival sponsorship, 87; Fête de la Musique, Berlin, 216–17; Roskilde Festival, 206–9; Sónar, 213
Reed, Lou, 93–94
Regev, Motti, 196–98
Re-Thinking Science (2001), 280
Rey, Lana Del, 109, 213, 214
Reykjavik (Iceland), 214–15
Reynolds, Simon, 57, 224, 225
Ridder, Willem de, 136
Riefenstahl, Leni, 176
Robinson, Roxy, 157, 160, 164
Rogers, Holly, 242–43
Rolf, Malte, 175–77
Roskilde Festival: and Anglophone global culture, 199–208, 217; author's collabo-

ration with, 221; ethics and ideology, 195; type of festival, 61t, 199, 218
Rottbøll, Jens, 148–49
Rousseau, Jean-Jacques, 168–70, 277
Royal Arena (Copenhagen), 150, 151
Rubin, Jerry, 183, 185, 188

Sassatelli, Monica, 166–67
Sassatelli, Roberta, 31–32, 237
Savages, The, 112f
Schechner, Richard, 42, 55, 256, 258
Schlösser, Cor, 136–38
Schneider, Rolf, 178
Schorske, Carl, 66
Scott, Dereck, 38, 44
Secret Project Robot, 82
Sensation White, 235, 247
SFX, 17, 23, 226, 229, 232, 235, 254
Shankar, Ravi, 5, 185, 199
Sheeran, Ed, 15, 109, 158
Silent Language, The (1959), 53
Sillerman, Robert, 229
Skov, Leif, 199, 200, 201
Smith, Neil, 91–92, 96, 102
Smith, Patti, 91, 109, 122
Sombart, Werner, 23
Sónar: case study of, 211–14; conception and typology of, 210; evolution of festival cinematography, 245
Sound of the City, The (1970), 67–69
South by Southwest, 200, 231
St. John, Graham, 58, 225–26
Super Bowl, 62, 201, 278
Swedish House Mafia, the, 220, 225
Swier, Michael, 39, 76, 100–111, 117
Sziget, 61t, 195, 208–9, 218, 221, 227–28

Taubman, Howard, 13
Taylor, Timothy, 26
Terminal 5, 109, 110, 111
Theberge, Nancy, 49
Thornton, Sarah, 12–13
Throsby, David, 130
Thunderdome, 235
Tiësto, 224, 235, 247
Tomorrowland: case study of, 239–61; corporate ownership of, 226, 248, 254–55; experience industry product, 228; in festival typology, 61t; inspired by Sensation White, 235; marketers and marketing, 235, 248–255; peak years of EDM pop, the, 224; 2011 aftermovie, 240, 251–52, 258; on YouTube, 206, 248–54
TomorrowWorld, 232, 254
Trips Festival, 191
Turner, Bryan, 48–49
2A (bar), 104–5

Ubiquitous Listening (2013), 47
UNESCO's City of Music program, 18
Urban Blues (1966), 67–68

Vega, 131–36, 144–46, 148–53
Vernallis, Carol, 242
Vienna (Austria), 66, 72

Walter, Bruno, 180
Weber, Max, 27, 28, 30, 49
Webster Hall, 103, 109, 115, 134
Weibel, Samuel, 168, 172–74
Wilber, Edan, 78, 80, 83–85
Woodstock: influence on festival history, 199, 208, 245; movie, 191–92, 244–45; peak of hippie festival movement, 184, 191; worldview of, 184–85, 191–93
World Federation of Democratic Youth, 177–79
World Festival of Youth and Students, 177–79

"Yesterday is history. Today is a gift. Tomorrow is mystery," 247–48
YouTube: evolutions in television culture, 234, 242, 253; globalization, 24, 194, 234; Roskilde, 206; Sziget, 209; Tomorrowland, 235, 240, 245, 250–54

Ziółkowski, Mikołaj, 24, 209
ZZ Top, 200

Index of Subjects

Page numbers followed by "t" refer to tables.

aftermovies and trailers, 235, 240, 245–46, 251–52, 254, 256–58. *See also* cinematography of cultural festivity

amateur music contests, 34–35

Anglophone global culture: and corporations, 23–24, 273, 276; and cultural diversity in northwest Continental Europe, 128; English language, 202, 204, 207, 216; in European modernity, 8–9, 141, 168, 193–93; festivals as institutions of, 9, 183, 208; globalization, 9, 23–24; globalization theory, 183, 196–98; media flows and geography of the field, 3, 5, 23–24; and small country mentality, 145; worldview of, 183–219

Anglophone popular music: commercial institutionalization of, 3, 5; and cultural diversity in northwest Continental Europe, 128, 219; and the decline of national European traditions, 141, 153; ethno-racial boundaries of, 5, 16, 21, 128; in European public policy, 128, 153; industry of, 17; live music as, 16–22, 131; worldviews of Anglophone popular music festivals, 183–219

architecture: ballroom-style, 100, 109, 117, 123; Barcelona, 211; constitutive role of, 52–54; and consumption, 31, 34, 51, 56, 195; East Village, 97; flagship, 55, 125, 129–31, 134, 138, 151; found spaces, 85, 102; and gentrification, 99, 102–3, 134; historical aura, 103–4; indoor vs. outdoor, 55–56; and performance culture, 36, 46t; professional concert aesthetics, 102–3; and public policy of performance, 152–53; ritual logic of, 54–58; standardization of, 34, 52, 152, 228; underground aesthetics of, 81

area literatures and area studies, 4, 10, 22, 24, 72, 159, 263, 264, 265, 277

arenas: boundaries with festival main stage, 200–201, 225, 228, 235, 278; and the Bowery Presents, 109–10; and clubs in northwest Continental Europe, 138, 150–51; and concert industry in 1970s and 1980s, 16, 193; and mass media, 37; not a performance institution, 32–33; scale and aesthetics, 53–54

artificial scarcity, 51

audiovisual music studies, 242

bars: in commercial concert clubs, 56, 98, 118; in gentrification, 84, 98–99; in indie rock clubs, 81, 83, 103; in

bars (*continued*)
neighborhood scenes, 33, 38, 78, 91, 93, 105; nondescript, 97; "we have live music," 13

camping, 205, 229, 247, 272. *See also* festivals: design
capitalism: aesthetics and entrepreneurialism, 103–5; changing conditions of life in, 119–22; defined, 26; evolutions in, 22–23; and festivals in Central and Eastern Europe, 193, 208–9; neoliberal, 22, 23, 26, 193, 263, 275
cinematography of cultural festivity: history of festival cinematography, 244–46; postcinematic aesthetics, 242, 252; Riefenstahl's, 176; sexualized, 235, 251–52. *See also* music festival video
civic: associations, 8, 39–40, 66, 169, 172–73, 265; authenticity and becoming, 8, 18, 39, 158, 167–75; civic and consumer values, 267; ownership, 27, 175
city, the: architecture and planning, 55; branding of, 18; bureaucracy of, 31; class and race, 37, 67–68, 71, 84, 88–96, 119–20, 139, 144, 270; as domain of cultural production, 36–40; elites in, 66, 89, 95, 125, 231–32; events in, 18, 59, 61t, 231–32, 277; genre cities, 68–70; immigration, 124, 205, 217; leisure in industrial-era metropolis, 66–67; leisure institutions in, 27, 38, 67, 76; Migration, Great, 67–68; migration (diasporic), 70–71; music histories of, 65–73; as site of extraordinary cultural achievements, 66. *See also* gentrification, urban ethnomusicology; urban musicology
city music history ("städtische Musikgeschichte"), 66
class, gender, and race: in the city, 37, 67–68, 71, 84, 88–96, 119–20, 139, 144, 219; in festival culture, 184–85, 197, 203, 205, 218, 230, 241, 259, 270, 278; in festival industry, 49–50; in live music discourse, 15–16, 21, 264
class of 2001/2002, 107, 121
clubs: architectural design, 55–56, 134; concert industry clubs, 98; decline of DIY and scene clubs, 83–84; DIY conception of, 76–82; events in, 52; evolution of rock clubs in Manhattan, 90–91; feeder, 106–7; house and techno, 57; indie rock concert theatre model of, 76, 111–22; industrial organization of, 131; as an institution, 2–3, 27, 33, 35–40, 74–153; institutionalization of DIY clubs, 85–88; music programming, 134–35; rock bar model of, 98, 105; small clubs as breeding grounds, 106–7; sound and crowd experience, 48; and utopian imagination at frontier, 79–80, 92
"club law" (Denmark), 146–48
commercial institutionalization, areas of: the body in performance, 50–51; country music, 222–23; EDM, 225–26; indie rock, performance culture, and urban life, 116–21; leisure; live music discourse, 16–19; musical performance, 32–35; the popular music festival, 157–58, 220–38, 270–74; the rock club in New York and in Europe, 74–153, 267–70. *See also* commercial institutionalization, forms of
commercial institutionalization, forms of: aesthetic transformation into glamor and pleasure for casual consumers, 9, 11, 23, 31, 33, 35, 39–40, 103, 117, 222–23, 229, 235, 236, 239, 242, 251–52, 259, 273; aesthetic transformation into soft-shell forms, 222–23; organizational strategy for aesthetic dimension of, 220–23, 226, 237–38; organizational transformation into bureaucratic structures, 11, 21, 27, 30–31, 49, 100, 109–11, 220, 266, 279. *See also* commercial institutionalization, areas of; institutionalization
concert halls: ambitions of clubs, 102, 134,

143, 145, 152; Ancienne Belgique in the 1950s and 1960s, 141; Bowery Presents expanding into, 109; design, 52, 55; Elbphilharmonie, 130; and festivals, 157, 173; institution of, 3, 27, 28, 29, 38, 157, 188; musical ritual, 56–57; organization vs. building, 134; rock music in, 121. *See also* clubs; venues

concert industry: artists frustrated with, 54; DIY in opposition to, 78; evolving into the club field, 76, 98; evolving into the festival field, 221, 227–30, 271, 274–75; expansion in the city, 23–24, 132–34, 137–38; formatting for new and broader market demographics (*see* commercial institutionalization, forms of); and gentrification, 104, 110–11, 119, 135–36, 148–51; rebranding of, 12, 16–17, 263; subsidized, 137

conditions of music, life and humanity: atomistic understandings of, 28; in city, 76, 119–22, 266, 269, 274; general findings in this book, 274–78; humanist knowledge interests in, 40, 59, 273–75, 283; moral philosophy of the good society, 277–78

conferences of the live music industry: author's participation in, 221; *Billboard*'s International Talent Forum, 16; *Billboard* Live Music Summit, 17; International Live Music Forum (ILMF), 16–17, 200; South by Southwest, 200, 231

consumer culture: the club and the festival as institutions of, 3; glamorous, 9, 11, 23, 31, 33, 35, 117, 229, 235, 236, 239, 242, 251–52, 259, 273; institutionalization of music into, 3; as social construction, 2

corporate institutionalization: of humanities, 279; of indie rock clubs, 100–122; of musical performance, 21, 30, 33–34; of popular music festivals, 220–38

counterculture: conceptions of festive events, 187–93; disassociation from, 136–37, 218, 230; and history of the independent European pop festival, 218; influence on New York rock scenes, 78, 81, 91–93, 190; La Movida Madrileña, 194; Lower East Side, 78, 91–93, 190; Nashestvie, 210; origin of popular music festivals, 33, 40; and public policy of popular music, 124–25, 136–37; ritual celebration of, 192; Roskilde Festival, 199; San Francisco, 70, 184, 186–88, 190–92, 218, 225, 271; Sziget Festival, 208–9; whiteness of, 184–86; worldviews of, 183–93

Counter-Enlightenment, 168

cult of silence, 56

cultural festivity. *See* festival vs. festivity

cultural policy. *See* public policy

cultural worldview: Anglophone global culture, 194–95, 198; Berlin in the 2010s, 216–19; bourgeois music festival, 172–74; hippie movement, 184–92; Nazism, 175; postcolonial humanism, 181–82; postwar international humanism, 177–81; Roskilde Festival, Sziget, and Nashestvie, 198–210; Sónar and Iceland Airwaves, 210–15; and theory of cultural festivity, 164–68; totalitarian, 175–76

culture of production. *See under* sociology

diaspora, 70–71

discipline and disciplinarity: area studies and disciplinary reflexivity, 72; challenge, the book's disciplinary, 6, 22–27; disciplinary authority, 283; ethnomusicology, 181–82; European Research Council policy of, 281–83; interdisciplinary vs. transdisciplinary, 282, 283; knowledge transmission, 283–84; logics of disciplines, 22, 284; media events literature, 60; music sociology, 22; sociology of the body, 49; urban ethnomusicology, 70–71; urban musicology, 66; urban music studies, 65, 72

Disney-style festival design, 241, 247

EDM pop: celebrity, teenage, and tabloid culture of, 224, 237; corporatization of, 229; embraced by city elites, 231–32; evolution of, 223–26; expansion of the popular music festival industry, 24, 40; festival industry, 226, 229; festivals, 61t, 225–26; ID&T's trajectory into, 234–35; into rock festivals, 201, 224, 230; media and festival culture of, 239–61; sexuality, 239, 242, 251–52, 255, 259; superstar DJs, 201; terminology, 224; visual culture of, 239; worldview, 165

entrepreneurs and entrepreneurialism, 78, 104–6, 125

epistemology and methodology, 4, 262–84

ethnic-racial issues: industry biases, 16, 197; industry segregation, 6. *See also* whiteness and white patriarchy

ethnography: author's, 4, 7, 9, 75–77, 100, 221–22, 240–41, 243–44; in cultural research, 74; popular music studies, 68, 71, 225

ethnomusicology: economic ethnomusicology, 26; historiography of self and other, 181–82; postcolonialism, 181–82; as social study of music, 6, 22, 24; theory of performance in, 44–45; urban, 70–71

events: be-ins and love-ins, 187–88; in city, 18, 211, 230–31; concept of, 58—62; concert events, 119; concert event spectacles, 130; as a decontextualized commodity, 16; economy of performance events, 2; festival as a cultural event, 39–40, 46t, 58–62, 157–64; in French Revolution, 171–72; the happening, 188–90; in hippie movement, 187–93; mega-events, 158, 201, 253–54; performance events, 46t, 52–58; in public policy, 8; as a resource of civic becoming, 8, 18, 27, 39–40, 66, 167–75, 177, 180, 208, 219, 238, 260, 265, 267, 273, 276–78; Roman carnival, 172; seasonal, 160–62; symbolic world and worldview of, 164–68; typology, 61t

eventful city, the, 18, 211, 230–31

event management, 59, 160

event studies, 4, 6, 227, 232; in media studies, 60–62; in tourism studies, 58–60

fan culture: in EDM pop, 224–25, 239–41; history of, 44; Tomorrowland, 239–41

fascism, 175, 178

festivals: broad pop festivals, 9, 198–99; cathedral festivals, 172; civic music festivals, 172; design, 5, 51, 62, 160, 198, 200, 201, 202, 226, 229, 232, 239, 241, 244, 246, 248, 251, 275; disciplinarity and methodology, 242; fashion culture and industry, 232–33; festive function, 160–62; general theory of, 157–67; as institution, 2–3, 27, 33, 35–40, 161, 220, 237–38, 271, 278–79; institutional function, 162–64; international niche festivals, 9, 198, 210–11; main stage culture, 200; and modernity, 157–82, 218–19, 238, 271–73; one-day tickets, 228; plenum, 192; postwar revival of, 180–81; and racial boundaries, 185; sexualized marketing of, 50, 196, 234, 239, 242, 246, 251–52; teenage and tabloid culture of, 233; worldview theory of, 164–68

festival vs. festivity: basic definition, 167; in Christianity, 170; in Counter-Enlightenment philosophy, 168–71; festive function of festivals, 160–62; in French Revolution, 168–72; overall argument about, 8, 167; outline of the festive summer season, 35, 39–40; relaxation of social rules and ethical norms, 50; weekend club culture, 52

"fest" to "festival," 169

fields: Anglophone popular music fields in the live music industry boom, 1, 13, 15, 16–19, 34, 151–52, 165, 263, 266; Bourdieu's theory of, 38; corporatization of the popular music field, 34; corporatization of the EDM pop festival field, 226; cultural vs. organizational,

38; fields and institutions as agents in music history and society, 4, 34, 263, 266; formation of the popular music festival field, 227; organizational fields, 9, 11, 27–30; policy influence on discourse in European club fields, 123–56; structuration of, 28, 211; transformations in the nineteenth-century bourgeois festival field in Germany, 173; value systems in the club field, 139, 151–52
fitness gyms, 31–33, 76, 265
Flemish cultural institutions, 140–44
Fluxus movement, 189
framework, theoretical, 6, 27–40, 263–67

gentrification: and bureaucracy, 31; class and race, 37, 67–68, 71, 84, 88–96, 119–20, 139, 144, 219; and cultural policy in Europe, 125, 137; growing culture markets in, 23–24, 127, 128–29, 132–33t, 134, 150; Lower East Side, 88; Ludlow Street area, 98–99; and music history, 7, 12, 71, 74; and music sociology, 25; and neighborhood difference, 37; and new conditions of cultural production, 75–76, 104, 119–22; and new formations in the cultural field, 76, 102–22; and rock club, 75–76; and scenes, 39, 71, 76, 95, 104; and subcultural theory of urbanism, 115; urban frontier of, 91–92; Williamsburg, 78, 83–84
globalization: corporate transculturalism, 196–97; cultural globalization, 9, 23–24, 193–94; genres as templates of, 197–98; globalization theory, 183, 196–98; media proximity, 198; pop culture internationalism, 197–98. *See also* Anglophone global culture
government control and regulation: argument for tighter regulation of capitalism, 12, 27, 226, 269–70; deregulation of media markets, 23, 196–97; effects of freedom from control, 79; preventing festivals, 192, 225
growth spiral: nineteenth century, 34, 173; twenty-first century, 33

happening, the, 188–90
headliners: in clubs, 33, 39, 75, 108, 113, 115, 118–19, 126, 133–35, 137–38, 149, 269; economy of, 228–29, 236–37; in festivals, 11, 158, 200–204, 227–30, 236, 237, 257, 260, 271
hierarchy and festival worldviews, 166, 204
high-fidelity, 13, 53
hippie festival movement, 33, 184–93
historicism and historical sociology, 120, 165, 267
humanities: area studies and disciplinary reflexivity, 72; changing approaches to musical culture in, 47; commercial institutionalization of, 279–83; ethnography in, 74; history and continued relevance of, 262–63; history of thinking about performance in, 42; prestige of research topics, 240; this book's position in, 283–84; uncritical adoption of live music discourse, 20–22

industry growth: architectural expansion of clubs, 52, 134, 137–38; in clubs and festivals, 23–24, 50–51, 111, 132–33t, 134, 199; and developments into larger stages and venues, 52, 110, 137–38, 150–53, 214, 225, 251; entrepreneurialism, 125, 138, 149; growth spiral in the nineteenth century, 34, 173; growth spiral in the twenty-first century, 33, 220–38; implications for the field of study, 5; industry-driven growth, 220–38; and policy interest, 18–19, 230–32
institutionalization, 29–31, 265, 267: of Ancienne Belgique and other clubs in Belgium, 135, 141–44, 151–53; of DIY culture, 85–88; of Melkweg and other clubs in Holland, 136–40, 151–53; of Vega and other clubs in Denmark, 146–53. *See also* commercial

institutionalization (*continued*)
institutionalization, areas of; commercial institutionalization, forms of; corporate institutionalization
institutions: atomistic understandings of the social institution, 27–28; institutional theory, 27–31; and domains, 35–40, 267–74; performance institutions, 27–31, 35–40

jazz: Ancienne Belgique, 143–44; and Anglophone global culture, 135, 139, 193–94; class and race, 67; club, 53, 57, 90, 133; festivals, 40, 183, 186–87, 202, 209, 233, 244–45; and the Lower East Side, 93, 99, 110; scene, 34, 70, 71

leisure: and changing conditions of labor, 121, 267; commercial institutionalization of, 31–32, 265; evolutions in modernity, 31; in industrial-era metropolis, 66–67; leisure time, 157
live ideology, 12–13
live music: and capitalism, 1–40, 263; discourse and terminology, 6, 16–22, 131, 262–64, 284; institutionalization of discourse, 16–19; literature, 19–22, 263–64; as a marketing invention, 2, 16–19; and modernity, 1–3, 5, 11, 36; political economy of live music scholarship, 21–22, 263, 283; reconstruction of the study object, 1, 6, 20, 263–64. *See also* bars; clubs; festivals; performance culture
"live music experience," 11, 20–21, 145
live music industry: economy of scale, 34, 54; ethics of, 179; genealogy and branding of, 1, 15–17, 23, 263, 275; live and recording sectors, 1, 15; and nonprofit clubs, 125, 144, 148, 150, 151; policy of, 19, 124; structuration of, 33–34, 220–38
lottery celebrity, 35

market dynamics: expansion of live music market into Eastern Europe, 24, 194, 209; expansion of Lower East Side rock field, 105; implications for the field of study, 5; international market expansion, 5; and live music industry boom, 131, 149, 152, 207, 226; strategies for market control, 34; and structuration of organizational fields, 28, 31, 275. *See also* industry growth
marketing: artificial scarcity, 51; cinematography, 9, 235–36, 239–61; city marketing, 18, 69, 72, 125, 150, 208, 230–32, 275; in club organizations, 131; experience discourse, 145; influence on the body in performance, 50–51; as an instrument of commercial institutionalization, 31, 33–34, 237; live music as a marketing term, 16–19, 21; only communicating for marketing purposes, 100–101, 120; Red Bull and festivals, 87, 206–9, 213, 216–17, 234; sexualized images in, 50, 196, 234, 239, 242, 246, 251–52; theming and visual branding of events, 232–61; transforming aura and image of musical performance, 31, 33–34, 50–51. *See also individual clubs and festivals*
media-centrism, 14, 20
mega-events, 158, 201, 253–54
methodology and epistemology, 4, 261–84
mode 1 and 2 knowledge production, 279–84
musical performance. *See* performance culture; performance institution
music festival videos: in annual festival cycle, 255–59; anticipatory function of, 256–57; consumption of, 236, 241–42, 255–59, 248; consumption, stimulus, 31, 241–42, 256, 258; evolution at Tomorrowland, 248–55; history of festival cinematography, 244–46; liminal function of, 257–58; and mediated life, 259–61; memory function of, 258
music studies and musicology: ignorance of festivals in, 159; knowledge

transmission, 283–84; music studies vs. musicology, 24; performative turn in musicology, 42–43; relevance and implications of ontology for, 6; urban musicology, 66; textualism in musicology, 41

Nazism, 175–76, 217. *See also* totalitarianism
New Institutionalism in organizational sociology, 29–30
"new universities," 280. *See also* university institution

ontology: of performance culture, 41–62; of performance event, 51–58; of performance in a cultural event, 58–62; of performing bodies, 44–51
oratorios, 173, 181

performance culture: analytical emphasis in this book, 11; and architecture, 54–56; and bureaucracy; conceptualization of, 41–62; and the conditions of urban life, 118–22; and cultural events, 58–62; definition of, 41–62, 264; discourse on, 1–2; of EDM pop, 235; fetishization of, 260; and the gentrified cities, 103; institutional theory of, 27–31, 267; and live music, 20–21; and media culture, 36–37, 116, 254, 260; mediatization of, 12, 36, 121, 236, 260; micromanagement of, 108; and modernity, 1–2; and music video scholarship, 242; ontologies of, 46t; policy of, 151–53; and reality TV, 34–35; and social change, 75, 85, 118–22, 124; and social movements, 42, 92, 174, 179, 184, 186, 193, 195, 208, 271, 274; unauthorized organization of, 79
performance institution, definition of, 28. *See also* institutionalization; institutions
pop podiums, 138
populism, right-wing, 128, 217–19
post-hippie festival culture, 195, 201, 210, 218–19
poverty, 88, 91, 97, 177, 262, 267
productivism, 237–38
promoters: as analytical focal point, 76; as auteur, 80–81, 85; authority in media event, 256; corporate, 100–101, 120; interest in EDM pop, 235; internal vs. external, 126, 138; large national EDM promoters, 226; motivations, 186; and real estate capitalism, 104–5; role in performance institution, 29; and the structuration of the festival field, 227. *See also individual promoters in Index of Names*
psychedelic culture, 57, 82, 116, 184, 190, 192, 210, 225
public culture, 8, 119–20, 125, 135, 140–44, 147, 152–53, 166, 269–70
public policy: arts policy of culture, 128; arts policy of music (musical arts policy), 7, 128, 140, 146–48, 150–53, 207; of clubs, 125; developments in Europe, 127–30; diversity and multiculturalism, 128, 137, 143–44; economic policy of culture, 129–30; and institutionalization of the nonprofit rock club, 125; musical arts policy (arts policy of music), 7, 128, 140, 146–48, 150–53, 207; of popular music, 124–25, 141; social policy of culture, 128–29; and values of nonprofit clubs, 125–26

racism, 50, 176
reality TV, 34–35, 197
reconstruction of live music as a study object, 1, 6, 20, 263–64
recording sector of the music industry, and recession, 1
religion, 28, 49, 68, 171, 187, 256
research question, 3
ritual, 11, 28, 38, 41–42, 52–58, 68, 80; and be-ins and love-ins in the 1960s, 187; and commercial institutionalization of the club, 111, 117–18, 121, 152; cooling

ritual (*continued*)
off, 258; dynamics of festival video, 242, 255–58, 260; and French Revolution, 171–72; and the happening, 188–90; and hippie festivals, 192; logic of architecture, 54–56; music vs. social, 56–58, 102–3; of nonviolent civil obedience, 187; reconstruction and reenactment of, 181; waving flags, 253
roots music, 115, 117

scene: Brooklyn warehouse scene, 77–88, 106, 116–18, 120; vs. commercial institutions, 34, 75, 77, 116–18, 121; concept of, 69–70, 95; vs. consumer purpose, 33; cultural, 78; death of, 76, 95, 119, 269, 275; East Village scene in the 1960s and 1970s, 89–95, 105, 112; era of, 76, 269, 275; expertise, 16; and festivals, 184, 186–91, 208, 211, 217, 218, 229, 238; in gentrification, 39, 71, 76, 95, 104; literature on, 43; Ludlow Street area scene, 98; microscene, 71
sexual harassment, 50, 196
"show," as term, 16, 81, 108
singer-songwriters, 111, 115, 209
social movements: history of music in cultural festivity, 174; and industrialization of musical performance culture, 9, 40, 121–22, 178–79, 195, 218, 271, 274; mythology of performance institutions, 92, 208; Occupy Wall Street, 121–22; rise of performance studies, 42; worldviews in festivals, 183–84, 186, 208
social study: of music, 24–27; of musical performance, 24, 26, 262; of music festivals, 158–60, 163–64; of music in cities, 65, 72; of music video, 241–43
sociology: of the body, 48–51; of cultural production, 37–39, 222, 243; of festive events. 165–67; historical, 165, 267; of industry-driven popularization, 222; of music, 22, 24–27; of musical performance, 20; organizational, 27–31
song and singing: Beyoncé Knowles at Coachella 2018, 278–79; contests, 35, 58, 177, 182; in Counter-Enlightenment philosophy, 168–71; in country music performance, 45; in EDM pop, 225, 239, 240; in the French Revolution, 168–69; love, 45, 121, 170; in music video scholarship, 242, 255; and the performing body, 45–46; in reality television, 35
sound: and architectural design, 52–53; at Berghain, 52; and the body, 45, 47–48; at the Bowery Ballroom, 52, 108, 117; at Burning Man, 58; and club experience; at Death by Audio, 79, 83; indoor vs. outdoor, 55–56; at Mercury Lounge, 107–8; Michael Swier's approach to, 102; at Ministry of Sound, 52; modalities, 44; optimization in European clubs, 134, 145; requirement of sound checks before recording, 207; Todd Patrick's DIY approach to, 86, 102; at Vega, 145; visualization of, 130
"Spielstätten" and "spillesteder," 131
sponsorship, 145, 208, 228–29, 233–37, 242, 253, 274
standardization, 2, 23, 24, 33–34, 52, 133, 152–53, 171, 218, 228, 265

totalitarianism, 171, 174–76, 177, 194

university institution, 279–83
urban ethnomusicology, 70–71
urban musicology, 66
urban music studies, 65, 72

venues: ambitions of clubs, 102, 134, 143, 145, 152; architectural design of clubs in northwest Continental Europe, 134; organization vs. building, 134; state-of-the-art, ideal of, 100, 102, 108, 134, 141, 143, 145, 152. *See also* clubs; concert halls

whiteness and white patriarchy: in Anglophone global culture, 197, 203, 205,

218–19, 230; and black popular music, 67–68; in Brussels, 144; in the cultural industries, 197; exotic gaze of, 5, 93, 103, 204–5; and gentrification, 71, 84, 96; in the hippie festival movement, 184–86; in historiography of music in cities, 67–68, 72; in Holland, 139; in live music discourse, 15–16, 21; in neo-bohemian scenes, 88–89, 91–93; in performance institutions, 5–6, 49–50; in popular music festivals, 203, 205, 218–19, 230, 241, 264, 278